Taste of Home's
Light&Tasty
Annual Recipes 2004

PICTURED ABOVE AND ON FRONT COVER: Halibut with Kiwi Salsa (page 176) and Chocolate Layer Cake (page 224).

Annual Recipes 2004

Editor: Julie Schnittka
Senior Art Director: Linda Dzik
Food Editor: Janaan Cunningham
Associate Editors: Jean Steiner, Heidi Reuter Lloyd
Cover Food Photographers: Rob Hagen, Dan Roberts
Senior Food Photography Artist: Stephanie Marchese
Food Photography Artist: Julie Ferron
Graphic Art Associates: Ellen Lloyd, Catherine Fletcher

Executive Editor: Kathy Pohl
Food Editor: Janaan Cunningham
Associate Food Editors: Diane Werner RD, Coleen Martin
Managing Editor: Julie Kastello
Art Director: Julie Wagner
Associate Editors: Mark Hagen, Sharon Selz, Barbara Schuetz, Ann Kaiser
Proofreader: Jean Steiner
Recipe Editor: Janet Briggs
Test Kitchen Director: Karen Johnson RD
Senior Home Economist: Mark Morgan RD
Home Economists: Wendy Stenman, Peggy Fleming RD, Pat Schmeling,
Amy Welk RD, Karen Wright
Test Kitchen Assistants: Suzanne Kern, Megan Taylor
Editorial Assistants: Ursula Maurer, Joanne Weid, Barb Czysz, Mary Ann Koebernik
Food Photographers: Rob Hagen, Dan Roberts
Food Stylists: Julie Herzfeldt, Kristin Koepnick
Senior Food Photography Artist: Stephanie Marchese
Food Photography Artist: Julie Ferron
Photo Studio Manager: Anne Schimmel
Graphic Art Associates: Ellen Lloyd, Catherine Fletcher

Chairman and Founder: Roy Reiman
President: Russell Denson

Taste of Home Books
© 2004 Reiman Media Group, Inc.
5400 S. 60th Street, Greendale WI 53129

International Standard Book Number: 0-89821-405-X
International Standard Serial Number: 1537-3134

To order additional copies of this book, write: *Taste of Home* Books,
P.O. Box 908, Greendale WI 53129; call toll-free 1-800/344-2560 to order
with a credit card. Or visit our Web site at **www.reimanpub.com**.

Contents

Low-Fat, Flavorful Foods For the Whole Family!

AT ONE TIME or another, each of us has undoubtedly made a New Year's resolution to cut back on the fat and calories in the foods we eat. Unfortunately, many folks have fallen victim to fad diets, only to have gained back any lost weight—if not more.

That's why I—and more than 1 million subscribers—love *Light & Tasty* magazine. You see, unlike most other food magazines, *Light & Tasty* takes a *common sense* approach to calorie-wise eating. It's not a diet magazine, so it doesn't lecture or urge diet and exercise but instead suggests simple options with lighter ingredient choices.

The recipes in *Light & Tasty* are lean on fat and calories. But most important, they're full of flavor. So getting your family to eat healthy meals is easy. It's no wonder that folks who are lightening up their menus have come to rely on *Light & Tasty*, even when they're cooking for finicky eaters.

And now all 518 light-done-right recipes from the third year of *Light & Tasty* magazine are at your fingertips in this timeless cookbook, *2004 Light & Tasty Annual Recipes*.

Many of the dishes are family-favorites of our readers, so they're guaranteed to offer great, home-style flavor. The taste is still there…these recipes have just been lightened up a bit with less fat, calories, cholesterol, etc.

Yet, these dishes won't leave you hungry. You'll find lots of great-tasting comfort foods, like Vegetable Beef Stew, Crispy Baked Chicken, Au Gratin Red Potatoes, Apricot Breakfast Rolls, Chocolate Chip Cheesecake and much more. Each of these mouth-watering dishes is leaner on fat, calories or sodium…but not leaner on flavor.

In addition, every recipe has been reviewed by a registered dietitian and includes Nutritional Analysis, plus Diabetic Exchanges where appropriate.

With *2004 Light & Tasty Annual Recipes*, healthy eating for the whole family has never been easier…or more enjoyable!

Diane Werner, R.D.

Associate Food Editor, *Light & Tasty*

What's Inside These Recipe-Packed Pages?

AS IF 518 great-tasting recipes aren't enough reasons to love *2004 Light & Tasty Annual Recipes*, the following helpful features will certainly make this big book a valued reference in your kitchen for years to come.

Here's What's New! If you are on a special diet—or someone you cook for is—finding suitable recipes is even easier!

That's because color-coded triangles now identify low-fat dishes (△) with 3 grams of fat or less per serving…and low-sodium dishes (▲) with 140 milligrams of sodium or less per serving. Plus, meatless entrees, side dishes and appetizers are marked with a red triangle (▲).

You'll find these helpful symbols throughout the book below an appropriate recipe's nutritional information.

User-Friendly Chapters. To assist in your menu planning, we've compiled all 518 recipes into 15 convenient chapters, such as Light Bites & Beverages, Beefed-Up Main Dishes, Chicken & Turkey Entrees, Meatless Main Dishes, Side Dishes & Condiments and Dazzling Desserts. (For a complete listing of chapters, turn back to page 3.)

Mouth-Watering Meals. You'll find 15 complete meals (including pictures!), which are perfect for either weekend entertaining (page 239) or weekday family dining (page 252).

De-Light-Ful Dinner Planner. In addition to the meal chapters mentioned above, we've created 27 menu plans. (See the De-Light-Ful Dinner Planner on page 7.) Each meal features at least two recipes found inside the book, as well as suggestions for "appealing partners" (side dishes, desserts or beverages) and meal-preparation pointers.

Hundreds of Color Photos. *More than half* of the 518 recipes in this timeless collection are shown in full color. So you can be sure these full-flavored foods not only taste terrific but are eye-appealing as well.

Easy-to-Use Indexes. Finding all 518 recipes is a snap with two simple-to-use indexes. The general index lists every recipe by food category, major ingredient and/or cooking technique. The alphabetical recipe listing is perfect for folks looking for a specific family favorite.

There's also a reference index that directs you to the many helpful kitchen tips and healthy-eating hints throughout the book. (The indexes begin on page 272.)

Nutritional Analysis Nuggets

EVERY RECIPE in *2004 Light & Tasty Annual Recipes* has been reviewed by a registered dietitian and includes Nutritional Analysis, plus Diabetic Exchanges where appropriate.

The Nutritional Analysis gives you the breakdown for calories, fat, saturated fat, cholesterol, sodium, carbohydrate, fiber and protein.

How we calculated the Nutritional Analysis.

- Whenever a choice of ingredients is given in a recipe (such as 1/3 cup of sour cream or plain yogurt), the first ingredient listed is the one calculated in the Nutritional Analysis.
- When a range is given for an ingredient (such as 2 to 3 teaspoons), we calculate the first amount given.
- Only the amount of marinade absorbed during preparation is calculated.
- Garnishes listed in recipes are generally included in our calculations.
- The nutritional values used in our calculations either come from The Food Processor, Version 8.1 (ESHA Research) or are provided by food manufacturers.

Key ingredients used in our recipe testing.

The following are the standard ingredients we use in recipe testing and in Nutritional Analysis unless otherwise indicated in a recipe:

- Large eggs
- 90% lean ground beef
- Regular long grain white rice
- Nonstick cooking spray (used on cookware)
- Farm-raised salmon and catfish (available in most grocery stores)
- Meat trimmed of all visible fat

Use symbols to find suitable recipes.

To help folks on restricted diets find appropriate dishes in a snap, we've included colored triangles after the nutritional information for many recipes throughout the book. Here's what they symbolize:

△ *Low-fat* (3 grams or less per serving)

▲ *Low-sodium* (140 milligrams or less per serving)

▲ *Meatless* (appetizer, side dish or main dish)

Daily Nutrition Guide

	Women 25-50	Women over 50	Men over 24
Calories	2,100	1,900 or less	2,700
Fat	47-82 g	42-74 g	60-105 g
Saturated Fat	23 g or less	21 g or less	30 g or less
Cholesterol	300 mg or less	300 mg or less	300 mg or less
Sodium	2,400 mg or less	2,400 mg or less	2,400 mg or less
Carbohydrates	about 300 g	about 275 g	about 385 g
Fiber	25-35 g	25-35 g	30-40 g
Protein	55 g	50 g	70 g

This chart is only a guide. Calorie requirements vary, depending on size, weight and amount of activity. Children's calorie and protein needs vary as they grow.

Your Serving Size Guide

Grains Group

1 bread slice, pancake or waffle

Half of an average bagel (the size of a hockey puck)

1 cup dry cereal

1/2 cup cooked cereal, rice or pasta

Vegetable Group

1 cup raw leafy greens

1/2 cup of any chopped vegetable, raw or cooked

6-ounce glass of vegetable juice

1 small potato

Fruit Group

1 medium piece of fruit

1/2 cup sliced fruit

6-ounce glass of orange juice or any 100% fruit juice

Milk Group

8-ounce container of yogurt

1 cup cottage cheese

2 ounces soft cheese (mozzarella)

1-1/2 ounces hard cheese (cheddar) (size of two dominoes)

8-ounce glass of milk

Meat and Beans Group

3 ounces cooked lean meat, poultry or fish (size of a deck of cards)

2 tablespoons peanut butter

1/2 cup beans

De-Light-ful Dinner Planner

To make meal planning easy,
turn to these 27 tasty menu suggestions
featuring recipes from this book, "appealing
partners" to round out the dinners and
meal-preparation pointers.

Traditional Tastes (page 8)

Skillet Supper

Start off your workweek with **Saucy Steak Strips** (p. 106) from Lacey Cook of Nedrow, New York. She sautes tender sirloin and crisp beans in a tasty sauce.

Accompany the main dish with a salad topped with **Creamy Buttermilk Dressing** (p. 62) from Emily Hockett of Federal Way, Washington.

Appealing Partners

- Steamed sliced carrots
- Dinner rolls

Practical Tips

We suggest serving the Saucy Steak Strips over rice, but it's just as delicious served on top of your favorite pasta.

To save time, chop a whole onion when preparing this meal. Store leftovers in the fridge to use later in the week or freeze for longer storage.

When you pick up fixings for the salad drizzled with Creamy Buttermilk Dressing, get salad greens as well as other vegetables like cucumbers and tomatoes.

Comforting Combo

From Louisville, Illinois, Ruth Hastings shares **Ham and Noodle Casserole** (p. 151). The pasta bake gets its creamy texture from cottage cheese.

Snuggle up to warm mugs of **Orange Spiced Cider** (p. 18) shared by Erika Reinhard of Colorado Springs, Colorado. Her heart-warming beverage is a delightful treat during cold weather.

Appealing Partners

- Tomato soup
- Fat-free pound cake

Practical Tips

When making the casserole, you can substitute cubed cooked chicken for the ham and dried oregano for the dill.

Erika uses a few Jolly Rancher "fire" candies instead of red hots in her cider. The individually wrapped hard candies have an intense cinnamon taste.

The cider recipe can easily be doubled for large gatherings, but be sure to use a 5-quart slow cooker.

Traditional Tastes

Get the taste of fried chicken with less fat when you prepare **Crispy Baked Chicken** (p. 129). Angela Capettini of Boynton Beach, Florida creates the crisp coating on her juicy chicken by baking it in the oven instead of frying it on the stove.

Corn Bread Squares (p. 194) from Amanda Andrews of Mansfield, Texas are a classic Southern accompaniment to the main dish.

Appealing Partners

- Vegetable sticks
- Rainbow Melon Julep (p. 44)

Practical Tips

For the Crispy Baked Chicken recipe, you'll need about 3-1/2 cups of cornflakes to make 1 cup crushed cereal.

There are several ways to crush cornflakes quickly. Process them in a blender or food processor, place them in a plastic bag and crush them with a rolling pin, or place them in a bowl and crush them with the bottom of a glass.

To add some zip to the corn bread, stir a chopped jalapeno pepper or 1/8 teaspoon of hot pepper sauce into the batter before baking.

Slow-Cooked Roast

Don't pour your extra coffee down the drain. It's the key to **Slow-Cooked Coffee Beef Roast** (p. 110) from Charles Trahan of San Dimas, California.

From Jensen, Utah, Connie Thomas sends her recipe for **Spanish Potatoes** (p. 77). This simple skillet side dish complements the tender beef and gravy, or most any entree.

Appealing Partners

◆ Sugar snap peas
◆ Low-fat ice cream with strawberry sauce

Practical Tips

👉 If you don't have any leftover brewed coffee to make the roast, you can stir 2 rounded teaspoons of instant coffee granules into 1-1/2 cups hot water.

👉 For a tasty substitute, use rosemary instead of oregano when fixing the Spanish Potatoes.

👉 To make the side dish suitable for vegetarians, we've offered vegetable bouillon granules as an option to the chicken bouillon. Look for it alongside other bouillon products in the soup aisle of your grocery store.

Microwave Meal

The microwave makes **Turkey with Orange Sauce** (p. 131) a speedy solution for weeknights. Gaye O'Dell of Binghamton, New York jazzes up moist turkey tenderloins with a thick orange sauce.

For a simple skillet side dish, try **Roasted Ginger Green Beans** (p. 75) shared by Kathy Jackson of Arlington, Virginia. Ginger comes through nicely in this pleasant treatment for fresh beans.

Appealing Partners

◆ Marvelous Melon (p. 61)
◆ Low-fat brownies

Practical Tips

👉 Gaye sometimes grills the turkey instead of cooking it in the microwave. She prepares the orange sauce in the microwave and serves it with the turkey.

👉 The sauce would also be good over chicken breasts or pork chops.

👉 Grated fresh gingerroot will perk up the green beans more than ground ginger. Look for fresh gingerroot in your produce section. Store leftover unpeeled gingerroot in a bag in the fridge for up to 3 weeks or tightly wrapped in the freezer for up to 1 year.

Swift Stir-Fry

Families are sure to enjoy **Sweet 'n' Sour Sausage Stir-Fry** (p. 134) shared by Wendy Wendler of Satellite Beach, Florida. The colorful combo features hearty sausage slices, sweet pineapple chunks and pretty carrot shreds.

For a good-for-you treat that tastes good, too, whip up **Quick Crispy Snack Bars** (p. 20). These chewy snacks from Ursula Maurer of Wauwatosa, Wisconsin have an appealing peanut butter flavor, yet they're not too sweet.

Appealing Partners

◆ Green peas
◆ Fat-free milk

Practical Tips

👉 We suggest serving Sweet 'n' Sour Sausage Stir-Fry over long grain rice. If your family prefers, substitute brown rice, couscous or angel hair pasta.

👉 Ursula suggests chilling the snack bars until set. But be sure to take them out of the fridge before serving or storing them. They're best enjoyed at room temperature.

No-Fuss Fare

You can get a head start on dinner when you assemble the ingredients for **Beef Vegetable Soup** (p. 36) the night before. In the morning, just combine them in the slow cooker, switch it on and let it simmer all day.

Shared by Jean Hutzell of Dubuque, Iowa, this satisfying soup is full of ground beef, carrots, potatoes and tomatoes.

No one will suspect that the secret ingredient in this moist loaf is yogurt. **Rustic Round Herb Bread** (p. 197), from Patricia Vatta of Norwood, Ontario, doesn't taste a bit light.

Appealing Partners

◆ Spinach salad
◆ Lime sherbet

Practical Tips

👉 Jean says the slow-cooked soup can be varied by using lean ground turkey instead of the ground beef.

👉 When seasoning Rustic Round Herb Bread, Patricia suggests trying different combinations of herbs, including basil, oregano and parsley.

Skillet Specialty

Jorie Welch of Acworth, Georgia prepares **Easy Barbecued Pork Chops** (p. 148) when she needs a quick-and-easy meal for her busy family. She says the saucy stovetop dish is so versatile that it can be adapted to fit most everyone's taste buds.

From Beverly Scalise of Bend, Oregon comes this healthy alternative to pasta and potato salads. **Asparagus Pepper Salad** (p. 52) is a refreshing medley that's a snap to toss together.

Appealing Partners

◆ Corn muffins
◆ Oven-baked steak fries

Practical Tips

👉 Jorie suggests a streamlined version of the entree. "If I'm in a hurry, I substitute cubed cooked chicken for the pork," she explains. "Also, the spiciness can be toned down by adding more brown sugar and less chili powder."

👉 When assembling Asparagus Pepper Salad, feel free to experiment with another flavor of store-bought or homemade vinaigrette. And if asparagus isn't your family's favorite vegetable, try cut green beans.

Steak 'n' Salad

For a sure-to-please entree, try **Onion-Rubbed Flank Steak** (p. 110) from Margaret Grant of Russellville, Arkansas. The flavorful beef is tender when sliced thinly across the grain.

From Trout Creek, Montana, Helen Meadows shares the recipe for **Broccoli Tomato Salad** (p. 56). Nicely coated with a mild mayonnaise dressing, the simple salad is especially good with fresh cherry tomatoes from the garden.

Appealing Partners

◆ Baked potatoes
◆ Fruit cup

Practical Tips

👉 When preparing the marinade-like mixture for the steak, you can use 1 tablespoon of dried minced onion in place of the chopped onion. Margaret recommends this treatment for sirloin steak, too.

👉 If weather allows, grill the steak instead of broiling it.

👉 If you don't have cherry tomatoes for the salad, you can substitute 2-3 medium tomatoes that have been seeded and chopped.

Stuffed Pizza Supper

Spinach lovers will delight in **Spinach-Stuffed Pizza** (p. 183), a meatless main dish. Nancy Gilmour of Sumner, Iowa uses frozen bread dough to hurry along this family-pleasing pizza.

Round out dinner with make-ahead **Mango Lemon Sorbet** (p. 230). Our Test Kitchen used just four ingredients to create this light and luscious dessert.

Appealing Partners

♦ Garden salad with low-fat dressing
♦ Sugar cookies

Practical Tips

👌 After assembling the pizza, Nancy divides the leftover dough into six portions, rolls them into breadsticks and bakes them until golden.

👌 When choosing mangoes for the sorbet, look for plump yellow fruit blushed with red. To prepare, use a sharp knife to cut the fruit from both sides of the large flat seed, then remove the peel and cut the fruit into chunks.

Better Burgers

You'll never miss the beef in these full-flavored burgers sent in by Jane Harris of Framingham, Massachusetts. Grated lemon peel and crushed caraway seeds pleasantly season the moist **Lemon Turkey Burgers** (p. 123).

To complete the meal, serve **Carrot Apple Salad** (p. 68). Kim Jones of Collinsville, Illinois says she likes to toss the crunchy combination together a day early for the best flavor.

Appealing Partners

♦ Relish platter
♦ Lemon iced tea

Practical Tips

👌 You'll need a fresh lemon for the turkey burgers. Wash it before grating the peel you need, then squeeze the juice. (A large lemon yields about 1 tablespoon peel and 3 tablespoons juice.)

👌 To crush caraway seed, place seeds in a plastic bag and set the bag on a cutting board. Use the flat side of a meat mallet to crush the seeds.

👌 Use leaf lettuce to top each burger, but save several lettuce leaves to use in a salad later in the week.

Mexican Menu

A Tex-Mex supper is a fun and flavorful addition to your weekday menu. Start with **White Chicken Enchiladas** (p. 129) from Sharon Welsh of Onsted, Michigan.

Continue the theme with **Southwestern Barley Salad** (p. 66) from Tommi Roylance. The Charlo, Montana cook includes corn, peas, tomatoes and black beans in her colorful grain salad.

Appealing Partners

♦ Cut fruit
♦ Limeade

Practical Tips

👌 The recipe for White Chicken Enchiladas calls for 4 cups of cooked chicken. Poach, microwave or grill 1-1/2 pounds of boneless chicken breasts, then cube it for the recipe.

👌 To cut down on last-minute preparation for the salad, prepare a big batch of barley ahead of time. (A 16-ounce package will yield about 9 cups cooked barley.) Then divide it into 1-cup portions, place it in labeled freezer bags or containers, and store in the freezer until needed. It will keep for up to 3 months.

Backyard Barbecue

Get a jump on dinner when you prepare **Grilled Sirloin Steak** (p. 115) from Jennie Sauvageot in Pialba, Queensland in Australia. She begins marinating the beef the night before, so it picks up the perfect blend of sweetness and spice.

Accompany the entree with **Garden Vegetable Salad** (p. 60) from Ramona Sailor. The Buhl, Idaho cook tosses colorful veggies in a tangy cooked dressing. Ramona says she always gets requests for the recipe.

Appealing Partners

♦ Grilled corn on the cob
♦ Apple slices with fat-free caramel sauce

Practical Tips

👌 The marinade for Grilled Sirloin Steak would also be good on pork chops.

👌 If you'd prefer not to grill the steak, broil it 4 inches from the heat for the same amount of time or until it reaches the desired doneness.

👌 When preparing the salad, feel free to toss in or substitute other veggies, such as carrots, zucchini, summer squash or mushrooms.

Thanksgiving Flavor

Don't wait for a Sunday dinner to enjoy the great taste of roasted turkey. Lynn Laux of Ballwin, Missouri takes advantage of her slow cooker to prepare moist **Lemony Turkey Breast** (p. 137).

Turn this supper into a special occasion with **Garlic-Rosemary Mashed Potatoes** (p. 82) from Kathy Rairigh of Milford, Indiana. The fluffy mashed spuds taste so good, your family won't even need to add butter.

Appealing Partners

♦ Sauteed yellow summer squash
♦ Fresh fruit salad

Practical Tips

👌 The entree makes a lot, so make the most of the leftovers. Extra cooked turkey can be stored in the refrigerator for 1-2 days or in the freezer for up to 3 months. Use it to make sandwiches, salads, casseroles or quick stir-fries.

👌 Kathy freezes a good deal of rosemary each summer with the mashed potato recipe in mind. To freeze rosemary, rinse whole sprigs, then pat dry with paper towels. Place a few sprigs in each of several small plastic freezer bags.

Fresh Summer Fare

For a south-of-the-border twist on a traditional favorite, try **Mexican-Style Stuffed Peppers** (p. 116). LaDonna Reed of Ponca City, Oklahoma adds salsa and green chilies to perk up the filling.

Cap off the meal with **Cinnamon Peach Crisp** (p. 236) shared by Leona Luecking, West Burlington, Iowa. A sweet golden topping over fresh sliced peaches tastes so delicious that folks will never know it's lower in fat.

Appealing Partners

♦ Light Guacamole with vegetables or fat-free chips (p. 30)
♦ Fresh squeezed lemonade

Practical Tips

👌 You'll need 1 cup of uncooked rice to make the 3 cups cooked rice for the stuffed pepper recipe. If you make a big batch of rice, you can store the rest in the fridge for 1 week or in the freezer for 6-8 months.

👌 It's easy to peel fresh peaches. Dip them, one at a time, in boiling water for 20-30 seconds, then place in a container of ice water. Use a paring knife to easily peel off the skin.

Choice Chicken Menu

In Suisun City, California, Kara De la vega needs just a few ingredients to throw together the flavorful breading for **Crumb-Coated Chicken Thighs** (p. 140).

Round out the meal with colorful **Zucchini Corn Saute** (p. 86). The speedy side dish from Barbara Lundgren of New Brighton, Minnesota has a mild flavor that balances the spicy chicken.

Appealing Partners

◆ Coleslaw
◆ Sliced watermelon

Practical Tips

👉 If you don't have dry bread crumbs for the chicken, make your own. Bake bread slices at 300° until dry and lightly browned, break into pieces and process in a food processor or blender.

👉 To cut fresh corn from the cob for the side dish, cut off the tip of the cob and discard it. Then stand that end on a cutting board. Use a knife to cut down the side of the ear, turning it to remove all the kernels. One ear yields about 1/2 cup kernels.

👉 If you prefer, measure 1-1/2 cups from a 16-ounce package of frozen corn.

Pleasing Pasta

Thought you couldn't eat healthy and enjoy pasta carbonara, too? Try this slimmed-down version from Mary Jo Nikolaus of Mansfield, Ohio. **Light Linguine Carbonara** (p. 153) has a creamy sauce and attractive color from peas and red pepper.

Hope Ralph of Woburn, Massachusetts jazzes up fresh greens with pears and dried cherries for **Fruity Green Salad** (p. 56). But her sweet-tart vinaigrette makes this medley a winner.

Appealing Partners

◆ Breadsticks
◆ Rainbow sherbet

Practical Tips

👉 You'll need two strips of bacon for the pasta dish. So fry two strips, then wrap and freeze the rest of the package for up to 1 month.

👉 When preparing the entree, Mary Jo sometimes uses 1/2 cup frozen mixed vegetables in place of the peas.

👉 Dried cherries for the salad can be found near the raisins in larger grocery stores. Or, use dried cranberries or golden raisins instead.

Pan-Fried Favorites

Pretzel and whole-wheat bread crumbs create the unusual coating on pan-fried **Spicy Salmon Patties** (p. 177). Barbara Coston of Little Rock, Arkansas adds chopped jalapeno pepper to give them just the right amount of kick.

For a swift side dish, try **Sauteed Spinach and Peppers** (p. 88) from Mary Lou Moon of Beaverton, Oregon. It's a snap to cook on the stovetop.

Appealing Partners

◆ Dijon Tartar Sauce (p. 93)
◆ Rice pilaf

Practical Tips

👉 The Spicy Salmon Patties include chopped green pepper. To save time later in the week, chop the whole pepper, use 1/3 cup for the patties and place the rest in a plastic bag in the freezer. When assembling the meal, take out just the amount of chopped pepper you need for the stuffed shells.

👉 Not familiar with the salt-free spicy seasoning blend in the recipe for the salmon patties? It's available under the brand name Mrs. Dash Extra Spicy in the spice aisle of most grocery stores.

Creamy Casserole

Carol Lepak of Sheboygan, Wisconsin combines popular Mexican and Italian flavors in one oven-baked dish. Her **Southwest Pasta Bake** (p. 115) is mildly seasoned to appeal to the pickiest of palates.

Cap off the meal by drizzling ice cream, cake or fruit with thick **Buttermilk Chocolate Sauce** (p. 230). Leah Ramage of Saskatoon, Saskatchewan simmers the smooth sauce on the stovetop for several minutes before serving it warm.

Appealing Partners

◆ Sliced fresh pears
◆ Spiced tea

Practical Tips

👌 Does your family like foods on the spicy side? Add some zip to the casserole by using medium or hot picante sauce, increasing the chili powder or adding some cayenne pepper.

👌 If you don't have buttermilk on hand for the chocolate sauce, Leah suggests this substitute. Place 1 tablespoon of vinegar in a 1-cup measure, then add enough 1% milk to measure 3/4 cup. Stir and let stand for 5 minutes before using.

Slow-Simmered Stew

Ease the dinnertime rush by assembling **Vegetable Beef Stew** (p. 107) the night before. Then just plug in the slow cooker before you leave the house in the morning. When you return home, this hearty entree from Ruth Rodriguez of Fort Myers Beach, Florida will be ready.

For a quick accompaniment, bake a batch of **Buttermilk Biscuits** (p. 194). Buttermilk lends tenderness to these lightly browned biscuits shared by Patricia Kile of Greentown, Pennsylvania.

Appealing Partners

◆ Tossed garden salad
◆ Apple cider

Practical Tips

👌 Ruth sometimes prepares the stew on her stovetop. To do that, brown the beef in a large saucepan, add the vegetables and seasonings, and bring to a boil. Reduce the heat and simmer until the meat and vegetables are tender. Then combine the cornstarch and water, add to the pan with the parsley and cook and stir until thickened.

👌 For the stew, feel free to use cubed acorn squash in place of butternut.

Down-Home Dinner

From Roselle, Illinois, Marge Wagner shares the recipe for **Oven Barbecued Chicken** (p. 141). With its sweet and tangy sauce, the tender chicken breasts are great for a busy weeknight meal or a special weekend supper for company.

To complement the entree, our Test Kitchen home economists came up with **Potato 'n' Pea Salad** (p. 65). The red pepper, red potato skins and green peas provide this medley with pretty color.

Appealing Partners

◆ Baked beans
◆ Tropical fruit salad

Practical Tips

👌 Marge usually serves Oven Barbecued Chicken with a fresh green salad and steamed red potatoes tossed with butter, dill, salt and pepper. "Corn bread is also a good accompaniment if we feel like splurging a little," she notes.

👌 If you don't have the salt-free garlic seasoning blend called for in the potato salad recipe, use an equal amount of regular salt-free seasoning blend and add between 1/8 and 1/4 teaspoon of garlic powder.

Super Stuffed Shells

Serve your family **Ham-Stuffed Jumbo Shells** (p. 156) for dinner and they will never realize they are eating lighter. Leona Reuer of Medina, North Dakota tucks a creamy filling with diced ham and Swiss cheese into pasta shells.

For a simple side dish, fix **Green Beans with Tomatoes** (p. 90) sent in by Clara Coulston of Washington Court House, Ohio. She spruces up fresh green beans with tomatoes, onion, allspice and garlic.

Appealing Partners

◆ Romaine lettuce salad
◆ Fruit juice bars

Practical Tips

👌 When preparing Ham-Stuffed Jumbo Shells, Leona often uses manicotti instead of jumbo pasta shells.

👌 The main dish calls for 3 cups cubed fully cooked lean ham. You can cut up a ham steak or cut a portion from a small boneless ham and save the rest for other meals. In a hurry? Pick up two 1-pound packages of ham that's already been cubed.

Satisfying Supper

Looking to add a little spark to your menu? Serve steaming bowls of the savory soup sent in by Denise Kilgore of Lino Lakes, Minnesota. Taco seasoning adds zip to her hearty **Turkey Barley Tomato Soup** (p. 39).

Round out the meal with **Ham 'n' Swiss-Topped Potatoes** (p. 162). Jill Hayes of Westerville, Ohio spoons a generous portion of tasty topping over baked potato halves for delicious results.

Appealing Partners

◆ Corn muffins
◆ Orange sherbet

Practical Tips

👌 Feel free to use lean ground beef instead of ground turkey in the soup.

👌 When preparing the stuffed potatoes, Jill suggests using a 10-ounce package of frozen asparagus when fresh asparagus is not in season.

👌 The stuffed potatoes are a tasty way to use up 2 cups leftover ham. If you don't have leftovers, buy a 3/4-pound chunk of deli ham as suggested on the grocery list...or cut up a ham slice that weighs about 12 ounces...or use part of a 1-pound package of cubed ham.

Perfect Pork

Chopped red and green peppers give a festive look to **Sweet 'n' Tangy Pork Chops** (p. 157) from Michelle Bishop of Peru, Indiana. The tender chops are simmered in an easy sauce on the stovetop, so they're perfect for busy weeknights.

For dessert, enjoy the old-fashioned flavor of **Raisin Cinnamon Bars** (p. 230). Jean Morgan of Roscoe, Illinois tops the warm snack cake with a sweet glaze, making it a sweet finale to any meal.

Appealing Partners

◆ Stir-fry vegetable blend
◆ Baked sweet potato

Practical Tips

👌 Michelle suggests serving the pork chops over no-yolk noodles, but they are also good with rice.

👌 You can use bone-in pork chops instead of boneless, but it may take a bit longer. Cook them until a meat thermometer reads 160°.

Stovetop Salmon

For moist and tender fillets, Nancy Deans cooks **Coriander Salmon** (p. 178) in a skillet. The Rochester, New York cook mildly seasons the fish with coriander, garlic, lime juice and a dash of hot pepper sauce.

Connie Thomas of Jensen, Utah jazzes up red potatoes to create her simple side dish. **Herbed Potato Wedges** (p. 94) take just minutes to cook in the microwave, so they're on the table in no time.

Appealing Partners

♦ Green Beans 'n' Celery (p. 92)
♦ Fat-free pound cake with chocolate syrup

Practical Tips

🍎 Many grocery stores offer fresh salmon in or near the meat department. Choose moist fillets that are not brown around the edges. The fish should feel firm and spring back when pressed with your finger. It should have a clean sea breeze smell, not a strong fishy odor.

🍎 When preparing the Herbed Potato Wedges, use basil or rosemary instead of thyme for a different flavor.

Fabulous Fajitas

Amy Trinkle of Milwaukee, Wisconsin needs just a few ingredients to fix family-pleasing **Baked Chicken Fajitas** (p. 145). Using the oven streamlines preparation of this tasty chicken mixture.

From Exton, Pennsylvania, Laura Perry shares **Peppered Cilantro Rice** (p. 91). The colorful side dish has Southwestern flair without a lot of spice.

Appealing Partners

♦ Guacamole
♦ Lime sherbet

Practical Tips

🍎 The fajitas can be made with beef sirloin instead of chicken. You might need to shorten the baking time to cook the beef to the desired doneness.

🍎 Many grocery stores carry a variety of flour tortillas. Try tortillas made with tomato, spinach or other veggies and seasoned with garlic and herbs.

🍎 When time is short, use instant rice in the side dish. You may want to saute the vegetables an extra minute or two before adding 1-1/2 cups each of instant rice and water. Then cook the rice according to package directions.

Savory Sandwiches

In Wilton, North Dakota, Lori Bergquist takes advantage of her slow cooker to prepare **Shredded Beef Barbecue** (p. 116). The beef roast simmers in a flavorful sauce all day, then it's a snap to shred for moist barbecue sandwiches.

For an appealing accompaniment, toss together **Vegetable Slaw** (p. 72). A simple dressing of mayonnaise and sour cream lightly coats this crunchy combination of veggies from Julie Copenhaver of Morganton, North Carolina.

Appealing Partners

♦ Relish platter
♦ Low-fat cookies

Practical Tips

🍎 If you have any leftover shredded beef, freeze it to use later as a filling for burritos or a topping for nachos.

🍎 To save time when preparing the Vegetable Slaw, buy a package of prepared coleslaw mix instead of shredding the cabbage yourself.

🍎 You can substitute three medium tomatoes, seeded and chopped, for the five plum tomatoes called for in the salad recipe.

Light Bites &
Beverages

The next time you're in the mood for a
satisfying snack or a thirst-quenching beverage,
try one of the tempting treats or refreshing
drinks on the following pages. They're
anything but lightweight in taste!

Savory Herb Cheesecake (page 28)

Cheesy Artichoke Mini Tarts

This recipe proves that good-for-you things come in tasty little packages! Wonton wrappers form the crisp cups that hold the cheddary artichoke filling in these cute appetizers.
—*Barbara Nowakowski, North Tonawanda, New York*

36 wonton wrappers
1 package (8 ounces) reduced-fat cream cheese
1 cup (4 ounces) shredded reduced-fat cheddar cheese
1 tablespoon Dijon mustard
1/4 to 1/2 teaspoon cayenne pepper
1 can (14 ounces) water-packed artichoke hearts, drained and chopped
1/4 cup chopped sweet red pepper
Fresh dill *or* tarragon sprigs, optional

Gently press wonton wrappers into miniature muffin cups coated with nonstick cooking spray, allowing edges to extend above cups. Spritz edges with nonstick cooking spray. In a mixing bowl, combine the cream cheese, cheddar cheese, mustard and cayenne until blended. Stir in artichokes and red pepper; mix well. Spoon into wonton cups.

Bake at 350° for 18-20 minutes or until cheese mixture is set and wontons are lightly browned. Garnish with dill or tarragon if desired. **Yield:** 3 dozen.

Nutritional Analysis: One serving (3 filled wontons) equals 157 calories, 5 g fat (3 g saturated fat), 18 mg cholesterol, 483 mg sodium, 19 g carbohydrate, 2 g fiber, 8 g protein.
Diabetic Exchanges: 1 starch, 1 vegetable, 1 fat.
▲ *Meatless*

Sugar 'n' Spice Popcorn

Our family can't get enough of this light cinnamon-sweet popcorn. The baked kernels are wonderfully crunchy and coated just right. Try mixing some up to have on hand as an anytime nibble.
—*Naomi Yoder, Leesburg, Indiana*

4 quarts air-popped popcorn
3 tablespoons butter *or* stick margarine
1/4 cup sugar
1 tablespoon water
1 teaspoon ground cinnamon
1/4 teaspoon salt

Place popcorn in a large roasting pan coated with non-stick cooking spray. In a saucepan, melt butter over low heat. Add the sugar, water, cinnamon and salt; cook and stir over low heat until sugar is dissolved. Pour over popcorn; toss to coat. Bake, uncovered, at 300° for 10-15 minutes. Serve immediately. **Yield:** 4 quarts.

Nutritional Analysis: One serving (1 cup) equals 62 calories, 2 g fat (1 g saturated fat), 6 mg cholesterol, 59 mg sodium, 9 g carbohydrate, 1 g fiber, 1 g protein.
Diabetic Exchanges: 1/2 starch, 1/2 fat.
△ *Low-fat*
▲ *Low-sodium*
▲ *Meatless*

Orange Spiced Cider

(Pictured above)

Every time I serve this wonderful hot beverage, someone asks for the recipe. Orange juice adds a bit of sweetness while red-hot candies are a fun substitute for traditional cinnamon sticks.
—*Erika Reinhard, Colorado Springs, Colorado*

4 cups unsweetened apple juice
1 can (12 ounces) orange juice concentrate, thawed
1/2 cup water
1 tablespoon red-hot candies
1/2 teaspoon ground nutmeg
1 teaspoon whole cloves
Fresh orange slices and cinnamon sticks, optional

In a slow cooker, combine the first five ingredients. Place cloves in a double thickness of cheesecloth; bring up corners of cloth and tie with kitchen string to form a bag. Add bag to slow cooker. Cover and cook on low for 2-3 hours or until heated through. Before serving, discard spice bag and stir cider. Garnish with orange slices and cinnamon sticks if desired. **Yield:** 8 servings.

Nutritional Analysis: One serving (3/4 cup) equals 128 calories, trace fat (trace saturated fat), 0 cholesterol, 6 mg sodium, 31 g carbohydrate, 1 g fiber, 1 g protein.
Diabetic Exchange: 2 fruit.
△ *Low-fat*
▲ *Low-sodium*

Banana Cream Smoothies

You can serve this thick, nutritious smoothie, flavored with bananas and raspberries, for breakfast or as a snack. And with only four ingredients, it's a breeze to prepare. This light, refreshing beverage looks beautiful served in tall glasses.
—Susan Burkholder, Leola, Pennsylvania

2 medium ripe bananas, peeled and sliced
1 can (8 ounces) unsweetened crushed pineapple
1/2 cup unsweetened frozen raspberries
1 cup fat-free plain yogurt

In a blender, combine all ingredients; cover and process for 30 seconds or until smooth. Stir if necessary. Pour into chilled glasses; serve immediately. **Yield:** 3 servings.

Nutritional Analysis: One serving (1 cup) equals 170 calories, 1 g fat (trace saturated fat), 2 mg cholesterol, 52 mg sodium, 40 g carbohydrate, 4 g fiber, 4 g protein.
Diabetic Exchanges: *2 fruit, 1/2 fat-free milk.*
△ *Low-fat*
▲ *Low-sodium*

Tortellini Appetizers

3ppt

These cute kabobs will lend a little Italian flavor to any get-together. Cheese tortellini is marinated in salad dressing, then skewered onto toothpicks along with stuffed olives, salami and cheese.
—Pat Schmidt, Sterling Heights, Michigan

18 refrigerated cheese tortellini, cooked, drained and cooled
1/4 cup fat-free Italian salad dressing
6 thin slices (4 ounces) reduced-fat provolone cheese
6 thin slices (2 ounces) Genoa salami
18 large stuffed olives

In a resealable plastic bag, combine the tortellini and salad dressing. Seal and refrigerate for 4 hours. Drain and discard dressing. Place a slice of cheese on each slice of salami; roll up tightly. Cut into thirds. For each appetizer, thread a tortellini, salami piece and olive on a toothpick. **Yield:** 1-1/2 dozen.

Nutritional Analysis: One serving (2 appetizers) equals 92 calories, 6 g fat (3 g saturated fat), 16 mg cholesterol, 453 mg sodium, 5 g carbohydrate, trace fiber, 7 g protein.
Diabetic Exchanges: *1 lean meat, 1 fat.*

Almond Tea

Don't be surprised if guests propose a toast to the iced tea at your next party! Almond and vanilla extract liven up this time-honored beverage while ginger ale adds sparkle to each refreshing sip.
—Susan Wilson, Lamesa, Texas

2 cups diet ginger ale, chilled
2 cups cold water
1/4 cup sugar-free instant lemon iced tea mix

1/2 teaspoon almond extract
1/2 teaspoon vanilla extract

In a pitcher, combine all ingredients. Serve immediately over ice. **Yield:** 4 servings.

Nutritional Analysis: One serving (1 cup) equals 11 calories, 0 fat (0 saturated fat), 0 cholesterol, 18 mg sodium, 2 g carbohydrate, 0 fiber, 0 protein.
Diabetic Exchange: *Free food.*
△ *Low-fat*
▲ *Low-sodium*
▲ *Meatless*

Spiced Honey Pretzels

3ppt

(Pictured below)

If your tastes run to sweet and spicy, you'll love these zesty pretzels with a twist. The coating is so yummy, you won't need a fattening dip to enjoy them! They're a great snack for munching, without feeling a bit guilty.
—Mary Lou Moon, Beaverton, Oregon

4 cups thin pretzel sticks
3 tablespoons honey
2 teaspoons butter *or* stick margarine, melted
1 teaspoon onion powder
1 teaspoon chili powder

Line a 15-in. x 10-in. x 1-in. baking pan with foil; coat the foil with nonstick cooking spray. Place pretzels in a large bowl. In a small bowl, combine the honey, butter, onion powder and chili powder. Pour over pretzels; toss to coat evenly. Spread into prepared pan. Bake at 350° for 8 minutes, stirring once. Cool on a wire rack, stirring gently several times to separate. **Yield:** 8 servings.

Nutritional Analysis: One serving (1/2 cup) equals 98 calories, 1 g fat (1 g saturated fat), 3 mg cholesterol, 487 mg sodium, 20 g carbohydrate, 1 g fiber, 2 g protein.
Diabetic Exchange: *1-1/2 starch.*
△ *Low-fat*
▲ *Meatless*

1/2 teaspoon ground cinnamon
1/8 teaspoon ground nutmeg
1/2 teaspoon vanilla extract
  5 flour tortillas (8 inches), warmed
1/3 cup shredded reduced-fat cheddar cheese
TOPPING:
1/2 teaspoon sugar
Dash ground cinnamon
 10 tablespoons reduced-fat whipped topping

In a small saucepan, melt butter over medium-low heat; stir in brown sugar until dissolved. Add the apples, raisins, cinnamon and nutmeg. Cook and stir over medium heat until apples are tender. Remove from the heat; stir in vanilla. Cool slightly.

Place each tortilla on a 12-in. square piece of foil. Top with about 1/4 cup apple mixture; sprinkle with cheese. Fold in sides of tortilla and roll up. Wrap in foil. Bake at 350° for 10-12 minutes or until heated through. Combine sugar and cinnamon; sprinkle over wraps. Serve warm with whipped topping. **Yield:** 5 servings.

Nutritional Analysis: One serving (1 wrap with 2 table-spoons whipped topping) equals 302 calories, 8 g fat (3 g saturated fat), 9 mg cholesterol, 313 mg sodium, 54 g carbohydrate, 2 g fiber, 6 g protein.
▲ *Meatless*

Quick Crispy Snack Bars

(Pictured above)

My daughters have loved these nutritious snacks since they were in grade school. Now, both are adults and still make these bars when they want a quick treat.
—*Ursula Maurer, Wauwatosa, Wisconsin*

1/2 cup honey
1/2 cup reduced-fat chunky peanut butter
1/2 cup nonfat dry milk powder
  4 cups crisp rice cereal

In a large saucepan, combine the honey, peanut butter and milk powder. Cook and stir over low heat until blended. Remove from the heat; stir in cereal. Press into an 8-in. square baking dish coated with nonstick cooking spray. Let stand until set. Cut into bars. **Yield:** 1 dozen.

Nutritional Analysis: One bar equals 144 calories, 4 g fat (1 g saturated fat), 1 mg cholesterol, 144 mg sodium, 25 g carbohydrate, 1 g fiber, 5 g protein.
Diabetic Exchanges: *1-1/2 starch, 1/2 fat.*
▲ *Meatless*

Apple Cheese Wraps

These tortilla-wrapped apple and cheese treats are a light alternative to apple pie. They're also a fun brunch item.
—*Grace Malone, Lafayette, Colorado*

1 tablespoon butter *or* stick margarine
1/4 cup packed brown sugar
  3 cups thinly sliced peeled Golden Delicious *or* other cooking apples (about 2 medium)
1/4 cup golden raisins

Fruit Slush

The original recipe for this frosty drink is from our church cookbook. I altered it by using different fruits and cutting the sugar in half. It's so refreshing!
—*Stephanie Gilmer, Anniston, Alabama*

5 frozen unsweetened whole strawberries
1 cup frozen blueberries
1 can (6 ounces) frozen orange juice concentrate
1/2 cup reduced-sugar sliced peaches, drained
1/2 cup sugar
3/4 cup water
  2 tablespoons lemon juice

Place all ingredients in a food processor or blender; cover and process until smooth. Pour into chilled glasses; serve immediately. **Yield:** 4 servings.

Nutritional Analysis: One serving (3/4 cup) equals 206 calories, trace fat (trace saturated fat), 0 cholesterol, 4 mg sodium, 52 g carbohydrate, 2 g fiber, 1 g protein.
Diabetic Exchanges: *2-1/2 fruit, 1 starch.*
△ *Low-fat*
▲ *Low-sodium*

Stuffed Mushrooms

I first tasted these fun mushroom appetizers at a support group meeting for diabetics. I couldn't believe how yummy they were. Since then, I've shared the recipe with friends and co-workers.
—*Beth Ann Howard, Verona, Pennsylvania*

1 pound large fresh mushrooms
3 tablespoons seasoned bread crumbs
3 tablespoons fat-free sour cream

2 tablespoons grated Parmesan cheese
2 tablespoons chopped chives
2 tablespoons reduced-fat mayonnaise
2 teaspoons balsamic vinegar
2 to 3 drops hot pepper sauce, optional

Remove stems from mushrooms; set caps aside. Chop stems, reserving 1/3 cup (discard remaining stems or save for another use). In a bowl, combine the bread crumbs, sour cream, Parmesan cheese, chives, mayonnaise, vinegar, hot pepper sauce if desired and reserved mushroom stems; mix well.

Place mushroom caps on a baking sheet coated with nonstick cooking spray; stuff with crumb mixture. Broil 4-6 in. from the heat for 5-7 minutes or until lightly browned. **Yield:** 6 servings.

Nutritional Analysis: One serving (3 stuffed mushrooms) equals 66 calories, 3 g fat (1 g saturated fat), 4 mg cholesterol, 173 mg sodium, 8 g carbohydrate, 1 g fiber, 4 g protein.
Diabetic Exchanges: *1/2 starch, 1/2 fat.*
  △ ***Low-fat***
  ▲ ***Meatless***

Apple Pie Tartlets
4ppt

(Pictured below)

Sweet and cinnamony, these mouth-watering morsels are a delightful addition to a dessert buffet or snack tray. For convenience, you can prebake the shells a day or two ahead of serving.
—*Mary Kelley, Minneapolis, Minnesota*

1 sheet refrigerated pie pastry
1 tablespoon sugar
Dash ground cinnamon

FILLING:
  2 teaspoons butter *or* stick margarine
  2 cups diced peeled tart apples
  3 tablespoons sugar
  3 tablespoons fat-free caramel ice cream topping
  2 tablespoons all-purpose flour
  1/2 teaspoon ground cinnamon
  1/2 teaspoon lemon juice
  1/8 teaspoon salt

Roll out pastry on a lightly floured surface; cut into twenty 2-1/2-in. circles. Press onto the bottom and up the sides of miniature muffin cups coated with nonstick cooking spray. Prick pastry with a fork. Spray lightly with nonstick cooking spray. Combine sugar and cinnamon; sprinkle over pastry. Bake at 350° for 6-8 minutes or until golden brown. Cool for 5 minutes before removing from pans to wire racks.

In a saucepan, melt butter. Add apples; cook and stir over medium heat for 4-5 minutes or until crisp-tender. Stir in the sugar, caramel topping, flour, cinnamon, lemon juice and salt. Bring to a boil; cook and stir for 2 minutes or until sauce is thickened and apples are tender. Cool for 5 minutes. Spoon into tart shells. **Yield:** 10 servings.

Nutritional Analysis: One serving (2 tartlets) equals 150 calories, 6 g fat (3 g saturated fat), 6 mg cholesterol, 126 mg sodium, 22 g carbohydrate, 1 g fiber, 1 g protein.
Diabetic Exchanges: *1-1/2 starch, 1 fat.*
  ▲ ***Low-sodium***
  ▲ ***Meatless***

Rosemary Zucchini Sticks

Our family loves zucchini, but fried zucchini has too much fat. So I baked these one day and everybody—even the grandchildren—thought they were great.
—*Betty Jackson, White Pine, Tennessee*

2 medium zucchini, peeled
1 cup seasoned bread crumbs
1 tablespoon minced fresh rosemary *or* 1 teaspoon dried rosemary, crushed
1 egg
1 tablespoon water

Cut each zucchini in half widthwise, then cut each half lengthwise into quarters. In a shallow bowl, combine bread crumbs and rosemary. In another bowl, beat egg and water. Dip zucchini in egg mixture, then coat with crumb mixture. Coat again in egg and crumbs. Arrange on a baking sheet coated with nonstick cooking spray. Bake at 375° for 20-25 minutes or until tender and golden, turning once. **Yield:** 4 servings.

Nutritional Analysis: One serving (4 zucchini sticks) equals 144 calories, 2 g fat (1 g saturated fat), 53 mg cholesterol, 814 mg sodium, 24 g carbohydrate, 2 g fiber, 7 g protein.
Diabetic Exchanges: *1-1/2 starch, 1/2 fat.*
  △ ***Low-fat***
  ▲ ***Meatless***

Bubble Pizza Loaf

3 ppt

Serve up these hearty pizza squares in your kitchen and get plenty of compliments in return! I trimmed excess calories from another recipe by substituting turkey pepperoni and reduced-fat cheese.
—Pam Peterson, Loveland, Colorado

      2 tubes (10 ounces *each*) refrigerated pizza crust
1-1/2 cups pizza sauce
      1 medium onion, chopped
      1 medium sweet red pepper, diced
   1/2 pound fresh mushrooms, sliced
      1 package (6 ounces) sliced turkey pepperoni
      3 cups (12 ounces) shredded part-skim mozzarella cheese, *divided*

Cut dough into 1-in. cubes; place in a large bowl. Add pizza sauce; toss to coat. In a nonstick skillet coated with nonstick cooking spray, saute the onion, red pepper and mushrooms for 4-5 minutes or until crisp-tender. Add to the dough mixture. Sprinkle with pepperoni and 1-1/2 cups mozzarella cheese; gently toss.

Transfer to a 13-in. x 9-in. x 2-in. baking dish coated with nonstick cooking spray. Sprinkle with remaining cheese. Bake, uncovered, at 350° for 30-35 minutes or until golden brown. Cool for 5 minutes before cutting. **Yield:** 28 servings.

Nutritional Analysis: One serving (2-in. square) equals 110 calories, 3 g fat (1 g saturated fat), 14 mg cholesterol, 370 mg sodium, 12 g carbohydrate, 1 g fiber, 7 g protein.
   Diabetic Exchanges: *1 starch, 1 lean meat.*
   △ **Low-fat**

Pretzel Snackers

4 ppt

I first served this snack when my husband's aunt came to visit and she asked for the recipe—even though she's in her 80s and lives in a convent. She has since reported that all her fellow nuns enjoy it as much as we do! The recipe can easily be doubled or tripled.
—Elissa Armbruster, Medford, New Jersey

      2 packages (16 ounces *each*) sourdough pretzel nuggets
      1 envelope ranch salad dressing mix
1-1/2 teaspoons dried oregano
      1 teaspoon lemon-pepper seasoning
      1 teaspoon dill weed
   1/2 teaspoon garlic powder
   1/2 teaspoon onion powder
   1/4 cup olive *or* canola oil

Place pretzels in a large bowl. In a small bowl, combine the dressing mix, oregano, lemon-pepper, dill weed, garlic powder and onion powder. Sprinkle over pretzels; toss gently to combine. Drizzle with oil; toss until well coated.

Spread in a 15-in. x 10-in. x 1-in. baking pan coated with nonstick cooking spray. Bake, uncovered, at 350° for 10 minutes. Stir and bake 5 minutes longer. Cool completely. Store in airtight containers. **Yield:** 10 cups.

Nutritional Analysis: One serving (1/2 cup) equals 158 calories, 3 g fat (trace saturated fat), 0 cholesterol, 601 mg sodium, 28 g carbohydrate, 2 g fiber, 3 g protein.
   Diabetic Exchange: *2 starch.*
   △ **Low-fat**
   ▲ **Meatless**

Creamy Parsley Veggie Dip

3 ppt

(Pictured below)

Whether you use fat-free or reduced-fat ingredients in this creamy dip for fresh vegetables, it makes no difference in taste. It's wonderful. I think it's best if made the night before.
—Joyce Ochsenwald, Coral Springs, Florida

      1 cup fat-free mayonnaise
      1 cup (8 ounces) reduced-fat sour cream
   1/3 cup minced fresh parsley
      2 tablespoons finely chopped onion
      1 tablespoon Dijon mustard
      1 garlic clove, minced
   1/2 teaspoon salt
   1/4 teaspoon pepper
Assorted fresh vegetables

In a bowl, combine the first eight ingredients. Cover and refrigerate for at least 2 hours. Serve with vegetables. **Yield:** 9 servings.

Nutritional Analysis: One serving (1/4 cup dip) equals 58 calories, 2 g fat (2 g saturated fat), 9 mg cholesterol, 379 mg sodium, 8 g carbohydrate, trace fiber, 2 g protein.
   Diabetic Exchanges: *1/2 starch, 1/2 fat.*
   △ **Low-fat**
   ▲ **Meatless**

Cut bread in half lengthwise; place on a baking sheet. In a nonstick skillet, saute 2 garlic cloves in 2 tablespoons oil until tender. Brush over cut side of bread.

In the same skillet, saute the red peppers, onion, Italian seasoning and remaining garlic in remaining oil until vegetables are tender; remove from the heat. Add 2 tablespoons basil, parsley and oregano; cool slightly. Place in a blender or food processor; cover and process until pureed. Spread over bread.

Top with tomato slices and cheeses. Sprinkle with remaining basil. Bake at 400° for 10-13 minutes or until cheese is melted and edges of bread are golden brown. **Yield:** 12 servings.

Nutritional Analysis: One serving (1 slice) equals 190 calories, 7 g fat (2 g saturated fat), 8 mg cholesterol, 309 mg sodium, 24 g carbohydrate, 2 g fiber, 8 g protein.
Diabetic Exchanges: 1-1/2 starch, 1-1/2 fat.
▲ *Meatless*

Italian Red Pepper Bruschetta

5ppt

(Pictured above)

To make this easy appetizer, I halve a loaf of Italian bread, then top it with a blend of fresh basil, oregano, garlic and red peppers, tomatoes and cheeses. It's hard to eat just one slice!
—*Josephine Devereaux Piro, Easton, Pennsylvania*

```
    1 loaf (1 pound) unsliced Italian bread
    3 garlic cloves, minced, divided
    3 tablespoons olive or canola oil, divided
    2 large sweet red peppers, chopped
    1 medium onion, chopped
1-1/2 teaspoons Italian seasoning
    2 tablespoons plus 1/4 cup coarsely chopped
        fresh basil, divided
    2 tablespoons minced fresh parsley
    1 tablespoon minced fresh oregano
    6 plum tomatoes, sliced
  3/4 cup shredded part-skim mozzarella cheese
  1/2 cup shredded reduced-fat provolone cheese
  1/4 cup shredded Parmesan cheese
```

Fruit Salsa with Ginger Chips

Pineapple, mango and kiwifruit give fruit salsa a tropical twist. This combination of fruity salsa and crisp gingery chips is wonderful on a hot day. I like to serve this with pineapple iced tea, which I make by simply adding some of the drained pineapple juice from this recipe to a pitcher of tea.
—*Christy Johnson, Columbus, Ohio*

```
    1 can (20 ounces) unsweetened crushed
        pineapple
    1 large mango or 2 medium peaches, peeled and
        chopped
    2 medium kiwifruit, peeled and chopped
  1/4 cup chopped macadamia nuts
4-1/2 teaspoons brown sugar
4-1/2 teaspoons flaked coconut
    8 flour tortillas (8 inches)
    1 tablespoon water
  1/4 cup sugar
    1 to 2 teaspoons ground ginger
```

Drain pineapple, reserving 3 tablespoons juice. In a bowl, combine the pineapple, mango, kiwi, nuts, brown sugar, coconut and reserved juice. Cover and refrigerate for at least 1 hour.

For chips, lightly brush one side of each tortilla with water. Combine sugar and ginger; sprinkle over the moistened side of tortillas. Cut each into six wedges. Place in a single layer on ungreased baking sheets. Bake at 400° for 5-7 minutes or until golden brown and crisp. Cool on wire racks. Serve with salsa. **Yield:** 12 servings.

Nutritional Analysis: One serving (1/4 cup salsa with 4 chips) equals 190 calories, 4 g fat (1 g saturated fat), 0 cholesterol, 173 mg sodium, 35 g carbohydrate, 1 g fiber, 3 g protein.
Diabetic Exchanges: 1-1/2 starch, 1 fruit, 1/2 fat.
▲ *Meatless*

Garlic Bean Dip

There isn't a bean that my family does not like.
In fact, I serve one kind or another almost every day.
This is one of our favorite dips.
—Nancy Testin, Harrington, Delaware

> 1 can (15 ounces) white kidney *or* cannellini
>   beans, rinsed and drained
> 1 tablespoon cider vinegar
> 2 garlic cloves, minced
> 1/2 teaspoon salt
> 1/2 teaspoon ground cumin
> 1/3 cup reduced-fat mayonnaise
> 2 tablespoons minced fresh parsley
> Baked pita chips *or* assorted raw vegetables

In a food processor, combine the beans, vinegar, garlic, salt and cumin; cover and process until almost smooth. Add mayonnaise and parsley; cover and process just until blended. Serve with pita chips or vegetables. **Yield:** 6 servings.

Nutritional Analysis: One serving (1/4 cup dip) equals 102 calories, 5 g fat (1 g saturated fat), 4 mg cholesterol, 450 mg sodium, 11 g carbohydrate, 3 g fiber, 3 g protein.
Diabetic Exchanges: 1 starch, 1 fat.
▲ *Meatless*

🍎 Keen on Cannellini Beans

ITALIAN cuisine is big on cannellini beans. First cultivated in Argentina by Italian immigrants, the beans were later taken back to Italy where they are now widely grown and exported.

Due to their creamy color and elongated shape, cannellinis are also called Italian white kidney beans. They have a fluffy texture and mild nutty taste that melds well with other flavors.

Cannellinis can be added to soups, stews, chilies and pasta dishes...cooked, marinated and tossed into cold salads...or pureed and served as a spread or dip.

Tropical Fruit Dip

This fruity dip is easy to prepare and so refreshing for summer get-togethers or brunches. The secret ingredient is the lemon-lime soda. It adds a little extra zing. Crushed pineapple and coconut extract bring a hint of the tropics to the creamy dip. Serve it with strawberries, grapes and bite-size melon pieces.
—Linda Venema, Fulton, Illinois

> 1 can (8 ounces) crushed unsweetened
>   pineapple, undrained
> 3/4 cup cold fat-free milk
> 1/2 cup reduced-fat sour cream
> 2 tablespoons diet lemon-lime soda
> 2 drops coconut extract
> 1 package (1 ounce) sugar-free instant vanilla
>   pudding mix
> Assorted fruit

In a blender or food processor, combine the first six ingredients; cover and process for 1 minute or until smooth. Cover and refrigerate for at least 1 hour. Serve with fruit. **Yield:** 2 cups.

Nutritional Analysis: One serving (1/4 cup dip) equals 49 calories, 1 g fat (1 g saturated fat), 5 mg cholesterol, 170 mg sodium, 7 g carbohydrate, trace fiber, 2 g protein.
Diabetic Exchange: 1/2 starch.
△ *Low-fat*
▲ *Meatless*

Coconut Pineapple Pops

With their sunny color and creamy texture, these pops from our Test Kitchen home economists just might be your hottest fresh-from-the-freezer treat!

> 1-1/2 cups cold 2% milk
> 1 can (6 ounces) unsweetened pineapple juice
> 1 can (8 ounces) unsweetened crushed pineapple
> 1 package (3.4 ounces) instant coconut cream
>   pudding mix
> 14 plastic cups *or* Popsicle molds (3 ounces *each*)
> 14 Popsicle sticks

In a blender or food processor, combine the milk, pineapple juice and pineapple; cover and process until smooth. Pour into a bowl; whisk in pudding mix for 2 minutes. Pour 1/4 cup into each cup or mold; insert Popsicle sticks. Freeze until firm. **Yield:** 14 ice pops.

Nutritional Analysis: One ice pop equals 56 calories, 1 g fat (trace saturated fat), 2 mg cholesterol, 96 mg sodium, 12 g carbohydrate, trace fiber, 1 g protein.
Diabetic Exchange: 1 starch.
△ *Low-fat*
▲ *Low-sodium*
▲ *Meatless*

Orange Cream Pops

For a lower-fat alternative to ice cream-filled pops, try slurping this citrus novelty that was created by our home economists.

> 1 package (3 ounces) orange gelatin
> 1 cup boiling water
> 1 cup (8 ounces) reduced-fat vanilla yogurt
> 1/2 cup 2% milk
> 1/2 teaspoon vanilla extract
> 10 plastic cups *or* Popsicle molds (3 ounces *each*)
> 10 Popsicle sticks

In a large bowl, dissolve gelatin in boiling water. Cool to room temperature. Stir in the yogurt, milk and vanilla. Pour 1/4 cup into each cup or mold; insert Popsicle sticks. Freeze until firm. **Yield:** 10 ice pops.

Nutritional Analysis: One ice pop equals 57 calories, 1 g fat (trace saturated fat), 2 mg cholesterol, 40 mg sodium, 11 g carbohydrate, 0 fiber, 2 g protein.
Diabetic Exchange: 1 starch.
△ *Low-fat*
▲ *Low-sodium*
▲ *Meatless*

Striped Fruit Pops

(Pictured above)

Our home economists layered these frosty favorites with fresh strawberries, kiwifruit and peaches.

> **2 cups sliced fresh strawberries**
> **3/4 cup honey, *divided***
> **12 plastic cups *or* Popsicle molds (3 ounces *each*)**
> **6 kiwifruit, peeled and sliced**
> **12 Popsicle sticks**
> **1-1/3 cups sliced fresh ripe peaches**

In a blender or food processor, place the strawberries and 1/4 cup honey; cover and process until smooth. Pour into cups or molds. Freeze for 30 minutes or until firm.

In a blender or food processor, place kiwi and 1/4 cup honey; cover and process until smooth. Pour over frozen strawberry layer; insert Popsicle sticks. Freeze until firm. Repeat with peaches and remaining honey; pour over kiwi layer. Freeze until firm. **Yield:** 1 dozen.

Nutritional Analysis: One ice pop equals 106 calories, trace fat (trace saturated fat), 0 cholesterol, 1 mg sodium, 27 g carbohydrate, 2 g fiber, 1 g protein.
Diabetic Exchange: *2 fruit.*
△ **Low-fat**
▲ **Low-sodium**
▲ **Meatless**

Cantaloupe Ice Pops

(Pictured above)

Your reminders to "eat your fruit" will stick, once kids take a lick of these melony snacks from our Test Kitchen. A perfect use for over-ripe cantaloupe, these pops make a light dessert or healthy between-meal refresher.

> **4 cups cubed cantaloupe**
> **1/4 cup sugar**
> **2 tablespoons lemon juice**
> **1 tablespoon chopped fresh mint *or* 1 teaspoon dried mint**
> **1/2 teaspoon grated lemon peel**
> **12 plastic cups *or* Popsicle molds (3 ounces *each*)**
> **12 Popsicle sticks**

In a blender or food processor, combine the first five ingredients; cover and process until smooth. Pour 1/4 cup into each cup or mold; insert Popsicle sticks. Freeze until firm. **Yield:** 1 dozen.

Nutritional Analysis: One ice pop equals 36 calories, trace fat (trace saturated fat), 0 cholesterol, 5 mg sodium, 9 g carbohydrate, trace fiber, trace protein.
Diabetic Exchange: *1/2 fruit.*
△ **Low-fat**
▲ **Low-sodium**
▲ **Meatless**

orange juice and spices is wonderful as the
punch simmers in the slow cooker.
—Susan Smith, Forest, Virginia

    4 cups apple cider *or* unsweetened apple juice
2-1/4 cups water
    3/4 cup orange juice concentrate
    3/4 teaspoon ground nutmeg
    3/4 teaspoon ground ginger
      3 whole cloves
      2 cinnamon sticks
      4 orange slices, halved

In a 3-qt. slow cooker, combine the apple cider, water, orange juice concentrate, nutmeg and ginger. Place cloves
and cinnamon sticks on a double thickness of cheesecloth; bring up corners of cloth and tie with string to form a
bag. Place bag in slow cooker. Cover and cook on low for 4-
5 hours or until heated through. Remove and discard
spice bag. Garnish with orange slices. **Yield:** 8 servings.

*Nutritional Analysis: One serving (3/4 cup) equals 108 calo-
ries, trace fat (trace saturated fat), 0 cholesterol, 13 mg sodium, 26
g carbohydrate, trace fiber, 1 g protein.*
Diabetic Exchange: *2 fruit.*
△ **Low-fat**
▲ **Low-sodium**

Ranch Yogurt Dip

(Pictured above)

*This creamy concoction is the perfect dip for a variety
of colorful veggies. Served in a cabbage bowl,
it's sure to draw attention on a buffet table.*
—Carol Gaus, Itasca, Illinois

  1 cup (8 ounces) fat-free plain yogurt
2/3 cup fat-free sour cream
1/3 cup reduced-fat mayonnaise
  1 tablespoon dried parsley flakes
  1 tablespoon minced chives
  1 tablespoon cider vinegar
  1 teaspoon sugar
  1 teaspoon onion powder
  1 teaspoon garlic powder
1/2 teaspoon salt
1/2 teaspoon celery seed
1/2 teaspoon ground mustard
1/4 teaspoon white pepper
Assorted raw vegetables

In a bowl, whisk together the first 13 ingredients. Cover and
refrigerate for at least 3 hours. Serve with raw vegetables.
Refrigerate leftovers. **Yield:** 8 servings.

*Nutritional Analysis: One serving (1/4 cup dip) equals 79 calo-
ries, 5 g fat (2 g saturated fat), 11 mg cholesterol, 257 mg sodium, 6 g carbohydrate, trace fiber, 3 g protein.*
Diabetic Exchanges: *1 fat, 1/2 fat-free milk.*
▲ **Meatless**

Warm Spiced Cider Punch

*This is a nice warm-up punch that I like to serve when
there is a nip in the air. The aroma of the apple cider,*

🍎 Attractive Celery Slices

I LOVE to serve those cute little peeled carrots on
veggie trays when I'm entertaining. To make the celery look just as nice, I wash the ribs, then cut them
on a diagonal into 1-inch slices. I find it's quick to
do, and my guests comment on how nice the celery
looks alongside the baby carrots. —*Ardis Brands
Glencoe, Minnesota*

Easy Smoked Salmon

*This has become my favorite way to prepare salmon.
It adds a bit of elegance to a holiday gathering.*
—Norma Fell, Boyne City, Michigan

  1 salmon fillet (about 2 pounds)
  2 tablespoons brown sugar
  2 teaspoons salt
1/2 teaspoon pepper
  1 to 2 tablespoons Liquid Smoke

Place salmon, skin side down, in an 11-in. x 7-in. x 2-in. baking pan coated with nonstick cooking spray. Sprinkle fish
with brown sugar, salt and pepper. Drizzle with Liquid
Smoke. Cover and refrigerate for 4-8 hours.

Drain and discard liquid. Bake at 350° for 35-45 minutes or until fish flakes easily with a fork. Cool to room
temperature. Cover and refrigerate 8 hours or overnight.
Yield: 16 servings.

*Nutritional Analysis: One serving (2 ounces) equals 110 calo-
ries, 6 g fat (1 g saturated fat), 33 mg cholesterol, 327 mg sodium, 2 g carbohydrate, trace fiber, 11 g protein.*
Diabetic Exchanges: *2 lean meat.*

Really Good Snack Mix

I grew tired of my family picking through a snack mix for their favorite items and leaving the rest. So I experimented using only their favorites and came up with this recipe. Now there's never any left!
—*Lori Genske, Waldo, Wisconsin*

    2 cups bite-size Shredded Wheat cereal
    2 cups corn Chex cereal
    2 cups Crispix cereal
1-1/2 cups salted cashew halves
    3 tablespoons butter *or* stick margarine, melted
    1 tablespoon canola oil
    4 teaspoons Worcestershire sauce
    1 teaspoon seasoned salt
1/2 teaspoon garlic powder

In a bowl, combine the cereals and cashews. In a small bowl, combine the butter, oil, Worcestershire sauce, salt and garlic powder. Pour over cereal mixture; toss to evenly coat. Transfer to a 15-in. x 10-in. x 1-in. baking pan coated with nonstick cooking spray. Bake at 250° for 45 minutes, stirring every 15 minutes. Store in airtight containers. **Yield:** 7-1/2 cups.

Nutritional Analysis: One serving (1/2 cup) equals 158 calories, 10 g fat (3 g saturated fat), 6 mg cholesterol, 298 mg sodium, 16 g carbohydrate, 1 g fiber, 3 g protein.
Diabetic Exchanges: *2 fat, 1 starch.*
▲ **Meatless**

Creamy Herb Appetizer Pockets

(Pictured at right)

I combined a creamy cheese sauce and an artichoke dip to come up with these bite-size morsels. The filling is tucked into triangles made from crescent roll dough. It's the perfect no-mess appetizer!
—*Tina Scarpaci, Chandler, Arizona*

    1 carton (4.4 ounces) reduced-fat garlic-herb cheese spread*
    4 ounces reduced-fat cream cheese
    2 tablespoons half-and-half cream
    1 garlic clove, minced
    1 tablespoon dried basil
    1 teaspoon dried thyme
1/2 teaspoon celery salt
1/4 teaspoon dill weed
1/4 teaspoon salt
1/4 teaspoon pepper
    3 to 4 drops hot pepper sauce
1/2 cup chopped canned water-packed artichoke hearts
1/4 cup chopped roasted red peppers
    2 tubes (8 ounces *each*) refrigerated reduced-fat crescent rolls

In a small mixing bowl, beat the cheese spread, cream cheese, cream and garlic until blended. Beat in the herbs, salt, pepper and hot pepper sauce. Fold in artichokes and red peppers. Cover and refrigerate for at least 1 hour.

Unroll both tubes of crescent roll dough. On a lightly floured surface, form each tube of dough into a long rectangle; seal seams and perforations. Roll each into a 16-in. x 12-in. rectangle. Cut lengthwise into four strips and widthwise into three strips; separate squares.

Place 1 rounded tablespoon of filling in the center of each square. Fold in half, forming triangles. Crimp edges to seal; trim if necessary. Place on ungreased baking sheets. Bake at 375° for 10-15 minutes or until golden brown. Serve warm. **Yield:** 2 dozen.

***Editor's Note:** This recipe was tested with Boursin Light Cheese Spread with garlic and fine herbs. One carton contains about 7 tablespoons of cheese spread.

Nutritional Analysis: One appetizer equals 96 calories, 5 g fat (2 g saturated fat), 7 mg cholesterol, 302 mg sodium, 10 g carbohydrate, trace fiber, 3 g protein.
Diabetic Exchanges: *1 starch, 1 fat.*
▲ **Meatless**

Mini Shrimp Rolls

(Pictured below)

These tasty tidbits make a great appetizer or even a mini meal. Plus, they're healthier than deep-fried egg rolls. I experimented with various ingredients to come up with the creamy filling...then baked the egg rolls to keep the fat lower.
—Jennifer Jones, Pine City, New York

  1 pound medium cooked shrimp, peeled and deveined
  6 ounces reduced-fat cream cheese
  1 cup (4 ounces) shredded part-skim mozzarella cheese
1-1/2 cups finely chopped cabbage
  3 green onions, finely chopped
1/2 cup shredded carrot
  1 tablespoon reduced-sodium soy sauce
  2 garlic cloves, minced
 48 wonton wrappers
  2 tablespoons all-purpose flour
  3 tablespoons water

Chop shrimp; set aside. In a mixing bowl, beat cream cheese until smooth. Add mozzarella cheese; mix well. Stir in the cabbage, onions, carrot, soy sauce, garlic and shrimp.

For each shrimp roll, place 1 tablespoon of shrimp mixture across the bottom third of a wonton wrapper to within 1/4 in. of bottom and side edges. Combine flour and water until smooth; brush a 1/4-in.-wide strip on side edges and fold side edges over 1/4 in. Brush side edges and top edge with water mixture. Fold bottom third of wonton wrapper over filling, then bring top over and pinch edges to seal completely.

Lightly spray rolls with nonstick cooking spray. Place on a baking sheet coated with nonstick cooking spray. Bake at 400° for 15-18 minutes or until golden brown, turning once. Serve warm. **Yield:** 4 dozen.

Nutritional Analysis: *One serving (3 shrimp rolls) equals 153 calories, 4 g fat (2 g saturated fat), 70 mg cholesterol, 317 mg sodium, 16 g carbohydrate, 1 g fiber, 11 g protein.*
Diabetic Exchanges: *1 starch, 1 very lean meat, 1 fat.*

Savory Herb Cheesecake

(Pictured on page 17)

I came across the recipe for this scrumptious appetizer while taking an herb gardening course. It was the hit of the buffet at our "End of Class" party.
—Lee-Anne Hamilton, Louisburg, Kansas

  3 packages (8 ounces *each*) reduced-fat cream cheese, cubed
  2 cups (16 ounces) reduced-fat sour cream, *divided*
  1 can (10-3/4 ounces) reduced-fat condensed cream of broccoli soup, undiluted
3/4 cup egg substitute
1/2 cup grated Romano cheese
  2 to 4 tablespoons minced fresh basil
  1 to 2 tablespoons minced fresh thyme
  1 tablespoon cornstarch
  1 to 2 teaspoons minced fresh tarragon
  2 garlic cloves, minced
1/2 teaspoon coarsely ground pepper
  3 tablespoons *each* chopped sweet red, yellow and orange pepper
  3 tablespoons minced chives
Assorted crackers *or* fresh vegetables

In a large mixing bowl, combine the cream cheese, 1 cup sour cream and soup; beat until smooth. Add egg substitute; beat on low just until combined. Add the Romano cheese, basil, thyme, cornstarch, tarragon, garlic and pepper; beat just until blended.

Pour into a 9-in. springform pan coated with nonstick cooking spray. Place pan on a baking sheet. Bake at 350° for 35-45 minutes or until center is almost set. Turn oven off; leave cheesecake in oven with door ajar for 30 minutes.

Remove from oven. Carefully run a knife around edge of pan to loosen. Cool 1 hour longer. Refrigerate overnight. Remove sides of pan. Just before serving, spread with remaining sour cream. Garnish with chopped peppers and chives. Serve with crackers or fresh vegetables. **Yield:** 24 servings.

Nutritional Analysis: *One serving (1/4 cup cheesecake, calculated without crackers or vegetables) equals 114 calories, 8 g fat (5 g saturated fat), 25 mg cholesterol, 211 mg sodium, 5 g carbohydrate, trace fiber, 6 g protein.*
Diabetic Exchanges: *1 lean meat, 1 fat.*
▲ **Meatless**

Creamy Taco Dip

(Pictured above)

Layered in a pizza pan, this taco dip makes a pretty presentation. I prepare this yummy spread often.
—Janet Vrieselaar, Rosedale, British Columbia

1 package (8 ounces) fat-free cream cheese
1/2 cup reduced-fat sour cream
1/4 cup fat-free mayonnaise
2 teaspoons taco seasoning
1 cup taco sauce
2 cups (8 ounces) shredded part-skim mozzarella cheese
1 medium green pepper, diced
3 green onions, chopped
1 medium tomato, diced
Baked tortilla chips

In a mixing bowl, beat the cream cheese, sour cream, mayonnaise and taco seasoning until smooth. Spread onto a 12-in. round serving plate. Spread with taco sauce; sprinkle with mozzarella cheese, green pepper, onions and tomato. Cover and refrigerate until serving. Serve with tortilla chips. **Yield:** 2 cups.

Nutritional Analysis: One serving (2 tablespoons dip) equals 78 calories, 3 g fat (2 g saturated fat), 12 mg cholesterol, 274 mg sodium, 5 g carbohydrate, trace fiber, 6 g protein.
Diabetic Exchanges: 1 lean meat, 1/2 starch.
△ *Low-fat*
▲ *Meatless*

Sugar-Free Cocoa Mix

Here's a delicious winter warmer-upper featuring a tasty blend of cinnamon and cocoa. Keep the cocoa mix on hand to enjoy on cold winter days...or package it in a pretty tin and give it as a gift. Family and friends will appreciate this sugar-free alternative to soda.
—Louise Clough, West Fork, Arkansas

2 cups nonfat dry milk powder
1/2 cup fat-free powdered nondairy creamer
1/2 cup baking cocoa
Sugar substitute equivalent to 1/2 cup sugar*
3/4 teaspoon ground cinnamon

In a bowl, combine all of the ingredients; mix well. Store in an airtight container in a cool dry place for up to 6 months. **Yield:** 2-3/4 cups (about 8 servings).

To prepare hot cocoa: Dissolve 1/3 cup mix in 1 cup boiling water; stir well. **Yield:** 1 serving.

*Editor's Note: This recipe was tested with Splenda No Calorie Sweetener. Look for it in the baking aisle of your grocery store.

Nutritional Analysis: One serving (1 cup prepared hot cocoa) equals 101 calories, 1 g fat (trace saturated fat), 3 mg cholesterol, 94 mg sodium, 17 g carbohydrate, 2 g fiber, 7 g protein.
Diabetic Exchange: 1 fat-free milk.
△ *Low-fat*
▲ *Low-sodium*

Light Guacamole

Feel guilty dipping into guacamole?
This lower-fat version is a yummy alternative.
—Marlene Tokarski, Mesa, Arizona

    2 large ripe avocados, peeled, *divided*
    1 cup (8 ounces) fat-free sour cream
  1/4 cup chopped onion
    3 jalapeno peppers, seeded and chopped*
    6 tablespoons minced fresh cilantro *or* parsley
    4 teaspoons lemon juice
  1/2 teaspoon salt
  1/2 teaspoon ground cumin
  1/8 teaspoon pepper
    1 large tomato, seeded and chopped
Baked tortilla chips *or* raw vegetables

In a food processor, combine one avocado, sour cream, onion, jalapenos, cilantro, lemon juice, salt, cumin and pepper; cover and process until smooth. In a serving bowl, mash the remaining avocado with a fork. Stir in the pureed avocado mixture. Gently fold in tomato. Serve with tortilla chips or vegetables. **Yield:** 12 servings.

*Editor's Note: When cutting or seeding hot peppers, use rubber or plastic gloves to protect your hands. Avoid touching your face.

Nutritional Analysis: One serving (1/4 cup dip) equals 79 calories, 5 g fat (1 g saturated fat), 2 mg cholesterol, 119 mg sodium, 7 g carbohydrate, 2 g fiber, 2 g protein.
Diabetic Exchanges: 1 fat, 1 vegetable.
  ▲ *Low-sodium*
  ▲ *Meatless*

Sweet 'n' Spicy Snack Mix

This yummy snack mix was concocted by our
Test Kitchen. It's sure to spice up your next
party or festive gathering.

    4 cups miniature pretzels
2-1/3 cups reduced-fat cheese-flavored baked snack
        crackers
    2 cups Wheat Chex cereal
    3 tablespoons butter *or* stick margarine, melted
    1 tablespoon reduced-sodium soy sauce
    2 teaspoons chili powder
    1 teaspoon barbecue seasoning
    3 cups Corn Pops cereal

In a large bowl, combine the pretzels, crackers and Chex cereal. In a small bowl, combine the butter, soy sauce, chili powder and barbecue seasoning. Pour over cereal mixture; toss to evenly coat. Transfer to a 15-in. x 10-in. x 1-in. baking pan coated with nonstick cooking spray. Bake at 250° for 45 minutes, stirring every 15 minutes. Stir in corn cereal. Store in airtight containers. **Yield:** 10 cups.

Nutritional Analysis: One serving (3/4 cup) equals 160 calories, 5 g fat (2 g saturated fat), 8 mg cholesterol, 484 mg sodium, 26 g carbohydrate, 1 g fiber, 3 g protein.
Diabetic Exchanges: 1-1/2 starch, 1 fat.
  ▲ *Meatless*

Canadian Bacon Potato Skins

(Pictured above)

Whether you're looking for a fun appetizer or a tasty
side dish, these potato skins are sure to fill the bill!
Top potato shells with Canadian bacon,
chopped tomato and reduced-fat cheese.
—Mary Plummer, De Soto, Kansas

    6 large baking potatoes (12 ounces *each*)
    2 teaspoons canola oil
  1/8 teaspoon hot pepper sauce
    1 teaspoon chili powder
    1 medium tomato, seeded and finely chopped
  2/3 cup chopped Canadian bacon
    2 tablespoons finely chopped green onion
    1 cup (4 ounces) shredded reduced-fat cheddar
        cheese
  1/2 cup reduced-fat sour cream

Place potatoes on a microwave-safe plate; prick with a fork. Microwave, uncovered, on high for 18-22 minutes or until tender but firm, turning once. Let stand for 5 minutes. Cut each potato in half lengthwise. Scoop out pulp, leaving a 1/4-in. shell (discard pulp or save for another use).

Combine oil and hot pepper sauce; brush over potato shells. Sprinkle with chili powder. Cut each potato shell in half lengthwise. Place on baking sheets coated with nonstick cooking spray. Sprinkle with tomato, bacon, onion and cheese. Bake at 450° for 12-14 minutes or until heated through and cheese is melted. Serve with sour cream. **Yield:** 8 servings.

Editor's Note: This recipe was tested in an 850-watt microwave.

Nutritional Analysis: One serving (3 wedges with 1 tablespoon sour cream) equals 211 calories, 7 g fat (4 g saturated fat), 21 mg cholesterol, 309 mg sodium, 29 g carbohydrate, 5 g fiber, 11 g protein.
Diabetic Exchanges: 2 starch, 1 lean meat, 1/2 fat.

Simmer Up a Souper Bowl!

Soups are naturally nutritious, oh-so flavorful
and sure to please in any season. Whether
it's a cool soup in summer or a steaming
pot of hearty chili on a winter's day,
soup is good for the body—and the spirit!

White Bean 'n' Barley Soup (page 37)

Nutritional Analysis: One serving (1-1/2 cups) equals 194 calories, 2 g fat (trace saturated fat), 16 mg cholesterol, 1,187 mg sodium, 32 g carbohydrate, 7 g fiber, 14 g protein.
Diabetic Exchanges: 3 vegetable, 2 very lean meat, 1 starch.
△ **Low-fat**

Beef Barley Lentil Soup

It's easy to fill up your slow cooker and forget about supper...until the kitchen is filled with a wonderful aroma, that is! I've served this soup often to family and friends on cold nights, along with homemade rolls and a green salad. For variety, substitute jicama (a starchy root vegetable found in the produce department of many grocery stores) for the potatoes.
—Judy Metzentine, The Dalles, Oregon

1 pound lean ground beef
1 medium onion, chopped
2 cups cubed red potatoes (1/4-inch pieces)
1 cup chopped celery
1 cup diced carrots
1 cup dry lentils, rinsed
1/2 cup medium pearl barley
8 cups water
2 teaspoons beef bouillon granules
1 teaspoon salt
1/2 teaspoon lemon-pepper seasoning
2 cans (14-1/2 ounces *each*) stewed tomatoes

In a nonstick skillet, cook beef and onion over medium heat until meat is no longer pink; drain. Transfer to a 5-qt. slow cooker. Layer with the potatoes, celery, carrots, lentils and barley. Combine the water, bouillon, salt and lemon-pepper; pour over vegetables. Cover and cook on low for 6 hours or until vegetables and barley are tender. Add the tomatoes; cook 2 hours longer. **Yield:** 10 servings.

Nutritional Analysis: One serving (1-1/2 cups) equals 241 calories, 5 g fat (2 g saturated fat), 17 mg cholesterol, 660 mg sodium, 33 g carbohydrate, 9 g fiber, 18 g protein.
Diabetic Exchanges: 2 lean meat, 1-1/2 starch, 1 vegetable.

Spicy Kielbasa Soup

(Pictured above)

Red pepper flakes bring a little zip to this hearty soup that's full of good-for-you ingredients. Should you have any left over, this soup is great reheated, after the flavors have had time to blend. I like to serve steaming bowls of it with rye bread.
—Carol Custer, Clifton Park, New York

1/2 pound reduced-fat smoked turkey kielbasa, sliced
1 medium onion, chopped
1 medium green pepper, chopped
1 celery rib with leaves, thinly sliced
4 garlic cloves, minced
2 cans (14-1/2 ounces *each*) reduced-sodium chicken broth
1 can (15-1/2 ounces) great northern beans, rinsed and drained
1 can (14-1/2 ounces) stewed tomatoes, cut up
1 small zucchini, sliced
1 medium carrot, shredded
1 tablespoon dried parsley flakes
1/4 teaspoon crushed red pepper flakes
1/4 teaspoon pepper

In a nonstick skillet, cook kielbasa over medium heat until lightly browned. Add the onion, green pepper, celery and garlic. Cook and stir for 5 minutes or until vegetables are tender. Transfer to a slow cooker. Stir in the remaining ingredients. Cover and cook on low for 8-9 hours. **Yield:** 5 servings.

Clam Chowder

I make this chowder for our annual Souper Bowl luncheon at work, and everyone loves it! I've slimmed it down by using both reduced-fat margarine and mushroom soup. Tender chunks of red potatoes add color and texture.
—Chris Sheetz, Olmsted Falls, Ohio

2 cups sliced fresh mushrooms
4 celery ribs with leaves, chopped
1 medium onion, chopped
2 tablespoons reduced-fat margarine*
2 cans (10-3/4 ounces *each*) reduced-fat reduced-sodium condensed cream of mushroom soup, undiluted
1 bottle (8 ounces) clam juice
1/2 cup white wine *or* chicken broth

6 medium unpeeled red potatoes, cubed
1/2 teaspoon salt
1/4 teaspoon white pepper
3 cans (6-1/2 ounces *each*) minced clams, undrained

In a Dutch oven or soup kettle, saute the mushrooms, celery and onion in margarine until tender. In a bowl, whisk the soup, clam juice and wine or broth; stir into vegetable mixture. Add the potatoes, salt and pepper. Bring to a boil. Reduce heat; cover and simmer for 25 minutes. Add clams; cover and simmer for 5-15 minutes or until potatoes are tender. **Yield:** 10 servings.

*Editor's Note: This recipe was tested with Parkay Light stick margarine.

Nutritional Analysis: One serving (1 cup) equals 202 calories, 4 g fat (1 g saturated fat), 43 mg cholesterol, 497 mg sodium, 24 g carbohydrate, 2 g fiber, 17 g protein.
Diabetic Exchanges: 2 very lean meat, 1-1/2 starch, 1/2 fat.

Taco Twist Soup

(Pictured below)

I lightened up this soup recipe by substituting black beans for the ground beef originally called for...and by topping off bowlfuls with reduced-fat sour cream and cheese. Spiral pasta adds a fun twist.
—Colleen Zertler, Cedar Falls, Wisconsin

1 medium onion, chopped
2 garlic cloves, minced
2 teaspoons olive *or* canola oil

3 cups reduced-sodium beef broth *or* vegetable broth
1 can (15 ounces) black beans, rinsed and drained
1 can (14-1/2 ounces) diced tomatoes
1-1/2 cups picante sauce
1 cup uncooked spiral pasta
1 small green pepper, chopped
2 teaspoons chili powder
1 teaspoon ground cumin
1/2 cup shredded reduced-fat cheddar cheese
3 tablespoons reduced-fat sour cream

In a large saucepan, saute onion and garlic in oil until tender. Add the broth, beans, tomatoes, picante sauce, pasta, green pepper and seasonings. Bring to a boil, stirring frequently. Reduce heat; cover and simmer for 10-12 minutes or until pasta is tender, stirring occasionally. Serve with cheese and sour cream. **Yield:** 6 servings.

Nutritional Analysis: One serving (1 cup) equals 216 calories, 5 g fat (2 g saturated fat), 12 mg cholesterol, 1,052 mg sodium, 33 g carbohydrate, 6 g fiber, 10 g protein.
Diabetic Exchanges: 2 vegetable, 1-1/2 starch, 1 lean meat, 1/2 fat.
▲ **Meatless**

Creamy Chicken Rice Soup

I combined three recipes to come up with this take on the classic creamy chicken rice soup. I cut down on the butter, increased the vegetables and eliminated the half-and-half cream. This lower-fat version is truly delicious...and no one can tell it's light!
—Marge Wagner, Roselle, Illinois

1/2 cup chopped carrot
1/3 cup finely chopped onion
1/3 cup chopped celery
2 tablespoons butter *or* stick margarine
1/4 cup all-purpose flour
2 cans (14-1/2 ounces *each*) reduced-sodium chicken broth
2 cups cooked long grain rice
1 cup cubed cooked chicken
1/2 teaspoon salt
1/4 teaspoon pepper
1/8 teaspoon garlic powder
1 cup 2% milk
2 tablespoons lemon juice
1 tablespoon white wine, optional

In a large saucepan, saute the carrot, onion and celery in butter until tender. Stir in flour until blended. Gradually stir in broth. Add the rice, chicken, salt, pepper and garlic powder; bring to a boil. Reduce heat; cover and simmer for 10-15 minutes or until vegetables are tender. Reduce heat to low. Stir in the milk, lemon juice and wine if desired. Cook and stir for 5 minutes or until heated through. **Yield:** 6 servings.

Nutritional Analysis: One serving (1 cup) equals 203 calories, 6 g fat (3 g saturated fat), 33 mg cholesterol, 648 mg sodium, 24 g carbohydrate, 1 g fiber, 13 g protein.
Diabetic Exchanges: 1-1/2 starch, 1 lean meat, 1/2 fat.

Hearty Split Pea Soup

This slow-cooker soup is one of my favorite meals to make during the busy workweek. When I get home, I just add the milk...and supper is served!
—Deanna Waggy, South Bend, Indiana

4 pts

- **1 package (16 ounces) dried split peas**
- **2 cups diced fully cooked lean ham**
- **1 cup diced carrots**
- **1 medium onion, chopped**
- **2 garlic cloves, minced**
- **2 bay leaves**
- **1/2 teaspoon salt**
- **1/2 teaspoon pepper**
- **5 cups boiling water**
- **1 cup hot milk**

In a slow cooker, layer the first nine ingredients in order listed (do not stir). Cover and cook on high for 4-5 hours or until vegetables are tender. Stir in milk. Discard bay leaves before serving. **Yield:** 9 servings.

Nutritional Analysis: One serving (1 cup) equals 214 calories, 3 g fat (1 g saturated fat), 16 mg cholesterol, 542 mg sodium, 31 g carbohydrate, 11 g fiber, 17 g protein.
Diabetic Exchanges: 2 lean meat, 1-1/2 starch, 1 vegetable.
△ **Low-fat**

Black Bean Chili

For a quick satisfying meal, ladle up big bowlfuls of vegetarian chili. Fresh corn bread is a delicious accompaniment.
—Pat Stanley, Canby, Minnesota

5 pts

- **2 cups chopped sweet onions**
- **2 tablespoons canola oil**
- **1/2 pound fresh mushrooms, sliced**
- **1 large green pepper, chopped**
- **1 large sweet yellow pepper, chopped**
- **1 large sweet red pepper, chopped**
- **3 garlic cloves, minced**
- **2 cans (15 ounces *each*) black beans, rinsed and drained**
- **2 cans (14-1/2 ounces *each*) diced tomatoes, undrained**
- **1 can (15 ounces) tomato sauce**
- **1 can (6 ounces) tomato paste**
- **2 tablespoons brown sugar**
- **2 to 3 teaspoons chili powder**
- **2 teaspoons ground cumin**

Dash hot pepper sauce

In a Dutch oven or soup kettle, saute onions in oil for 5 minutes. Add the mushrooms, peppers and garlic; saute for 5-6 minutes or until vegetables are tender. Stir in the remaining ingredients; bring to a boil. Reduce heat; cover and simmer for 20-25 minutes or until heated through. **Yield:** 7 servings.

Nutritional Analysis: One serving (about 1-1/2 cups) equals 253 calories, 5 g fat (trace saturated fat), 0 cholesterol, 751 mg sodium, 42 g carbohydrate, 10 g fiber, 11 g protein.
Diabetic Exchanges: 3 vegetable, 1-1/2 starch, 1 lean meat.
▲ **Meatless**

Chilled Cucumber Soup

(Pictured below)

This is a wonderful way to use up all those cucumbers that seem to be ready at the same time. It's so refreshing on hot summer days.
—Shirley Kidd, New London, Minnesota

3 pts

- **2 medium cucumbers**
- **2 cups 1% buttermilk**
- **1/2 cup reduced-fat sour cream**
- **1-1/2 teaspoons sugar**
- **1 teaspoon dill weed**
- **1/2 teaspoon salt**
- **1/8 teaspoon white pepper**
- **2 green onions, chopped**

Fresh dill, optional

Cut four thin slices of cucumber; set aside for garnish. Peel and finely chop remaining cucumbers. In a bowl, combine the buttermilk, sour cream, sugar, dill, salt, pepper, green onions and chopped cucumbers; mix well. Refrigerate for 4 hours or overnight. Garnish with cucumber slices and fresh dill if desired. **Yield:** 4 servings.

Nutritional Analysis: One serving (1 cup) equals 110 calories, 4 g fat (3 g saturated fat), 15 mg cholesterol, 445 mg sodium, 13 g carbohydrate, 1 g fiber, 7 g protein.
Diabetic Exchanges: 1 vegetable, 1/2 reduced-fat milk.
▲ **Meatless**

White Bean Fennel Soup

(Pictured above)

Even when my garden is snow-covered, its bounty crops up in the steaming bowls I pass around the table. This filling soup is a favorite with our family and is often requested for company dinners. A hint of fennel accents the flavor of this quick-to-fix bean soup.
—Donna Quinn, Salem, Wisconsin

3 pts

- 1 large onion, chopped
- 1 small fennel bulb, thinly sliced
- 1 tablespoon olive *or* canola oil
- 5 cups reduced-sodium chicken broth *or* vegetable broth
- 1 can (15 ounces) white kidney *or* cannellini beans, rinsed and drained
- 1 can (14-1/2 ounces) diced tomatoes, undrained
- 1 teaspoon dried thyme
- 1/4 teaspoon pepper
- 1 bay leaf
- 3 cups shredded fresh spinach

In a large saucepan, saute onion and fennel in oil until tender. Add the broth, beans, tomatoes, thyme, pepper and bay leaf; bring to a boil. Reduce heat; cover and simmer for 30 minutes or until fennel is tender. Discard bay leaf. Add spinach; cook 3-4 minutes longer or until spinach is wilted. **Yield:** 5 servings.

Nutritional Analysis: *One serving (1-1/2 cups) equals 152 calories, 3 g fat (trace saturated fat), 0 cholesterol, 976 mg sodium, 23 g carbohydrate, 7 g fiber, 8 g protein.*
Diabetic Exchanges: *1 starch, 1 vegetable, 1 very lean meat.*

△ **Low-fat**
▲ **Meatless**

Vegetable Beef Soup

(Pictured above)

Your crew will chase away winter's chill with a spoon when you cook up this hearty soup. It has such a rich flavor…and it's full of nutritious vegetables and chunks of tender steak.
—Brigitte Schultz, Barstow, California

4 pts

- 1 pound boneless beef sirloin steak, cut into 1/2-inch cubes
- 1/4 teaspoon pepper, *divided*
- 2 teaspoons olive *or* canola oil
- 2 cans (14-1/2 ounces *each*) beef broth
- 2 cups cubed peeled potatoes
- 1-1/4 cups water
- 2 medium carrots, sliced
- 1 tablespoon onion soup mix (28 oz)
- 1 tablespoon dried basil + 1 can diced tomatoes
- 1/2 teaspoon dried tarragon x
- 2 tablespoons cornstarch
- 1/2 cup white wine *or* additional beef broth

Sprinkle steak with 1/8 teaspoon pepper. In a Dutch oven, brown steak in batches in oil over medium heat. Add the broth, potatoes, water, carrots, onion soup mix, basil, tarragon and remaining pepper; bring to a boil. Reduce heat; cover and simmer for 20-25 minutes or until vegetables are tender. In a small bowl, combine the cornstarch and wine or additional broth until smooth; stir into soup. Bring to a boil; cook and stir for 2 minutes or until thickened. **Yield:** 7 servings.

Nutritional Analysis: *One serving (1 cup) equals 192 calories, 6 g fat (2 g saturated fat), 44 mg cholesterol, 633 mg sodium, 15 g carbohydrate, 2 g fiber, 17 g protein.*
Diabetic Exchanges: *2 lean meat, 1 starch.*

Beef Vegetable Soup

(Pictured below)

This nicely seasoned soup tastes so good. It's convenient, too, since it simmers all day in the slow cooker.
—Jean Hutzell, Dubuque, Iowa

- 1 pound lean ground beef
- 1 medium onion, chopped
- 1/2 teaspoon salt
- 1/4 teaspoon pepper
- 3 cups water
- 3 medium potatoes, peeled and cut into 3/4-inch cubes
- 1 can (14-1/2 ounces) Italian diced tomatoes, undrained
- 1 can (11-1/2 ounces) V8 juice
- 1 cup chopped celery
- 1 cup sliced carrots
- 2 tablespoons sugar
- 1 tablespoon dried parsley flakes
- 2 teaspoons dried basil
- 1 bay leaf

In a nonstick skillet, cook beef and onion over medium heat until meat is no longer pink; drain. Stir in salt and pepper. Transfer to a 5-qt. slow cooker. Add the remaining ingredients. Cover and cook on low for 9-11 hours or until vegetables are tender. Discard bay leaf before serving. **Yield:** 7 servings.

Nutritional Analysis: One serving (1-1/3 cups) equals 210 calories, 5 g fat (2 g saturated fat), 32 mg cholesterol, 537 mg sodium, 26 g carbohydrate, 3 g fiber, 15 g protein.
Diabetic Exchanges: 2 lean meat, 2 vegetable, 1 starch.

A Tomato's True Colors

WHAT MAKES a tomato show its true colors? According to J.W. Scott, a tomato breeder with the University of Florida, the answer is more than skin-deep.

Tomato color depends on the amount of carotene pigments in its flesh and skin. Most varieties are high in lycopene, the pigment that makes tomatoes red. Some, however, have a gene that shuts off lycopene, resulting in yellow tomatoes.

Yellow tomatoes taste a shade sweeter or milder since they have less acid than red varieties. Yellow tomatoes are lower in vitamin A due to low beta-carotene—an orange pigment found in red tomatoes that converts into vitamin A.

Sunset Tomato Soup

The secret to the beautiful orange color of this chunky soup I created is the mix of garden-fresh yellow tomatoes, red plum tomatoes and carrots.
—Emily Beebe, Stoughton, Wisconsin

- 4 medium carrots, sliced
- 1 medium onion, chopped
- 1 tablespoon olive *or* canola oil
- 3 to 4 large yellow tomatoes, peeled and coarsely chopped
- 4 plum tomatoes, peeled and coarsely chopped
- 1 can (14-1/2 ounces) reduced-sodium chicken broth *or* vegetable broth
- 1/2 teaspoon salt
- 1/4 teaspoon pepper
- 1-1/2 teaspoons snipped fresh dill *or* 3/4 teaspoon dill weed

In a Dutch oven or large kettle, saute carrots and onion in oil until onion is tender. Add the tomatoes, broth, salt and pepper. Bring to a boil. Reduce heat; simmer, uncovered, for 45-60 minutes or until liquid is slightly reduced. Stir in dill; simmer 15 minutes longer. **Yield:** 4 servings.

Nutritional Analysis: One serving (1-1/2 cups) equals 125 calories, 4 g fat (1 g saturated fat), 0 cholesterol, 650 mg sodium, 20 g carbohydrate, 5 g fiber, 5 g protein.
Diabetic Exchanges: 4 vegetable, 1/2 fat.
▲ **Meatless**

Tortellini Soup

*I like to top bowls of this tasty soup with a
little grated Parmesan cheese...and serve it with
crusty bread to round out the meal.*
—Donna Morgan, Hend, Tennessee

2 garlic cloves, minced
1 tablespoon butter *or* stick margarine
**3 cans (14-1/2 ounces *each*) reduced-sodium
chicken broth *or* vegetable broth**
**1 package (9 ounces) refrigerated cheese
tortellini**
**1 package (10 ounces) frozen chopped spinach,
thawed and squeezed dry**
**1 can (14-1/2 ounces) diced tomatoes with green
chilies, undrained**

In a saucepan, saute the garlic in butter until tender. Stir in
the broth. Bring to a boil. Add tortellini; cook for 5-6 minutes or until tender. Stir in the spinach and tomatoes; heat
through. **Yield:** 5 servings.

*Nutritional Analysis: One serving (1-1/2 cups) equals 242
calories, 6 g fat (4 g saturated fat), 25 mg cholesterol, 1,181 mg
sodium, 33 g carbohydrate, 4 g fiber, 13 g protein.*
*Diabetic Exchanges: 2 vegetable, 1-1/2 starch, 1 lean meat,
1/2 fat.*
▲ **Meatless**

HOME MADE SOUP (3 pts)
= 1 1/2 cups
4 MED. CARROTS, CHOPPED
1 MED ONION, CHOPPED
1-28 oz. CAN DICED TOMATO
2 CANS BEEF BROTH
4 CANS WATER
2 pkg. CHICKEN OXO
2 celery ribs, chopped
1/2 cup BARLEY
1 CAN WHITE KIDNEY BEAN
1 TSP SALT
-COOK IN CROCK POT
OVERNIGHT ON LOW-

Blackberry Soup

*This recipe for chilled soup stars a bounty
of berries. I have several blackberry bushes,
and they yielded an abundance of berries one year.
I came up with this recipe by adapting
another fruit soup recipe I had on hand.*
—Julie Ann Hillman, Cheney, Kansas

4 cups frozen blackberries, thawed
1 cup pear juice
1/2 cup honey
1/4 cup water
1 lime *or* lemon wedge
1/4 teaspoon ground cinnamon
1/4 teaspoon vanilla extract
Dash ground nutmeg
1 carton (8 ounces) fat-free vanilla yogurt

In a heavy saucepan, combine the first eight ingredients.
Cook, uncovered, over low heat for 20 minutes or until
berries are softened. Remove and discard lime wedge.
Strain berry mixture, reserving juice. Press blackberry
mixture through a fine meshed sieve; discard seeds. Add
pulp to juice. Cover and chill.
Set aside 2 tablespoons of the yogurt for the garnish.
Combine the blackberry mixture and remaining yogurt in a
food processor or blender; cover and process until smooth.
Ladle into soup bowls and dollop with reserved yogurt.
Yield: 4 servings.

*Nutritional Analysis: One serving (3/4 cup) equals 308 calo-
ries, 1 g fat (trace saturated fat), 1 mg cholesterol, 47 mg sodium,
76 g carbohydrate, 8 g fiber, 5 g protein.*
△ **Low-fat**
▲ **Low-sodium**
▲ **Meatless**

White Bean 'n' Barley Soup

(Pictured above and on page 31)

A friend of mine gave me this recipe, and it's delicious.
—Stephanie Land, Sudbury, Ontario

1-1/2 cups dried great northern beans
1 large onion, chopped
2 garlic cloves, minced
1 tablespoon olive *or* canola oil
4 cups chicken *or* vegetable broth
4 cups water
3 medium carrots, sliced
2 medium sweet red peppers, diced
2 celery ribs, chopped
1/2 cup medium pearl barley
1/2 cup minced fresh parsley, *divided*
2 bay leaves
1 teaspoon salt
1/2 teaspoon dried thyme
1/2 teaspoon pepper
1 can (28 ounces) diced tomatoes, undrained

Place beans in a Dutch oven or soup kettle; add enough water to cover beans by 2 in. Bring to a boil; boil for 2 minutes. Remove from the heat; cover and let stand for 1
hour.
Drain and rinse beans, discarding liquid. In a Dutch oven,
saute onion and garlic in oil. Add the broth, water, beans,
carrots, red peppers, celery, barley, 1/4 cup parsley, bay
leaves, salt, thyme and pepper. Bring to a boil. Reduce heat;
cover and simmer for 1 hour or until beans are tender. Add
the tomatoes; heat through. Discard bay leaves. Sprinkle
with remaining parsley. **Yield:** 9 servings.

*Nutritional Analysis: One serving (1-1/2 cups) equals 193
calories, 3 g fat (trace saturated fat), 0 cholesterol, 831 mg sodium, 35 g carbohydrate, 9 g fiber, 10 g protein.*
*Diabetic Exchanges: 2 vegetable, 1-1/2 starch, 1 very lean
meat.*
△ **Low-fat**
▲ **Meatless**

Creamy Asparagus Soup

This asparagus soup tastes just like spring! Pureed to a smooth and creamy texture, it is nicely seasoned with thyme…and is sure to please asparagus lovers.
—Adele Long, Sterling Heights, Michigan

2 green onions, chopped
1 garlic clove, minced
1 tablespoon butter *or* stick margarine
2 cans (14-1/2 ounces *each*) reduced-sodium chicken broth *or* vegetable broth
1 pound fresh asparagus, trimmed and cut into 1-inch pieces
1/2 teaspoon salt
1/2 to 3/4 teaspoon dried thyme
1/8 teaspoon pepper
1 bay leaf
2 tablespoons all-purpose flour
3 tablespoons water
1/4 cup reduced-fat sour cream
1 teaspoon grated lemon peel

In a large saucepan, saute onions and garlic in butter. Add the broth, asparagus, salt, thyme, pepper and bay leaf. Bring to a boil. Reduce heat; cover and simmer for 8-10 minutes or until asparagus is tender. Drain asparagus, reserving cooking liquid. Discard bay leaf. Cool slightly.

In a food processor, combine asparagus and 1/2 cup cooking liquid; cover and process until smooth. Return pureed asparagus and remaining cooking liquid to pan. Combine flour and water until smooth; stir into soup. Bring to a boil; cook and stir for 1-2 minutes or until thickened. Garnish each serving with sour cream and lemon peel. **Yield:** 4 servings.

Nutritional Analysis: One serving (1 cup soup with 1 tablespoon sour cream) equals 107 calories, 4 g fat (3 g saturated fat), 13 mg cholesterol, 876 mg sodium, 11 g carbohydrate, 3 g fiber, 7 g protein.
Diabetic Exchanges: *1 vegetable, 1 fat, 1/2 starch.*
▲ **Meatless**

Minestrone Soup

(Pictured above)

Brimming with a harvest of garden bounty, this quick-to-fix soup is fresh-tasting and nutritious. The tomato-based broth is chock-full of everything from carrots and zucchini to garbanzo beans and elbow macaroni.
—Heather Ryan, Brown Deer, Wisconsin

4 medium carrots, chopped
1 medium zucchini, sliced
1/4 cup chopped onion
1 garlic clove, minced
1 tablespoon olive *or* canola oil
2 cans (14-1/2 ounces *each*) vegetable broth
3 cups V8 juice
1 can (15 ounces) garbanzo beans *or* chickpeas, drained
1 can (14-1/2 ounces) diced tomatoes, undrained
1 cup frozen cut green beans
1/2 cup uncooked elbow macaroni
1 teaspoon dried basil
1 tablespoon minced fresh parsley

In a Dutch oven, cook the carrots, zucchini, onion and garlic in oil for 7 minutes or until onion is tender. Add the broth, V8 juice, garbanzo beans, tomatoes, green beans, macaroni and basil. Bring to a boil. Reduce heat; simmer, uncovered, for 15 minutes. Stir in parsley. Cook 5 minutes longer or until macaroni is tender. **Yield:** 8 servings.

Nutritional Analysis: One serving (1-1/2 cups) equals 166 calories, 3 g fat (trace saturated fat), 0 cholesterol, 900 mg sodium, 30 g carbohydrate, 5 g fiber, 6 g protein.
Diabetic Exchanges: *3 vegetable, 1 starch, 1/2 fat.*
△ **Low-fat**
▲ **Meatless**

 Give Garbanzos a Go

LOOKING FOR a well-traveled legume? You'll find garbanzo beans getting into hot water in pots from the Middle East, India, North Africa and Spain to Italy, France and the U.S.

Also called chickpeas, garbanzos are slightly larger than peas and have a round, irregular shape, firm texture and mild nut-like flavor. They are an excellent source of protein and fiber, rich in calcium and iron and low in sodium.

Although garbanzos can be reddish or black, the buff-colored variety is most common. Look for pale tan ones with a uniform color. They are available dried or canned year-round. Garbanzos are delicious in soups, stews, salads and casseroles.

Turkey Barley Tomato Soup

(Pictured below)

This low-calorie soup is so quick to prepare and tastes so good. It's a real stomach-filler and warms us up on cold winter days.
—Denise Kilgore, Lino Lakes, Minnesota

1 pound lean ground turkey
3/4 cup sliced *or* baby carrots
1 medium onion, chopped
1 celery rib, chopped
1 garlic clove, minced
1 envelope reduced-sodium taco seasoning, *divided*
3-1/2 cups water
1 can (28 ounces) Italian diced tomatoes, undrained
3/4 cup quick-cooking barley
1/2 teaspoon minced fresh oregano *or* 1/8 teaspoon dried oregano

In a Dutch oven, cook the turkey, carrots, onion, celery, garlic and 1 tablespoon taco seasoning over medium heat until meat is no longer pink. Stir in the water, tomatoes and remaining taco seasoning; bring to a boil. Reduce heat; cover and simmer for 20 minutes. Add barley; cover and simmer for 15-20 minutes longer or until barley is tender. Stir in oregano. **Yield:** 6 servings.

Nutritional Analysis: *One serving (1-1/2 cups) equals 275 calories, 7 g fat (2 g saturated fat), 60 mg cholesterol, 923 mg sodium, 36 g carbohydrate, 6 g fiber, 18 g protein.*
Diabetic Exchanges: *2 lean meat, 2 vegetable, 1-1/2 starch.*

Two-Bean Soup

(Pictured above)

My husband, David, and I volunteer at our American Legion post, cooking dinner on Friday nights. David, who loves beans, concocted this hearty soup that combines limas and great northerns with cubes of ham and chopped vegetables.
—Lee Hawk, San Diego, California

1/2 pound dried baby lima beans
1/2 pound dried great northern beans
1 can (49-1/2 ounces) reduced-sodium chicken broth
1-1/2 cups cubed fully cooked lean ham
1 medium onion, chopped
2 celery ribs with leaves, chopped
2 medium carrots, sliced
3 garlic cloves, minced
1/8 teaspoon ground ginger
2 green onions, sliced

Place beans in a large saucepan or Dutch oven; add water to cover by 2 in. Bring to a boil; boil for 2 minutes. Remove from the heat; cover and let stand for 1 hour.

Drain and rinse beans, discarding liquid. Return beans to pan. Add broth and ham; bring to a boil. Reduce heat; cover and simmer for 1 hour. Add the onion, celery, carrots, garlic and ginger; return to a boil. Reduce heat; cover and simmer 30 minutes longer or until beans and vegetables are tender. Garnish with green onions. **Yield:** 7 servings.

Nutritional Analysis: *One serving (1-1/2 cups) equals 215 calories, 2 g fat (1 g saturated fat), 9 mg cholesterol, 895 mg sodium, 31 g carbohydrate, 10 g fiber, 19 g protein.*
Diabetic Exchanges: *2 lean meat, 1-1/2 starch, 1 vegetable.*
△ **Low-fat**

Celery Zucchini Soup

There's a harvest of flavor in this pleasant celery soup. I concocted the recipe at the end of the growing season with leftover vegetables from our garden.
—Alyson Sprague, Sewickley, Pennsylvania

- 3 green onions, thinly sliced
- 2 garlic cloves, minced
- 2 tablespoons butter *or* stick margarine
- 4 celery ribs, chopped
- 2 medium carrots, chopped
- 2 cups water
- 1 tablespoon reduced-sodium chicken bouillon granules *or* 3 vegetable bouillon cubes
- 3/4 teaspoon salt
- 3/4 teaspoon dried thyme
- 5 medium red potatoes, cut into small chunks (about 1 pound)
- 3 cups fat-free milk
- 2 cups shredded zucchini
- 2 tablespoons cornstarch
- 1/4 cup cold water

In a large saucepan, saute onions and garlic in butter until tender. Add celery and carrots; cook and stir for 4 minutes. Stir in the water, bouillon, salt and thyme. Add potatoes. Bring to a boil. Reduce heat; cover and simmer about 15 minutes or until potatoes are tender. Stir in milk and zucchini. Bring to a boil. In a small bowl, combine cornstarch and cold water until smooth. Gradually whisk into soup. Return to a boil; cook and stir for 2 minutes or until slightly thickened. **Yield:** 6 servings.

Nutritional Analysis: One serving (1-1/2 cups) equals 175 calories, 4 g fat (2 g saturated fat), 13 mg cholesterol, 651 mg sodium, 28 g carbohydrate, 3 g fiber, 7 g protein.
Diabetic Exchanges: 1 starch, 1 vegetable, 1 fat, 1/2 fat-free milk.

▲ **Meatless**

Taco Soup

(Pictured above right)

Savory and satisfying, this thick chili-like soup has mild taco flavor and eye-appealing color. It comes together quickly and always brings compliments. A meal in itself, the recipe can easily be doubled to make more servings.
—Marylou von Scheele, University Place, Washington

- 1 pound lean ground beef
- 1 medium onion, chopped
- 1 medium green pepper, chopped
- 1 envelope reduced-sodium taco seasoning
- 2/3 cup water
- 4 cups reduced-sodium V8 juice
- 1 cup chunky salsa
TOPPINGS:
- 3/4 cup shredded lettuce
- 6 tablespoons chopped fresh tomato
- 6 tablespoons reduced-fat shredded cheddar cheese
- 1/4 cup chopped green onions
- 1/4 cup fat-free sour cream
Baked tortilla chips, optional

In a large saucepan coated with nonstick cooking spray, cook the beef, onion and pepper over medium heat until meat is no longer pink and vegetables are tender; drain. Stir in taco seasoning and water; cook and stir for 5 minutes or until liquid is reduced.

Add V8 juice and salsa; bring to a boil. Reduce heat; simmer, uncovered, for 5 minutes or until heated through. Top each serving with 2 tablespoons of lettuce, 1 tablespoon of tomato and cheese, and 2 teaspoons of green onions and sour cream. Serve with tortilla chips if desired. **Yield:** 6 servings.

Nutritional Analysis: One serving (1-1/3 cups soup with toppings, calculated without chips) equals 229 calories, 7 g fat (3 g saturated fat), 43 mg cholesterol, 726 mg sodium, 20 g carbohydrate, 3 g fiber, 19 g protein.
Diabetic Exchanges: 3 vegetable, 2 lean meat, 1/2 starch.

White Turkey Chili

I came up with this dish by combining several recipes I liked and changing the flavors until it was just right. It's so simple to make.
—Tina Barrett, Puerto La Cruz, Venezuela

- 2 cups cubed cooked turkey breast
- 2 cans (15 ounces *each*) white kidney *or* cannellini beans, rinsed and drained
- 1 can (10-3/4 ounces) reduced-fat reduced-sodium condensed cream of chicken soup, undiluted
- 1-1/3 cups fat-free milk
- 1 can (4 ounces) chopped green chilies, drained
- 1 tablespoon dried minced onion
- 1 tablespoon minced fresh cilantro *or* parsley
- 1 teaspoon garlic powder
- 1 teaspoon ground cumin

1 teaspoon dried oregano
6 tablespoons fat-free sour cream

In a large saucepan, combine the first 10 ingredients; bring to a boil. Reduce heat; cover and simmer for 25-30 minutes or until heated through. Garnish with sour cream. **Yield:** 6 servings.

Nutritional Analysis: One serving (1 cup) equals 250 calories, 2 g fat (1 g saturated fat), 47 mg cholesterol, 510 mg sodium, 31 g carbohydrate, 6 g fiber, 23 g protein.
Diabetic Exchanges: 3 very lean meat, 2 starch.
△ *Low-fat*

Fennel Carrot Soup

2 pts

This recipe for soup is perfect as a first course for a special-occasion dinner. The pretty pumpkin-orange soup gets delicious flavor from toasted fennel seeds—a pleasant complement to the carrots, apple and sweet potato.
—*Marlene Bursey, Waverley, Nova Scotia*

1/2 teaspoon fennel seed
1 tablespoon butter *or* stick margarine
1-1/2 pounds carrots, sliced
1 medium sweet potato, peeled and cubed
1 medium apple, peeled and cubed
3 cans (14-1/2 ounces *each*) vegetable broth
2 tablespoons uncooked long grain rice
1/4 teaspoon curry powder
1 bay leaf
1 tablespoon lemon juice
1 teaspoon salt
1/4 teaspoon white pepper
2 tablespoons minced fresh parsley

In a large saucepan, saute fennel seed in butter for 2-3 minutes or until lightly toasted. Add the carrots, sweet potato and apple; saute for 5 minutes. Stir in the broth, rice, curry powder and bay leaf; bring to a boil. Reduce heat; cover and simmer for 30 minutes or until rice and vegetables are very tender.

Remove from the heat and cool slightly. Discard bay leaf. In a blender or food processor, process soup in batches until pureed. Return to saucepan. Stir in the lemon juice, salt and pepper. Cook for 5 minutes or until heated through. Sprinkle with parsley. **Yield:** 8 servings (2 quarts).

Nutritional Analysis: One serving (1 cup) equals 117 calories, 2 g fat (1 g saturated fat), 4 mg cholesterol, 989 mg sodium, 23 g carbohydrate, 3 g fiber, 3 g protein.
Diabetic Exchanges: 2 vegetable, 1 starch.
△ *Low-fat*
▲ *Meatless*

Brown Rice Turkey Soup

5 pts

(Pictured below)

I don't recall where I got this recipe, but it's my all-time favorite turkey soup. Everyone who has tried it agrees. The sweet red pepper is what gives the soup its distinctive flavor.
—*Bobby Langley, Rocky Mount, North Carolina*

1 cup diced sweet red pepper
1/2 cup chopped onion
1/2 cup sliced celery
2 garlic cloves, minced
2 tablespoons butter *or* stick margarine
3 cans (14-1/2 ounces *each*) reduced-sodium chicken broth
3/4 cup white wine *or* additional reduced-sodium chicken broth
1 teaspoon dried thyme
1/4 teaspoon pepper
2 cups cubed cooked turkey breast
1 cup instant brown rice
1/4 cup sliced green onions

In a Dutch oven, saute the red pepper, onion, celery and garlic in butter for 5-7 minutes or until vegetables are tender. Add the broth, wine or additional broth, thyme and pepper. Bring to a boil. Reduce heat; cover and simmer for 5 minutes. Stir in turkey and rice. Bring to a boil; simmer, uncovered, for 5 minutes or until rice is tender. Garnish with green onions. **Yield:** 5 servings.

Nutritional Analysis: One serving (1-1/2 cups) equals 259 calories, 8 g fat (4 g saturated fat), 55 mg cholesterol, 766 mg sodium, 20 g carbohydrate, 2 g fiber, 22 g protein.
Diabetic Exchanges: 3 lean meat, 1 starch, 1 vegetable.

Zippy Slow-Cooked Chili

(Pictured below)

Serve up steaming bowls of this chili to warm your family on a cold winter's day...and you'll get plenty of compliments! This recipe for nicely spiced chili simmers all day in the slow cooker.
—Travis Skroch, Stratford, Wisconsin

- 1 pound lean ground beef
- 1 can (28 ounces) diced tomatoes, undrained
- 1 medium onion, chopped
- 1 medium green pepper, chopped
- 1 can (15 ounces) fat-free vegetarian chili
- 1 can (8 ounces) tomato sauce
- 2 tablespoons chili powder
- 2 tablespoons minced fresh parsley
- 1 tablespoon dried basil
- 2 teaspoons ground cumin
- 4 garlic cloves, minced
- 1 teaspoon dried oregano
- 3/4 teaspoon pepper
- 1/8 teaspoon hot pepper sauce
- 6 tablespoons shredded reduced-fat cheddar cheese
- 1 tablespoon minced chives

In a nonstick skillet, cook beef over medium heat until no longer pink; drain. Transfer to a 3-qt. slow cooker. Add the tomatoes, onion, green pepper, chili, tomato sauce, chili powder, parsley, basil, cumin, garlic, oregano, pepper and hot pepper sauce. Cover and cook on low for 6-8 hours. Sprinkle with cheese and chives before serving. **Yield:** 6 servings.

Nutritional Analysis: One serving (1-1/3 cups) equals 266 calories, 8 g fat (3 g saturated fat), 42 mg cholesterol, 759 mg sodium, 27 g carbohydrate, 8 g fiber, 23 g protein.
Diabetic Exchanges: 3 lean meat, 3 vegetable, 1/2 starch.

Orzo Chicken Soup

(Pictured above)

For a different twist on noodle soup, add orzo— small rice-like grains of pasta. It cooks up nicely with tender chunks of chicken.
—Betty Rench, Eaton, Indiana

- 1/2 cup chopped onion
- 1 tablespoon butter *or* stick margarine
- 3 cans (14-1/2 ounces *each*) reduced-sodium chicken broth, *divided*
- 1/2 cup sliced carrot
- 1/2 cup chopped celery
- 1 cup cubed cooked chicken breast
- 1/2 cup uncooked orzo pasta
- 1/4 teaspoon pepper
- Minced fresh parsley

In a large saucepan, saute onion in butter until tender. Add 1 can broth, carrot and celery; bring to a boil. Reduce heat; cover and simmer for 15 minutes. Add the chicken, orzo, pepper and remaining broth; return to a boil. Reduce heat; cover and simmer for 25-30 minutes or until orzo and vegetables are tender. Sprinkle with parsley. **Yield:** 4 servings.

Nutritional Analysis: One serving (1-1/2 cups) equals 225 calories, 5 g fat (2 g saturated fat), 38 mg cholesterol, 890 mg sodium, 26 g carbohydrate, 2 g fiber, 19 g protein.
Diabetic Exchanges: 2 very lean meat, 1-1/2 starch, 1 vegetable, 1/2 fat.

Step Up to The Salad Bar

Whether you're looking for a standout side dish to accompany a main course, a tangy take-along for the neighborhood barbecue or an appealing addition to your lunchtime lineup, nothing beats garden-fresh salads!

Black Bean Chicken Salad (page 64)

Rainbow Melon Julep

(Pictured below)

Three different kinds of melons make up this colorful fruit medley. Lime juice and soda, plus a hint of mint, season this pretty citrus salad.
—Sue Ross, Casa Grande, Arizona

       3 cups watermelon balls
       3 cups honeydew balls
       2 cups cantaloupe balls
       1/2 cup orange juice
       1/2 cup lime juice
    Sugar substitute equivalent to 1/4 cup sugar*
       2 tablespoons minced fresh mint *or* 2 teaspoons dried mint
       2 teaspoons grated orange peel
       2 teaspoons grated lime peel
       1 cup diet lemon-lime soda

In a large bowl, combine the melon balls. In a small bowl, combine the orange juice, lime juice, sugar substitute, mint, orange peel and lime peel. Pour over melon; toss gently to coat. Cover and refrigerate for 2 hours or until chilled. Just before serving, add soda and toss gently. **Yield:** 8 servings.

*Editor's Note: This recipe was tested with Splenda No Calorie Sweetener. Look for it in the baking aisle of your grocery store.

Nutritional Analysis: One serving (1 cup) equals 72 calories, trace fat (trace saturated fat), 0 cholesterol, 16 mg sodium, 20 g carbohydrate, 1 g fiber, 1 g protein.
Diabetic Exchange: *1-1/2 fruit.*
△ **Low-fat**
▲ **Low-sodium**
▲ **Meatless**

Pineapple Grapefruit Salad

This sweet-tart salad, nicely coated in a yogurt dressing, makes a refreshing light luncheon dish. I usually put a scoop of low-fat cottage cheese in the center of the plate and surround it with the salad.
—Rosemarie Kondrk, Old Bridge, New Jersey

       1 can (20 ounces) unsweetened pineapple tidbits, drained
       1 medium pink grapefruit, peeled, sectioned and cut into bite-size pieces
       1/2 cup fat-free plain yogurt
    Sugar substitute equivalent to 4-1/2 teaspoons sugar*
       1/2 teaspoon vanilla extract
       5 maraschino cherries

In a bowl, combine pineapple and grapefruit. Refrigerate until chilled. Drain if necessary. Just before serving, combine the yogurt, sugar substitute and vanilla. Pour over fruit; toss to coat. Top each serving with a cherry. **Yield:** 5 servings.

*Editor's Note: This recipe was tested with Splenda No Calorie Sweetener. Look for it in the baking aisle of your grocery store.

Nutritional Analysis: One serving (1/2 cup) equals 91 calories, 0 fat (0 saturated fat), 1 mg cholesterol, 20 mg sodium, 22 g carbohydrate, 4 g fiber, 2 g protein.
Diabetic Exchange: *1-1/2 fruit.*
△ **Low-fat**
▲ **Low-sodium**
▲ **Meatless**

Crunchy Apple-Pecan Slaw

This salad is so quick to put together using a convenient coleslaw mix. It is crunchy and flavorful...and the toasted pecans make it seem special. A friend shared the recipe.
—M.K. Bishop, North Platte, Nebraska

       5 cups shredded cabbage
       2 sweet apples, diced
       1/2 cup coarsely chopped pecans, toasted
       1/2 cup golden raisins
       3 green onions, chopped
       1/2 cup reduced-fat mayonnaise
       1/2 cup 1% buttermilk
       1 tablespoon lemon juice
       1 tablespoon honey
       1/4 to 1/2 teaspoon pepper

In a large bowl, toss the cabbage, apples, pecans, raisins and onions. In a small bowl, whisk the remaining ingredients. Pour over cabbage mixture and toss to coat. Cover and refrigerate until serving. **Yield:** 10 servings.

Nutritional Analysis: One serving (3/4 cup) equals 143 calories, 9 g fat (1 g saturated fat), 5 mg cholesterol, 118 mg sodium, 17 g carbohydrate, 3 g fiber, 2 g protein.
Diabetic Exchanges: *1-1/2 vegetable, 1 fruit, 1 fat.*
▲ **Low-sodium**
▲ **Meatless**

Mandarin Orange Chicken Salad

My sister-in-law introduced me to this colorful salad with a delicious homemade dressing. I reduced the oil and salt and switched to light soy sauce.
—Renee Heimerl, Oakfield, Wisconsin

3/4 pound boneless skinless chicken breasts, cubed
1/4 cup reduced-sodium teriyaki sauce
8 cups torn mixed salad greens
1 can (11 ounces) mandarin oranges, drained
1 medium carrot, shredded
1/4 cup slivered almonds, toasted
3 tablespoons thinly sliced green onions
DRESSING:
2 tablespoons white wine vinegar *or* cider vinegar
2 tablespoons olive *or* canola oil
1 tablespoon reduced-sodium soy sauce
2 teaspoons sugar
1/2 teaspoon ground ginger
1/4 teaspoon salt
1/4 teaspoon pepper

In a large resealable plastic bag, combine the chicken and teriyaki sauce. Seal the bag and turn to coat; refrigerate for 1-2 hours. Drain and discard the marinade. In a large nonstick skillet coated with nonstick cooking spray, cook and stir the chicken for 5-7 minutes or until no longer pink. Refrigerate until chilled.

In a large bowl, combine the salad greens, chicken, oranges, carrot, almonds and onions. In a jar with a tight-fitting lid, combine the dressing ingredients; shake well. Drizzle over the salad and toss to coat. **Yield:** 4 servings.

Nutritional Analysis: One serving (2 cups dressed salad) equals 262 calories, 12 g fat (1 g saturated fat), 49 mg cholesterol, 471 mg sodium, 16 g carbohydrate, 4 g fiber, 24 g protein.
Diabetic Exchanges: 3 lean meat, 1 vegetable, 1 fat, 1/2 fruit.

Sesame Chicken Couscous Salad

(Pictured above right)

I grow lots of the ingredients needed in this recipe. Fresh-tasting and crunchy, it's a perfect summer salad.
—Tari Ambler, Shorewood, Illinois

1-1/2 cups reduced-sodium chicken broth
3 teaspoons reduced-sodium soy sauce, *divided*
2 teaspoons sesame oil, *divided*
1 cup uncooked couscous
2 green onions, sliced
1-1/2 cups fresh *or* frozen sugar snap peas
3/4 cup fresh broccoli florets
1-1/2 cups cubed cooked chicken
1 large sweet red pepper, chopped
3/4 cup diced zucchini
2 tablespoons cider vinegar
1 tablespoon apple juice concentrate
1 tablespoon water
2 teaspoons canola oil
1/2 teaspoon ground ginger
1/4 teaspoon pepper
2 tablespoons slivered almonds, toasted
2 teaspoons sesame seeds, toasted

In a saucepan, combine the broth, 1 teaspoon soy sauce and 1 teaspoon sesame oil; bring to a boil. Stir in couscous. Cover and remove from the heat. Let stand for 5 minutes. Fluff with a fork. Stir in green onions. Cover and refrigerate until chilled.

Place pea pods in a steamer basket in a saucepan over 1 in. of water; bring to a boil. Cover and steam for 1 minute. Add broccoli; cover and steam 2 minutes longer or until crisp-tender. Rinse in cold water; drain. Transfer to a serving bowl; add chicken, red pepper and zucchini.

In a jar with a tight-fitting lid, combine the vinegar, apple juice concentrate, water, canola oil, ginger, pepper and remaining soy sauce and sesame oil. Shake well. Pour over chicken mixture and toss to coat. Cover and refrigerate for 30 minutes or until chilled. Serve over couscous. Sprinkle with almonds and sesame seeds. **Yield:** 4 servings.

Nutritional Analysis: One serving (1 cup chicken mixture with 3/4 cup couscous) equals 382 calories, 9 g fat (1 g saturated fat), 45 mg cholesterol, 451 mg sodium, 45 g carbohydrate, 6 g fiber, 26 g protein.
Diabetic Exchanges: 3 lean meat, 2 starch, 2 vegetable.

Hominy Bean Salad

(Pictured at right)

Chock-full of fresh and canned beans, this colorful salad is perfect for a potluck. I am a great-grandmother who loves to cook—from fancy meals for company to simple bean and corn bread suppers.
—De Loris Lawson, Carthage, Missouri

> 2 cups fresh green beans, cut into 2-inch pieces
> 1 can (16 ounces) kidney beans, rinsed and drained
> 1 can (15-1/2 ounces) hominy, rinsed and drained
> 1 can (15 ounces) black beans, rinsed and drained
> 1 cup thinly sliced celery
> 1 cup thinly sliced red onion
> 1 medium sweet red pepper, julienned
> 1/2 cup white wine vinegar *or* cider vinegar
> 1/2 cup minced fresh cilantro *or* parsley
> 1/4 cup olive *or* canola oil
> 2 teaspoons sugar
> 1 garlic clove, minced
> 1/2 teaspoon salt
> 1/2 teaspoon coarsely ground pepper

Place green beans in a saucepan and cover with water. Bring to a boil. Cook, uncovered, for 8-10 minutes or until crisp-tender; drain and rinse in cold water. In a serving bowl, combine the green beans, kidney beans, hominy, black beans, celery, onion and red pepper.

In a jar with a tight-fitting lid, combine the remaining ingredients; shake well. Pour over vegetables and stir gently to coat. Cover and refrigerate for at least 1 hour. **Yield:** 12 servings.

Nutritional Analysis: One serving (3/4 cup) equals 146 calories, 5 g fat (1 g saturated fat), 0 cholesterol, 425 mg sodium, 20 g carbohydrate, 6 g fiber, 5 g protein.
   Diabetic Exchanges: 1 starch, 1 vegetable, 1 fat.
   ▲ *Meatless*

Kiwi-Strawberry Spinach Salad

(Pictured at right)

This pretty salad is always a hit when I serve it. The recipe came from a cookbook, but I "doctored" it to personalize it. Sometimes just a small change in ingredients can make a big difference in taste.
—Laura Pounds, Andover, Kansas

> 12 cups torn fresh spinach
> 2 pints fresh strawberries, halved
> 4 kiwifruit, peeled and cut into 1/4-inch slices

> 1/3 cup sugar
> 1/4 cup canola oil
> 1/4 cup raspberry vinegar
> 1/4 teaspoon paprika
> 1/4 teaspoon Worcestershire sauce
> 2 green onions, chopped
> 2 tablespoons sesame seeds, toasted
> 1 tablespoon poppy seeds

In a large salad bowl, combine the spinach, strawberries and kiwi. In a blender or food processor, combine the sugar, oil, vinegar, paprika and Worcestershire sauce; cover and process for 30 seconds. Add onions, sesame seeds and poppy seeds. Pour over salad and toss to coat. Serve immediately. **Yield:** 12 servings.

Nutritional Analysis: One serving (1 cup) equals 121 calories, 6 g fat (trace saturated fat), 0 cholesterol, 64 mg sodium, 16 g carbohydrate, 4 g fiber, 3 g protein.
   Diabetic Exchanges: 1 fruit, 1 fat, 1/2 vegetable.
   ▲ *Low-sodium*
   ▲ *Meatless*

Barley Ham Salad

A pleasant alternative to pasta salad, this side dish combines barley, cubed ham and a medley of vegetables. Every time I make it for a crowd, I bring copies of the recipe. As a busy wife and mom of four, I like the fact that it can be made ahead of time.
—Sheryl Hershberger, Donalds, South Carolina

> 6 cups cooked medium pearl barley
> 1 cup (6 ounces) cubed fully cooked ham
> 2 celery ribs, diced
> 1/2 cup sliced water chestnuts
> 1/2 cup chopped green pepper
> 1 jar (4 ounces) diced pimientos, drained
> 1/2 cup sliced green onions
> 1/2 cup sliced fresh mushrooms
> **DRESSING:**
> 1/2 cup white vinegar
> 1/4 cup olive *or* canola oil
> 1/3 cup sugar
> 1 envelope (.7 ounce) Italian salad dressing mix

In a large bowl, combine the first eight ingredients. In a jar with a tight-fitting lid, combine the dressing ingredients; shake well. Pour over barley mixture and stir to coat. Cover and refrigerate for at least 2 hours, stirring occasionally. **Yield:** 12 servings.

Nutritional Analysis: One serving (3/4 cup) equals 234 calories, 7 g fat (1 g saturated fat), 4 mg cholesterol, 185 mg sodium, 38 g carbohydrate, 8 g fiber, 7 g protein.
   Diabetic Exchanges: 2 starch, 1 lean meat, 1 fat.

Cherry Gelatin Salad

Pineapple and cherries provide added interest to this cherry and lemon gelatin molded salad. With its cherry cola flavor, the salad is a fun take-along dish for a picnic, potluck or family reunion.
—Amy Olson, Louisville, Kentucky

1 can (8 ounces) unsweetened crushed
   pineapple, undrained
1/2 cup water
1 package (.3 ounce) sugar-free cherry gelatin
1 package (.3 ounce) sugar-free lemon gelatin
1 can (12 ounces) diet cola
1 can (15 ounces) water-packed pitted dark sweet
   cherries, drained and chopped

In a saucepan, bring pineapple and water to a boil. Stir in cherry and lemon gelatin until dissolved. Stir in cola and cherries. Pour into a 4-cup mold coated with nonstick cooking spray. Refrigerate until firm. **Yield:** 12 servings.

Nutritional Analysis: One serving equals 33 calories, trace fat (trace saturated fat), 0 cholesterol, 43 mg sodium, 7 g carbohydrate, 1 g fiber, 1 g protein.
Diabetic Exchange: *1/2 fruit.*
  △ *Low-fat*
  ▲ *Low-sodium*

Pineapple Coleslaw

This twist on traditional cabbage slaw gets a touch of sweetness from raisins and pineapple and a little zip from its horseradish dressing.
—Terri Webber, Miami, Florida

1 can (20 ounces) unsweetened pineapple tidbits
4 cups shredded cabbage
1/2 cup shredded carrot
1/3 cup raisins
2 tablespoons reduced-fat mayonnaise
1 tablespoon lemon juice
4 teaspoons prepared horseradish
1/2 teaspoon celery seed
1/2 teaspoon salt

Drain pineapple, reserving 2 tablespoons juice (discard remaining juice or save for another use). In a large bowl, combine the pineapple, cabbage, carrot and raisins. In a jar with a tight-fitting lid, combine the mayonnaise, lemon juice, horseradish, celery seed, salt and reserved pineapple juice; shake well. Pour over cabbage mixture and toss to coat. Cover and refrigerate for 2 hours. **Yield:** 8 servings.

Nutritional Analysis: One serving (3/4 cup) equals 78 calories, 1 g fat (trace saturated fat), 1 mg cholesterol, 195 mg sodium, 18 g carbohydrate, 2 g fiber, 1 g protein.
Diabetic Exchanges: *1 fruit, 1 vegetable.*
  △ *Low-fat*
  ▲ *Meatless*

Shrimp Shell Salad

(Pictured below)

My mother came up with this lovely salad when she lived in Anchorage, Alaska, and I modified it to make it lower in fat. Instead of buying small shrimp and chopping them, I often use salad shrimp.
—Adrienne Barbe, Litchfield, Connecticut

1 cup fat-free mayonnaise
1/2 cup seafood sauce
1 teaspoon prepared horseradish
1/2 teaspoon dried tarragon
1/2 teaspoon dried basil
1/4 teaspoon celery seed
1/8 teaspoon pepper
2 hard-cooked eggs
2 cups cooked small shrimp, *divided*
2 cups cooked small pasta shells
3 celery ribs with leaves, chopped
3 green onions, thinly sliced
5 lettuce leaves

For dressing, in a bowl, whisk the first seven ingredients. Cover and refrigerate until chilled. Cut eggs in half; discard yolks or save for another use. Chop egg whites. Set aside 10 shrimp for garnish; chop remaining shrimp.

In a bowl, combine the chopped shrimp, pasta, celery, egg whites and green onions. Add dressing and toss to coat. Serve on lettuce. Garnish with reserved shrimp. **Yield:** 5 servings.

Nutritional Analysis: One serving (1 cup) equals 214 calories, 1 g fat (trace saturated fat), 89 mg cholesterol, 835 mg sodium, 35 g carbohydrate, 1 g fiber, 16 g protein.
Diabetic Exchanges: *2 very lean meat, 2 starch, 1 vegetable.*
  △ *Low-fat*

Cucumber Fennel Salad

Our Test Kitchen home economists suggest this side dish as a cool addition to backyard barbecues.

**3 large cucumbers, sliced
1 medium sweet onion, thinly sliced
1 small fennel bulb, thinly sliced
3 tablespoons lemon juice
3 tablespoons olive *or* canola oil
3/4 teaspoon dill weed
1/2 teaspoon salt
1/4 teaspoon pepper
1/4 teaspoon grated lemon peel**

In a bowl, combine cucumber, onion and fennel. In a jar with a tight-fitting lid, combine remaining ingredients; shake well. Pour over salad; toss to coat. Chill. **Yield:** 8 servings.

Nutritional Analysis: One serving (1 cup) equals 80 calories, 5 g fat (1 g saturated fat), 0 cholesterol, 165 mg sodium, 8 g carbohydrate, 2 g fiber, 1 g protein.
Diabetic Exchanges: *1 vegetable, 1 fat.*
▲ *Meatless*

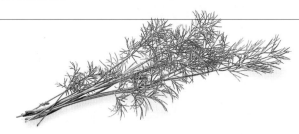

Watermelon Ambrosia

Colorful watermelon, pineapple, fruit cocktail, maraschino cherries and more are combined in this eye-catching fruit salad that's sure to take center stage at your next summer buffet!
—Sandy Leversee, Apache Junction, Arizona

**3 cups watermelon balls
1 can (20 ounces) unsweetened pineapple tidbits, drained
1 can (16 ounces) reduced-sugar fruit cocktail, drained
1 can (15 ounces) mandarin oranges, drained
1 jar (10 ounces) maraschino cherries, well drained
1 cup miniature marshmallows
1 cup diet lemon-lime soda, chilled
1/4 cup flaked coconut**

In a large bowl, combine watermelon balls, pineapple, fruit cocktail, oranges, cherries and marshmallows. Add soda and gently toss to coat. Cover and refrigerate for 2 hours or until chilled. Just before serving, stir in coconut. **Yield:** 10 servings.

Nutritional Analysis: One serving (3/4 cup) equals 116 calories, 1 g fat (1 g saturated fat), 0 cholesterol, 25 mg sodium, 28 g carbohydrate, 1 g fiber, 1 g protein.
Diabetic Exchange: *2 fruit.*
△ *Low-fat*
▲ *Low-sodium*
▲ *Meatless*

Chicken Bow Tie Salad

(Pictured above)

I first prepared this pasta salad for a family picnic at a national park and everyone really enjoyed it. I'm sure Mother Nature helped make that meal so memorable, but I still find myself serving this often during the summer. A zippy dressing lightly coats the tossed mixture of pasta, chicken, tomato and onion.
—Pam Guerin, Skowhegan, Maine

**8 ounces uncooked bow tie pasta
1 can (4 ounces) chopped green chilies, drained
3 tablespoons lime juice
3 tablespoons canola oil
2 garlic cloves, minced
1 teaspoon ground cumin
1/2 teaspoon sugar
1/2 teaspoon hot pepper sauce
2 cups cubed grilled *or* cooked chicken breast
2 large tomatoes, chopped
1/3 cup chopped red onion
3 tablespoons minced fresh cilantro *or* parsley**

Cook pasta according to package directions; rinse with cold water and drain. Cool completely. For dressing, combine the chilies, lime juice, oil, garlic, cumin, sugar and hot pepper sauce in a small bowl; stir well. In a large bowl, combine the pasta, chicken, tomatoes, onion and cilantro. Add dressing and toss gently to coat. Cover and refrigerate overnight. **Yield:** 6 servings.

Nutritional Analysis: One serving (1-1/2 cups) equals 294 calories, 10 g fat (1 g saturated fat), 40 mg cholesterol, 111 mg sodium, 32 g carbohydrate, 3 g fiber, 20 g protein.
Diabetic Exchanges: *2 starch, 2 lean meat, 1 fat.*
▲ *Low-sodium*

Roasted Garlic Vinaigrette

Our Test Kitchen came up with this full-flavored vinaigrette. Roasted garlic is blended with Italian seasoning, Dijon mustard, tarragon vinegar and lemon juice in the zesty dressing. Try it drizzled over crisp greens or cherry tomatoes.

3 large whole garlic bulbs
1 teaspoon plus 2 tablespoons olive *or* canola oil, *divided*
3 tablespoons tarragon vinegar
2 tablespoons water
1 tablespoon sugar
1 tablespoon lemon juice
1-1/2 teaspoons Italian seasoning
1/2 teaspoon Dijon mustard
1/4 teaspoon salt
1/8 teaspoon pepper

Remove papery outer skin from garlic (do not peel or separate cloves). Cut top off each garlic bulb. Brush with 1 teaspoon oil. Wrap bulbs in heavy-duty foil. Bake at 425° for 30-35 minutes or until softened. Cool for 10-15 minutes.

Squeeze softened garlic into a blender. Add the vinegar, water, sugar, lemon juice, Italian seasoning, mustard, salt, pepper and remaining oil; cover and process until smooth. Store in the refrigerator. **Yield:** 3/4 cup.

Nutritional Analysis: One serving (2 tablespoons) equals 83 calories, 5 g fat (1 g saturated fat), 0 cholesterol, 111 mg sodium, 8 g carbohydrate, trace fiber, 1 g protein.
Diabetic Exchanges: *1 vegetable, 1 fat.*
▲ **Low-sodium**
▲ **Meatless**

Kiwi Lime Gelatin

Our Test Kitchen broke the mold when they came up with this bright green gem of a salad featuring kiwifruit, oranges and lime. As the recipe specifies, be sure to cook the kiwi before it's added to the gelatin; otherwise, it won't set up.

6 kiwifruit, peeled, sliced and quartered
1 cup dry white wine *or* diet lemon-lime soda
2 packages (3 ounces *each*) lime gelatin
3 cups diet lemon-lime soda, chilled
2 tablespoons orange juice
1 can (11 ounces) mandarin oranges, drained

In a saucepan, bring the kiwi and wine or soda to a boil. Cook over medium heat for 5 minutes, stirring occasionally. Add the gelatin; stir until dissolved. Stir in chilled soda and orange juice. Refrigerate until partially set. Fold in the oranges. Pour into a 6-cup mold coated with nonstick cooking spray. Refrigerate until firm, about 8 hours or overnight. **Yield:** 8 servings.

Nutritional Analysis: One serving equals 81 calories, trace fat (trace saturated fat), 0 cholesterol, 31 mg sodium, 16 g carbohydrate, 2 g fiber, 1 g protein.
Diabetic Exchange: *1 fruit.*
△ **Low-fat**
▲ **Low-sodium**

Baby Corn Romaine Salad

(Pictured at right)

My kids really enjoy this green salad, made with romaine lettuce, broccoli, corn and crumbled bacon. It uses bottled dressing, so it's quick to fix, too.
—*Kathryn Maxson, Mountlake Terrace, Washington*

6 cups torn romaine
2 cups broccoli florets
1 can (15 ounces) whole baby corn, rinsed, drained and cut into 1/2-inch pieces *or* 1-1/2 cups frozen corn, thawed
3 tablespoons crumbled cooked bacon
1/2 cup fat-free Caesar *or* Italian salad dressing

In a large bowl, combine romaine, broccoli, corn and bacon. Drizzle with dressing and toss to coat. **Yield:** 6 servings.

Nutritional Analysis: One serving (1 cup) equals 43 calories, 2 g fat (1 g saturated fat), 3 mg cholesterol, 329 mg sodium, 4 g carbohydrate, 2 g fiber, 3 g protein.
Diabetic Exchanges: *1 vegetable, 1/2 fat.*
△ **Low-fat**

Sicilian Orange Salad

(Pictured at right)

Red onion and orange slices sprinkled with basil, oil and ground pepper make a pretty presentation that's bound to brighten any meal. This zesty salad is even more colorful when you use dark-red blood oranges.
—*Beverly Coyde, Gasport, New York*

6 large navel oranges, peeled and sliced
1 medium red onion, thinly sliced
8 fresh basil leaves, thinly sliced
2 tablespoons olive *or* canola oil
1/4 teaspoon coarsely ground pepper

On a serving platter, alternately arrange the orange and onion slices, with the slices slightly overlapping. Sprinkle with the basil. Drizzle with the oil and sprinkle with pepper. **Yield:** 6 servings.

Nutritional Analysis: One serving equals 133 calories, 5 g fat (1 g saturated fat), 0 cholesterol, 1 mg sodium, 23 g carbohydrate, 5 g fiber, 2 g protein.
Diabetic Exchanges: *1-1/2 fruit, 1 fat.*
▲ **Low-sodium**
▲ **Meatless**

🍎 Don't Douse It with Dressing!

INSTEAD of pouring dressing over a salad, serve the dressing on the side. Lightly dip your fork into the dressing, then gather several pieces of lettuce with it. I think you'll find you use less dressing this way.
—*Suzanne Ratkewicz, Grand Rapids, Michigan*

Kiwifruit Dressing

Here's a slightly sweet, refreshing dressing that lets the flavor of kiwifruit shine through. Combine the dressing with a medley of cut melons, apples, pears, strawberries, etc., for a bright side to breakfast, brunch or dinner.
—Edna Hoffman, Hebron, Indiana

  4 kiwifruit, peeled, sliced and quartered
1/2 cup white grape juice
1/4 cup canola oil
  2 tablespoons honey
  1 tablespoon lime juice
1/4 teaspoon salt
Assorted fruit

In a blender or food processor, combine the first six ingredients; cover and process until smooth. Serve over fruit. Store in the refrigerator. **Yield:** 2 cups.

Nutritional Analysis: One serving (2 tablespoons dressing) equals 55 calories, 4 g fat (trace saturated fat), 0 cholesterol, 38 mg sodium, 6 g carbohydrate, 1 g fiber, trace protein.
Diabetic Exchanges: 1/2 fruit, 1/2 fat.
▲ **Low-sodium**
▲ **Meatless**

Five-Bean Salad

Five kinds of beans star in this colorful classic featuring an oil-and-vinegar dressing. Everyone loves the variety of beans in this simple salad. My husband, Chuck, just can't get enough of it.
—Jeanette Simec, Ottawa, Illinois

  1 can (19 ounces) garbanzo beans *or* chickpeas, rinsed and drained
  1 can (16 ounces) kidney beans, rinsed and drained
  1 can (15-1/2 ounces) great northern beans, rinsed and drained
  1 can (14-1/2 ounces) cut wax beans, rinsed and drained
  1 package (10 ounces) frozen cut green beans, thawed
  2 small onions, chopped
  1 cup white vinegar
3/4 cup sugar
1/4 cup canola oil
  1 teaspoon salt
1/2 teaspoon pepper

In a large bowl, combine the first six ingredients. In another bowl, whisk the vinegar, sugar, oil, salt and pepper. Pour over bean mixture and toss to coat. Cover and refrigerate for several hours or overnight. Serve with a slotted spoon. **Yield:** 15 servings.

Nutritional Analysis: One serving (2/3 cup) equals 161 calories, 5 g fat (trace saturated fat), 0 cholesterol, 496 mg sodium, 28 g carbohydrate, 6 g fiber, 5 g protein.
Diabetic Exchanges: 1-1/2 starch, 1 fat.
▲ **Meatless**

Asparagus Pepper Salad

(Pictured below)

I made up this recipe when I needed a last-minute potluck dish and I had a lot of asparagus on hand. This salad went over so well that I serve it again and again. No one seems to get tired of it.
—Beverly Scalise, Bend, Oregon

 10 cups water
  1 pound fresh asparagus, trimmed and cut into 1-inch pieces
1/2 cup *each* chopped green, sweet red and yellow pepper
  2 green onions (white portion only), thinly sliced
1/3 cup reduced-fat raspberry salad dressing

In a large saucepan, bring water to a boil. Add asparagus; cover and boil for 3 minutes. Drain and immediately place asparagus in ice water. Drain and pat dry. In a bowl, combine the peppers, onions and asparagus. Drizzle with salad dressing; toss to coat. Cover and refrigerate for 3-4 hours before serving. **Yield:** 4 servings.

Nutritional Analysis: One serving (1 cup) equals 73 calories, 3 g fat (trace saturated fat), trace cholesterol, 154 mg sodium, 9 g carbohydrate, 2 g fiber, 4 g protein.
Diabetic Exchanges: 2 vegetable, 1/2 fat.
△ **Low-fat**
▲ **Meatless**

Tomato Herb Salad Dressing

A handful of herbs perks up the low-sodium tomato juice used in this refreshing salad dressing.
—*Mary Kretschmer, Miami, Florida*

1-1/2 cups low-sodium tomato juice
1/4 cup chopped onion
2 tablespoons chopped green pepper
3 teaspoons sugar
2 teaspoons lemon juice
1 teaspoon garlic salt
1 teaspoon Worcestershire sauce
3/4 teaspoon dried basil
1/4 teaspoon dried marjoram
1/4 teaspoon dried savory
1/4 teaspoon celery seed
1 tablespoon canola oil

Place all ingredients in a blender; cover and process until smooth. Chill for at least 4 hours before serving. Store leftovers in the refrigerator. **Yield:** 1-1/2 cups.

Nutritional Analysis: One serving (2 tablespoons) equals 23 calories, 1 g fat (trace saturated fat), 0 cholesterol, 102 mg sodium, 3 g carbohydrate, trace fiber, trace protein.
Diabetic Exchange: 1/2 fat.
△ *Low-fat*
▲ *Low-sodium*
▲ *Meatless*

Chili-Cumin Bean Salad

This bean salad has lots of texture and gets a little kick from the chili powder and cumin.
—*Michelle Smith, Running Springs, California*

4 cups chopped tomatoes
1 can (15-1/2 ounces) hominy, rinsed and drained
1 can (15 ounces) black beans, rinsed and drained
1 can (15 ounces) pinto beans, rinsed and drained
1-1/2 cups chopped red onion
1 cup minced fresh cilantro *or* parsley
1/4 cup lime juice
3 tablespoons olive *or* canola oil
2-1/2 teaspoons chili powder
2-1/2 teaspoons ground cumin
1 teaspoon pepper
1/2 teaspoon salt

In a large bowl, combine the tomatoes, hominy, beans, onion and cilantro. In a jar with a tight-fitting lid, combine the remaining ingredients; shake well. Pour over salad and toss to coat. Refrigerate for at least 2 hours before serving. **Yield:** 12 servings.

Nutritional Analysis: One serving (3/4 cup) equals 140 calories, 5 g fat (1 g saturated fat), 0 cholesterol, 413 mg sodium, 21 g carbohydrate, 6 g fiber, 5 g protein.
Diabetic Exchanges: 1-1/2 starch, 1 fat.
▲ *Meatless*

Cannellini Bean Salad

(Pictured above)

Here's a perfect side dish for a backyard picnic or barbecue. Celery and red pepper accent this bean salad that's dressed with a mild oil and vinegar dressing.
—*Dorothy Majewski, Vienna, Virginia*

2 cans (15 ounces *each*) cannellini *or* white kidney beans, rinsed and drained
3 celery ribs with leaves, sliced
3/4 cup chopped red onion
1/2 cup chopped sweet red pepper
1/2 cup minced fresh parsley
1/4 cup chopped green onions
2 tablespoons olive *or* canola oil
2 tablespoons balsamic vinegar
1/2 teaspoon salt
1/4 teaspoon pepper

In a large bowl, toss the beans, celery, red onion, red pepper, parsley and green onions. In a small bowl, combine the oil, vinegar, salt and pepper. Pour over salad and toss to coat. Cover and refrigerate for 1 hour or until chilled. **Yield:** 7 servings.

Nutritional Analysis: One serving (3/4 cup) equals 145 calories, 4 g fat (1 g saturated fat), 0 cholesterol, 440 mg sodium, 21 g carbohydrate, 6 g fiber, 5 g protein.
Diabetic Exchanges: 1 starch, 1 vegetable, 1 fat.
▲ *Meatless*

Beef Tenderloin Salad

Slices of tender beef, fresh asparagus and juicy tomatoes highlight this attractive main-dish salad from our Test Kitchen.

    1/4 cup fat-free mayonnaise
      2 tablespoons Dijon mustard
      1 tablespoon fat-free milk
      2 teaspoons white wine vinegar *or* cider vinegar
      1 teaspoon prepared horseradish
1-1/4 teaspoons sugar
    3/8 teaspoon salt, *divided*
    1/4 teaspoon pepper, *divided*
      8 cups water
      1 pound fresh asparagus, cut into 2-inch pieces
      4 beef tenderloin steaks (4 ounces *each*)
      1 large garlic clove, peeled and halved
      6 cups torn mixed salad greens
      2 large ripe tomatoes, cut into wedges

For salad dressing, in a bowl, whisk the mayonnaise, mustard, milk, vinegar, horseradish, sugar, 1/8 teaspoon salt and 1/8 teaspoon pepper. Cover and refrigerate. In a large saucepan, bring water to a boil. Add asparagus; cover and boil for 3 minutes. Drain and immediately place asparagus in ice water; drain and pat dry. Cover and refrigerate.

If grilling the steaks, coat grill rack with nonstick cooking spray before starting the grill. Rub steaks with garlic; discard garlic. Sprinkle with remaining salt and pepper. Grill steaks, covered, over medium heat or broil 4-6 in. from the heat for 6-8 minutes on each side or until meat reaches desired doneness (for rare, a meat thermometer should read 140°; medium, 160°; well-done, 170°).

On four serving plates, arrange the greens, tomatoes and asparagus. Thinly slice beef; place over salad. Drizzle with dressing. **Yield:** 4 servings.

Nutritional Analysis: One serving with 2 tablespoons dressing equals 259 calories, 10 g fat (3 g saturated fat), 72 mg cholesterol, 610 mg sodium, 14 g carbohydrate, 4 g fiber, 29 g protein.
Diabetic Exchanges: *3 lean meat, 3 vegetable.*

Layered Taco Salad

(Pictured at right)

I invented this taco salad to please the kids. I've made it with ground beef, ground turkey or ground chicken and it's equally good—so you can easily adjust it to fit your family's preferences. It's quick to make and everyone seems to like it!
—*Betty Nickels, Tampa, Florida*

      1 cup salsa
      1 tablespoon lime juice
      1 pound lean ground beef
      2 tablespoons reduced-sodium taco seasoning
      6 ounces baked tortilla chips (about 60 chips)
    12 cups sliced iceberg lettuce
      6 plum tomatoes, seeded and chopped

      1 can (15 ounces) black beans, rinsed and drained
1-1/2 cups (6 ounces) shredded reduced-fat Mexican cheese blend
      1 large sweet yellow *or* red pepper, thinly sliced
      1 medium red onion, thinly sliced
    1/3 cup fat-free sour cream

In a small bowl, combine the salsa and lime juice; set aside. In a large nonstick skillet, cook beef over medium heat until no longer pink; drain. Sprinkle with taco seasoning; stir to coat. Remove from the heat. Divide tortilla chips among six plates. Layer with the lettuce, tomatoes, beans, cheese, yellow pepper, beef mixture, onion, salsa mixture and sour cream. Serve immediately. **Yield:** 6 servings.

Nutritional Analysis: One serving equals 433 calories, 12 g fat (5 g saturated fat), 49 mg cholesterol, 1,117 mg sodium, 51 g carbohydrate, 10 g fiber, 32 g protein.
Diabetic Exchanges: *3 lean meat, 2-1/2 starch, 2 vegetable, 1/2 fat.*

Cottage Cheese Cantaloupe Salad

(Pictured at right)

You can easily wedge this pretty melon salad into any meal plan. For variety, drizzle a little reduced-fat French salad dressing over the sweet combination of cantaloupe, cottage cheese, granola, raisins and nuts.
—*Margaret Wagner Allen, Abingdon, Virginia*

      2 cups (16 ounces) 1% cottage cheese
    1/2 cup raisins
    1/4 cup chopped walnuts
      1 medium cantaloupe, quartered and seeded
    1/4 cup reduced-fat granola
      2 kiwifruit, peeled and sliced
Leaf lettuce

In a bowl, combine the cottage cheese, raisins and walnuts; mix well. Spoon into cantaloupe wedges. Sprinkle with granola; top with kiwi. Serve immediately on lettuce-lined plates. **Yield:** 4 servings.

Nutritional Analysis: One serving equals 282 calories, 7 g fat (1 g saturated fat), 5 mg cholesterol, 500 mg sodium, 41 g carbohydrate, 4 g fiber, 18 g protein.
Diabetic Exchanges: *2-1/2 fruit, 2 very lean meat, 1 fat, 1/2 starch.*
▲ **Meatless**

🍎 Light and Lively Salad Idea

FOR A QUICK SALAD, grate some carrots and add a handful or two of golden raisins. Toss with the juice of one or two oranges. This combination is simple and nutritious. For a little different taste, sprinkle with cinnamon.
—*Marie Roberts*
Lakes Charles, Louisiana

Fruity Green Salad

(Pictured at right)

As a beekeeper, I'm always looking for new ways to use honey. I've found that when I put honey in dressing, I don't need to add oil, which cuts down on the fat. This salad goes well with any entree.
—Hope Ralph, Woburn, Massachusetts

6 cups torn mixed salad greens *or* 1 package (10 ounces) fresh spinach, torn
2 medium ripe pears, thinly sliced
1/3 cup dried cherries *or* cranberries
1/4 cup balsamic vinegar
2 tablespoons honey, warmed
1/4 teaspoon salt
1/8 teaspoon pepper

In a salad bowl, toss the greens, pears and cherries. In a small bowl, combine the vinegar, honey, salt and pepper. Drizzle over salad and toss to coat. Serve immediately. **Yield:** 4 servings.

Nutritional Analysis: One serving (1-1/2 cups) equals 134 calories, 1 g fat (trace saturated fat), 0 cholesterol, 170 mg sodium, 32 g carbohydrate, 5 g fiber, 2 g protein.
Diabetic Exchanges: *2 fruit, 1 vegetable.*
  △ **Low-fat**
  ▲ **Meatless**

Broccoli Tomato Salad

I found this recipe over 25 years ago. I made a few changes to it and our family has enjoyed it ever since. The colorful combination is perfect for the holidays, but it's equally nice at a summer picnic.
—Helen Meadows, Trout Creek, Montana

5 cups broccoli florets
1 tablespoon water
1 pint cherry tomatoes, cut in half
2 tablespoons chopped green onion
1/4 cup fat-free mayonnaise
1/4 cup reduced-fat sour cream
1 tablespoon lemon juice
1/2 teaspoon salt
1/4 teaspoon pepper

Place broccoli and water in a 2-qt. microwave-safe bowl. Cover and microwave on high for 2-3 minutes or until crisp-tender, stirring once; drain. Cool completely.
Place broccoli in a serving bowl; gently stir in tomatoes and onion. In a small bowl, combine the mayonnaise, sour cream, lemon juice, salt and pepper; pour over vegetables and stir gently. Cover and refrigerate for 1 hour. **Yield:** 6 servings.
Editor's Note: This recipe was tested in an 850-watt microwave.

Nutritional Analysis: One serving (3/4 cup) equals 49 calories, 2 g fat (1 g saturated fat), 4 mg cholesterol, 303 mg sodium, 8 g carbohydrate, 3 g fiber, 3 g protein.
Diabetic Exchanges: *1 vegetable, 1/2 fat.*
  △ **Low-fat**
  ▲ **Meatless**

Overnight Vegetable Salad

Frozen mixed vegetables and canned kidney beans come together in this fresh-tasting salad that's tossed in a zippy sweet-sour dressing. This make-ahead dish is sure to please at your next potluck.
—Shirley Doyle, Mt. Prospect, Illinois

1 package (16 ounces) frozen mixed vegetables
1 can (16 ounces) kidney beans, rinsed and drained
1 cup chopped celery
1 cup chopped green pepper
1 medium onion, chopped
1/4 cup plus 2 tablespoons sugar
1 tablespoon all-purpose flour
3/4 teaspoon salt
1/4 teaspoon pepper
1/2 cup white vinegar
1 tablespoon prepared mustard

Place mixed vegetables in a steamer basket over 1 in. of water in a saucepan. Bring to a boil. Cover and steam for 6-8 minutes or until crisp-tender. Transfer to a large bowl. Add the kidney beans, celery, green pepper and onion; mix well.
In a small saucepan, combine the sugar, flour, salt and pepper. Stir in the vinegar and mustard until blended. Bring to a boil; cook and stir for 2 minutes or until thickened. Cool. Pour over vegetables and toss to coat. Cover and refrigerate overnight. Serve with a slotted spoon. **Yield:** 8 servings.

Nutritional Analysis: One serving (3/4 cup) equals 102 calories, trace fat (trace saturated fat), 0 cholesterol, 475 mg sodium, 21 g carbohydrate, 6 g fiber, 5 g protein.
Diabetic Exchanges: *3 vegetable, 1/2 starch.*
  △ **Low-fat**
  ▲ **Meatless**

Onion Bulgur Salad

I use homegrown ingredients from our garden to put together this refreshing salad. Onion, tomato and cucumber blend beautifully with the chewy texture of bulgur.
—Evelyn Lewis, Independence, Missouri

3/4 cup bulgur*
2 cups boiling water
3/4 cup finely chopped red onion
1 teaspoon salt
1/2 teaspoon ground allspice
1 cup diced seeded cucumber
1 cup diced seeded tomato
1/2 cup minced fresh basil
1/2 cup minced fresh parsley
1/2 cup chopped green onions
1/4 cup minced fresh mint
1/4 cup lemon juice

Rinse and drain bulgur; place in a bowl. Stir in the boiling water. Cover and let stand for 1 hour or until liquid is absorbed. Meanwhile, in a large bowl, combine the onion, salt and allspice; let stand for 30 minutes. Drain bulgur and squeeze dry; add bulgur and remaining ingredients to onion mixture. Toss gently to combine. Serve or refrigerate. **Yield:** 8 servings.

*Editor's Note: Look for bulgur in the cereal, rice or organic food aisle of your grocery store.

Nutritional Analysis: One serving (3/4 cup) equals 64 calories, trace fat (trace saturated fat), 0 cholesterol, 302 mg sodium, 14 g carbohydrate, 4 g fiber, 2 g protein.
Diabetic Exchanges: *1 vegetable, 1/2 starch.*
△ **Low-fat**
▲ **Meatless**

Red Beans and Rice Salad

Mango lends a sweet tropical twist to our Test Kitchen's version of red beans and rice.

2 cups cooked brown rice
1 can (16 ounces) kidney beans, rinsed and drained
3/4 cup finely chopped green pepper
1/2 cup cubed peeled mango *or* peaches (1/2-inch cubes)
1/2 cup finely chopped red onion
1/2 cup salsa, well drained
1/2 teaspoon salt
1/8 teaspoon pepper
2 tablespoons minced fresh cilantro *or* parsley

In a large bowl, combine the first eight ingredients. Cover and refrigerate for 1 hour or until chilled. Sprinkle with cilantro before serving. **Yield:** 4 servings.

Nutritional Analysis: One serving (1-1/4 cups) equals 245 calories, 1 g fat (trace saturated fat), 0 cholesterol, 623 mg sodium, 49 g carbohydrate, 9 g fiber, 11 g protein.
Diabetic Exchanges: *2 starch, 2 vegetable, 1 very lean meat.*
△ **Low-fat**
▲ **Meatless**

Rainbow Pasta Salad

(Pictured below)

I like to serve this colorful salad over a bed of leafy green lettuce for a pretty look. With its rich dressing of sour cream and dill, it makes a great change-of-pace pasta salad.
—Julie Wilson, Chetek, Wisconsin

2 cups uncooked tricolor spiral pasta
1 cup (8 ounces) fat-free sour cream
1/2 cup reduced-fat mayonnaise *or* salad dressing
1 tablespoon dill weed
1/2 teaspoon garlic salt
1/2 teaspoon ground mustard
Dash pepper
1/2 pound fresh asparagus, trimmed
1 tablespoon water
1 cup cubed fully cooked lean ham
1 small onion, chopped
1 small sweet red pepper, chopped
1/2 cup cubed reduced-fat cheddar cheese
Leaf lettuce

Cook pasta according to package directions. Meanwhile, for dressing, combine the sour cream, mayonnaise, dill, garlic salt, mustard and pepper in a bowl; set aside. Rinse pasta in cold water and drain well; set aside.

Cut the tips off six asparagus spears; chop the remaining asparagus. Place chopped asparagus and tips and water in a microwave-safe dish. Cover and microwave on high for 1-2 minutes or until crisp-tender. Rinse with cold water; pat dry. Set aside asparagus tips for garnish.

In a large bowl, combine the pasta, chopped asparagus, ham, onion, red pepper and cheese. Add dressing and toss to coat. Refrigerate until serving. Serve in a lettuce-lined bowl; garnish with asparagus tips. **Yield:** 6 servings.

Nutritional Analysis: One serving (1 cup salad with 1 cup lettuce) equals 293 calories, 9 g fat (2 g saturated fat), 22 mg cholesterol, 684 mg sodium, 36 g carbohydrate, 4 g fiber, 16 g protein.
Diabetic Exchanges: *1-1/2 starch, 1 vegetable, 1 lean meat, 1 fat, 1/2 fat-free milk.*

Grape Broccoli Salad

(Pictured at right)

This tempting toss-up of vegetables, fruit and a sweet tangy dressing is a tasty alternative to pasta salads.
—*Peggy Cathey, McKinney, Texas*

1 cup fresh broccoli florets
3/4 cup halved seedless red grapes
1/3 cup chopped celery
1/3 cup chopped green onions
1/3 cup sliced water chestnuts
1/4 cup raisins
1/2 cup fat-free plain yogurt
2 tablespoons reduced-fat mayonnaise
1 teaspoon honey

In a large bowl, combine the broccoli, grapes, celery, onions, water chestnuts and raisins. In a small bowl, combine the yogurt, mayonnaise and honey. Pour over broccoli mixture and toss to coat. Cover and refrigerate for at least 1 hour or until chilled. **Yield:** 3 servings.

Nutritional Analysis: One serving (1 cup) equals 129 calories, 4 g fat (1 g saturated fat), 4 mg cholesterol, 127 mg sodium, 24 g carbohydrate, 3 g fiber, 3 g protein.
Diabetic Exchanges: 1 fruit, 1/2 starch, 1/2 fat.
▲ *Low-sodium*
▲ *Meatless*

Orange Chicken Salad

(Pictured at right)

This refreshing salad makes a wonderful light supper on a warm summer evening. Or leave out the chicken and serve it as a side dish to enhance any main course.
—*Sue McKenney, Eagle, Michigan*

4 boneless skinless chicken breast halves (1 pound)
1/3 cup raspberry vinegar
1/4 cup sugar
3 tablespoons orange juice
2 tablespoons olive *or* canola oil
2 tablespoons minced fresh parsley
1/2 teaspoon salt
1/4 teaspoon coarsely ground pepper
1/4 teaspoon hot pepper sauce
6 cups torn mixed salad greens
2 celery ribs, thinly sliced
1 cup orange sections
1/2 cup thinly sliced red onion
1/4 cup dried cranberries
1/4 cup slivered almonds, toasted

Grill chicken, uncovered, over medium heat for 6-8 minutes on each side or until juices run clear. Slice and set aside. In a small bowl, combine the vinegar, sugar, orange juice, oil, parsley, salt, pepper and hot pepper sauce; set aside.

In a large bowl, combine the salad greens, celery, orange sections, onion and cranberries. Divide among individual serving plates. Top with chicken. Drizzle with dressing. Sprinkle with almonds. **Yield:** 4 servings.

Nutritional Analysis: One serving (2 cups) equals 352 calories, 14 g fat (2 g saturated fat), 63 mg cholesterol, 393 mg sodium, 30 g carbohydrate, 5 g fiber, 27 g protein.
Diabetic Exchanges: 3 lean meat, 1 fruit, 1 vegetable, 1 fat, 1/2 starch.

Citrus Melon Mingle

A hint of mint, honey and ginger adds subtle flavor to delicious fruit salad.
—*Doris Heath, Franklin, North Carolina*

1-1/2 cups cubed cantaloupe
1-1/2 cups cubed honeydew
2 medium grapefruit, peeled and sectioned
2 medium navel oranges, peeled and sectioned
1 can (8 ounces) unsweetened pineapple chunks, undrained
2 medium firm bananas, sliced
1/2 cup orange juice
2 tablespoons honey
1 tablespoon minced fresh mint *or* 1 teaspoon dried mint
1/4 teaspoon ground ginger *or* 1 teaspoon minced fresh gingerroot

In a large bowl, combine all ingredients. Cover and refrigerate until serving. **Yield:** 8 servings.

Nutritional Analysis: One serving (3/4 cup) equals 125 calories, trace fat (trace saturated fat), 0 cholesterol, 10 mg sodium, 31 g carbohydrate, 3 g fiber, 2 g protein.
Diabetic Exchange: 2 fruit.
△ *Low-fat*
▲ *Low-sodium*
▲ *Meatless*

Tuna Pasta Salad

You can dress up this scrumptious salad and take it most anywhere. It's a real crowd-pleaser in hot weather.
—*Patricia Smith, Canby, Oregon*

3 cups uncooked spiral pasta
3 plum tomatoes, seeded and chopped
2 cups frozen peas, thawed
1 cup (4 ounces) cubed reduced-fat cheddar cheese
1 cup sliced ripe olives
1 cup chopped dill pickles
2 hard-cooked eggs, chopped
1 can (6 ounces) light water-packed tuna, drained
1/2 cup reduced-fat Italian salad dressing
1/2 cup pickle juice

Cook pasta according to package directions; drain and rinse in cold water. Place in a large bowl; add the tomatoes, peas, cheese, olives, pickles, eggs and tuna. Combine salad dressing and pickle juice; pour over pasta mixture and toss to coat. Refrigerate until serving. **Yield:** 13 servings.

Nutritional Analysis: One serving (3/4 cup) equals 173 calories, 6 g fat (2 g saturated fat), 45 mg cholesterol, 533 mg sodium, 20 g carbohydrate, 2 g fiber, 10 g protein.
Diabetic Exchanges: 1 starch, 1 lean meat, 1 vegetable, 1/2 fat.

Black Bean Bow Tie Salad

Even people who don't like beans compliment me on this delicious salad. The slimmed-down dressing gets a little kick from cilantro and lime.
—*Teresa Smith, Huron, South Dakota*

8 ounces uncooked bow tie pasta
2/3 cup reduced-sodium chicken broth *or* vegetable broth
3 garlic cloves, sliced
1 can (15 ounces) black beans, rinsed and drained, *divided*
1/2 cup fresh cilantro *or* parsley
3 tablespoons lime juice
2 tablespoons olive *or* canola oil
1 tablespoon tomato paste
1-1/2 teaspoons dried oregano
3/4 teaspoon salt
1 medium zucchini, cut in half lengthwise and sliced
1 medium sweet red pepper, chopped
1 medium green pepper, chopped
1/3 cup chopped red onion

Cook pasta according to package directions. Rinse with cold water and drain; set aside. In a small saucepan, bring broth and garlic to a boil. Reduce heat; simmer, uncovered, for 5 minutes or until garlic is tender. Cool slightly.

Transfer to a food processor. Add 1/4 cup black beans, cilantro, lime juice, oil, tomato paste, oregano and salt; cover and process until smooth. Transfer to a large serving bowl. Add the pasta, zucchini, peppers, onion and remaining beans; toss gently to coat. Refrigerate until serving. **Yield:** 10 servings.

Nutritional Analysis: One serving (1 cup) equals 159 calories, 4 g fat (1 g saturated fat), 0 cholesterol, 352 mg sodium, 26 g carbohydrate, 4 g fiber, 6 g protein.
Diabetic Exchanges: *1-1/2 starch, 1 vegetable, 1/2 fat.*
▲ *Meatless*

Christmas Ribbon Salad

Spirits are light at holiday time around home— and so are many of the meals I serve. I make this dish every year at Christmas. It's one of my husband's favorites. I slimmed down the recipe by using sugar-free gelatin and reduced-fat topping.
—*Debra Stoner, Carlisle, Pennsylvania*

2 packages (.3 ounce *each*) sugar-free lime gelatin
5 cups boiling water, *divided*
4 cups cold water, *divided*
2 packages (.3 ounce *each*) sugar-free lemon gelatin
1 package (8 ounces) reduced-fat cream cheese, cubed
1 can (8 ounces) crushed pineapple, undrained
1/4 cup chopped pecans
2 cups reduced-fat whipped topping
2 packages (.3 ounce *each*) sugar-free cherry gelatin

In a bowl, dissolve lime gelatin in 2 cups boiling water. Add 2 cups cold water; stir. Pour into a 13-in. x 9-in. x 2-in. dish coated with nonstick cooking spray. Refrigerate until almost set, about 2 hours.

In a bowl, dissolve lemon gelatin in 1 cup boiling water; whisk in cream cheese until smooth. Stir in pineapple and pecans. Fold in whipped topping. Spoon over first layer. Refrigerate until firm, about 1 hour.

In a bowl, dissolve cherry gelatin in remaining boiling water. Add remaining cold water; stir. Chill until syrupy and slightly thickened. Carefully spoon over second layer. Refrigerate until set, about 4 hours. **Yield:** 15 servings.

Nutritional Analysis: One square equals 92 calories, 5 g fat (3 g saturated fat), 8 mg cholesterol, 140 mg sodium, 5 g carbohydrate, trace fiber, 3 g protein.
Diabetic Exchanges: *1 fat, 1/2 starch.*
▲ *Low-sodium*

Garden Vegetable Salad

When I got married, I wrote down all of my mother's favorite recipes, including this one. The salad is good in any season, but it's especially tasty made with homegrown vegetables.
—*Ramona Sailor, Buhl, Idaho*

6 medium tomatoes, quartered
1 medium green pepper, julienned
1 medium onion, sliced and separated into rings
1/3 cup cider vinegar
1/4 cup sugar
1-1/2 teaspoons celery seed
1-1/2 teaspoons prepared mustard
1/2 teaspoon salt
1 large cucumber, peeled and sliced

In a bowl, combine the tomatoes, green pepper and onion. In a small saucepan, combine the vinegar, sugar, celery seed, mustard and salt; bring to a boil. Boil for 1 minute. Pour over vegetables. Let stand until mixture comes to room temperature. Stir in the cucumber. Cover and refrigerate for 2 hours or until chilled. **Yield:** 6 servings.

Nutritional Analysis: One serving (3/4 cup) equals 84 calories, 1 g fat (trace saturated fat), 0 cholesterol, 226 mg sodium, 20 g carbohydrate, 3 g fiber, 2 g protein.
Diabetic Exchanges: *2 vegetable, 1/2 starch.*
△ *Low-fat*
▲ *Meatless*

Marvelous Melon

(Pictured above)

*Kids love these cantaloupe wedges filled with
fruit-flavored gelatin and fresh strawberries.
For different looks, I experiment with other
combinations of melons, gelatin and fruit.*
—*Jillian Surman, Wisconsin Dells, Wisconsin*

  1 large cantaloupe
  1 package (3 ounces) strawberry banana gelatin
  1 cup boiling water
1/2 cup unsweetened applesauce
  1 cup sliced fresh strawberries

Cut melon in half lengthwise from bud to stem end; discard seeds. Cut a thin slice off the bottom of each half so melon sits level; pat dry. In a bowl, dissolve gelatin in boiling water. Stir in applesauce and strawberries. Pour into melon halves (discard any remaining gelatin mixture or save for another use). Cover with plastic wrap and refrigerate overnight. Just before serving, slice each melon half into three wedges. **Yield:** 6 servings.

   Nutritional Analysis: One serving equals 72 calories, trace fat (trace saturated fat), 0 cholesterol, 21 mg sodium, 17 g carbohydrate, 2 g fiber, 2 g protein.
   Diabetic Exchange: *1 fruit.*
  △ **Low-fat**
  ▲ **Low-sodium**

Green Bean 'n' Pea Salad

(Pictured above)

*Diced pimientos add a dash of color, and the
sweet-sour dressing adds flavor to this appealing toss.*
—*Pat Walter, Pine Island, Minnesota*

  1 package (16 ounces) frozen peas, thawed
  3 cups frozen French-style green beans, thawed
  1 cup chopped celery
1/2 cup chopped green pepper
1/3 cup finely chopped onion
1/4 cup diced pimientos
3/4 cup sugar
1/3 cup cider vinegar
  2 tablespoons water
1/2 teaspoon salt

In a large bowl, combine the first six ingredients. In a small bowl, combine the sugar, vinegar, water and salt; stir until sugar is dissolved. Pour over vegetables; toss to coat. Refrigerate for 3-4 hours. Serve with a slotted spoon. **Yield:** 8 servings.

   Nutritional Analysis: One serving (3/4 cup) equals 137 calories, trace fat (trace saturated fat), 0 cholesterol, 229 mg sodium, 31 g carbohydrate, 4 g fiber, 4 g protein.
   Diabetic Exchanges: *1-1/2 starch, 1 vegetable.*
  △ **Low-fat**
  ▲ **Meatless**

Zesty Potato Salad

I adjusted the original recipe for this cold, creamy salad to better suit my tastes. The cilantro comes through nicely...while green chilies and chili powder add a little kick and a hint of color.
—Raquel Haggard, Edmond, Oklahoma

2 pounds red potatoes, cubed
3/4 cup fat-free mayonnaise *or* salad dressing
1/3 cup reduced-fat sour cream
1/3 cup minced fresh cilantro *or* parsley
1 can (4 ounces) chopped green chilies
3 green onions, finely chopped
1 tablespoon lemon juice
1 teaspoon chili powder
1/2 teaspoon salt
1/4 teaspoon pepper
Dash garlic powder

Place potatoes in a saucepan and cover with water. Bring to a boil. Reduce heat; cover and cook for 15 minutes or just until tender. Drain and rinse with cold water. In a small bowl, combine the remaining ingredients. Place potatoes in a large bowl. Add dressing and toss to coat. Cover and refrigerate for 2 hours or until chilled. **Yield:** 6 servings.

Nutritional Analysis: One serving (3/4 cup) equals 162 calories, 2 g fat (1 g saturated fat), 7 mg cholesterol, 693 mg sodium, 32 g carbohydrate, 4 g fiber, 4 g protein.
Diabetic Exchange: *2 starch.*
△ **Low-fat**
▲ **Meatless**

Creamy Buttermilk Dressing

(Pictured above)

This thick ranch-like dressing doesn't taste light. I used it to prepare a cold chicken and pasta salad. After trying it, a friend begged me for the recipe.
—Emily Hockett, Federal Way, Washington

1 cup reduced-fat mayonnaise
1/2 cup reduced-fat sour cream
1/2 cup 1% buttermilk
1 teaspoon onion powder
1 teaspoon cider vinegar
1/2 teaspoon garlic powder
1/2 teaspoon salt
1/8 teaspoon pepper

Place all ingredients in a blender or food processor; cover and process until smooth. Cover and refrigerate for at least 1 hour before serving. **Yield:** 2 cups.

Nutritional Analysis: One serving (2 tablespoons) equals 64 calories, 6 g fat (1 g saturated fat), 8 mg cholesterol, 206 mg sodium, 2 g carbohydrate, trace fiber, 1 g protein.
Diabetic Exchange: *1 fat.*
▲ **Meatless**

Garbanzo Bean Salad

In this simple bean salad recipe, fresh herbs and a citrusy dressing add extra zest. Chilling it lets the flavors blend...and gives you time to tend to the rest of the meal.
—Donna Smith, Victor, New York

1 can (15 ounces) garbanzo beans *or* chickpeas, rinsed and drained
1/2 cup chopped red onion
2 tablespoons minced fresh parsley
1 tablespoon minced fresh mint
2 tablespoons lemon juice
2 tablespoons olive *or* canola oil
1 garlic clove, minced
1/2 teaspoon sugar
1/2 teaspoon salt
1/4 teaspoon pepper
Leaf lettuce

In a bowl, combine the beans, onion, parsley and mint. In a jar with a tight-fitting lid, combine the lemon juice, oil, garlic, sugar, salt and pepper; shake well. Pour over salad and toss to coat. Cover and refrigerate for at least 2 hours. Serve on lettuce-lined plates. **Yield:** 4 servings.

Nutritional Analysis: One serving (1/2 cup) equals 167 calories, 8 g fat (1 g saturated fat), 0 cholesterol, 616 mg sodium, 19 g carbohydrate, 5 g fiber, 6 g protein.
Diabetic Exchanges: *1-1/2 fat, 1 starch.*
▲ **Meatless**

Favorite Pasta Salad Made Lighter

PASTA SALAD is a popular addition to summer menus, and Danielle Carpenter's recipe is no exception. "My children love Pizza Pasta Salad, but I would like to reduce the fat in it," shares the Vienna, West Virginia cook.

"I know that using reduced-fat cheddar cheese and turkey pepperoni will help, but can you help more?" she asks.

Our Test Kitchen staff members were eager to try. As Danielle suggested, they cut some fat by replacing the regular pepperoni with turkey pepperoni.

By reducing the amount of cheese and switching to reduced-fat cheddar and part-skim mozzarella, they further trimmed the fat.

To limit the fat in the dressing, our home economists reduced the amount of oil and substituted olive or canola oil. They combined cornstarch and water and heated it to thicken the mixture. The heat helped melt the grated Parmesan cheese a little and blend it with the other ingredients.

These changes cut the fat in half, reduced the calories and cholesterol by a third and reduced the sodium by a fifth. Yet there's still plenty of flavor in Makeover Pizza Pasta Salad to please Danielle's family...and yours!

Pizza Pasta Salad

    8 ounces uncooked spiral pasta
    6 tablespoons vegetable oil
1/3 cup grated Parmesan cheese
1/4 cup red wine vinegar *or* cider vinegar
    1 teaspoon dried oregano
1/2 teaspoon salt
1/2 teaspoon garlic powder
1/8 teaspoon pepper
    1 cup halved cherry tomatoes
    1 cup (4 ounces) cubed cheddar cheese
    1 cup (4 ounces) cubed mozzarella cheese
1/2 cup sliced green onions
1/2 cup sliced pepperoni (about 1-1/2 ounces)

Cook pasta according to package directions. In a jar with a tight-fitting lid, combine the oil, Parmesan cheese, vinegar, oregano, salt, garlic powder and pepper; shake well. Drain pasta; rinse in cold water. In a large bowl, combine the remaining ingredients. Add pasta and dressing; toss to coat. Cover and refrigerate for at least 1 hour before serving. **Yield:** 7 servings.

Nutritional Analysis: *One serving (1 cup) equals 382 calories, 25 g fat (9 g saturated fat), 38 mg cholesterol, 517 mg sodium, 25 g carbohydrate, 2 g fiber, 14 g protein.*

Makeover Pizza Pasta Salad

(Pictured below)

    8 ounces uncooked spiral pasta
1/2 teaspoon cornstarch
1/3 cup water
1/4 cup grated Parmesan cheese
1/4 cup red wine vinegar *or* cider vinegar
    2 tablespoons olive *or* canola oil
    1 teaspoon dried oregano
1/2 teaspoon salt
1/2 teaspoon garlic powder
1/8 teaspoon pepper
1-1/2 cups halved cherry tomatoes
3/4 cup shredded reduced-fat cheddar cheese
3/4 cup shredded part-skim mozzarella cheese
1/2 cup sliced green onions
1/2 cup sliced turkey pepperoni (about 1-1/2 ounces)

Cook pasta according to package directions. In a small saucepan, combine the cornstarch and water until smooth. Bring to a boil; cook and stir for 1-2 minutes or until thickened. Remove from heat; stir in Parmesan cheese, vinegar, oil, oregano, salt, garlic powder and pepper; mix well. Drain pasta; rinse in cold water.

In a large bowl, combine the remaining ingredients. Add pasta and dressing; toss to coat. Cover and refrigerate for at least 1 hour before serving. **Yield:** 7 servings.

Nutritional Analysis: *One serving (1 cup) equals 255 calories, 11 g fat (5 g saturated fat), 26 mg cholesterol, 403 mg sodium, 25 g carbohydrate, 2 g fiber, 14 g protein.*
Diabetic Exchanges: *1-1/2 starch, 1-1/2 fat, 1 lean meat.*

Creamy Lime Potato Salad

(Pictured below)

*Not only is this salad good served cold,
but it is absolutely fantastic when it's warmed a tad.
The recipe came from my daughter, who likes to use
lime juice and lime peel for a unique flair.*
—Angela Accorinti, Okeana, Ohio

    4 cups cubed red potatoes
    1/3 cup reduced-fat mayonnaise
    1/4 cup reduced-fat sour cream
    2 tablespoons lime juice
    1 tablespoon minced fresh thyme *or* 1 teaspoon
       dried thyme
    1/2 teaspoon grated lime peel
    1/2 teaspoon salt
    1/2 teaspoon pepper

Place the potatoes in a saucepan and cover with water.
Bring to a boil. Reduce heat; cover and cook for 13-18
minutes or until potatoes are tender. Drain. Cool potatoes
for 10 minutes.

Meanwhile, in a bowl, combine the mayonnaise, sour
cream, lime juice, thyme, lime peel, salt and pepper. Pour
over potatoes; toss gently to coat. Serve warm or chilled.
Yield: 5 servings.

*Nutritional Analysis: One serving (3/4 cup) equals 158 calo-
ries, 6 g fat (2 g saturated fat), 10 mg cholesterol, 376 mg sodium, 22 g carbohydrate, 2 g fiber, 3 g protein.*
Diabetic Exchanges: *1-1/2 starch, 1 fat.*
▲ *Meatless*

🍎 Slim Down with Sunny Citrus

THINKING of adding snappy citrus to your meal
plan? It's easy! Keep the following in mind when
preparing your family's favorites:
• Stir a little lemon peel into waffle batter or replace
  some of the milk in your pancake recipe with orange juice.
• You can't go wrong when working citrus into
  seafood dishes. Marinate fish fillets, tuna steaks or
  shrimp in freshly squeezed lime or grapefruit
  juice. Discard the marinade before cooking.
• Substitute the vinegar called for in a salad dressing
  with lemon juice and toss a few orange or grapefruit sections into green salads.
• Hold off on the butter, and season steamed or
  broiled veggies by squeezing a lime or lemon over
  them before serving.
• Forget the can of soda and enjoy a healthy glass
  of chilled orange or grapefruit juice instead. Or, try
  combining citrus juice with cranberry or pineapple juice for a refreshing change-of-pace beverage.

Black Bean Chicken Salad

(Pictured on page 43)

*A refreshing mix of beans, garden veggies and chicken
is tossed with a light lime vinaigrette in this satisfying
salad that's sure to be a winner on hot summer days!*
—Jean Ecos, Hartland, Wisconsin

    6 cups torn lettuce
    1-1/2 cups cubed cooked chicken breast
    1 can (15 ounces) black beans, rinsed and
       drained
    1 cup chopped seeded tomatoes
    1 cup chopped green pepper
    1/2 cup sliced red onion
    1/2 cup shredded reduced-fat cheddar cheese
    LIME VINAIGRETTE:
    1/4 cup minced fresh cilantro *or* parsley
    1/4 cup chopped seeded tomato
    1 tablespoon cider vinegar
    1 tablespoon olive *or* canola oil
    1 tablespoon lime juice
    1/2 teaspoon grated lime peel
    1 garlic clove, minced
    1/4 teaspoon salt
    1/4 teaspoon pepper
    1/4 teaspoon chili powder

In a large serving bowl, combine the lettuce, chicken,
beans, tomatoes, green pepper, onion and cheese. In a
blender or food processor, combine the vinaigrette ingredients; cover and process until smooth. Pour over salad and
toss to coat. **Yield:** 4 servings.

*Nutritional Analysis: One serving (2 cups salad with 2 table-
spoons vinaigrette) equals 298 calories, 9 g fat (3 g saturated
fat), 55 mg cholesterol, 672 mg sodium, 26 g carbohydrate, 10 g
fiber, 28 g protein.*
Diabetic Exchanges: *3 lean meat, 2 vegetable, 1 starch.*

Potato 'n' Pea Salad

A nicely seasoned dressing made with sour cream and yogurt coats tender potatoes, green peas and sweet red pepper in this chilled salad developed by our Test Kitchen home economists. It's sure to be popular at a potluck or picnic.

9 unpeeled small red potatoes (1-1/4 pounds)
1/3 cup fat-free plain yogurt
1/3 cup reduced-fat sour cream
 3 tablespoons chopped green onions
 3 teaspoons minced fresh parsley, *divided*
3/4 teaspoon dried basil
1/2 teaspoon *each* **salt and salt-free garlic seasoning blend**
Dash paprika
3/4 cup fresh *or* **frozen peas, thawed**
1/2 cup chopped sweet red pepper

Place potatoes in a large saucepan and cover with water. Bring to a boil. Reduce heat; cover and cook for 15-20 minutes or until tender. Drain and cool; slice potatoes.

In a large bowl, combine the yogurt, sour cream, onions, 1 teaspoon parsley, basil, salt, seasoning blend and paprika. Add the potatoes, peas and red pepper; toss to coat. Sprinkle with remaining parsley. Cover and refrigerate for at least 1 hour. **Yield:** 6 servings.

Nutritional Analysis: One serving (1-1/2 cups) equals 115 calories, 1 g fat (1 g saturated fat), 5 mg cholesterol, 246 mg sodium, 22 g carbohydrate, 3 g fiber, 5 g protein.
Diabetic Exchange: *1-1/2 starch.*
 △ *Low-fat*
 ▲ *Meatless*

Minestrone Pasta Salad

My husband's favorite soup is minestrone. But during warmer weather, we enjoy this pasta salad. It goes great with anything grilled.
—*Rosemary Swope, Springfield, Missouri*

3 cups uncooked medium pasta shells
1 can (16 ounces) kidney beans, rinsed and drained
1 can (15 ounces) garbanzo *or* **chickpeas, rinsed and drained**
1 can (14-1/2 ounces) Italian diced tomatoes, drained
1 medium green pepper, chopped
2/3 cup fat-free Italian salad dressing
1/2 cup grated Parmesan cheese
 1 can (2-1/4 ounces) sliced ripe olives, drained
1/4 cup chopped green onions

Cook pasta according to package directions. In a large bowl, combine remaining ingredients. Drain pasta and rinse in cold water; add to bean mixture and toss to coat. Cover and refrigerate for 3-4 hours before serving. **Yield:** 13 servings.

Nutritional Analysis: One serving (3/4 cup) equals 210 calories, 3 g fat (1 g saturated fat), 3 mg cholesterol, 665 mg sodium, 37 g carbohydrate, 6 g fiber, 10 g protein.
Diabetic Exchanges: *2 starch, 1 lean meat, 1 vegetable.*
 △ *Low-fat*
 ▲ *Meatless*

Spinach Berry Salad

(Pictured above)

My mother shared this recipe with me because of my passion for light dishes. Delicious and colorful, it is as pleasing to the eye as it is to the palate. It wins me compliments whenever I serve it.
—*Lisa Lorenzo, Willoughby, Ohio*

4 cups packed torn fresh spinach
1 cup sliced fresh strawberries
1 cup fresh *or* **frozen blueberries**
1 small sweet onion, sliced
1/4 cup chopped pecans, toasted
CURRY SALAD DRESSING:
 2 tablespoons white wine vinegar *or* **cider vinegar**
 2 tablespoons balsamic vinegar
 2 tablespoons honey
 2 teaspoons Dijon mustard
 1 teaspoon curry powder
1/4 teaspoon salt
1/8 teaspoon pepper

In a large salad bowl, toss together the spinach, strawberries, blueberries, onion and pecans. In a jar with a tight-fitting lid, combine the dressing ingredients; shake well. Pour over salad and toss to coat. Serve immediately. **Yield:** 4 servings.

Nutritional Analysis: One serving (1-1/2 cups) equals 141 calories, 6 g fat (1 g saturated fat), 0 cholesterol, 250 mg sodium, 22 g carbohydrate, 4 g fiber, 3 g protein.
Diabetic Exchanges: *1 fruit, 1 vegetable, 1 fat.*
 ▲ *Meatless*

Southwestern Barley Salad

Cilantro comes through in this colorful side salad that's zesty but not too spicy. It also makes a great luncheon dish when served with sesame breadsticks, sherbet and sugar cookies. It's sure to satisfy!
—*Tommi Roylance, Charlo, Montana*

    3 cups cooked medium pearl barley
    1 can (15 ounces) black beans, rinsed and
       drained
1-1/2 cups frozen corn, thawed
1-1/2 cups diced seeded tomatoes
    1 cup frozen peas, thawed
  1/4 cup minced fresh cilantro *or* parsley
    1 teaspoon salt
  1/4 teaspoon pepper
  1/2 cup water
    3 tablespoons lemon juice
    1 tablespoon finely chopped onion
    1 tablespoon canola oil
    2 garlic cloves, minced
    8 lettuce leaves
    1 ripe avocado, peeled and sliced
    2 medium tomatoes, cut into wedges

In a bowl, combine the first eight ingredients. In a jar with a tight-fitting lid, combine the water, lemon juice, onion, oil and garlic; shake well. Pour over barley mixture and toss to coat. Serve on lettuce-lined plates. Garnish with avocado and tomatoes. **Yield:** 8 servings.

Nutritional Analysis: One serving (1 cup) equals 233 calories, 7 g fat (1 g saturated fat), 0 cholesterol, 490 mg sodium, 38 g carbohydrate, 9 g fiber, 7 g protein.
Diabetic Exchanges: *2 starch, 1 vegetable, 1 fat.*
▲ *Meatless*

Cantaloupe Chicken Salad

(Pictured at right)

Apples add sweet-tart flavor and crunch to this lightened-up chicken salad that's lovely mounded on melon rings. Curry powder gives this fruity chicken a unique flavor and golden hue.
—*Nancy Daugherty, Cortland, Ohio*

    3 cups cubed cooked chicken breast
    2 cups chopped tart green apples
  3/4 cup chopped celery
  1/4 cup sliced green onions
  1/4 cup chopped pecans
  1/2 cup fat-free reduced-sugar vanilla yogurt

  1/4 cup reduced-fat mayonnaise
  1/2 teaspoon curry powder
  1/4 teaspoon salt
    1 medium cantaloupe
    6 lettuce leaves

In a large bowl, combine the chicken, apples, celery, onions and pecans. Combine the yogurt, mayonnaise, curry and salt; add to chicken mixture and toss to coat. Cover and refrigerate for 2 hours or until chilled.

Meanwhile, place cantaloupe on its side; cut into six rings. Discard seeds and ends. With a sharp knife, cut off rind. To serve, place cantaloupe rings on lettuce-lined plates. Top with chicken salad. **Yield:** 6 servings.

Nutritional Analysis: One serving (1 cantaloupe ring with 1 cup salad) equals 287 calories, 10 g fat (2 g saturated fat), 63 mg cholesterol, 276 mg sodium, 25 g carbohydrate, 3 g fiber, 24 g protein.
Diabetic Exchanges: *3 lean meat, 1 fruit, 1/2 starch, 1/2 fat.*

Chef's Spinach Salad

(Pictured at right)

This salad is eye-catching enough to make any chef proud! It's served with a tangy buttermilk dressing that gets a little zip from white wine vinegar.
—*Loretta Matzen, Coram, New York*

    1 small red onion, thinly sliced
    2 tablespoons white wine vinegar *or* cider
       vinegar
    1 teaspoon sugar
    1 package (6 ounces) fresh baby spinach
    1 cup quartered cherry tomatoes
    1 cup fresh *or* frozen corn, thawed
    4 ounces fully cooked lean ham, cut into thin
       strips
    4 ounces sliced cooked turkey, cut into thin
       strips
    1 piece (2 ounces) reduced-fat cheddar cheese,
       cut into thin strips
DRESSING:
  1/2 cup 1% buttermilk
    2 tablespoons minced chives
    1 tablespoon reduced-fat mayonnaise
    2 teaspoons white wine vinegar *or* cider vinegar
    2 teaspoons Dijon mustard
  1/4 teaspoon minced garlic
  1/4 teaspoon salt
  1/4 teaspoon pepper

In a small bowl, combine onion, vinegar and sugar; let stand for 15 minutes. On a serving platter, arrange spinach, tomatoes, corn, ham, turkey and cheese. Drain onion mixture and place onions over salad. In a bowl, whisk dressing ingredients. Serve with salad. **Yield:** 4 servings.

Nutritional Analysis: One serving (2 cups salad with 3 tablespoons dressing) equals 172 calories, 6 g fat (3 g saturated fat), 44 mg cholesterol, 783 mg sodium, 10 g carbohydrate, 2 g fiber, 21 g protein.
Diabetic Exchanges: *2 lean meat, 1 vegetable, 1/2 starch.*

Carrot Apple Salad

Deciding to start eating healthy, I took a classic carrot and raisin salad recipe and lightened it up, then added apples for extra flavor. I took this dish to a weight-loss group meeting...and they loved it!
—Kim Jones, Collinsville, Illinois

> 1 can (8 ounces) unsweetened crushed pineapple
> 2 medium tart apples, diced
> 3 cups shredded carrots
> 3 tablespoons raisins
> 3 tablespoons flaked coconut
> 1/3 cup fat-free reduced-sugar vanilla yogurt
> 1/3 cup fat-free plain yogurt
> 3 tablespoons reduced-fat mayonnaise *or* salad dressing
> 1 tablespoon lemon juice

Drain pineapple, reserving juice in a bowl. Add apples to the juice; toss to coat. Let stand for 5 minutes; drain. In a large bowl, combine the pineapple, carrots, raisins, coconut and apples. In a small bowl, combine the remaining ingredients. Pour over carrot mixture and toss to coat. Cover and refrigerate for 3-4 hours or until chilled. **Yield:** 6 servings.

Nutritional Analysis: One serving (3/4 cup) equals 138 calories, 4 g fat (1 g saturated fat), 3 mg cholesterol, 101 mg sodium, 26 g carbohydrate, 3 g fiber, 2 g protein.
Diabetic Exchanges: 1 fruit, 1 vegetable, 1/2 starch, 1/2 fat.
▲ *Low-sodium*
▲ *Meatless*

Mediterranean Pasta Salad

(Pictured above)

This cold pasta salad is wonderful for warm days when you don't want to cook. I like to make it ahead so when we get home from work, it's ready to serve with fruit and whole-grain bread.
—Ruth Stone, Loyalton, California

> 6 ounces uncooked spinach fettuccine
> 1 can (3 ounces) light water-packed tuna, drained and flaked
> 1 medium tomato, cut into wedges
> 1/4 cup pitted ripe olives, halved
> 1/3 cup thinly sliced red onion
> **VINAIGRETTE:**
> 1/4 cup red wine vinegar *or* cider vinegar
> 4-1/2 teaspoons olive *or* canola oil
> 1 garlic clove, minced
> 1/2 teaspoon dried oregano
> 1/4 teaspoon salt
> 1/4 teaspoon dried basil
> **Dash pepper**

Cook fettuccine according to package directions; rinse in cold water and drain. Place in a large bowl; add the tuna, tomato, olives and onion. In a jar with a tight-fitting lid, combine the vinaigrette ingredients; shake well. Pour over salad and toss to coat. Cover and refrigerate for 1-2 hours. **Yield:** 4 servings.

Nutritional Analysis: One serving (1 cup) equals 242 calories, 8 g fat (1 g saturated fat), 9 mg cholesterol, 319 mg sodium, 33 g carbohydrate, 3 g fiber, 11 g protein.
Diabetic Exchanges: 2 starch, 1 very lean meat, 1 vegetable, 1 fat.

Chinese Chicken Salad

This chilled chicken salad has a slightly tangy taste and is a tasty alternative to the typical chicken salad. An added plus is that it is easy to prepare. I like to serve it with fresh fruit and a muffin (low-fat, of course!).
—Sandra Miller, Lexington, Kentucky

> 3 cups cubed cooked chicken breast
> 3 celery ribs, chopped
> 1 cup canned bean sprouts, rinsed and drained
> 1/2 cup reduced-fat French salad dressing
> 1/2 cup fat-free mayonnaise
> 2 tablespoons reduced-sodium soy sauce
> 1/4 teaspoon onion powder
> 1/4 teaspoon salt
> 1/8 teaspoon pepper
> 1/8 teaspoon Chinese five-spice powder
> 5 cups torn salad greens
> 2 tablespoons sliced ripe olives

In a large bowl, combine the first 10 ingredients; toss to coat. Refrigerate for at least 2 hours. Serve on salad greens; garnish with olives. **Yield:** 5 servings.

Nutritional Analysis: One serving (1 cup) equals 219 calories, 6 g fat (1 g saturated fat), 74 mg cholesterol, 919 mg sodium, 13 g carbohydrate, 3 g fiber, 28 g protein.
Diabetic Exchanges: 3 lean meat, 1 vegetable, 1/2 starch.

Favorite Salad Dressing Made Lighter

WHILE salad dressings lend lots of flavor to fresh greens, they often add plenty of fat, too. That's why Joan Dones asked us to revise her recipe for Honey French Dressing. The smooth thick dressing is a nice blend of tangy and sweet, with flavor reminiscent of a Western dressing.

"I got this recipe years ago when I worked as a cook in a high school cafeteria," notes the Las Vegas, Nevada cook. "Please reduce the fat without losing any flavor or causing the dressing to separate. I tried replacing some of the oil with water, but the dressing separated and tasted weak. I also tried adding applesauce instead of some of the oil, but it wasn't as tasty."

While our Test Kitchen staff applauded Joan's efforts, they were eager to try some other methods.

To trim the fat, they reduced the oil from 3/4 to 1/3 cup and called for mild-flavored canola oil. Then the sweetness of the honey came through too strongly, so they reduced that as well.

With less honey and oil, the dressing was thinner and yielded less, so they increased the amount of ketchup and onion and added a little apricot nectar to give it volume.

The finished product was so flavorful, they were able to reduce the salt, too. And, as Joan requested, the dressing does not separate upon standing.

Makeover Honey French Dressing has half the fat, about 40% fewer calories and a third less sodium. But it will still dress up salads with gusto.

Honey French Dressing

3/4 cup honey
1/3 cup ketchup
1/3 cup cider vinegar
1/3 cup chopped onion
  3 garlic cloves, minced
  1 teaspoon salt
  1 teaspoon paprika
1/2 teaspoon celery seed
3/4 cup vegetable oil

In a blender or food processor, combine the first eight ingredients; cover and process until blended. While processing, add oil in a steady stream. Process until thickened. Store in the refrigerator. **Yield:** 2 cups.

Nutritional Analysis: One serving (2 tablespoons) equals 147 calories, 10 g fat (1 g saturated fat), 0 cholesterol, 210 mg sodium, 15 g carbohydrate, trace fiber, trace protein.
▲ *Meatless*

Makeover Honey French Dressing

(Pictured below)

1/2 cup ketchup
1/2 cup honey
1/2 cup chopped onion
1/3 cup cider vinegar
1/4 cup apricot nectar
  3 garlic cloves, minced
  1 teaspoon paprika
1/2 teaspoon celery seed
1/4 teaspoon salt
1/3 cup canola oil

3 PPV

In a blender or food processor, combine the first nine ingredients; cover and process until blended. While processing, add oil in a steady stream. Process until thickened. Store in the refrigerator. **Yield:** 2 cups.

Nutritional Analysis: One serving (2 tablespoons) equals 87 calories, 5 g fat (trace saturated fat), 0 cholesterol, 133 mg sodium, 12 g carbohydrate, trace fiber, trace protein.
Diabetic Exchanges: 1 fruit, 1 fat.
▲ *Low-sodium*
▲ *Meatless*

Tart Orange Gelatin Salad

Here's a fun and fruity salad that's sure to disappear at picnics and family gatherings. The creamy pudding topping nicely balances the tart orange gelatin layer.
—Mary Martzke, Shawano, Wisconsin

> 2 packages (.3 ounce *each*) sugar-free orange gelatin
> Sugar substitute equivalent to 3 tablespoons sugar*
> 2 cups boiling water
> 1 can (6 ounces) frozen orange juice concentrate, thawed
> 1 cup cold water
> 1 can (20 ounces) unsweetened pineapple tidbits, drained
> 1 can (11 ounces) mandarin oranges, drained
> 1 cup cold fat-free milk
> 1 package (1 ounce) sugar-free instant vanilla pudding mix
> 1 teaspoon grated lemon peel
> 2 cups reduced-fat whipped topping

In a bowl, dissolve gelatin and sugar substitute in boiling water. Stir in orange juice concentrate and cold water. Add pineapple and oranges; mix well. Pour into a 13-in. x 9-in. x 2-in. dish; refrigerate until set. In a bowl, whisk the milk and pudding mix for 2 minutes. Add lemon peel; mix well. Let stand for 2 minutes or until soft-set. Fold in whipped topping; spread over gelatin. Refrigerate until set. **Yield:** 12 servings.

*Editor's Note: This recipe was tested with Splenda No Calorie Sweetener. Look for it in the baking aisle of your grocery store.

Nutritional Analysis: One piece equals 99 calories, 1 g fat (1 g saturated fat), trace cholesterol, 149 mg sodium, 18 g carbohydrate, 1 g fiber, 2 g protein.
Diabetic Exchanges: 1/2 fruit, 1/2 starch.
△ **Low-fat**

Strawberry-Honey Salad Dressing

(Pictured at right)

This salad dressing is good for you and delicious. It makes your fruit salad taste heavenly! The mild, sweet strawberry yogurt dressing brings a pretty pink tint to the fruit it's draped over... and chopped walnuts add nice crunch.
—Andrea Pollock, Jordan, New York

> 1/2 cup fat-free reduced-sugar strawberry yogurt
> 1/2 cup fat-free plain yogurt
> 1/4 cup fresh *or* frozen unsweetened whole strawberries, thawed and mashed
> 1 tablespoon honey
> 1 tablespoon chopped walnuts
> Assorted fresh fruit
> Additional walnuts, optional

In a bowl, combine the first five ingredients. Serve with assorted fresh fruit and additional nuts if desired. **Yield:** 10 servings.

Nutritional Analysis: One serving (2 tablespoons) equals 28 calories, 1 g fat (trace saturated fat), 1 mg cholesterol, 17 mg sodium, 4 g carbohydrate, trace fiber, 1 g protein.
Diabetic Exchange: 1/2 fruit.
△ **Low-fat**
▲ **Low-sodium**
▲ **Meatless**

Chicken Pasta Salad

(Pictured at right)

Served warm, this satisfying salad combines pasta, chicken, lettuce, mandarin oranges and romaine and is tossed with a slightly tart dressing. My daughter-in-law gave me a basic dressing recipe, and I adapted it to suit our tastes.
—Diane Conrad, Glide, Oregon

> 2 tablespoons cider vinegar
> 2 tablespoons reduced-sodium soy sauce
> 4-1/2 teaspoons olive *or* canola oil, *divided*
> 1 tablespoon sugar
> 1 garlic clove, minced
> 1 medium onion, coarsely chopped
> 1 medium green pepper, cut into 1/2-inch pieces
> 1 medium sweet red pepper, cut into 1/2-inch pieces
> 1/2 pound fresh mushrooms, sliced
> 3/4 pound boneless skinless chicken breasts, cut into cubes
> 4 cups cooked rigatoni *or* large tube pasta
> 4 cups torn romaine lettuce
> 1 can (11 ounces) mandarin oranges, drained
> 1 can (6 ounces) pitted ripe olives, drained

In a jar with a tight-fitting lid, combine the vinegar, soy sauce, 1-1/2 teaspoons oil, sugar and garlic; shake well. In a nonstick skillet, saute onion, peppers and mushrooms in 1-1/2 teaspoons oil until tender. Remove and keep warm. In same skillet, saute chicken in remaining oil until juices run clear; drain.

In a large bowl, combine pasta, lettuce, oranges, olives, onion mixture and chicken. Pour dressing over lettuce mixture; toss to coat. Serve immediately. **Yield:** 6 servings.

Nutritional Analysis: One serving (2 cups) equals 332 calories, 9 g fat (1 g saturated fat), 48 mg cholesterol, 464 mg sodium, 37 g carbohydrate, 4 g fiber, 24 g protein.
Diabetic Exchanges: 2 lean meat, 2 vegetable, 1-1/2 starch, 1/2 fruit, 1/2 fat.

Grandma's Fruit Salad

I can't believe how easy this pretty salad is to make. The colorful blend of bananas, pineapple, pears, peaches and grapes is tossed with a creamy pudding sauce. People of all ages enjoy this dish.
—Carolyn Tomatz, Jackson, Wisconsin

1 can (20 ounces) unsweetened pineapple chunks
1 can (15 ounces) reduced-sugar sliced pears, drained
1 can (15 ounces) reduced-sugar sliced peaches, drained
1-1/2 cups seedless red grapes
1 package (3 ounces) cook-and-serve vanilla pudding mix
2 medium firm bananas
3 tablespoons lemon juice
1 jar (10 ounces) maraschino cherries, well drained

Drain pineapple, reserving juice in a 1-cup measuring cup. In a bowl, combine the pineapple, pears, peaches and grapes. Cover and chill. Add enough water to pineapple juice to measure 1 cup. Pour into a small saucepan. Whisk in pudding mix. Bring to a boil over medium heat, stirring constantly. Remove from the heat; set aside to cool to room temperature.

Slice bananas into a bowl. Drizzle with lemon juice; gently toss to coat. Let stand for 5 minutes; drain. Add bananas and cherries to chilled fruit. Add cooled pudding; toss gently to combine. Refrigerate until serving. Refrigerate leftovers. **Yield:** 12 servings.

Nutritional Analysis: One serving (1/2 cup) equals 126 calories, trace fat (trace saturated fat), 0 cholesterol, 59 mg sodium, 33 g carbohydrate, 2 g fiber, 1 g protein.
Diabetic Exchange: *2 fruit.*
△ **Low-fat**
▲ **Low-sodium**
▲ **Meatless**

Vegetable Slaw

We've nicknamed this crunchy salad "Christmas slaw" because of its pretty mix of red and green vegetables. But it's tasty anytime. It's a great light lunch when stuffed into a whole wheat pita.
—Julie Copenhaver, Morganton, North Carolina

3 cups shredded cabbage
5 plum tomatoes, seeded and chopped
1 cup fresh broccoli florets, cut into small pieces
1 cup cauliflowerets, cut into small pieces
1/2 cup chopped red onion
1/2 cup fat-free sour cream
1/4 cup reduced-fat mayonnaise
1 tablespoon cider vinegar
3/4 teaspoon salt
1/4 teaspoon pepper

In a bowl, combine the cabbage, tomatoes, broccoli, cauliflower and onion. In a small bowl, combine the sour cream, mayonnaise, vinegar, salt and pepper. Pour over cabbage mixture; toss to coat evenly. Cover and refrigerate until chilled. **Yield:** 6 servings.

Nutritional Analysis: One serving (3/4 cup) equals 84 calories, 5 g fat (1 g saturated fat), 7 mg cholesterol, 402 mg sodium, 10 g carbohydrate, 3 g fiber, 3 g protein.
Diabetic Exchanges: *2 vegetable, 1 fat.*
▲ **Meatless**

Mandarin Couscous Salad

(Pictured below)

I help teach a healthy lifestyles program and often share this recipe. Instead of mandarin oranges, you can add fresh chopped oranges.
—Debbie Anderson, Hillsdale, Michigan

1-1/3 cups water
1 cup uncooked couscous
1 can (11 ounces) mandarin oranges, drained
1 cup frozen peas, thawed
1/2 cup slivered almonds, toasted
1/3 cup chopped red onion
3 tablespoons cider *or* white vinegar
2 tablespoons olive *or* canola oil
1 tablespoon sugar
1/4 teaspoon salt
1/4 teaspoon hot pepper sauce

Place water in a saucepan; bring to a boil. Stir in couscous. Cover and remove from the heat; let stand for 5 minutes. Fluff with a fork. Cover and refrigerate for at least 1 hour.

In a bowl, combine the oranges, peas, almonds, onion and couscous. In a jar with a tight-fitting lid, combine the vinegar, oil, sugar, salt and hot pepper sauce; shake well. Pour dressing over couscous mixture; toss to coat. **Yield:** 7 servings.

Nutritional Analysis: One serving (3/4 cup) equals 221 calories, 8 g fat (1 g saturated fat), 0 cholesterol, 108 mg sodium, 31 g carbohydrate, 4 g fiber, 6 g protein.
Diabetic Exchanges: *1-1/2 starch, 1-1/2 fat, 1/2 fruit.*
▲ **Low-sodium**
▲ **Meatless**

Side Dishes & Condiments

In this chapter, you'll find just the right accompaniment for your meals...from fresh vegetables, pleasing pasta and hearty potatoes to satisfying rice, mouth-watering relishes and perfectly seasoned sauces.

Oven-Roasted Root Vegetables (page 94)

Salt-Free Herb Blend

I combine a handful of seasonings, from paprika to poppy seeds, to make this salt-free mix that will perk up poultry, meat and vegetables, too.
—Eva Bailey, Olive Hill, Kentucky

    4 teaspoons sesame seeds
    2 teaspoons celery seed
    2 teaspoons dried marjoram
    2 teaspoons poppy seeds
    2 teaspoons coarsely ground pepper
1-1/2 teaspoons dried parsley flakes
    1 teaspoon onion powder
    1 teaspoon dried thyme
1/2 teaspoon garlic powder
1/2 teaspoon paprika

In a small bowl, combine all ingredients. Store in an airtight container for up to 6 months. **Yield:** 1/3 cup.

Nutritional Analysis: One serving (1/4 teaspoon) equals 3 calories, trace fat (trace saturated fat), 0 cholesterol, trace sodium, trace carbohydrate, trace fiber, trace protein.
Diabetic Exchange: Free food.
△ *Low-fat*
▲ *Low-sodium*
▲ *Meatless*

Venezuelan Black Beans

My husband and I are missionaries in Venezuela, South America. I found this recipe in a missionary ladies' cookbook. This dish is traditionally served with cornmeal pancakes and plantains (cooked bananas).
—Casandra Falls, Venezuela, South America

    2 cups (1 pound) dried black beans
1/4 cup ketchup
1/4 cup chopped onion
    1 teaspoon beef *or* vegetable bouillon granules
    1 teaspoon salt
1/4 teaspoon dried oregano
1/4 teaspoon garlic powder
1/4 teaspoon ground cumin
1/4 teaspoon pepper

Place beans in a Dutch oven or soup kettle; add water to cover by 2 in. Bring to a boil; boil for 2 minutes. Remove from the heat; cover and let stand for 1 hour. Drain and rinse beans, discarding liquid. Return beans to the pan; add water to cover by 2 in. Bring to a boil. Reduce heat; cover and simmer for 1 hour or until the beans are almost tender.

Drain beans and reserve 2 cups liquid. Return beans and reserved liquid to Dutch oven. Stir in remaining ingredients. Remove half of the bean mixture and mash well; return to the pan. Bring to a boil. Reduce heat; cover and simmer for 30 minutes or until beans reach desired consistency. **Yield:** 12 servings.

Nutritional Analysis: One serving (1/2 cup) equals 126 calories, 1 g fat (trace saturated fat), trace cholesterol, 328 mg sodium, 23 g carbohydrate, 8 g fiber, 8 g protein.
Diabetic Exchanges: 1 very lean meat, 1 starch.
△ *Low-fat*
▲ *Meatless*

 ## Secret to Sauteing

WHEN a recipe calls for sauteing vegetables such as mushrooms or onions, I do it in the microwave. Instead of sauteing them in butter, margarine or oil, I just add a little water to the veggies and cover the dish before cooking.
—Bridget Perrine
Hartfield, Virginia

Winter Floret Medley

(Pictured below)

Our family loves broccoli and cauliflower. This simple stovetop side dish is quick and easy to make. Crisp-tender florets are mildly seasoned with garlic.
—Joyce Davis, Marshfield, Missouri

    1 garlic clove, minced
    1 tablespoon olive *or* canola oil
    2 cups broccoli florets
    2 cups cauliflowerets
1/4 cup water
1/4 teaspoon salt
Dash pepper

In a large nonstick skillet, saute garlic in oil for 1 minute. Add the remaining ingredients. Bring to a boil. Reduce heat; cover and simmer for 8-10 minutes or until vegetables are tender. **Yield:** 4 servings.

Nutritional Analysis: One serving (3/4 cup) equals 53 calories, 4 g fat (trace saturated fat), 0 cholesterol, 310 mg sodium, 5 g carbohydrate, 1 g fiber, 2 g protein.
Diabetic Exchanges: 1 vegetable, 1/2 fat.
▲ *Meatless*

Quick Picante Sauce

Hot pepper sauce and a jalapeno pepper give this snappy sauce just the right amount of zip. It makes a great dip for tortilla chips or a tangy sauce for tacos and fajitas. This is always a big hit at parties and office gatherings. I even make it for my mother when she needs to bring a dip to a party.
—Barbara Sellers, Shreveport, Louisiana

1 can (14-1/2 ounces) whole tomatoes, drained
1/2 cup coarsely chopped onion
1/2 cup minced fresh cilantro *or* parsley
1 jalapeno pepper, seeded and halved*
3 tablespoons lime juice
1 tablespoon chili powder
1 garlic clove, halved
1/2 teaspoon salt
1/4 teaspoon grated lime peel
5 drops hot pepper sauce
Baked tortilla chips

In a blender or food processor, combine the first 10 ingredients; cover and process until smooth. Serve with tortilla chips. **Yield:** 5 servings.

Editor's Note: When cutting or seeding hot peppers, use rubber or plastic gloves to protect your hands. Avoid touching your face.

Nutritional Analysis: One serving (1/4 cup sauce) equals 35 calories, trace fat (trace saturated fat), 0 cholesterol, 404 mg sodium, 7 g carbohydrate, 2 g fiber, 1 g protein.
Diabetic Exchange: *1 vegetable.*
△ **Low-fat**
▲ **Meatless**

Cheesy Spinach Casserole

This quiche-like casserole is a wonderful way to include good-for-you spinach in your menu. Made with eggs and reduced-fat cheese, the easy-to-cut side dish would be a welcome addition to a breakfast or brunch buffet.
—Marilyn Paradis, Woodburn, Oregon

3/4 cup chopped onion
1 tablespoon butter *or* stick margarine
2 eggs
1 egg white
1 package (10 ounces) frozen chopped spinach, thawed and squeezed dry
2 cups small-curd 2% cottage cheese
1 cup (4 ounces) shredded reduced-fat cheddar cheese
3 tablespoons all-purpose flour
1/8 teaspoon salt

In a small nonstick skillet, saute onion in butter until tender. In a large bowl, combine the eggs, egg white and spinach. Stir in the cottage cheese, cheddar cheese, flour, salt and onion mixture. Pour into a 1-1/2-qt. baking dish coated with nonstick cooking spray. Bake, uncovered, at 350° for 50-60 minutes or until set. **Yield:** 6 servings.

Nutritional Analysis: One serving equals 199 calories, 9 g fat (5 g saturated fat), 95 mg cholesterol, 440 mg sodium, 10 g carbohydrate, 2 g fiber, 20 g protein.
Diabetic Exchanges: *2 lean meat, 1 vegetable, 1 fat.*
▲ **Meatless**

Roasted Ginger Green Beans

(Pictured above)

My husband, Michael, is the cook in our house and discovered this simple treatment for green beans. I hope you like its pleasant flavor as much as we do.
—Kathy Jackson, Arlington, Virginia

1 tablespoon olive *or* canola oil
1 teaspoon sesame oil
3/4 teaspoon salt
1 garlic clove, minced
1/4 teaspoon minced fresh thyme *or* dash dried thyme
1 pound fresh green beans
3/4 teaspoon ground ginger *or* 1 tablespoon minced fresh gingerroot

In a large bowl, combine the first five ingredients. Add beans; toss to coat. Transfer to a 15-in. x 10-in. x 1-in. baking pan coated with nonstick cooking spray. Bake, uncovered, at 400° for 16-20 minutes or until beans are crisp-tender, stirring occasionally. Sprinkle with ginger. **Yield:** 4 servings.

Nutritional Analysis: One serving (3/4 cup) equals 77 calories, 5 g fat (1 g saturated fat), 0 cholesterol, 443 mg sodium, 8 g carbohydrate, 3 g fiber, 2 g protein.
Diabetic Exchanges: *1 vegetable, 1 fat.*
▲ **Meatless**

Herbed Vegetable Bake

My husband has high cholesterol, so I've had to revise some of his favorite recipes. I've found that adding herbs to vegetables is a good way to replace some of those yummy cheese and dairy-rich cream sauces. And since the veggies in this dish are baked, they retain most of their nutrients.
—*Sandra Cooper, Calgary, Alberta*

3 cups broccoli florets
2 cups cauliflowerets
2 medium carrots, thinly sliced
1 medium red onion, thinly sliced
1 celery rib, thinly sliced
1/2 teaspoon Italian seasoning
1/2 teaspoon dried basil
1/2 teaspoon garlic salt
2 tablespoons water
2 tablespoons reduced-fat stick margarine*

Place the vegetables in a 9-in. square baking dish coated with nonstick cooking spray. Sprinkle with Italian seasoning, basil, garlic salt and water. Dot with margarine. Cover and bake at 450° for 20-25 minutes or until vegetables are tender. **Yield:** 6 servings.

*Editor's Note: This recipe was tested with Parkay Light stick margarine.

Nutritional Analysis: One serving (3/4 cup) equals 55 calories, 2 g fat (trace saturated fat), 0 cholesterol, 139 mg sodium, 8 g carbohydrate, 3 g fiber, 2 g protein.
Diabetic Exchanges: 1 vegetable, 1/2 fat.
△ **Low-fat**
▲ **Low-sodium**
▲ **Meatless**

Squash and Bean Saute

(Pictured above)

We like to include meatless dishes in our diet. This nicely seasoned vegetable medley is easy to prepare and really delicious. Sometimes we even enjoy it as a main entree.
—*Ellie Vorous, Seaford, Delaware*

1 large onion, sliced
2 garlic cloves, minced
1 teaspoon salt
1/4 teaspoon pepper
1/4 teaspoon dried thyme
1/4 teaspoon rubbed sage
1 tablespoon canola oil
1 pound fresh green beans, trimmed
1 pound small yellow summer squash, sliced
1/3 cup water
3 large plum tomatoes, peeled and chopped
3 tablespoons minced fresh parsley

In a large nonstick skillet, saute the onion, garlic and seasonings in oil until onion is tender. Add the beans, squash and water; bring to a boil. Reduce heat; cover and simmer for 8-10 minutes or until just tender. Add tomatoes and parsley; cover and simmer 5 minutes longer or until vegetables are tender. Serve with a slotted spoon. **Yield:** 6 servings.

Nutritional Analysis: One serving (3/4 cup) equals 76 calories, 3 g fat (trace saturated fat), 0 cholesterol, 398 mg sodium, 12 g carbohydrate, 4 g fiber, 3 g protein.
Diabetic Exchanges: 2 vegetable, 1/2 fat.
△ **Low-fat**
▲ **Meatless**

Parsley Pesto Spaghetti

Fresh parsley, Parmesan cheese and a variety of herbs pack plenty of flavor into this well-seasoned side dish.
—*Jeanette Simec, Ottawa, Illinois*

3 tablespoons olive *or* canola oil
1 cup packed fresh parsley leaves
1 teaspoon *each* dried basil, oregano and marjoram
1 teaspoon salt
1/2 teaspoon garlic powder
1/2 teaspoon pepper
12 ounces uncooked spaghetti
1/4 cup chopped walnuts, toasted
1/4 cup shredded Parmesan cheese

For pesto, combine the oil, parsley and seasonings in a blender or food processor; cover and process until blended. Cook spaghetti according to package directions; drain. Transfer to a serving bowl and add the walnuts, Parmesan cheese and pesto. Toss to coat; serve immediately. **Yield:** 6 servings.

Nutritional Analysis: One serving (1 cup) equals 328 calories, 12 g fat (2 g saturated fat), 3 mg cholesterol, 479 mg sodium, 44 g carbohydrate, 2 g fiber, 10 g protein.
Diabetic Exchanges: 3 starch, 2 fat.
▲ **Meatless**

Spanish Potatoes

(Pictured below)

I keep my kitchen stocked with fruits and vegetables. Potatoes are great to have on hand because they're nutritious and low in fat. Oregano seasons this side dish dressed up with onions, peppers and tomatoes.
—Connie Thomas, Jensen, Utah

1-1/4 pounds small red potatoes, quartered
1-1/2 cups chopped onions
   1 cup sliced green pepper
1/2 cup water
   1 tablespoon olive *or* canola oil
   1 teaspoon chicken *or* vegetable bouillon
     granules
   1 cup chopped fresh tomatoes
1/2 teaspoon dried oregano

Place potatoes in a large saucepan and cover with water. Bring to a boil. Reduce heat; cover and cook for 15 minutes or until tender.

Meanwhile, in a small saucepan, combine the onions, green pepper, water, oil and bouillon. Bring to a boil. Reduce heat; cover and simmer for 8-10 minutes or until vegetables are tender. Drain potatoes; add onion mixture, tomatoes and oregano. Stir gently to coat. **Yield:** 6 servings.

Nutritional Analysis: One serving (1 cup) equals 113 calories, 3 g fat (trace saturated fat), trace cholesterol, 199 mg sodium, 21 g carbohydrate, 2 g fiber, 2 g protein.
  Diabetic Exchanges: 1 starch, 1 vegetable, 1/2 fat.
  △ *Low-fat*
  ▲ *Meatless*

Old-Fashioned Corn Relish

This was the first "country" recipe I received after moving away from the city—a farm wife neighbor shared it. I've made a few additions to it and gotten quite a few compliments. It's wonderful made with garden-fresh ingredients.
—Jean Peterson, Mulliken, Michigan

   2 cups fresh *or* frozen corn
   2 cups chopped onions
   2 cups chopped tomatoes
   2 cups chopped seeded cucumber
   1 large green pepper, chopped
   1 cup sugar
   1 cup cider vinegar
1-1/2 teaspoons celery seed
1-1/2 teaspoons mustard seed
   1 teaspoon salt
1/2 teaspoon ground turmeric

In a large saucepan, combine all of the ingredients. Bring to a boil. Reduce heat; simmer, uncovered, for 20-30 minutes or until thickened. Store in the refrigerator for up to 3 weeks. **Yield:** 6-1/2 cups.

Nutritional Analysis: One serving (2 tablespoons) equals 53 calories, trace fat (trace saturated fat), 0 cholesterol, 94 mg sodium, 13 g carbohydrate, 1 g fiber, 1 g protein.
  Diabetic Exchange: 1 starch.
  △ *Low-fat*
  △ *Low-sodium*

Raisin Brown Rice Pilaf

I dress up nutritious brown rice with onion, garlic, raisins and almonds in this flavorful pilaf.
—Michele Doucette, Stephenville, Newfoundland

   1 medium onion, chopped
   1 garlic clove, minced
   1 teaspoon olive *or* canola oil
   1 cup uncooked brown rice
1/2 cup raisins *or* dried currants
   1 cinnamon stick (1 inch)
2-1/2 cups vegetable broth
1/2 teaspoon salt
1/4 cup sliced almonds, toasted

In a large saucepan, saute onion and garlic in oil until tender. Stir in rice, raisins and cinnamon stick; saute until rice is golden. Add broth and salt. Bring to a boil. Reduce heat; cover and simmer for 1 hour or until liquid is absorbed and rice is tender. Discard cinnamon stick. Sprinkle with almonds. **Yield:** 6 servings.

Nutritional Analysis: One serving (2/3 cup) equals 193 calories, 4 g fat (trace saturated fat), 0 cholesterol, 621 mg sodium, 36 g carbohydrate, 3 g fiber, 5 g protein.
  Diabetic Exchanges: 2 starch, 1/2 fruit, 1/2 fat.
  ▲ *Meatless*

Greek Seasoning

Can't find Greek seasoning at the grocery store? Our Test Kitchen home economists came up with their own rendition of the ethnic blend.

1-1/2 teaspoons dried oregano
1 teaspoon dried mint
1 teaspoon dried thyme
1/2 teaspoon dried basil
1/2 teaspoon dried marjoram
1/2 teaspoon dried minced onion
1/4 teaspoon dried minced garlic

In a small bowl, combine all ingredients. Store in an airtight container in a cool dry place for up to 6 months. **Yield:** 2 tablespoons.

Nutritional Analysis: One serving (1/2 teaspoon) equals 2 calories, trace fat (0 saturated fat), 0 cholesterol, 1 mg sodium, trace carbohydrate, trace fiber, trace protein.
Diabetic Exchanges: Free food.
△ *Low-fat*
▲ *Low-sodium*
▲ *Meatless*

Spicy Green Bean Saute

Perk up everyday green beans with this snappy saute recipe. It's great alongside thinly sliced beef or chicken.
—Mary Tallman, Arbor Vitae, Wisconsin

2 teaspoons cornstarch
3/4 cup reduced-sodium chicken broth *or* vegetable broth
1/4 cup reduced-sodium teriyaki sauce
1/8 teaspoon cayenne pepper
1 pound fresh green beans, cut into 2-inch pieces
1 medium onion, thinly sliced
1/2 cup chopped sweet red pepper
1 teaspoon garlic powder
1/2 teaspoon ground ginger *or* 2 teaspoons minced fresh gingerroot
1 tablespoon canola oil

In a bowl, combine the cornstarch, broth, teriyaki sauce and pepper until smooth; set aside. In a large nonstick skillet or wok, saute the green beans, onion, red pepper, garlic and ginger in oil until crisp-tender. Stir cornstarch mixture and add to the pan. Bring to a boil; cook and stir for 2 minutes until thickened. **Yield:** 4 servings.

Nutritional Analysis: One serving (1 cup) equals 111 calories, 4 g fat (trace saturated fat), 0 cholesterol, 438 mg sodium, 17 g carbohydrate, 5 g fiber, 4 g protein.
Diabetic Exchanges: 2 vegetable, 1/2 starch, 1/2 fat.
▲ *Meatless*

Sweet 'n' Tangy Barbecue Sauce

(Pictured below)

Jalapeno pepper, cayenne and chili powder lend a bit of a bite to this low-sodium sauce from our Test Kitchen home economists. Try it on pork, chicken, beef ribs and more.

1 large onion, chopped
1 jalapeno pepper, seeded and chopped*
1 tablespoon olive *or* canola oil
1-1/2 cups water
1 can (6 ounces) tomato paste
1/2 cup packed brown sugar
1/2 cup cider vinegar
1/4 cup honey
2 tablespoons chili powder
1 tablespoon molasses
2 teaspoons chicken bouillon granules
1 teaspoon garlic powder
1/2 teaspoon onion powder
1/2 teaspoon ground cumin
1/4 teaspoon pepper
1/4 teaspoon cayenne pepper
1/2 to 1 teaspoon Liquid Smoke, optional

In a saucepan, cook onion and jalapeno in oil over medium heat until tender and lightly browned. Add the next 13 ingredients. Bring to a boil. Reduce heat; simmer, uncovered, for 30 minutes or until thickened, stirring occasionally. Remove from the heat. Stir in Liquid Smoke if desired. Store in the refrigerator for up to 2 weeks. **Yield:** 2-1/2 cups.

*Editor's Note: When cutting or seeding hot peppers, use rubber or plastic gloves to protect your hands. Avoid touching your face.

Nutritional Analysis: One serving (2 tablespoons) equals 56 calories, 1 g fat (trace saturated fat), trace cholesterol, 126 mg sodium, 12 g carbohydrate, trace fiber, 1 g protein.
Diabetic Exchange: 1 starch.
△ *Low-fat*
▲ *Low-sodium*

Scalloped Basil Tomatoes

If your garden is flooded with tomatoes, be sure to try this scrumptious baked side dish. It goes over big at family, church and club dinners. Cubes of French bread are combined with mildly seasoned tomatoes, then sprinkled with Parmesan cheese and baked. Every bite captures the flavor of summer.
—Edna Apostol, Savannah, Missouri

  16 plum tomatoes
   2 cups cubed crustless French bread (1/2-inch cubes)
   1 tablespoon olive *or* canola oil
   1 tablespoon sugar
   3 garlic cloves, minced
 1/2 teaspoon salt
 1/8 teaspoon pepper
 1/4 cup thinly sliced fresh basil leaves
   3 tablespoons shredded Parmesan cheese

Peel tomatoes and cut into 1/2-in. cubes; drain. In a large nonstick skillet, cook bread in oil over medium heat for 5-7 minutes or until lightly browned. Add the tomatoes, sugar and garlic; cook and stir for 5 minutes. Stir in the salt, pepper and basil. Pour into a 1-1/2-qt. baking dish. Sprinkle with cheese. Bake, uncovered, at 350° for 35-40 minutes or until bubbly. **Yield:** 6 servings.

Nutritional Analysis: One serving (2/3 cup) equals 103 calories, 4 g fat (1 g saturated fat), 2 mg cholesterol, 325 mg sodium, 15 g carbohydrate, 2 g fiber, 4 g protein.
Diabetic Exchanges: 1 vegetable, 1 fat, 1/2 starch.
▲ *Meatless*

German Baked Beans

Canned baked beans never tasted so good! I dress them up in style with sauerkraut, applesauce and brown sugar. These beans are always requested for the monthly dinners at our senior center.
—Mary Nieburger, Laughlin, Nevada

  2 cans (15 ounces *each*) pork and beans
  1 can (14 ounces) sauerkraut, rinsed and well drained
  1 cup unsweetened applesauce
1/2 cup packed brown sugar
1/2 teaspoon salt
1/2 teaspoon ground mustard

In a large bowl, combine all ingredients. Transfer to a 2-qt. baking dish coated with nonstick cooking spray. Bake, uncovered, at 400° for 1 to 1-1/2 hours or until bubbly. **Yield:** 8 servings.

Nutritional Analysis: One serving (3/4 cup) equals 185 calories, 2 g fat (1 g saturated fat), 7 mg cholesterol, 890 mg sodium, 40 g carbohydrate, 8 g fiber, 6 g protein.
Diabetic Exchange: 2-1/2 starch.
△ *Low-fat*

Confetti Barley Pilaf

(Pictured above)

This pilaf is both colorful and tasty. The slightly chewy texture of the barley, the tender vegetables and lively spices make it special enough for company. I love to cook and experiment in the kitchen— especially with grains and veggies.
—Kris Erickson, Everett, Washington

   1 large onion, finely chopped
   1 garlic clove, minced
   1 tablespoon canola oil
   1 cup medium pearl barley
   1 cup sliced fresh mushrooms
 1/2 cup shredded carrot
 1/2 cup coarsely shredded cabbage
 1/2 cup chopped sweet red pepper
   1 teaspoon dried basil
   1 teaspoon dried oregano
2-1/2 cups chicken broth *or* vegetable broth

In a large nonstick skillet, saute onion and garlic in oil until tender. Add barley; saute for 3-5 minutes or until lightly browned. Add the mushrooms, carrot, cabbage, red pepper, basil and oregano. Cook and stir until vegetables are crisp-tender, about 3 minutes. Stir in broth; bring to a boil. Reduce heat; cover and simmer for 40-45 minutes or until liquid is absorbed and barley is tender. **Yield:** 6 servings.

Nutritional Analysis: One serving (2/3 cup) equals 169 calories, 3 g fat (trace saturated fat), 0 cholesterol, 507 mg sodium, 32 g carbohydrate, 7 g fiber, 5 g protein.
Diabetic Exchanges: 1-1/2 starch, 1 vegetable, 1/2 fat.
△ *Low-fat*
▲ *Meatless*

Gingered Carrots 'n' Onions

A little ginger goes a long way in this dish. It gives the carrots and onions wonderful flavor. This side is so pretty...and it goes well with any meat.
—*Sarah Rodgers, Pittsburgh, Pennsylvania*

1-3/4 pounds carrots
1-1/3 cups chopped onions
   2 teaspoons olive *or* canola oil
   1/2 teaspoon salt
   1/8 to 1/4 teaspoon ground ginger
   1/8 teaspoon pepper

Cut carrots in half lengthwise; thinly slice. Place in a large nonstick skillet; cover with water. Bring to a boil; cook for 9 minutes or until crisp-tender. Drain and keep warm. In the same skillet, saute onions in oil until tender. Stir in the carrots, salt, ginger and pepper. **Yield:** 6 servings.

Nutritional Analysis: One serving (3/4 cup) equals 93 calories, 2 g fat (trace saturated fat), 0 cholesterol, 266 mg sodium, 18 g carbohydrate, 4 g fiber, 2 g protein.
Diabetic Exchanges: 2 vegetable, 1/2 starch.
△ *Low-fat*
▲ *Meatless*

Chunky Pear Applesauce

Here's a quick way to dress up store-bought applesauce...and it is equally good served as a side dish or a light dessert. Chopped apples and pears add texture, while wine spices up the mixture a bit.
—*Mary Eckles, Kirkwood, Missouri*

   2 medium red pears, peeled, cored and chopped
   1 medium apple, peeled, cored and chopped
1/2 cup white wine *or* white grape juice
   1 jar (23 ounces) unsweetened applesauce
Ground cinnamon, optional

In a saucepan, combine pears, apple and wine or grape juice. Bring to a boil. Reduce heat; simmer, uncovered, for 40 minutes or until liquid is absorbed. Place applesauce in a bowl; stir in pear mixture. Sprinkle with cinnamon if desired. Serve warm or chilled. **Yield:** 6 servings.

Nutritional Analysis: One serving (2/3 cup) equals 96 calories, trace fat (trace saturated fat), 0 cholesterol, 3 mg sodium, 24 g carbohydrate, 3 g fiber, trace protein.
Diabetic Exchange: 1-1/2 fruit.
△ *Low-fat*
▲ *Low-sodium*
▲ *Meatless*

Garlic Brussels Sprouts

These brussels sprouts are special enough for company—I like to serve them for Thanksgiving dinner. If you can't find fresh sprouts, try using the frozen ones.
—*Myra Innes, Auburn, Kansas*

1-1/2 pounds fresh brussels sprouts
   4 garlic cloves, chopped
   3 teaspoons butter *or* stick margarine, *divided*
   2 teaspoons olive *or* canola oil
1/2 cup reduced-sodium chicken broth
1/4 teaspoon salt
1/8 teaspoon pepper

Cut an X in the core end of each brussels sprout; set aside. In a large saucepan, saute garlic in 1 teaspoon butter and oil for 2-3 minutes or until golden brown. Add sprouts; toss to coat. Add the broth, salt and pepper; cover and cook for 12-14 minutes or until sprouts are tender. Drain; add the remaining butter and toss until melted. **Yield:** 6 servings.

Nutritional Analysis: One serving (2/3 cup) equals 83 calories, 3 g fat (1 g saturated fat), 5 mg cholesterol, 198 mg sodium, 11 g carbohydrate, 4 g fiber, 4 g protein.
Diabetic Exchanges: 2 vegetable, 1/2 fat.
△ *Low-fat*

Winter Veggie Stir-Fry

(Pictured at right)

My husband and I own and operate a 160-Holstein dairy in western Washington. He commutes one way to the dairy, and I drive the other way to my job in Kent. Even with our busy schedules, we still find time to share our favorite hobby—vegetable gardening. We enjoy our bounty year-round in dishes like this delicious stir-fry.
—*Julie DeRuwe, Olympia, Washington*

   1 cup sliced carrots
   1 cup sliced parsnips
1/2 cup sliced onion, separated into rings
   1 tablespoon olive *or* canola oil
   1 cup julienned potatoes
   1 cup julienned sweet potatoes
3/4 teaspoon ground ginger *or* 1 tablespoon minced fresh gingerroot
1/2 cup vegetable broth
   2 teaspoons orange juice concentrate
1/2 teaspoon salt
1/8 teaspoon crushed red pepper flakes

In a large nonstick skillet or wok, stir-fry the carrots, parsnips and onion in hot oil for 2 minutes. Add potatoes, sweet potatoes and ginger. Stir-fry for 5-7 minutes or until vegetables are crisp-tender. Add the broth, orange juice concentrate, salt and red pepper flakes. Cover and cook for 5-7 minutes or until vegetables are tender. Uncover; cook and stir until sauce is thickened, about 2 minutes. **Yield:** 6 servings.

Nutritional Analysis: One serving (3/4 cup) equals 102 calories, 3 g fat (trace saturated fat), 0 cholesterol, 293 mg sodium, 19 g carbohydrate, 3 g fiber, 2 g protein.
Diabetic Exchanges: 1 starch, 1 vegetable.
△ *Low-fat*
▲ *Meatless*

Barbecued Baked Beans

*To enliven convenient canned pork and beans,
our Test Kitchen starts with bottled barbecue sauce,
then stirs in brown sugar, vinegar, Liquid Smoke and
spices. These hearty oven-baked beans will
perk up your next summer picnic.*

1/2 cup finely chopped onion
2 garlic cloves, minced
2 teaspoons canola oil
4 cans (15 ounces *each*) pork and beans
3/4 cup barbecue sauce
1/4 cup packed brown sugar
2 tablespoons lemon juice
2 tablespoons balsamic vinegar *or* cider vinegar
2 tablespoons chili powder
2 tablespoons finely chopped jalapeno pepper*
1/2 to 1 teaspoon cayenne pepper
1/8 teaspoon Liquid Smoke

In a Dutch oven, saute onion and garlic in oil until tender. Stir in the remaining ingredients. Bake, uncovered, at 325° for 1-1/2 to 2 hours or until thickened and bubbly. **Yield:** 11 servings.

*Editor's Note: When cutting or seeding hot peppers, use rubber or plastic gloves to protect your hands. Avoid touching your face.

Nutritional Analysis: *One serving (1/2 cup) equals 205 calories, 4 g fat (1 g saturated fat), 6 mg cholesterol, 656 mg sodium, 38 g carbohydrate, 8 g fiber, 7 g protein.*
Diabetic Exchanges: *2-1/2 starch, 1/2 fat.*

Garlic-Rosemary Mashed Potatoes

(Pictured above)

This is one of my favorite ways to fix mashed potatoes. In fact, I freeze rosemary each summer with this dish in mind. I increased the garlic from the original recipe, and my family hasn't complained a bit.
—Kathy Rairigh, Milford, Indiana

6 medium baking potatoes (about 3 pounds)
1 large whole garlic bulb
4-1/2 teaspoons olive *or* canola oil, *divided*
1 teaspoon minced fresh rosemary
3/4 cup fat-free milk
3/4 teaspoon salt

Scrub and pierce potatoes. Bake at 400° for 45-55 minutes or until tender. Meanwhile, remove papery outer skin from garlic bulb (do not peel or separate cloves); cut top off bulb. Place on a piece of heavy-duty foil; drizzle with 1/2 teaspoon oil. Wrap foil around bulb. Bake at 400° for 30-35 minutes or until softened. Cool for 10 minutes.

Squeeze softened garlic into a large mixing bowl. Cut potatoes in half; scoop out pulp and add to garlic. Discard potato skins. Mash potatoes. In a small saucepan, saute rosemary in remaining oil for 2 minutes; add to potato mixture. Add milk and salt; beat until fluffy. **Yield:** 8 servings.

Nutritional Analysis: *One serving (3/4 cup) equals 153 calories, 3 g fat (trace saturated fat), trace cholesterol, 239 mg sodium, 30 g carbohydrate, 2 g fiber, 4 g protein.*
Diabetic Exchanges: *2 starch, 1/2 fat.*
△ *Low-fat*
▲ *Meatless*

Garden Twists

I love to serve this in summer when carrots, onions and peppers are fresh from my garden. If I prepare the vegetables ahead of time, I can fix supper in minutes! My whole family enjoys this satisfying dish.
—Sarah Bartel, Kewaunee, Wisconsin

2 medium carrots
2-1/4 cups uncooked spiral pasta
1 medium onion, chopped
1 medium green *or* sweet red pepper, chopped
2 teaspoons dried basil
1/4 teaspoon garlic powder
1/8 teaspoon crushed red pepper flakes
2 tablespoons butter *or* stick margarine
1 tablespoon cornstarch
1-1/4 cups cold water
2 teaspoons chicken *or* vegetable bouillon granules
2 tablespoons lemon juice

Using a vegetable peeler, slice carrots into curls. Cook pasta according to package directions. Meanwhile, in a large nonstick skillet, saute the carrots, onion, pepper, basil, garlic powder and pepper flakes in butter for 3 minutes or until vegetables are crisp-tender.

Combine the cornstarch, water and bouillon until smooth; add to vegetable mixture. Bring to a boil; cook and stir for 2 minutes or until thickened. Drain pasta. Stir pasta and lemon juice into vegetable mixture. **Yield:** 7 servings.

Nutritional Analysis: One serving (2/3 cup) equals 176 calories, 4 g fat (2 g saturated fat), 9 mg cholesterol, 376 mg sodium, 31 g carbohydrate, 3 g fiber, 5 g protein.
  Diabetic Exchanges: 1-1/2 starch, 1 vegetable, 1/2 fat.
▲ *Meatless*

Broccoli Brown Rice Pilaf

(Pictured below)

This is one of my favorite low-fat dishes—it's delicious! Rosemary, garlic, almonds and sunflower kernels flavor the broccoli and rice.
—*Marie Condit, Brooklyn Center, Minnesota*

      1 cup uncooked brown rice
2-1/4 cups reduced-sodium chicken broth *or*
          vegetable broth
      2 tablespoons minced fresh rosemary *or* 2
          teaspoons dried rosemary, crushed
      2 garlic cloves, minced
      2 cups chopped fresh broccoli
   1/4 cup slivered almonds
   1/4 cup unsalted sunflower kernels
   1/2 teaspoon salt
   1/8 teaspoon pepper

In a large nonstick skillet coated with nonstick cooking spray, saute rice until lightly browned. Add the broth, rosemary and garlic; bring to a boil. Reduce heat; cover and simmer for 40 minutes or until rice is almost tender.

Stir in the broccoli, almonds, sunflower kernels, salt and pepper. Cover and cook 3-5 minutes longer or until rice

is tender and broccoli is crisp-tender. Fluff with a fork. **Yield:** 6 servings.

Nutritional Analysis: One serving (2/3 cup) equals 202 calories, 6 g fat (1 g saturated fat), 0 cholesterol, 414 mg sodium, 31 g carbohydrate, 2 g fiber, 7 g protein.
  Diabetic Exchanges: 2 starch, 1 fat.
▲ *Meatless*

Pepper Potato Gratin

I like to serve this aromatic potato and peppers gratin with roasted chicken.
—*Evelyn Plyler, Apple Valley, California*

      2 pounds potatoes, peeled and thinly sliced
      1 *each* medium green, sweet red and yellow
          pepper, julienned
1-1/2 to 2 teaspoons dried thyme
      1 teaspoon salt
   1/2 teaspoon pepper
   1/2 cup grated Parmesan cheese, *divided*
      6 teaspoons olive *or* canola oil, *divided*
   1/3 cup chicken *or* vegetable broth
   1/3 cup dry white wine *or* additional chicken *or*
          vegetable broth

In a 2-qt. baking dish coated with nonstick cooking spray, arrange a third of the potatoes in overlapping rows. Top with half of the peppers. Combine the thyme, salt and pepper; sprinkle a third over peppers. Sprinkle with a third of the Parmesan cheese and 2 teaspoons oil. Repeat layers.

Top with remaining potatoes; pour broth and wine or additional broth over potatoes. Sprinkle with remaining thyme mixture and oil. Cover and bake at 375° for 45 minutes. Uncover; bake 30 minutes longer or until potatoes are tender and golden. Sprinkle with remaining Parmesan. **Yield:** 6 servings.

Nutritional Analysis: One serving equals 202 calories, 7 g fat (2 g saturated fat), 7 mg cholesterol, 650 mg sodium, 32 g carbohydrate, 4 g fiber, 8 g protein.
  Diabetic Exchanges: 1-1/2 starch, 1-1/2 fat, 1 vegetable.
▲ *Meatless*

🍎 A Grain of Truth About Rice

RICE is a staple for two-thirds of the world's population. It is nutritious, versatile, economical, easy to prepare and tastes good, too!

Wondering what's the difference between brown and white rice? Brown rice is the least processed form of rice. It has the outer hull removed but still retains the bran layers that give it that characteristic tan color and nut-like flavor. It has a chewier texture than white rice.

Both brown and white rice are nutritious. Brown rice provides slightly more fiber, vitamin E, phosphorus and calcium. Most white rice sold in the U.S. is enriched. White rice actually provides more thiamine and iron than brown rice.

Vegetable Rice Casserole

This is my family's very favorite side dish any time of year. It's especially good when fresh produce is in season. Brown sugar adds a hint of sweetness to the rice and vegetables in this colorful casserole.
—Marcia Nelson, Ponca City, Oklahoma

1/4 cup uncooked rice
1 pound zucchini, sliced
1 pound yellow summer squash, sliced
1 large onion, sliced
3 tablespoons minced fresh basil, *divided*
1 medium green pepper, julienned
4 celery ribs with leaves, chopped
2 large tomatoes, sliced
1/4 cup packed brown sugar
1/2 teaspoon salt
1/8 teaspoon pepper
2 tablespoons olive *or* canola oil

Spread the rice into a 13-in. x 9-in. x 2-in. baking dish coated with nonstick cooking spray. Layer with zucchini, yellow squash, onion and half of the basil; top with green pepper, celery and tomatoes. Combine the brown sugar, salt and pepper; sprinkle over vegetables. Drizzle with oil. Cover and bake at 350° for 1 hour or until tender. Sprinkle with remaining basil. **Yield:** 8 servings.

Nutritional Analysis: One serving (1 cup) equals 122 calories, 4 g fat (1 g saturated fat), 0 cholesterol, 176 mg sodium, 22 g carbohydrate, 3 g fiber, 2 g protein.
Diabetic Exchanges: 2 vegetable, 1/2 starch, 1/2 fat.
▲ *Meatless*

Mediterranean Herb Rub

Whether you're monitoring your sodium intake or not, you'll want to try this robust rub on fish, poultry or pork. Or fill a shaker with this savory blend to sprinkle on veggies. This seasoning rub is great, especially on grilled pork chops.
—Jacqueline Thompson Graves, Lawrenceville, Georgia

1 tablespoon dried thyme
1 tablespoon dried oregano
1-1/2 teaspoons poultry seasoning
1 teaspoon dried rosemary, crushed
1 teaspoon dried marjoram
1 teaspoon dried basil
1 teaspoon dried parsley flakes
1/8 teaspoon pepper

In a small bowl, combine all ingredients. Store in an airtight container in a cool dry place for up to 6 months. **Yield:** 1/4 cup.

Nutritional Analysis: One serving (1/2 teaspoon) equals 2 calories, trace fat (trace saturated fat), 0 cholesterol, trace sodium, trace carbohydrate, trace fiber, trace protein.
Diabetic Exchange: Free food.
△ *Low-fat*
▲ *Low-sodium*
▲ *Meatless*

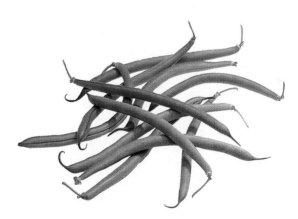

Greek Green Beans

(Pictured below)

In an effort to eat healthier, I'm trying to serve more vegetables. So I substituted green beans for the pasta in one of my favorite Greek dishes. It's even better than the original!
—Kathleen Law, Pullman, Washington

1-1/2 pounds fresh green beans, cut into 1-1/2-inch pieces
1 tablespoon olive *or* canola oil
1 tablespoon minced fresh garlic
1/4 teaspoon salt
1/2 cup feta *or* mozzarella cheese

In a microwave-safe dish, combine the beans, oil, garlic and salt. Cover and microwave on high for 7-9 minutes or until tender, stirring twice. Stir in cheese. Serve immediately. **Yield:** 5 servings.

Editor's Note: This recipe was tested in an 850-watt microwave.

Nutritional Analysis: One serving (3/4 cup) equals 107 calories, 6 g fat (3 g saturated fat), 13 mg cholesterol, 285 mg sodium, 9 g carbohydrate, 5 g fiber, 4 g protein.
Diabetic Exchanges: 2 vegetable, 1 fat.
▲ *Meatless*

Lima Bean Medley

Here's a tasty medley of beans and veggies that harmonizes perfectly with healthy meal plans. This mildly spiced succotash makes a colorful side that goes well with many main dishes.
—Dianne Spurgeon, London, Ontario

1 large green pepper, chopped
1 medium onion, chopped
2 garlic cloves, minced
2 teaspoons olive *or* canola oil
1-1/2 cups chopped fresh tomatoes
1 cup cooked fresh *or* frozen lima beans
1 cup fresh *or* frozen corn
1/2 cup minced fresh basil
1/2 teaspoon salt
1/8 teaspoon pepper

In a large nonstick skillet, saute the green pepper, onion and garlic in oil until tender. Add tomatoes. Reduce heat; simmer, uncovered, for 5 minutes. Stir in lima beans and corn; cover and simmer 10 minutes longer or until vegetables are tender. Stir in the basil, salt and pepper. **Yield:** 4 servings.

Nutritional Analysis: One serving (3/4 cup) equals 145 calories, 3 g fat (trace saturated fat), 0 cholesterol, 370 mg sodium, 27 g carbohydrate, 6 g fiber, 5 g protein.
Diabetic Exchanges: 2 vegetable, 1 starch, 1/2 fat.
△ **Low-fat**
▲ **Meatless**

Asparagus Linguine

(Pictured above)

Pasta and asparagus are tossed together in this side dish that makes an appealing partner to poultry or fish. I lightened up the original recipe by reducing the amount of butter and substituting olive oil.
—Carolyn DiPasquale, Middletown, Rhode Island

6 ounces uncooked linguine
1 small onion, chopped
2 garlic cloves, minced
1 tablespoon olive *or* canola oil
2 teaspoons butter *or* stick margarine
1/2 pound fresh asparagus, trimmed and cut into
  1/2-inch pieces
2 tablespoons white wine *or* chicken broth
2 tablespoons grated Parmesan cheese
1 tablespoon lemon juice
1/4 teaspoon salt
1/8 teaspoon pepper

Cook linguine according to package directions. Meanwhile, in a nonstick skillet, saute the onion and garlic in oil and butter until tender. Add asparagus; cook and stir for 2 minutes or until crisp-tender. Add wine or broth; cook and stir for 1-2 minutes or until liquid is reduced. Remove from the heat.

Drain linguine; add to the asparagus mixture. Add the remaining ingredients; toss to coat. Serve immediately. **Yield:** 4 servings.

Nutritional Analysis: One serving (1 cup) equals 245 calories, 7 g fat (2 g saturated fat), 7 mg cholesterol, 217 mg sodium, 36 g carbohydrate, 3 g fiber, 8 g protein.
Diabetic Exchanges: 2 starch, 1 vegetable, 1 fat.
▲ **Meatless**

Light Pesto

I adapted this recipe by substituting fresh lemon juice for olive oil—cutting the fat, but not the flavor. The pesto keeps up to 5 days in the refrigerator and also freezes well. Try serving it once with pasta and again later with shrimp.
—Cynthia Nardi, Uhrichsville, Ohio

4 ounces Romano cheese, cut into 1-inch pieces
6 garlic cloves
2-2/3 cups loosely packed fresh basil
1/3 cup chopped walnuts
3/4 teaspoon salt
1/8 teaspoon pepper
1/4 cup lemon juice
Hot cooked spaghetti

In a food processor, combine Romano cheese and garlic; cover and process for 30 seconds. Add the basil, nuts, salt and pepper; cover and process until combined, about 15 seconds. While processing, add the lemon juice; process about 15 seconds longer or until combined. Toss with spaghetti. **Yield:** 5 servings.

Nutritional Analysis: One serving (1/4 cup pesto) equals 155 calories, 11 g fat (4 g saturated fat), 24 mg cholesterol, 626 mg sodium, 5 g carbohydrate, 2 g fiber, 9 g protein.
Diabetic Exchanges: 2 fat, 1 vegetable.
▲ **Meatless**

Zucchini Corn Saute

(Pictured above)

I enjoy ethnic cooking, so I usually serve this quick side dish with baked chile rellenos and diced fresh tomatoes. It's also good with a Moroccan-type meal.
—Barbara Lundgren, New Brighton, Minnesota

4-1/2 cups sliced zucchini (1/4-inch slices)
  1/4 cup diced onion
    1 tablespoon olive *or* canola oil
1-1/2 cups fresh *or* frozen corn, thawed
  1/2 teaspoon salt
  1/4 teaspoon ground cumin
  1/8 teaspoon pepper

In a nonstick skillet, saute zucchini and onion in oil for 4-5 minutes. Stir in corn; saute 2 minutes longer or until vegetables are tender. Sprinkle with salt, cumin and pepper. **Yield:** 4 servings.

Nutritional Analysis: One serving (3/4 cup) equals 104 calories, 4 g fat (1 g saturated fat), 0 cholesterol, 307 mg sodium, 16 g carbohydrate, 3 g fiber, 4 g protein.
  Diabetic Exchanges: 1 vegetable, 1/2 starch, 1/2 fat.
  ▲ *Meatless*

Ripe Tomato Relish

Here's a garden-fresh relish that's sure to turn a simple hot dog or burger into a delicacy. The sweet-tasting relish is thick and chunky, made with a bounty of tomatoes, peppers and onions.
—Patsy McKnight, Hot Springs, Arkansas

12 medium tomatoes, peeled and chopped (about 8 cups)

  4 medium onions, chopped (about 3-1/2 cups)
  3 medium green peppers, chopped (about 2 cups)
1-1/4 cups sugar
  1 cup white vinegar
  3 jalapeno peppers, seeded and chopped
  1 teaspoon celery salt
  1/2 teaspoon salt
  1/2 teaspoon ground cinnamon
  1/4 teaspoon ground allspice
  1/4 teaspoon ground cloves

In a large saucepan, combine all ingredients; bring to a boil. Reduce heat; simmer, uncovered, for 40-50 minutes or until thickened, stirring occasionally. Pack hot mixture into hot jars, leaving 1/2-in. headspace. Adjust caps. Process for 10 minutes in a boiling-water bath. **Yield:** 3 pints.

  Editor's Note: Unprocessed relish may be refrigerated for up to 1 week or frozen for up to 3 months.

Nutritional Analysis: One serving (2 tablespoons) equals 35 calories, trace fat (trace saturated fat), 0 cholesterol, 59 mg sodium, 9 g carbohydrate, 1 g fiber, 1 g protein.
  Diabetic Exchange: 2 vegetable.
  △ *Low-fat*
  ▲ *Low-sodium*

Raspberry Barbecue Sauce

Raspberries replace the traditional tomatoes in this unique barbecue sauce. Red pepper flakes add a little kick to the thick ruby-red sauce. This is great over chicken breasts or pork tenderloin. Brush on the sauce near the end of the grilling time.
—Garnet Pirre, Helena, Montana

  3 garlic cloves, peeled
  1/4 teaspoon olive *or* canola oil
1-1/4 cups unsweetened raspberries
  3 tablespoons brown sugar
  1 tablespoon balsamic vinegar
  1 tablespoon light corn syrup
  1 teaspoon molasses
  1/2 teaspoon lemon juice
  1/4 to 1/2 teaspoon crushed red pepper flakes
  1/8 teaspoon salt
  1/8 teaspoon pepper
Dash onion powder

Place garlic on a double thickness of heavy-duty foil; drizzle with oil. Wrap foil around garlic. Bake at 425° for 15-20 minutes. Cool for 10-15 minutes.

  Place softened garlic in a small saucepan. Add the remaining ingredients. Cook over medium-low heat for 15-20 minutes until sauce is thickened and bubbly. Remove from the heat; cool slightly. Transfer to a food processor or blender; cover and process until smooth. Strain seeds. Store in the refrigerator. **Yield:** 4 servings.

Nutritional Analysis: One serving (2 tablespoons) equals 83 calories, trace fat (trace saturated fat), 0 cholesterol, 86 mg sodium, 21 g carbohydrate, 3 g fiber, 1 g protein.
  Diabetic Exchange: 1-1/2 fruit.
  △ *Low-fat*
  ▲ *Low-sodium*

Spaghetti Squash Medley

*We grow spaghetti squash in our garden, and
I enjoy coming up with different ways to use it.*
— *Wanda Ivan, Salina, Kansas*

1 medium spaghetti squash (2-1/2 to 3 pounds)
2 cups chopped seeded tomatoes
1 tablespoon olive *or* canola oil
1 garlic clove, minced
2 tablespoons chopped fresh basil *or* 2
 teaspoons dried basil
1/2 teaspoon salt
1/4 teaspoon pepper
1-1/2 cups fresh broccoli florets
1 large carrot, thinly sliced
2 tablespoons water
2 ounces fresh *or* frozen snow peas, sliced
2 tablespoons grated Parmesan cheese

Pierce squash six times with a sharp knife. Place on a microwave-safe plate; microwave on high for 7 minutes. Turn squash; cook 7 minutes longer. Cover with an inverted bowl; let stand for 10 minutes.

Meanwhile, combine the tomatoes, oil and garlic in a microwave-safe bowl. Heat, uncovered, on high for 2-3 minutes or until tomatoes are softened, stirring once. Stir in the basil, salt and pepper. Place broccoli, carrot and water in another microwave-safe bowl. Cover and microwave on high for 2 minutes. Add peas; cover and cook 1-2 minutes longer or until vegetables are tender. Let stand for 5 minutes; drain. Add to tomato mixture.

Halve squash lengthwise; remove seeds. Using a fork, separate squash into strands; toss with tomato mixture. Serve with Parmesan cheese. **Yield:** 5 servings.

Editor's Note: This recipe was tested in an 850-watt microwave.

Nutritional Analysis: One serving (3/4 cup) equals 132 calories, 4 g fat (1 g saturated fat), 2 mg cholesterol, 336 mg sodium, 23 g carbohydrate, 6 g fiber, 4 g protein.
Diabetic Exchanges: 1 starch, 1 vegetable, 1/2 fat.
▲ *Meatless*

🍎 Snow Peas and Cues

EVERYTHING you love about fresh peas in a crisp green package, with no shelling—that's what's so appealing about snow peas!

● The snow pea is thin and crisp and has a nearly translucent bright-green pod with flat, small, sweet seeds inside. Best of all, it's entirely edible.

● Other names for this legume include Chinese snow pea, sugar pea and mange-tout, which means "eat it all" in French.

● Snow peas originated in the Mediterranean and were grown widely in England and Europe in the 19th century. The Chinese adopted them from the English.

● Snow peas provide vitamins A and C, iron, potassium and about 43 calories per 3-ounce serving.

● Very young snow peas are best for eating. They should be picked when seeds are barely visible in the pod.

Creamed Spinach

(Pictured below)

*The inspiration for this creamy side dish came from
a local restaurant. I lightened up the original recipe
by using fat-free half-and-half and cream cheese.
It goes great with most any entree.*
— *Susan Geddie, Harker Heights, Texas*

1/4 cup diced onion
1 garlic clove, minced
1 tablespoon butter *or* stick margarine
1 tablespoon all-purpose flour
1-1/4 cups fat-free half-and-half
4 ounces fat-free cream cheese, cubed
3/4 teaspoon salt
1/8 teaspoon ground nutmeg
1/8 teaspoon pepper
1 package (16 ounces) frozen leaf spinach,
 thawed and squeezed dry
1/4 cup plus 1 tablespoon shredded Parmesan
 cheese, *divided*

In a large nonstick skillet, saute onion and garlic in butter until tender. Stir in flour until blended. Gradually whisk in half-and-half until blended. Bring to a boil over medium-low heat; cook and stir for 2 minutes or until slightly thickened.

Add the cream cheese, salt, nutmeg and pepper, stirring until cream cheese is melted. Stir in spinach and 1/4 cup Parmesan cheese; heat through. Sprinkle with remaining Parmesan cheese. Serve immediately. **Yield:** 5 servings.

Nutritional Analysis: One serving (1/2 cup) equals 131 calories, 4 g fat (3 g saturated fat), 12 mg cholesterol, 704 mg sodium, 13 g carbohydrate, 2 g fiber, 10 g protein.
Diabetic Exchanges: 1 vegetable, 1 fat, 1/2 fat-free milk.
▲ *Meatless*

Candied Sweet Potatoes

This easy apple and sweet potato bake is a natural for holiday meals. You can substitute two 18-ounce cans of sweet potatoes, drained.
—Heidi Grant, Orangeville, Ontario

> 2 pounds sweet potatoes, peeled and cut into 1/2-inch slices
> 1/2 cup packed brown sugar
> 2 tablespoons unsweetened apple juice
> 1/4 teaspoon salt
> 1/8 teaspoon ground cinnamon
> 1 medium apple, peeled and sliced

Place sweet potatoes in a saucepan and cover with water; bring to a boil. Cover and cook for 10 minutes or until crisp-tender; drain. In a bowl, combine the brown sugar, apple juice, salt and cinnamon; set aside. Arrange sweet potato and apple slices in an 8-in. square baking dish coated with nonstick cooking spray. Drizzle with brown sugar mixture. Bake, covered, at 350° for 25 minutes. Uncover; bake 20-25 minutes longer, basting occasionally with pan juices. **Yield:** 6 servings.

Nutritional Analysis: One serving (2/3 cup) equals 178 calories, trace fat (trace saturated fat), 0 cholesterol, 114 mg sodium, 44 g carbohydrate, 3 g fiber, 2 g protein.
 △ **Low-fat**
 ▲ **Low-sodium**
 ▲ **Meatless**

Artichoke Orzo Pilaf

Canned artichoke hearts bring a tangy taste to tiny orzo pasta in this side dish.
—Stacy Crochet, Watertown, Connecticut

> 1 medium leek (white portion only), chopped
> 1 cup uncooked orzo pasta
> 2 tablespoons olive *or* canola oil
> 1 can (14-1/2 ounces) reduced-sodium chicken broth *or* vegetable broth
> 1 cup water
> 2 teaspoons Italian seasoning
> 1 can (14 ounces) water-packed artichoke hearts, drained and chopped
> 2 tablespoons grated Parmesan cheese

In a nonstick skillet, saute leek and orzo in oil for 3 minutes or until leek is tender. Add the broth, water and Italian seasoning; bring to a boil. Reduce heat; simmer, uncovered, for 15 minutes or until liquid is absorbed. Stir in artichoke hearts and Parmesan cheese. Serve immediately. **Yield:** 6 servings.

Nutritional Analysis: One serving (3/4 cup) equals 181 calories, 3 g fat (1 g saturated fat), 1 mg cholesterol, 382 mg sodium, 30 g carbohydrate, 1 g fiber, 7 g protein.
Diabetic Exchanges: 1-1/2 starch, 1 vegetable, 1/2 fat.
 △ **Low-fat**
 ▲ **Meatless**

Sauteed Spinach and Peppers

(Pictured above)

We often steam our fresh spinach and eat it plain. But this version dressed up with red pepper, onion and garlic is a nice change. It is really quick and tasty...and pretty, too.
—Mary Lou Moon, Beaverton, Oregon

> 1 large sweet red pepper, coarsely chopped
> 1 tablespoon olive *or* canola oil
> 1 small red onion, finely chopped
> 3 garlic cloves, minced
> 8 cups packed fresh spinach
> 1/2 teaspoon salt
> 1/4 teaspoon pepper
> 1/8 teaspoon sugar

In a large nonstick skillet, saute red pepper in oil for 1 minute. Add onion and garlic; saute until tender, about 1-1/2 minutes longer. Stir in the spinach, salt, pepper and sugar; saute for 1-2 minutes or until spinach is wilted and tender. Serve with a slotted spoon. **Yield:** 4 servings.

Nutritional Analysis: One serving (1/2 cup) equals 65 calories, 4 g fat (1 g saturated fat), 0 cholesterol, 342 mg sodium, 7 g carbohydrate, 3 g fiber, 2 g protein.
Diabetic Exchanges: 1 vegetable, 1/2 fat.
 ▲ **Meatless**

Favorite Potato Recipe Made Lighter

FAMILY GATHERINGS at Kathy Brandenburg's home in Elkhorn, Wisconsin wouldn't be the same without Au Gratin Hash Browns. The creamy crumb-topped casserole takes advantage of convenient frozen hash browns and has loads of comforting flavor.

"This recipe has been a family favorite since my mother first found it," Kathy says. "Now our son, a cheese lover, makes the side dish for nearly every family function. We love its rich taste, but we'd appreciate it if you could reduce the fat."

Our home economists were happy to help out. First, they tackled the creamy potato filling. They cut quite a bit of fat by substituting reduced-fat cheddar cheese and sour cream and by eliminating the butter. They also reduced the salt but boosted the filling's flavor by adding more onion.

Then they revamped the crunchy topping by simply cutting out most of the butter and reducing the amount of crushed cornflakes.

Makeover Au Gratin Hash Browns has nearly two-thirds less fat and saturated fat than the original recipe and 40% fewer calories! Cholesterol was reduced by more than half…and the sodium by more than a quarter.

Au Gratin Hash Browns

- 1 package (30 ounces) frozen shredded hash brown potatoes, thawed
- 2 cups (8 ounces) shredded cheddar cheese
- 1/4 cup chopped onion
- 1 teaspoon salt
- 1/2 teaspoon pepper
- 2 cups (16 ounces) sour cream
- 1 can (10-3/4 ounces) condensed cream of chicken soup, undiluted
- 1/2 cup butter *or* margarine, melted, *divided*
- 2 cups cornflakes, lightly crushed

In a large bowl, combine the hash browns, cheese, onion, salt and pepper. In another bowl, combine the sour cream, soup and 1/4 cup butter. Pour over potato mixture and mix gently to combine. Transfer to a greased 3-qt. baking dish. Toss cornflakes and remaining butter; sprinkle over the top. Bake, uncovered, at 350° for 45-55 minutes or until heated through. **Yield:** 12 servings.

Nutritional Analysis: One serving (3/4 cup) equals 324 calories, 23 g fat (14 g saturated fat), 59 mg cholesterol, 681 mg sodium, 22 g carbohydrate, 2 g fiber, 9 g protein.

Makeover Au Gratin Hash Browns

(Pictured below)

- 1 package (30 ounces) frozen shredded hash brown potatoes, thawed
- 2 cups (8 ounces) shredded reduced-fat cheddar cheese
- 1/2 cup chopped onion
- 3/4 teaspoon salt
- 1/2 teaspoon pepper
- 1-1/2 cups reduced-fat sour cream
- 1 can (10-3/4 ounces) reduced-fat reduced-sodium cream of chicken soup, undiluted
- 1-1/2 cups cornflakes, lightly crushed
- 1 tablespoon butter *or* stick margarine, melted
- 1 tablespoon minced fresh parsley

In a large bowl, combine the hash browns, cheese, onion, salt and pepper. In another bowl, combine the sour cream and soup. Pour over potato mixture and mix gently to combine. Transfer to a 3-qt. baking dish coated with nonstick cooking spray. Toss cornflakes and butter; sprinkle over the top. Bake, uncovered, at 350° for 45-55 minutes or until heated through. Sprinkle with parsley. **Yield:** 12 servings.

Nutritional Analysis: One serving (3/4 cup) equals 190 calories, 8 g fat (5 g saturated fat), 28 mg cholesterol, 492 mg sodium, 23 g carbohydrate, 2 g fiber, 9 g protein.
Diabetic Exchanges: 1-1/2 starch, 1 lean meat, 1 fat.

Special Spicy Seafood Sauce

*I've been serving this tangy seafood sauce for over
30 years, and I'm always asked for the recipe.
Low in fat and easy to make, it's a great seafood sauce
to serve with cold shrimp as an appetizer. The recipe
is easy to halve or double, too. I've found it's
usually smart to make extra. It goes so fast!*
—Carolyn Chapman, Snohomish, Washington

1-1/2 cups ketchup
  2 tablespoons finely chopped celery
  **2 tablespoons white wine vinegar *or* cider
    vinegar**
  2 teaspoons finely chopped green onion
  2 teaspoons water
  2 teaspoons Worcestershire sauce
  1 teaspoon prepared horseradish
1/2 teaspoon seasoned salt
1/2 teaspoon ground mustard
1/4 teaspoon cayenne pepper

In a bowl, combine all ingredients; mix well. Refrigerate for
at least 1 hour before serving. Refrigerate leftovers. **Yield:**
1-3/4 cups.

*Nutritional Analysis: One serving (2 tablespoons) equals 28
calories, trace fat (0 saturated fat), trace cholesterol, 445 mg
sodium, 7 g carbohydrate, trace fiber, trace protein.*
Diabetic Exchange: *1 vegetable.*
△ *Low-fat*

Zippy Rice Pilaf

*If I need a quick side dish that has flair and flavor,
I whip up this tasty pilaf in a jiffy on the stovetop. The
jalapeno pepper, herbs and spices season the rice nicely.
It's one of those side dishes that goes well with anything.*
—Elizabeth Perez, Flower Mound, Texas

  1 small onion, finely chopped
  3 garlic cloves, minced
  2 teaspoons butter *or* stick margarine
  1 cup uncooked long grain rice
  2 jalapeno peppers, seeded and chopped*
  **2 cups reduced-sodium chicken broth *or*
    vegetable broth**
1/2 teaspoon ground cumin
1/4 teaspoon salt
  1 tablespoon minced fresh cilantro *or* parsley

In a saucepan, saute onion and garlic in butter until tender. Add the rice and jalapenos; toss to coat. Stir in the
broth, cumin and salt; bring to a boil. Reduce heat; cover
and simmer for 20-25 minutes or until liquid is absorbed and
rice is tender. Add cilantro. Fluff with a fork; serve immediately. **Yield:** 6 servings.
*Editor's Note: When cutting or seeding hot peppers,
use rubber or plastic gloves to protect your hands. Avoid
touching your face.

*Nutritional Analysis: One serving (2/3 cup) equals 147 calo-
ries, 2 g fat (1 g saturated fat), 3 mg cholesterol, 319 mg sodium,
29 g carbohydrate, 1 g fiber, 4 g protein.*
Diabetic Exchange: *2 starch.*
△ *Low-fat*
▲ *Meatless*

Green Beans with Tomatoes

(Pictured below)

*This savory side dish goes well with a variety of entrees.
The crisp-tender beans are accented with chopped
tomatoes, onion, garlic and allspice.*
—Clara Coulston, Washington Court House, Ohio

**1/2 cup reduced-sodium chicken broth *or*
    vegetable broth**
  1 cup chopped onion
  2 garlic cloves, minced
  **2 pounds fresh green beans, cut into 2-inch
    pieces**
  4 medium ripe tomatoes, seeded and chopped
3/4 teaspoon seasoned salt
1/8 teaspoon ground allspice
1/8 teaspoon pepper

In a large nonstick skillet, bring the broth, onion and garlic
to a boil. Add beans; return to a boil. Reduce heat; cover and
simmer for 15 minutes. Add the tomatoes, seasoned salt,
allspice and pepper; cook 2-3 minutes longer or until beans
are tender. Serve with a slotted spoon. **Yield:** 8 servings.

*Nutritional Analysis: One serving (3/4 cup) equals 61 calo-
ries, trace fat (trace saturated fat), 0 cholesterol, 184 mg sodium,
12 g carbohydrate, 5 g fiber, 2 g protein.*
Diabetic Exchange: *2 vegetable.*
△ *Low-fat*
▲ *Meatless*

for 18-22 minutes or until the rice is tender. Remove from the heat. Add cilantro; fluff with a fork. **Yield:** 6 servings.

Nutritional Analysis: One serving (2/3 cup) equals 156 calories, 3 g fat (trace saturated fat), 0 cholesterol, 295 mg sodium, 30 g carbohydrate, 1 g fiber, 3 g protein.
Diabetic Exchange: 2 starch.
△ *Low-fat*
▲ *Meatless*

Peppered Cilantro Rice

(Pictured above)

This colorful confetti rice is a traditional dish in Puerto Rico. We enjoy it in the summer alongside grilled shrimp kabobs, but it's good with most any entree.
—Laura Perry, Exton, Pennsylvania

    1 small onion, finely chopped
1/2 cup finely chopped sweet red pepper
1/2 cup finely chopped sweet yellow pepper
    2 garlic cloves, minced
    1 tablespoon olive *or* canola oil
    2 cups water
    1 cup uncooked long grain rice
3/4 teaspoon salt
1/4 teaspoon pepper
    2 tablespoons minced fresh cilantro *or* parsley

In a saucepan, saute the onion, peppers and garlic in oil for 2-4 minutes or until crisp-tender. Add the water, rice, salt and pepper. Bring to a boil. Reduce heat; cover and simmer

🍎 Better Browned Potatoes

WE love fried potatoes, but not all the fat that comes with frying them in oil. So I came up with this method.

    I coat the sliced potatoes with nonstick cooking spray, then spritz a nonstick frying pan. I heat up the pan and add the potatoes. After browning them on both sides, I add a little water for moisture.

    I cover the pan and continue to cook until the potatoes are tender. They taste just like potatoes fried in oil...my husband can't tell the difference.
    —LaDonna Reed, Ponca City, Oklahoma

Salt-Free Seasoning Mix

We're on a low-salt diet, and this seasoning blend perks up everything. We especially like it on chicken and pork.
—Burva Caldwell, Cheyenne, Wyoming

    1 teaspoon *each* dried basil, marjoram, parsley flakes, thyme and savory
    1 tablespoon garlic powder
    1 teaspoon onion powder
    1 teaspoon rubbed sage
    1 teaspoon ground mace
    1 teaspoon pepper
1/8 teaspoon cayenne pepper

In a small bowl, crush the basil, marjoram, parsley, thyme and savory. Stir in the remaining ingredients. Store in an airtight container. **Yield:** about 1/4 cup.

Nutritional Analysis: One serving (1/2 teaspoon) equals 3 calories, trace fat (trace saturated fat), 0 cholesterol, 1 mg sodium, 1 g carbohydrate, trace fiber, trace protein.
Diabetic Exchange: Free food.
△ *Low-fat*
▲ *Low-sodium*

Almond Apricot Jam

There's no added sugar in this jam, so even if you're watching your diet, you can enjoy it on your morning toast. There's no need to wait for harvest season to make it either, since the recipe calls for dried apricots. I often give this chunky spread as a gift to my four grown children and 10 grandkids.
—Mary Fenske, Bricelyn, Minnesota

2-1/2 cups unsweetened apple juice
    1 cup diced dried apricots (8 ounces)
1/4 to 1/2 teaspoon almond extract
1/4 teaspoon ground cinnamon

In a saucepan, combine the apple juice and apricots; bring to a boil. Reduce heat; simmer, uncovered, for 20-25 minutes or until apricots are tender. Remove from heat. Mash until desired consistency. Stir in almond extract and cinnamon. Pour into a pint jar. Cover and refrigerate for up to 3 weeks. **Yield:** 2 cups.

Nutritional Analysis: One tablespoon equals 29 calories, trace fat (0 saturated fat), 0 cholesterol, 1 mg sodium, 7 g carbohydrate, trace fiber, trace protein.
Diabetic Exchange: 1/2 fruit.
△ *Low-fat*
▲ *Low-sodium*
▲ *Meatless*

Brown Rice Hot Dish

Enhance instant brown rice with celery, onion, mushrooms, seasonings and chopped pecans. With its stuffing-like flavor, this fluffy rice dish makes a perfect accompaniment for chicken or turkey.
—Dolores Kastello, Waukesha, Wisconsin

1-1/3 cups instant brown rice
   1 tablespoon butter *or* stick margarine, *divided*
1-1/2 cups chopped fresh mushrooms
1-1/4 cups finely chopped celery
   1/4 cup finely chopped onion
1-1/4 cups hot water
   1/3 cup chopped pecans
   3/4 teaspoon salt
   1/4 teaspoon dried marjoram
   1/4 teaspoon pepper
   1/8 teaspoon rubbed sage
   1/8 teaspoon dried thyme

In a nonstick skillet, saute rice in half of the butter until golden brown; transfer to a large bowl. In the same skillet, saute the mushrooms, celery and onion in remaining butter until tender; add to rice. Stir in the water, pecans, salt, marjoram, pepper, sage and thyme.

Transfer to a 1-1/2-qt. baking dish coated with nonstick cooking spray. Cover and bake at 350° for 25-30 minutes or until rice is tender and liquid is absorbed. Fluff with a fork before serving. **Yield:** 6 servings.

Nutritional Analysis: One serving (2/3 cup) equals 149 calories, 7 g fat (2 g saturated fat), 5 mg cholesterol, 340 mg sodium, 18 g carbohydrate, 2 g fiber, 3 g protein.
Diabetic Exchanges: 1-1/2 fat, 1 starch.
▲ *Meatless*

Savory Skillet Noodles

(Pictured above)

My daughter is a vegetarian, so I created this colorful side dish to serve with vegetables. She asks for it once a week. Chopped sweet peppers, onion and almonds accent the mild buttery noodles.
—Lucille Goers, Seminole, Florida

   8 ounces uncooked yolk-free noodles
   1 cup sliced fresh mushrooms
1/4 cup chopped sweet red pepper
1/4 cup chopped green pepper
   2 tablespoons chopped onion
   2 tablespoons butter *or* stick margarine
1/3 cup sliced almonds
   1 teaspoon chicken bouillon granules *or* 1
     vegetable bouillon cube, crushed
   2 tablespoons minced fresh parsley

Cook noodles according to package directions. Meanwhile, in a large nonstick skillet, saute the mushrooms, peppers and onion in butter until tender. Drain the noodles; add to skillet. Sprinkle with almonds and bouillon; mix gently to combine. Heat through. Garnish with the parsley. **Yield:** 8 servings.

Nutritional Analysis: One serving (2/3 cup) equals 160 calories, 5 g fat (2 g saturated fat), 8 mg cholesterol, 189 mg sodium, 22 g carbohydrate, 2 g fiber, 5 g protein.
Diabetic Exchanges: 1-1/2 starch, 1 fat.
▲ *Meatless*

Green Beans 'n' Celery

This quick side makes a nice complement to any entree, particularly Italian dishes.
—Marian Platt, Sequim, Washington

   1 pound fresh green beans, trimmed
   1 celery rib, chopped
   1 jar (2 ounces) diced pimientos, drained
   2 tablespoons sunflower kernels
   1 tablespoon butter *or* stick margarine
1/2 teaspoon salt
1/8 teaspoon pepper
   2 tablespoons shredded Parmesan cheese

Place beans and celery in a saucepan and cover with water; bring to a boil. Cook, uncovered, for 8-10 minutes or until crisp-tender. Drain. Add the pimiento, sunflower kernels, butter, salt and pepper; toss to coat. Garnish with Parmesan cheese. **Yield:** 5 servings.

Nutritional Analysis: One serving (3/4 cup) equals 87 calories, 5 g fat (2 g saturated fat), 8 mg cholesterol, 317 mg sodium, 7 g carbohydrate, 4 g fiber, 3 g protein.
Diabetic Exchanges: 1 vegetable, 1 fat.
▲ *Meatless*

Dijon Tartar Sauce

(Pictured below)

Fat-free mayonnaise mixed only with pickle relish seemed so tasteless, so I began experimenting and came up with my own recipe for tartar sauce. It adds lots of flavor to fish, but very few calories.
—Kristen Flaherty, South Portland, Maine

1/2 cup fat-free mayonnaise
3 tablespoons sweet pickle relish
3 tablespoons chopped onion
4 teaspoons Dijon mustard
2 teaspoons lemon juice
1/4 teaspoon sugar
1/4 teaspoon salt
1/8 teaspoon pepper

In a bowl, combine all ingredients. Store in the refrigerator for up to 1 week. **Yield:** 3/4 cup.

Nutritional Analysis: One serving (2 tablespoons) equals 31 calories, 1 g fat (trace saturated fat), 2 mg cholesterol, 392 mg sodium, 6 g carbohydrate, 1 g fiber, trace protein.
Diabetic Exchange: 1/2 starch.
△ *Low-fat*

Lo Mein Noodles

One of the things my husband and I share is a love of Oriental food. At the end of the week, I go through the fridge, looking for leftover vegetables and meats to use in my "leftovers chow mein". If I have leftover spaghetti noodles, I use them to make these stir-fried noodles. Otherwise, I just cook up a fresh pot.
—Kay Bergeron, Phoenix, Arizona

2 quarts water
1 tablespoon chicken bouillon granules
1 package (16 ounces) thin spaghetti
1/2 cup thinly sliced onion
1/4 cup canola oil
1 cup fresh snow peas
1 tablespoon reduced-sodium soy sauce
1 tablespoon reduced-sodium teriyaki sauce
1-1/2 teaspoons Chinese five-spice powder
1/8 teaspoon white pepper
1/2 cup chopped green onions

In a Dutch oven, bring water and bouillon to a boil. Add spaghetti. Return to a boil; cook, uncovered, for 6 minutes or until almost tender. Drain, reserving 1/2 cup cooking liquid. Set spaghetti and liquid aside.

In a large nonstick skillet or wok, saute onion in hot oil for 2 minutes. Add peas; saute 2 minutes longer. Stir in spaghetti. Combine the soy sauce, teriyaki sauce, five-spice powder, pepper and reserved cooking liquid; add to pan. Simmer, uncovered, for 3-4 minutes or until liquid is evaporated. Sprinkle with green onions. **Yield:** 8 servings.

Nutritional Analysis: One serving (3/4 cup) equals 304 calories, 8 g fat (1 g saturated fat), trace cholesterol, 530 mg sodium, 48 g carbohydrate, 3 g fiber, 9 g protein.
Diabetic Exchanges: 3 starch, 1-1/2 fat.

Pea Pod Carrot Medley

We grow pea pods, and I wanted to use them in something other than stir-fries...this fit the bill! I receive compliments on its pretty glaze.
—Josie Smith, Winamac, Indiana

1 cup sliced carrots
2 cups fresh sugar snap peas *or* snow peas
1 teaspoon cornstarch
1/3 cup orange juice
2 teaspoons reduced-sodium soy sauce
1/2 teaspoon grated orange peel
1/4 teaspoon salt

Place carrots in a small saucepan; cover with water. Bring to a boil. Reduce heat; cover and simmer for 5 minutes. Add the peas. Cover and simmer 2-4 minutes longer or until vegetables are crisp-tender. Drain; set aside and keep warm.

In the same saucepan, whisk the cornstarch and orange juice until smooth. Bring to a boil; cook and stir for 2 minutes or until thickened. Stir in the soy sauce, orange peel and salt. Pour over vegetables; toss to coat. **Yield:** 2 servings.

Nutritional Analysis: One serving (1 cup) equals 100 calories, trace fat (trace saturated fat), 0 cholesterol, 517 mg sodium, 21 g carbohydrate, 6 g fiber, 4 g protein.
Diabetic Exchanges: 2 vegetable, 1/2 fruit.
△ *Low-fat*
▲ *Meatless*

Oven-Roasted Root Vegetables

(Pictured on page 73)

All kinds of root vegetables star in this colorful medley. Fresh thyme and sage season the mix of rutabaga, parsnips and butternut squash. This side dish is satisfying any time of year. Besides being delicious, it's very easy to prepare.
—Mitzi Sentiff, Alexandria, Virginia

4 PPV

2 cups cubed peeled rutabaga
2 cups cubed peeled parsnips
2 cups cubed peeled butternut squash
2 medium onions, chopped
1 tablespoon olive *or* canola oil
1/2 teaspoon salt
1/8 teaspoon pepper
1 tablespoon minced fresh thyme *or* 1 teaspoon dried thyme
1 tablespoon minced fresh sage *or* 1 teaspoon rubbed sage

In a large bowl, combine the rutabaga, parsnips, squash and onions. Add the oil, salt and pepper; toss to coat. Arrange in a single layer in a 15-in. x 10-in. x 1-in. baking pan coated with nonstick cooking spray. Bake, uncovered, at 400° for 40-50 minutes, stirring occasionally. Sprinkle with herbs; toss to combine. **Yield:** 4 servings.

Nutritional Analysis: One serving (3/4 cup) equals 168 calories, 4 g fat (1 g saturated fat), 0 cholesterol, 319 mg sodium, 33 g carbohydrate, 9 g fiber, 3 g protein.
Diabetic Exchanges: 5 vegetable, 1/2 starch, 1/2 fat.
▲ *Meatless*

Herbed Potato Wedges

(Pictured below)

These potatoes are mildly seasoned with thyme, lemon juice and Parmesan cheese...and they are so good! Using the microwave makes them fast, too.
—Connie Thomas, Jensen, Utah

1-1/4 pounds medium red potatoes
2 teaspoons butter *or* stick margarine, melted
2 teaspoons lemon juice
1/4 cup grated Parmesan cheese
1 teaspoon dried thyme
1/2 teaspoon salt
1/4 teaspoon pepper

Cut potatoes in quarters. In a bowl, combine the butter and lemon juice; brush over cut surfaces of potatoes. Combine the remaining ingredients; dip coated sides of potatoes into cheese mixture. Place the potatoes, cut sides up, into a 2-qt. microwave-safe dish. Cover and microwave on high for 12-15 minutes or until potatoes are tender. **Yield:** 4 servings.

Editor's Note: This recipe was tested in an 850-watt microwave.

Nutritional Analysis: One serving (3/4 cup) equals 151 calories, 4 g fat (2 g saturated fat), 10 mg cholesterol, 446 mg sodium, 23 g carbohydrate, 3 g fiber, 6 g protein.
Diabetic Exchanges: 1-1/2 starch, 1 fat.
▲ *Meatless*

Wild Rice Casserole

Here's a fun way to jazz up wild rice. Soy sauce and chicken bouillon add plenty of flavor, while celery, mushrooms and water chestnuts help dress it up. My husband and two adult children love this delicious side dish. It's convenient, too, because you can make it a day ahead.
—Joyce Bodle, Enumclaw, Washington

2 tablespoons cornstarch
1 cup water
1/4 cup reduced-sodium soy sauce
1 teaspoon reduced-sodium chicken bouillon granules
2 cups sliced celery
1 medium onion, halved and sliced
1 cup sliced fresh mushrooms
2 tablespoons canola oil
2 cups coarsely shredded cabbage
1 can (8 ounces) sliced water chestnuts
2 cups cooked wild rice

Combine the cornstarch, water, soy sauce and bouillon until blended. In a nonstick skillet, saute the celery, onion and mushrooms in oil for 8 minutes. Add cabbage and saute 2-3 minutes longer or until cabbage is just crisp-tender; stir in water chestnuts.

Stir soy sauce mixture and add to the skillet. Bring to a boil; cook and stir over medium heat for 2 minutes or until thickened. Stir in rice.

Pour into an 11-in. x 7-in. x 2-in. baking dish coated with nonstick cooking spray. Cover and bake at 350° for 25-30 minutes or until heated through. **Yield:** 8 servings.

Nutritional Analysis: One serving (3/4 cup) equals 121 calories, 4 g fat (trace saturated fat), 0 cholesterol, 391 mg sodium, 19 g carbohydrate, 4 g fiber, 3 g protein.
Diabetic Exchanges: 1 starch, 1 vegetable, 1/2 fat.

Breakfast & Brunch

Breakfast boosts your energy level, which is
bound to give you a sunny outlook on the
day and help you perform your best. So
open your family's eyes to good eating
with these day-brightening recipes.

Apricot Breakfast Rolls and Confetti Scrambled Egg Pockets (page 100)

Breakfast Casserole

*This make-ahead dish is convenient for
serving overnight guests.*
—Mary Stoddard, Fountain Inn, South Carolina

12 ounces reduced-fat bulk pork sausage
1 medium onion, chopped
2 eggs
4 egg whites
2 cups fat-free milk
1-1/2 teaspoons ground mustard
1 teaspoon salt
1/4 teaspoon pepper
8 slices firm white bread, cubed
2 cups (8 ounces) shredded reduced-fat cheddar
  cheese

In a nonstick skillet, cook sausage and onion over medium heat until sausage is no longer pink; drain and cool. In a large bowl, beat the eggs, egg whites, milk, mustard, salt and pepper. Stir in the bread cubes, cheese and sausage mixture. Pour into a 13-in. x 9-in. x 2-in. baking dish coated with nonstick cooking spray. Cover and refrigerate overnight.

Remove from the refrigerator 30 minutes before baking. Bake, uncovered, at 350° for 35-40 minutes or until a knife inserted near the center comes out clean. Let stand for 5 minutes before cutting. **Yield:** 12 servings.

Nutritional Analysis: One serving equals 211 calories, 11 g fat (5 g saturated fat), 51 mg cholesterol, 690 mg sodium, 13 g carbohydrate, 1 g fiber, 15 g protein.
Diabetic Exchanges: 2 lean meat, 1 starch, 1 fat.

Hot Cross Buns

(Pictured at right)

*With their tender texture and pretty frosted crosses, these
Easter buns are both tasty and attractive. Add a little
orange juice to the frosting for a delicate citrusy flavor.*
—Dolores Skrout, Summerhill, Pennsylvania

4 to 5 cups all-purpose flour
1/3 cup sugar
1 package (1/4 ounce) active dry yeast
1-1/4 teaspoons ground cinnamon
1/2 teaspoon salt
1 cup fat-free milk
1/4 cup butter *or* stick margarine
2 eggs
3/4 cup raisins
1 egg yolk
2 tablespoons cold water

ICING:
1-1/2 cups confectioners' sugar
1/4 teaspoon grated orange peel
4 teaspoons orange juice

In a large mixing bowl, combine 2 cups flour, sugar, yeast, cinnamon and salt. In a saucepan, heat milk and butter to 120°-130°. Add to dry ingredients; beat just until moistened. Add eggs; beat until smooth. Stir in raisins and enough remaining flour to form a soft dough. Turn onto a floured surface; knead until smooth and elastic, about 6-8 minutes. Place in a bowl coated with nonstick cooking spray, turning once to coat top. Cover and let rise in a warm place until doubled, about 1 hour.

Punch dough down; turn onto a lightly floured surface. Divide into 18 pieces; shape each into a ball. Place in two 9-in. round baking pans coated with nonstick cooking spray. Using a sharp knife, cut a cross on top of each roll. Cover and let rise in a warm place until doubled, about 30 minutes.

Beat egg yolk and water; brush over buns. Bake at 375° for 18-22 minutes or until golden brown. Remove from pans to wire racks to cool. Combine icing ingredients; pipe crosses onto rolls. **Yield:** 1-1/2 dozen.

Nutritional Analysis: One bun equals 207 calories, 4 g fat (2 g saturated fat), 43 mg cholesterol, 107 mg sodium, 39 g carbohydrate, 1 g fiber, 5 g protein.
Diabetic Exchanges: 2 starch, 1/2 fruit, 1/2 fat.
▲ *Low-sodium*
▲ *Meatless*

Impossible Garden Pie

(Pictured at right)

*The biscuit mix in this "impossible" pie settles to the
bottom during baking to create a cheesy crust.*
—Barbara Gigliotti, Ocala, Florida

2 cups cut fresh asparagus (1-inch pieces)
1-1/2 cups chopped fresh tomatoes
1 medium onion, chopped
1 garlic clove, minced
1/4 teaspoon dried basil
1/4 teaspoon salt
1/4 teaspoon pepper
1 cup (4 ounces) shredded part-skim mozzarella
  cheese
1/2 cup grated Parmesan cheese
3/4 cup reduced-fat biscuit/baking mix
3 eggs
1-1/2 cups fat-free milk

In a bowl, combine the first seven ingredients. Transfer to an 8-in. square baking dish coated with nonstick cooking spray. Sprinkle with cheeses. In another bowl, whisk the biscuit mix, eggs and milk until smooth; pour over cheese. Bake, uncovered, at 400° for 30-35 minutes or until set and a thermometer inserted near the center reads 160°. Let stand for 5 minutes before cutting. **Yield:** 6 servings.

Nutritional Analysis: One serving equals 221 calories, 9 g fat (4 g saturated fat), 124 mg cholesterol, 553 mg sodium, 20 g carbohydrate, 2 g fiber, 15 g protein.
Diabetic Exchanges: 2 lean meat, 1 starch, 1 vegetable, 1/2 fat.
▲ *Meatless*

Lemon Blueberry Pancakes

(Pictured above)

Lemon yogurt gives these hearty pancakes a fluffy texture and delectable flavor. My son couldn't get enough of them the first time we had them for breakfast. Top each stack with extra yogurt and berries.
—Ann Flores, Seneca, Kansas

    1 egg
    1 cup low-fat lemon yogurt, *divided*
1/2 cup fat-free milk
    2 tablespoons canola oil
    1 teaspoon lemon juice
    1 cup all-purpose flour
Sugar substitute equivalent to 2 tablespoons sugar*
    1 teaspoon baking powder
1/2 teaspoon baking soda
1/2 teaspoon salt
1-1/4 cups blueberries, *divided*

In a small bowl, whisk egg, 1/2 cup yogurt, milk, oil and lemon juice until blended. Combine the flour, sugar substitute, baking powder, baking soda and salt. Make a well in the center. Pour yogurt mixture into the well; stir just until moistened. Gently fold in 1 cup blueberries.

Pour batter by 1/4 cupfuls onto a hot griddle coated with nonstick cooking spray. Turn when bubbles form on top of pancake; cook until second side is golden brown. Serve with remaining yogurt and blueberries. **Yield:** 8 pancakes.

*Editor's Note: This recipe was tested with Splenda No Calorie Sweetener. Look for it in the baking aisle of your grocery store.

Nutritional Analysis: One serving (2 pancakes with yogurt and blueberries) equals 283 calories, 10 g fat (1 g saturated fat), 57 mg cholesterol, 809 mg sodium, 41 g carbohydrate, 2 g fiber, 9 g protein.
Diabetic Exchanges: 2 starch, 1 fat, 1/2 reduced-fat milk, 1/2 fruit.
▲ *Meatless*

Best Turkey Sausage

I've had to cut the salt in my diet but love my family's recipe for homemade sausage. When I heat up these turkey sausage patties at work, everyone smells their wonderful aroma and begs for a taste.
—Kim Cook, Dade City, Florida

    1 pound lean ground turkey
    2 tablespoons water
    5 teaspoons butter-flavored sprinkles*
1/2 teaspoon *each* dried thyme, basil and rubbed sage
1/4 teaspoon *each* dried marjoram, oregano, cayenne pepper and ground cumin
1/8 teaspoon *each* garlic powder, pepper, ground ginger and nutmeg

Crumble turkey into a bowl. Add the remaining ingredients; mix well. Cover and refrigerate overnight. Shape into eight patties. In a nonstick skillet coated with nonstick cooking spray, cook patties over medium heat until no longer pink and a meat thermometer reads 160°. **Yield:** 8 patties.

*Editor's Note: This recipe was tested with Butter Buds butter-flavored sprinkles.

Nutritional Analysis: One patty equals 90 calories, 5 g fat (1 g saturated fat), 45 mg cholesterol, 129 mg sodium, 2 g carbohydrate, 0 fiber, 10 g protein.
Diabetic Exchange: 2 lean meat.
▲ *Low-sodium*

Ham and Apple Skillet

Here are all the breakfast favorites—hash browns, eggs, ham and cheese—baked together in one pan. Reduced-fat cheese, fat-free milk and lean meat help trim the fat, while chopped apple adds a hint of sweetness to this easy-to-fix skillet breakfast.
—Patty Kile, Greentown, Pennsylvania

    3 cups frozen O'Brien hash brown potatoes, thawed
    1 large apple, peeled, cored and chopped (about 1 cup)
1/4 cup chopped onion
1/2 to 1 teaspoon rubbed sage
    2 tablespoons water
    1 cup diced fully cooked lean ham
1/2 cup shredded reduced-fat cheddar cheese, *divided*
    4 eggs
1-1/2 cups fat-free milk
1/4 teaspoon salt

Press potatoes between paper towels to remove moisture; set aside. In a nonstick ovenproof skillet, cook the apple, onion and sage in water over medium heat until apple and onion are tender. Stir in potatoes and ham; heat through. Sprinkle with half of the cheese. Remove from the heat.

In a bowl, beat eggs, milk and salt; pour over potato mixture (do not stir). Sprinkle with remaining cheese. Bake, uncovered, at 350° for 35-40 minutes or until the center is set and a knife inserted near the center comes out clean. **Yield:** 6 servings.

Eggs Florentine

(Pictured below)

I wanted to impress my family with a holiday brunch, but keep it healthy, too. So I lightened up the hollandaise sauce in a classic egg recipe. No one could believe this tasty dish was good for them!
—*Bobbi Trautman, Burns, Oregon*

    2 tablespoons reduced-fat stick margarine*
    1 tablespoon all-purpose flour
    1/2 teaspoon salt, *divided*
1-1/4 cups fat-free milk
    1 egg yolk
    2 teaspoons lemon juice
    1/2 teaspoon grated lemon peel
    1/2 pound fresh spinach
    1/8 teaspoon pepper
    4 eggs
    2 English muffins, split and toasted
Dash paprika

In a saucepan, melt margarine. Stir in flour and 1/4 teaspoon salt until smooth. Gradually add milk. Bring to a boil; cook and stir for 1-2 minutes or until thickened. Remove from the heat. Stir a small amount of sauce into egg yolk; return all to the pan, stirring constantly. Bring to a gentle boil; cook and stir for 2 minutes. Remove from the heat; stir in lemon juice and peel. Set aside and keep warm.

Place spinach in a steamer basket. Sprinkle with pepper and remaining salt. Place in a saucepan over 1 in. of water. Bring to a boil; cover and steam for 3-4 minutes or until wilted and tender.

Meanwhile, in a skillet or omelet pan with high sides, bring 2 to 3 in. water to a boil. Reduce heat; simmer gently. Break cold eggs, one at a time, into a custard cup or saucer. Holding the dish close to the surface of the simmering water, slip the eggs, one at a time, into the water. Cook, uncovered, for 3-5 minutes or until whites are completely set and yolks begin to thicken. Lift out of the water with a slotted spoon.

Place spinach on each muffin half; top with an egg. Spoon 3 tablespoons sauce over each egg. Sprinkle with paprika. Serve immediately. **Yield:** 4 servings.

*Editor's Note: This recipe was tested with Parkay Light Stick Margarine.

Perfect Breakfast Parfait

FOR a quick, nourishing and filling breakfast, layer cottage cheese, yogurt and fruit in a glass or bowl. Sprinkle with a plain bran cereal like All-Bran for a lovely nutty crunch. This also makes a great snack.
—*Linda Humphrey, Bright, Ontario*

Toasted Muesli

Here's a healthy start to the day that can be made ahead; then the crisp mixture can be eaten quickly on the way to work or school.
—*Jennifer Wilson, Vancouver, British Columbia*

    2 cups old-fashioned oats
    1/4 cup sunflower kernels
    1/4 cup sliced almonds
    1/3 cup finely chopped dates
    2 tablespoons oat bran
    1 cup bran flakes
    1/4 cup toasted wheat germ
    1/4 cup raisins
    1 tablespoon sugar
1-3/4 cups fat-free milk, optional

In a 15-in. x 10-in. x 1-in. baking pan, combine the oats, sunflower kernels and almonds. Bake at 350° for 10-15 minutes or until almonds are golden. Place dates and oat bran in a large bowl; stir to coat dates with oat bran. Add the toasted oat mixture, bran flakes, wheat germ, raisins and sugar; stir gently to combine. Serve with milk if desired. Store in an airtight container. **Yield:** 7 servings.

Apple-Cinnamon Oatmeal Mix

*Oatmeal is a breakfast staple at our house.
It's a warm nutritious start to the day
that keeps us going all morning.*
—Lynne Van Wagenen, Salt Lake City, Utah

6 cups quick-cooking oats
1-1/3 cups nonfat dry milk powder
1 cup dried apples, diced
1/4 cup sugar
1/4 cup packed brown sugar
1 tablespoon ground cinnamon
1 teaspoon salt
1/4 teaspoon ground cloves
ADDITIONAL INGREDIENT (for each serving):
1/2 cup water

In a large bowl, combine the first eight ingredients. Store in an airtight container in a cool dry place for up to 6 months. **Yield:** 8 cups total.

To prepare oatmeal: Shake mix well. In a saucepan, bring water to a boil; slowly stir in 1/2 cup mix. Cook and stir over medium heat for 1 minute. Remove from the heat. Cover and let stand for 1 minute or until oatmeal reaches desired consistency. **Yield:** 1 serving.

Nutritional Analysis: One serving equals 176 calories, 2 g fat (trace saturated fat), 1 mg cholesterol, 185 mg sodium, 33 g carbohydrate, 4 g fiber, 7 g protein.
Diabetic Exchange: 2 starch.
△ *Low-fat*
▲ *Meatless*

Apricot Breakfast Rolls

(Pictured at right and on page 95)

I came up with this original recipe while trying to make cinnamon rolls without using butter, margarine or oil. It won first prize in the heart-healthy cooking contest at the Ozark Empire Fair one year.
—Connie Knudtson, Joplin, Missouri

1 package (1/4 ounce) active dry yeast
1/2 cup warm water (110° to 115°)
2 cups warm fat-free milk (110° to 115°)
1 teaspoon salt
1 cup whole wheat flour
3-1/2 to 4-1/2 cups all-purpose flour
1 jar (14-1/2 ounces) apricot spreadable fruit, divided
1/2 teaspoon ground cinnamon
1 cup confectioners' sugar
1/2 teaspoon cold fat-free milk

In a mixing bowl, dissolve yeast in warm water. Stir in warm milk, salt, whole wheat flour and 3 cups all-purpose flour; beat until smooth. Stir in enough remaining all-purpose flour to form a soft dough. Turn onto a floured surface; knead until smooth and elastic, about 6-8 minutes. Place in a bowl coated with nonstick cooking spray, turning once to coat top. Cover and let rise in a warm place until doubled, about 1-1/4 hours.

Punch dough down. Turn onto a floured surface; knead 8 times. Cover and let rest for 5 minutes. Roll into an 18-in. square. Spread 1 cup fruit spread to within 1/2 in. of edges; sprinkle with cinnamon. Roll up jelly-roll style; pinch seam to seal. Cut into 12 pieces; place in a 13-in. x 9-in. x 2-in. baking dish coated with nonstick cooking spray. Cover and let rise until doubled, about 30 minutes.

Bake at 350° for 30-35 minutes or until lightly browned. Cool on a wire rack for 30 minutes. For glaze, in a bowl, combine confectioners' sugar, cold milk and remaining fruit spread. Drizzle over rolls. **Yield:** 1 dozen.

Nutritional Analysis: One roll equals 271 calories, 1 g fat (trace saturated fat), 1 mg cholesterol, 225 mg sodium, 60 g carbohydrate, 2 g fiber, 7 g protein.
△ *Low-fat*
▲ *Meatless*

Confetti Scrambled Egg Pockets

(Pictured at right and on page 95)

*This sunny specialty is a colorful crowd-pleaser.
My eight grandchildren often enjoy these egg-packed
pitas for a Saturday morning brunch.*
—Dixie Terry, Goreville, Illinois

1 cup fresh or frozen corn
1/4 cup chopped green pepper
2 tablespoons chopped onion
1 jar (2 ounces) diced pimientos, drained
1 tablespoon butter or stick margarine
1-1/4 cups egg substitute
3 eggs
1/4 cup fat-free evaporated milk
1/2 teaspoon seasoned salt
1 medium tomato, seeded and chopped
1 green onion, sliced
3 whole wheat pita breads (6 inches), halved

In a large nonstick skillet, saute the corn, green pepper, onion and pimientos in butter for 5-7 minutes or until tender. Combine the egg substitute, eggs, milk and salt; pour into skillet. Cook and stir over medium heat until eggs are completely set. Stir in the tomato and green onion. Spoon about 2/3 cup into each pita half. **Yield:** 6 servings.

Nutritional Analysis: One serving (1 filled pita half) equals 207 calories, 6 g fat (2 g saturated fat), 112 mg cholesterol, 538 mg sodium, 28 g carbohydrate, 4 g fiber, 13 g protein.
Diabetic Exchanges: 1-1/2 starch, 1 lean meat, 1 vegetable, 1/2 fat.
▲ *Meatless*

Ginger-Pear Coffee Cake

(Pictured at right)

Chock-full of diced pears, raisins, walnuts and spices, this coffee cake ring from our Test Kitchen is a real taste treat. It takes some time to prepare, but the oohs and aahs from friends and family make it all worth it.

1 package (1/4 ounce) active dry yeast
1/4 cup warm water (110° to 115°)
1 cup warm buttermilk (110° to 115°)*
1/4 cup sugar
2 tablespoons butter *or* stick margarine, melted
1 teaspoon salt
3 to 3-1/2 cups all-purpose flour
1 egg
FILLING:
1-1/2 cups diced peeled fresh pears
1/2 cup raisins
1/3 cup chopped walnuts
1 tablespoon ground cinnamon
1/2 teaspoon ground ginger
1/2 teaspoon grated lemon peel
1/4 teaspoon ground cloves
1 tablespoon butter *or* stick margarine, softened
1/4 cup sugar
1 egg, lightly beaten
GLAZE:
1 cup confectioners' sugar
1/4 teaspoon vanilla extract
3 to 4 teaspoons milk

In a mixing bowl, dissolve yeast in warm water. Add buttermilk, sugar, butter, salt and 1-1/2 cups flour. Beat just until moistened. Add egg; beat for 2 minutes. Stir in enough remaining flour to form a soft dough. Turn onto a lightly floured surface; knead until smooth and elastic, about 6-8 minutes. Place in a bowl coated with nonstick cooking spray, turning once to coat top. Cover and let rise in a warm place until doubled, about 1 hour.

For filling, combine the first seven filling ingredients. Punch dough down. Turn onto a lightly floured surface. Roll into a 16-in. x 9-in. rectangle. Spread butter over dough. Sprinkle pear mixture to within 1/2 in. of edges. Sprinkle with sugar. Roll up jelly-roll style, starting with long side; pinch seams to seal. Place seam side down on a baking sheet coated with nonstick cooking spray. Pinch ends together to form a ring.

With scissors, cut from outside edge to two-thirds of the way toward center of ring at 1-in. intervals. Separate strips slightly; twist to allow filling to show. Cover and let rise in a warm place until doubled, about 50 minutes. Brush dough with egg. Bake at 375° for 20-25 minutes or until golden brown. Cool on a wire rack.

For glaze, combine confectioners' sugar, vanilla and enough milk to achieve drizzling consistency. Drizzle over ring. **Yield:** 14 servings.

*Editor's Note: Warmed buttermilk will appear curdled.

Nutritional Analysis: One piece equals 243 calories, 6 g fat (2 g saturated fat), 38 mg cholesterol, 222 mg sodium, 44 g carbohydrate, 2 g fiber, 5 g protein.
Diabetic Exchanges: 2 starch, 1 fat, 1 fruit.
▲ *Meatless*

Spinach Cheese Phyllo Squares

(Pictured at right)

A higher-fat version of this casserole was a big hit when my aunt and I ran a gourmet carryout business. My family loves this lighter version.
—Julie Remer, Gahanna, Ohio

6 sheets phyllo dough (14 inches x 9 inches)
1 package (10 ounces) frozen chopped spinach, thawed and squeezed dry
2-1/2 cups (10 ounces) shredded part-skim mozzarella cheese
1-1/2 cups (6 ounces) shredded reduced-fat cheddar cheese
1-1/2 cups fat-free cottage cheese
4 eggs
1-1/2 teaspoons dried parsley flakes
3/4 teaspoon salt
6 egg whites
1-1/2 cups fat-free milk

Layer three phyllo sheets in a 13-in. x 9-in. x 2-in. baking dish coated with nonstick cooking spray, lightly spraying the top of each sheet with nonstick cooking spray.

In a bowl, combine the spinach, cheeses, 2 eggs, parsley flakes and salt; spread over phyllo dough. Top with remaining phyllo sheets, lightly spraying the top of each sheet with nonstick cooking spray. Using a sharp knife, cut into 12 squares; cover and chill for 1 hour. Beat egg whites, milk and remaining eggs; pour over casserole. Cover and refrigerate overnight.

Remove from refrigerator 1 hour before baking. Bake, uncovered, at 375° for 40-50 minutes or until a knife inserted near center comes out clean and top is golden brown. Let stand 10 minutes before cutting. **Yield:** 12 servings.

Nutritional Analysis: One piece equals 187 calories, 9 g fat (5 g saturated fat), 97 mg cholesterol, 593 mg sodium, 9 g carbohydrate, 1 g fiber, 19 g protein.
Diabetic Exchanges: 2 lean meat, 1/2 starch, 1/2 fat.
▲ *Meatless*

Walnut Date Spread

This fruit and nut spread is wonderful on raisin toast.
—Leora Muellerleile, Turtle Lake, Wisconsin

1 cup pitted dates
2 tablespoons chopped walnuts
1/4 cup orange juice

In a food processor, combine dates and nuts; cover and process until finely chopped. While processor is running, add orange juice until blended. **Yield:** 7 servings.

Nutritional Analysis: One serving (2 tablespoons) equals 86 calories, 2 g fat (trace saturated fat), 0 cholesterol, 1 mg sodium, 19 g carbohydrate, 2 g fiber, 1 g protein.
Diabetic Exchange: 1 starch.
△ *Low-fat*
▲ *Low-sodium*
▲ *Meatless*

Pumpkin Spice Spread

(Pictured below)

With its hint of cinnamon, nutmeg and maple flavors, this thick and creamy pumpkin spread is sure to be gone in no time at your next brunch or special luncheon. Our Test Kitchen suggests spreading it on quick breads, bagels or homemade oven-toasted tortilla wedges.

1 package (8 ounces) fat-free cream cheese
1/2 cup canned pumpkin
Sugar substitute equivalent to 1/2 cup sugar*
1 teaspoon ground cinnamon
1 teaspoon vanilla extract
1 teaspoon maple flavoring
1/2 teaspoon pumpkin pie spice
1/2 teaspoon ground nutmeg
1 carton (8 ounces) reduced-fat frozen whipped topping, thawed

In a large mixing bowl, combine the cream cheese, pumpkin and sugar substitute; mix well. Beat in the cinnamon, vanilla, maple flavoring, pumpkin pie spice and nutmeg. Fold in whipped topping. Refrigerate until serving. **Yield:** 4 cups.

*Editor's Note: This recipe was tested with Splenda No Calorie Sweetener. Look for it in the baking aisle of your grocery store.

Nutritional Analysis: *One serving (2 tablespoons) equals 25 calories, 1 g fat (1 g saturated fat), 1 mg cholesterol, 34 mg sodium, 3 g carbohydrate, trace fiber, 1 g protein.*
Diabetic Exchange: *1/2 starch.*
△ **Low-fat**
▲ **Low-sodium**
▲ **Meatless**

Fruit 'n' Oat Yogurt

This combination of yogurt, oats, fruit and nuts is a delicious alternative to standard oatmeal. After sampling this yummy breakfast treat at my sister's, I had to have the recipe. It's healthy, quick to make and tastes so good!
—Susanne Melton, Mission Viejo, California

2 cups (16 ounces) fat-free vanilla yogurt
1 cup quick-cooking oats
1 can (8 ounces) crushed pineapple, undrained
1/2 cup slivered almonds, toasted
2 medium firm bananas, sliced

In a bowl, combine the yogurt, oats, pineapple and almonds; cover and refrigerate overnight. Serve with sliced bananas. **Yield:** 4 servings.

Nutritional Analysis: *One serving (3/4 cup) equals 370 calories, 10 g fat (1 g saturated fat), 2 mg cholesterol, 85 mg sodium, 58 g carbohydrate, 5 g fiber, 13 g protein.*
▲ **Low-sodium**
▲ **Meatless**

Blueberry Oatmeal Coffee Cake

There's a taste of summer in every slice of this bursting-with-blueberries cake. With its tender texture and slightly sweet streusel topping, it's the perfect way to end a special-occasion breakfast or brunch.
—Lori Buenger, Mountain Home, Arkansas

1-1/3 cups all-purpose flour
3/4 cup quick-cooking oats
1/3 cup sugar
2 teaspoons baking powder
1/2 teaspoon salt
1 egg
1/2 cup fat-free milk
1/4 cup canola oil
1/4 cup reduced-fat sour cream
1 cup fresh *or* frozen blueberries*
STREUSEL TOPPING:
1/4 cup quick-cooking oats
3 tablespoons all-purpose flour
3 tablespoons brown sugar
2 tablespoons cold butter *or* stick margarine

In a large bowl, combine the flour, oats, sugar, baking powder and salt. In another bowl, beat the egg, milk, oil and sour cream. Stir into dry ingredients just until moistened. Fold in blueberries. Pour into a 9-in. round baking pan coated with nonstick cooking spray.

For topping, in a small bowl, combine the oats, flour and brown sugar; cut in butter until crumbly. Sprinkle over batter. Bake at 400° for 20-25 minutes or until a toothpick inserted near the center comes out clean. Cool on a wire rack. **Yield:** 8 servings.

*Editor's Note: If using frozen blueberries, do not thaw before adding to the batter.

Nutritional Analysis: *One piece equals 297 calories, 12 g fat (3 g saturated fat), 37 mg cholesterol, 258 mg sodium, 42 g carbohydrate, 2 g fiber, 6 g protein.*
Diabetic Exchanges: *2-1/2 starch, 2 fat, 1/2 fruit.*
▲ **Meatless**

Beefed-Up Main Dishes

Even folks watching their diets can indulge
in a meaty entree. The secret is to select lean
beef cuts and to trim down the accompanying
sauces. No one will guess you cheated
these dishes out of fat and calories!

Italian Beef Kabobs (page 112)

Zucchini Beef Casserole

Everyone in our family always asks me to make this quick-and-easy microwave recipe. I use it as a side when I need a take-along dish or as a light one-dish supper at home.
—Lisa Bales, Peru, Indiana

 3/4 pound lean ground beef
 1 teaspoon garlic powder
1-1/2 cups diced zucchini
 1 can (14-1/2 ounces) diced tomatoes, drained
 1/2 cup instant rice
 1/2 cup water
 1/4 cup chopped onion
 1/4 cup reduced-sodium soy sauce
 3/4 teaspoon dried basil

Crumble beef into a 1-1/2-qt. microwave-safe dish; sprinkle with garlic powder. Cover and microwave on high for 2 minutes; stir. Heat 1-2 minutes longer or until no longer pink; drain. Stir in the remaining ingredients. Cover and microwave on high for 20-25 minutes or until vegetables and rice are tender, stirring twice. **Yield:** 4 servings.

Editor's Note: This recipe was tested in an 850-watt microwave.

Nutritional Analysis: One serving (1 cup) equals 230 calories, 8 g fat (3 g saturated fat), 31 mg cholesterol, 845 mg sodium, 17 g carbohydrate, 2 g fiber, 21 g protein.
Diabetic Exchanges: 3 lean meat, 1 starch.

Sirloin with Mushroom Sauce

(Pictured above)

*This steak is special enough to make for company...
and you can have it ready in no time!
Our Test Kitchen came up with the mouth-watering
combination of rich brown mushroom sauce
and tender strips of peppery steak.*

 1 boneless beef sirloin steak (1 pound and 3/4 inch thick)
 1 teaspoon coarse ground pepper
 2 teaspoons canola *or* vegetable oil
1-1/2 cups sliced fresh mushrooms
 1/2 cup beef broth
 1/2 cup dry red wine *or* additional beef broth

Rub steak with pepper. In a heavy ovenproof skillet over medium-high heat, brown steak in oil for about 4 minutes on each side. Bake, uncovered, at 450° for 4 minutes or until meat reaches desired doneness (for rare, a meat thermometer should read 140°; medium, 160°; well-done, 170°). Transfer steak to a warm serving platter. Let stand for 10 minutes.

In the same skillet, cook mushrooms over medium heat until golden brown. Add broth and wine or additional broth. Bring to a boil; cook until the liquid is reduced by about half. Thinly slice the steak; top with mushroom sauce. **Yield:** 4 servings.

Nutritional Analysis: One serving (3 ounces cooked beef with 1/4 cup mushroom sauce) equals 214 calories, 9 g fat (3 g saturated fat), 77 mg cholesterol, 161 mg sodium, 1 g carbohydrate, trace fiber, 27 g protein.
Diabetic Exchanges: 3 lean meat, 1/2 fat.

Saucy Steak Strips

Tomato and chili sauces lend nice flavor to this simple stir-fry of sirloin strips and crunchy green beans. You can serve it alone, but we like it over rice or noodles.
—Lacey Cook, Nedrow, New York

 3/4 pound lean boneless beef sirloin steak, trimmed and cut into thin strips
 1 tablespoon canola oil
1-1/2 cups sliced onions
 1 can (8 ounces) tomato sauce
 1/2 cup beef broth

1 tablespoon chili sauce
1 teaspoon sugar
1/4 teaspoon salt
1/4 teaspoon pepper
1 package (10 ounces) frozen cut green beans, thawed
Hot cooked rice *or* yolk-free noodles, optional

In a large nonstick skillet, brown steak in oil over medium heat. Remove and set aside. In the same skillet, saute onions in drippings until tender. Add the tomato sauce, broth, chili sauce, sugar, salt and pepper; cook and stir for 3 minutes.

Add the beans and beef. Cook and stir over medium heat until meat and beans are tender and sauce is slightly thickened. Serve over the rice or noodles if desired. **Yield:** 4 servings.

Nutritional Analysis: One serving (1 cup steak mixture, calculated without rice) equals 230 calories, 9 g fat (2 g saturated fat), 57 mg cholesterol, 779 mg sodium, 15 g carbohydrate, 4 g fiber, 22 g protein.
Diabetic Exchanges: 3 lean meat, 3 vegetable.

Herbed Beef Tenderloin

You don't need much seasoning to add flavor to this tender beef roast. The mild blending of rosemary, basil and garlic does the trick in this recipe.
—*Ruth Andrewson, Leavenworth, Washington*

1 whole beef tenderloin (3 pounds), trimmed
2 teaspoons olive *or* canola oil
2 garlic cloves, minced
1-1/2 teaspoons dried basil
1-1/2 teaspoons dried rosemary, crushed
1 teaspoon salt
1 teaspoon pepper

Tie tenderloin at 2-in. intervals with kitchen string. Combine oil and garlic; brush over meat. Combine the basil, rosemary, salt and pepper; sprinkle evenly over meat. Place on a rack in a shallow roasting pan. Bake, uncovered, at 425° for 40-50 minutes or until meat reaches desired doneness (for rare, a meat thermometer should read 140°; medium, 160°; well-done, 170°). Let stand for 10 minutes before slicing. **Yield:** 12 servings.

Nutritional Analysis: One serving (3 ounces cooked beef) equals 198 calories, 10 g fat (4 g saturated fat), 78 mg cholesterol, 249 mg sodium, 1 g carbohydrate, trace fiber, 25 g protein.
Diabetic Exchange: 3 lean meat.

Vegetable Beef Stew

(Pictured at right)

Here is a variation of a beef stew that I came across. We think its sweet flavor from apricots and squash gives it South American or Cuban flair. The addition of corn makes it even more hearty.
—*Ruth Rodriguez, Fort Myers Beach, Florida*

3/4 pound lean beef stew meat, cut into 1/2-inch cubes
2 teaspoons canola oil
1 can (14-1/2 ounces) beef broth
1 can (14-1/2 ounces) stewed tomatoes, cut up
1-1/2 cups cubed peeled butternut squash
1 cup frozen corn, thawed
6 dried apricot *or* peach halves, quartered
1/2 cup chopped carrot
1 teaspoon dried oregano
1/4 teaspoon salt
1/4 teaspoon pepper
2 tablespoons cornstarch
1/4 cup water
2 tablespoons minced fresh parsley

In a nonstick skillet, brown beef in oil over medium heat. Transfer to a slow cooker. Add the broth, tomatoes, squash, corn, apricots, carrot, oregano, salt and pepper. Cover and cook on high for 5-6 hours or until vegetables and meat are tender.

Combine cornstarch and water until smooth; stir into stew. Cover and cook on high for 30 minutes or until gravy is thickened. Stir in parsley. **Yield:** 4 servings.

Nutritional Analysis: One serving (1-1/2 cups) equals 278 calories, 9 g fat (3 g saturated fat), 53 mg cholesterol, 717 mg sodium, 32 g carbohydrate, 5 g fiber, 21 g protein.
Diabetic Exchanges: 2 vegetable, 2 lean meat, 1-1/2 starch, 1/2 fat.

Pizza Lasagna

My husband and I love pizza and lasagna. In this recipe, we have the best of both. Because we are both watching our weight, I trimmed down the fat so we could still enjoy this favorite dish.
—Vicki Melies, Glenwood, Iowa

1/2 pound lean ground beef
2 cans (14-1/2 ounces *each*) diced tomatoes, undrained
1 can (15 ounces) ready-to-serve creamy tomato soup*
1 can (6 ounces) tomato paste
1/2 cup water
1 medium onion, chopped
1 teaspoon *each* dried oregano and garlic powder
1/2 teaspoon salt
9 uncooked lasagna noodles
4 ounces sliced turkey pepperoni
1-1/2 cups (6 ounces) shredded part-skim mozzarella cheese, *divided*
1/2 pound fresh mushrooms, sliced
1 medium sweet red pepper, diced
6 green onions, chopped
1 can (2-1/4 ounces) sliced ripe olives, drained

In a nonstick skillet, cook the beef over medium heat until no longer pink; drain. For sauce, in a large bowl, combine the tomatoes, soup, tomato paste, water, onion and seasonings.

Spread 1/2 cup sauce in a 13-in. x 9-in. x 2-in. baking dish coated with nonstick cooking spray. Top with three noodles and a third of the sauce, then pepperoni. Sprinkle with 1 cup cheese. Top with three noodles and a third of the sauce. Top with mushrooms, red pepper, green onions and beef. Top with remaining noodles, sauce and cheese. Sprinkle with olives.

Cover and bake at 350° for 70-80 minutes or until the noodles are tender. Uncover; bake 10 minutes longer or until the cheese is melted. Let stand for 10 minutes. **Yield:** 12 servings.

*Editor's Note: This recipe was tested with Healthy Choice Creamy Tomato Soup.

Nutritional Analysis: One piece equals 191 calories, 6 g fat (3 g saturated fat), 29 mg cholesterol, 568 mg sodium, 22 g carbohydrate, 4 g fiber, 14 g protein.
Diabetic Exchanges: 3 vegetable, 2 lean meat, 1/2 starch.

Creamy Beef and Onions

If your family leans toward beef recipes, give this one a try. This stick-to-your-ribs mainstay gets its tang from a low-fat sauce of yogurt and gravy. Add a tossed salad and a basket of biscuits for a complete meal.
—Jennifer Rahe, St. Cloud, Minnesota

1 pound lean ground beef
2 cups sliced fresh mushrooms
2 medium onions, cut into thin wedges
1 garlic clove, minced
1 jar (12 ounces) fat-free beef gravy

2/3 cup reduced-fat plain yogurt
1 tablespoon Worcestershire sauce
1/4 teaspoon dried thyme
1/8 teaspoon pepper
Hot cooked noodles
4 teaspoons minced fresh parsley

In a nonstick skillet, cook the beef, mushrooms, onions and garlic over medium heat until meat is no longer pink; drain. In a bowl, combine the gravy, yogurt, Worcestershire sauce, thyme and pepper; pour over beef. Cook just until heated through. Serve over noodles; sprinkle with parsley. **Yield:** 4 servings.

Nutritional Analysis: One serving (1 cup beef mixture, calculated without noodles) equals 266 calories, 9 g fat (4 g saturated fat), 65 mg cholesterol, 588 mg sodium, 19 g carbohydrate, 2 g fiber, 26 g protein.
Diabetic Exchanges: 3 lean meat, 1 starch, 1 vegetable.

+ Rice (1cup = 5 ppts)

Teriyaki Beef Stir-Fry

(Pictured at right)

I often serve this delicious dish to family and friends. Try substituting chicken, shrimp or tofu for the beef, and add a healthy mix of water chestnuts, bean sprouts or nuts.
—Jennifer Wickes, Pine Beach, New Jersey

1/2 cup water
1/3 cup reduced-sodium soy sauce
1/4 cup honey
4 garlic cloves, minced
3/4 teaspoon ground ginger *or* 1 tablespoon minced fresh gingerroot
1 beef flank steak (3/4 pound), cut into thin strips
2 teaspoons canola oil
2 cups broccoli florets
1 medium onion, chopped
1/2 cup coarsely chopped green pepper
1/2 cup coarsely chopped sweet red pepper
1 cup sliced fresh mushrooms
1 teaspoon cornstarch
Hot cooked brown rice, optional

In a bowl, mix the first five ingredients. Pour 1/2 cup into a resealable plastic bag; add beef. Seal bag; turn to coat. Refrigerate for 1 hour. Refrigerate remaining marinade.

Drain and discard marinade from beef. In a large nonstick skillet or wok, stir-fry beef in batches in oil for 2-3 minutes or until no longer pink. Remove and keep warm.

Add broccoli, onion and peppers to the pan; stir-fry for 4 minutes. Add mushrooms; stir-fry for 1-2 minutes or until vegetables are tender. Return beef to the pan. Combine cornstarch and reserved marinade until smooth; stir into beef mixture. Bring to a boil; cook and stir until thickened. Serve over rice if desired. **Yield:** 3 servings.

Nutritional Analysis: One serving (1 cup beef mixture, calculated without rice) equals 320 calories, 11 g fat (4 g saturated fat), 59 mg cholesterol, 695 mg sodium, 29 g carbohydrate, 4 g fiber, 28 g protein.
Diabetic Exchanges: 3 lean meat, 3 vegetable, 1 starch.

Slow-Cooked Coffee Beef Roast

(Pictured below)

Day-old coffee is the key to this flavorful beef roast that simmers in the slow cooker until it's fall-apart tender. Try it once and I'm sure you'll cook it again.
—Charles Trahan, San Dimas, California

    1 boneless beef sirloin tip roast (2-1/2 pounds), cut in half
    2 teaspoons canola oil
1-1/2 cups sliced fresh mushrooms
    1/3 cup sliced green onions
    2 garlic cloves, minced
1-1/2 cups brewed coffee
    1 teaspoon Liquid Smoke, optional
    1/2 teaspoon salt
    1/2 teaspoon chili powder
    1/4 teaspoon pepper
    1/4 cup cornstarch
    1/3 cup cold water

In a large nonstick skillet, brown roast over medium-high heat on all sides in oil. Place in a 5-qt. slow cooker. In the same skillet, saute mushrooms, onions and garlic until tender; stir in the coffee, Liquid Smoke if desired, salt, chili powder and pepper. Pour over roast. Cover and cook on low for 8-10 hours or until meat is tender.

Remove the roast and keep warm. Pour the cooking juices into a 2-cup measuring cup; skim fat. In a saucepan, combine the cornstarch and water until smooth. Gradually stir in 2 cups cooking juices. Bring to a boil; cook and stir for 2 minutes or until thickened. Serve with sliced beef. **Yield:** 6 servings.

Nutritional Analysis: One serving (3 ounces cooked beef with 1/3 cup gravy) equals 209 calories, 7 g fat (2 g saturated fat), 82 mg cholesterol, 244 mg sodium, 6 g carbohydrate, trace fiber, 28 g protein.
Diabetic Exchanges: 3 lean meat, 1/2 starch.

Onion-Rubbed Flank Steak

(Pictured above)

This was always our three children's favorite. I'd set the table with china, crystal and cloth napkins, then serve this steak along with baked potatoes, a salad, a vegetable and rolls.
—Margaret Grant, Russellville, Arkansas

1/3 cup chopped onion
  1 tablespoon red wine vinegar *or* cider vinegar
  1 tablespoon canola oil
  1 teaspoon pepper
1/2 teaspoon salt
  1 garlic clove, minced
1/4 teaspoon dried rosemary, crushed
1/4 teaspoon dried basil
  1 beef flank steak (1-1/2 pounds)

In a bowl, combine the first eight ingredients; brush over both sides of steak. Place in a large resealable plastic bag; seal bag and refrigerate for 3-4 hours or overnight.

Place steak on a broiler pan. Broil 3-4 in. from the heat for 6-8 minutes on each side or until meat reaches desired doneness (for rare, a meat thermometer should read 140°; medium, 160°; well-done, 170°). Thinly slice across the grain. **Yield:** 6 servings.

Nutritional Analysis: One serving (3 ounces cooked beef) equals 208 calories, 11 g fat (4 g saturated fat), 59 mg cholesterol, 269 mg sodium, 2 g carbohydrate, trace fiber, 24 g protein.
Diabetic Exchanges: 3 lean meat, 1/2 fat.

Peppery Beef Stir-Fry

(Pictured at right)

This is a great dish for guests because you can easily do the prep work in advance. Everyone asks me for the recipe.
—Karla Hanson, Monona, Iowa

8 ounces uncooked linguine
1 tablespoon cornstarch
1 teaspoon pepper
1/4 teaspoon cayenne pepper
1 cup water
1/2 cup reduced-sodium soy sauce
1-1/2 pounds boneless beef sirloin steak, cut into thin strips
2 tablespoons canola oil
1/2 cup julienned green pepper
1/2 cup julienned sweet red pepper
2 to 3 garlic cloves, minced
2 cups fresh *or* frozen snow peas, thawed and halved
2 cups sliced fresh mushrooms

Cook linguine according to package directions; drain. In a small bowl, combine the cornstarch, pepper and cayenne. Stir in water and soy sauce until smooth; set aside.

In a large nonstick skillet or wok, stir-fry beef in hot oil for 4-5 minutes or until no longer pink. Using a slotted spoon, remove meat and set aside. Add the peppers and garlic; stir-fry for 1 minute. Add the snow peas and mushrooms; stir-fry for 2-3 minutes or until vegetables are crisp-tender.

Stir soy sauce mixture and add to vegetables. Bring to a boil; cook and stir for 2 minutes or until thickened. Stir in beef and linguine; heat through. **Yield:** 6 servings.

Nutritional Analysis: One serving (1-1/3 cups) equals 388 calories, 12 g fat (3 g saturated fat), 67 mg cholesterol, 879 mg sodium, 36 g carbohydrate, 3 g fiber, 33 g protein.
Diabetic Exchanges: 3 lean meat, 2 starch, 1 vegetable, 1 fat.

Meatballs with Bean Sauce

Since we like Tex-Mex food so much, I've transformed many of my recipes, including this one, to give them a more ethnic flavor.
—Gloria Warczak, Cedarburg, Wisconsin

1/2 cup quick-cooking oats
3 tablespoons finely chopped green onions
2 tablespoons minced fresh parsley
1 tablespoon minced fresh cilantro *or* additional parsley
1 tablespoon fat-free milk
1 tablespoon Worcestershire sauce
1 teaspoon chopped green chilies
1 teaspoon chili powder
1 teaspoon ground cumin
1 garlic clove, minced
1-1/2 pounds lean ground beef
1 cup (4 ounces) shredded reduced-fat cheddar cheese
1 tablespoon olive *or* canola oil
SAUCE:
1/2 cup finely chopped green pepper
2 cups salsa
1/2 cup beef broth
2 tablespoons lime juice
2 tablespoons tomato paste
2 teaspoons sugar
1 teaspoon chili powder
1 teaspoon minced fresh cilantro *or* parsley
1 can (16 ounces) kidney beans, rinsed and drained
6 cups hot cooked rice

In a large bowl, combine the first 10 ingredients. Crumble beef and cheese over mixture and mix well. Shape into 24 balls. In a large nonstick skillet, brown meatballs in oil in small batches over medium heat. Remove meatballs and set aside.

For sauce, add green pepper to skillet; saute for 3 minutes. Stir in the salsa, broth, lime juice, tomato paste, sugar, chili powder and cilantro. Cook and stir over medium heat for 5 minutes. Return meatballs to skillet. Reduce heat; cover and simmer for 15 minutes. Uncover and cook 10 minutes longer or until juices run clear. Stir in beans; heat through. Serve over rice. **Yield:** 6 servings.

Nutritional Analysis: One serving (3/4 cup sauce and 3 meatballs with 1 cup rice) equals 394 calories, 16 g fat (7 g saturated fat), 51 mg cholesterol, 797 mg sodium, 27 g carbohydrate, 6 g fiber, 36 g protein.
Diabetic Exchanges: 4 lean meat, 1-1/2 starch, 1 vegetable, 1/2 fat.

Italian Beef Kabobs

(Pictured on page 105)

Balsamic vinegar and fresh herbs are combined in a marinade that gives great flavor to the tender cubes of steak on these shish kabobs. Along with the beef, skewer mushrooms, zucchini and cherry tomatoes for an easy, well-balanced meal.
—Joyce Triggs, Thibodaux, Louisiana

1/2 cup balsamic vinegar
1/2 cup water
1 tablespoon olive *or* **canola oil**
4 garlic cloves, minced
2 tablespoons minced fresh oregano *or* **2 teaspoons dried oregano**
1 tablespoon minced fresh marjoram *or* **1 teaspoon dried marjoram**
2 teaspoons sugar
1-1/4 pounds boneless beef sirloin steak, cut into 1-inch cubes
3 medium zucchini, cut into 1/2-inch slices
32 small fresh mushrooms
1/2 teaspoon salt
8 cherry tomatoes

In a bowl, combine the first seven ingredients; mix well. Pour 2/3 cup marinade into a large resealable plastic bag; add the beef. Seal bag and turn to coat; refrigerate for 4 hours. Cover and refrigerate remaining marinade for basting.

Drain and discard marinade from beef. On four metal or soaked wooden skewers, alternately thread the beef, zucchini and mushrooms. Brush with reserved marinade; sprinkle with salt. Broil 4 in. from heat for 5 minutes on each side or until meat reaches desired doneness, turning once and basting frequently with reserved marinade. Place a tomato on each skewer before serving. **Yield:** 4 servings.

Nutritional Analysis: One serving (2 kabobs) equals 315 calories, 13 g fat (4 g saturated fat), 96 mg cholesterol, 379 mg sodium, 14 g carbohydrate, 3 g fiber, 37 g protein.
Diabetic Exchanges: 4 lean meat, 2 vegetable, 1 fat.

Garlic Ginger Beef

(Pictured at right)

This stir-fry takes a little longer to prepare, since the meat has to marinate first—but it's well worth the wait! Our Test Kitchen staff tossed together the pleasing combination.

4 tablespoons reduced-sodium soy sauce, *divided*
1 tablespoon balsamic vinegar
1-1/2 teaspoons minced garlic, *divided*
1 teaspoon brown sugar
3/4 teaspoon ground ginger *or* **3 teaspoons minced fresh gingerroot,** *divided*
1 pound boneless beef sirloin steak, cut into 1/4-inch strips
2 teaspoons cornstarch
1/2 cup beef broth
2 tablespoons ketchup
2 tablespoons sherry *or* **white wine vinegar**

1 tablespoon steak sauce
1/8 teaspoon cayenne pepper
4 teaspoons canola oil, *divided*
2 large sweet red peppers, cut into 1-inch pieces
6 green onions, cut into 2-inch pieces
8 ounces fresh snow peas
Hot cooked rice, optional

In a large resealable plastic bag, combine 2 tablespoons soy sauce, balsamic vinegar, 1 teaspoon garlic, brown sugar and 1/2 teaspoon ground ginger or 2 teaspoons gingerroot; mix well. Add the beef. Seal bag and turn to coat; refrigerate for at least 1 hour, turning once. In a bowl, combine the cornstarch, broth, ketchup, sherry or vinegar, steak sauce, cayenne and remaining soy sauce until smooth; set aside.

In a large nonstick skillet or wok, stir-fry beef in batches in 2 teaspoons hot oil until no longer pink. Remove and keep warm. In the same pan, stir-fry red peppers and onions in remaining oil for 2 minutes. Add the peas and remaining garlic and ginger; stir-fry for 2-3 minutes or until vegetables are crisp-tender. Return beef to the pan. Stir broth mixture and add to the pan. Bring to a boil; cook and stir for 2 minutes or until thickened. Serve with rice if desired. **Yield:** 4 servings.

Nutritional Analysis: One serving (1 cup stir-fry mixture, calculated without rice) equals 310 calories, 11 g fat (3 g saturated fat), 75 mg cholesterol, 934 mg sodium, 21 g carbohydrate, 4 g fiber, 30 g protein.
Diabetic Exchanges: 3 lean meat, 3 vegetable, 1/2 starch, 1/2 fat.

Marinated Steak

I took over the cooking when I retired, much to my wife's delight. Here's a marinade that's foolproof—I just dump all the ingredients into a container... and the steak comes out great every time!
—Gordon Richardson, Spring Hill, Florida

3/4 cup unsweetened pineapple juice
1/3 cup dry red wine *or* **beef broth**
1/4 cup reduced-sodium teriyaki sauce
1/4 cup reduced-sodium soy sauce
4 garlic cloves, minced
1 teaspoon ground ginger
1/4 teaspoon Worcestershire sauce
2 pounds boneless beef top round steak (1-1/2 inches thick)

In a bowl, combine the first seven ingredients; mix well. Pour 3/4 cup marinade into a large resealable plastic bag; add the steak. Seal bag and turn to coat; refrigerate for at least 4 hours. Cover and refrigerate remaining marinade.

Before starting the grill, spray grill rack with nonstick cooking spray. Drain and discard marinade from steak. Grill, covered, over medium heat for 10-12 minutes on each side or until meat reaches desired doneness (for rare, a meat thermometer should read 140°; medium, 160°; well-done, 170°). Baste with reserved marinade during the last 5 minutes of cooking. **Yield:** 6 servings.

Nutritional Analysis: One serving (4 ounces cooked beef) equals 242 calories, 6 g fat (2 g saturated fat), 94 mg cholesterol, 799 mg sodium, 7 g carbohydrate, trace fiber, 37 g protein.
Diabetic Exchanges: 4 lean meat, 1/2 fruit.

Garlic-Pepper Tenderloin Steaks

Give a little kick to these grilled tenderloin steaks with a zippy dry rub that combines paprika, thyme, ground mustard, chili powder and cayenne pepper.
—Vicki Atkinson, Kamas, Utah

1-1/2 teaspoons minced garlic
  1 teaspoon ground mustard
  1 teaspoon paprika
  1 teaspoon chili powder
  1 teaspoon pepper
1/2 teaspoon salt
1/2 teaspoon dried thyme
1/4 to 1/2 teaspoon cayenne pepper
  4 beef tenderloin steaks (4 ounces *each*)
  2 teaspoons olive *or* canola oil

In a small bowl, combine the first eight ingredients. Brush steaks with oil; rub in seasoning mixture. Cover and refrigerate for at least 1 hour.

If grilling the steaks, coat grill rack with nonstick cooking spray before starting the grill. Grill steaks, uncovered, over medium heat or broil 4-6 in. from the heat for 7-10 minutes on each side or until meat reaches desired doneness (for rare, a meat thermometer should read 140°; medium, 160°; well-done, 170°). **Yield:** 4 servings.

Nutritional Analysis: *One serving (3 ounces cooked beef) equals 209 calories, 11 g fat (3 g saturated fat), 70 mg cholesterol, 353 mg sodium, 2 g carbohydrate, 1 g fiber, 24 g protein.*
Diabetic Exchanges: *3 lean meat, 1/2 fat.*

Venison Stew

When I simmer a pot of this satisfying stew, I stir plenty of garlic and herbs into the hearty meat-and-vegetable mixture. This stew tastes great right off the stove, but it's even better if you make it ahead and reheat it.
—Rick Sullivan, Henryville, Indiana

  1 pound venison, cubed
  1 tablespoon olive *or* canola oil
  2 cans (14-1/2 ounces *each*) beef broth
  2 teaspoons dried thyme
  2 teaspoons dried marjoram
  2 teaspoons dried parsley flakes
  2 garlic cloves, minced
1/2 teaspoon salt
  6 to 8 whole peppercorns
  1 bay leaf
  2 cups cubed peeled potatoes
  1 large onion, chopped
  2 medium carrots, sliced
  2 celery ribs, chopped
  2 tablespoons all-purpose flour
  3 tablespoons water
1/8 to 1/4 teaspoon browning sauce

In a Dutch oven, brown venison in oil over medium-high heat; drain. Stir in the broth, thyme, marjoram, parsley, garlic and salt. Place peppercorns and bay leaf on a double thickness of cheesecloth; bring up corners of cloth and tie with kitchen string to form a bag. Add to pan. Bring to a boil. Reduce heat; cover and simmer for 30 minutes.

Add the potatoes, onion, carrots and celery; return to a boil. Reduce heat; cover and simmer for 30-35 minutes or until meat and vegetables are tender. Discard herb bag. In a small bowl, combine flour, water and browning sauce until smooth; stir into stew. Bring to a boil; cook and stir for 2 minutes or until thickened. **Yield:** 4 servings.

Nutritional Analysis: *One serving (1-1/2 cups) equals 306 calories, 7 g fat (2 g saturated fat), 96 mg cholesterol, 1,104 mg sodium, 29 g carbohydrate, 4 g fiber, 31 g protein.*
Diabetic Exchanges: *3 lean meat, 1-1/2 starch, 1 vegetable.*

Italian Beef

(Pictured below)

I make this beef in the slow cooker when I'm having a party so I don't have to spend the whole time in the kitchen. The meat smells so delicious, I can hardly keep my husband from helping himself ahead of time! For a robust sandwich, serve the shredded beef on a roll spread with horseradish sauce.
—Lori Hayes, Venice, Florida

  1 boneless beef top round roast (4 pounds)
  2 cups water
  2 tablespoons Italian seasoning
  1 teaspoon *each* salt, dried oregano, dried basil, garlic powder, dried parsley flakes and pepper
  1 bay leaf
14 French rolls (5 inches long)

Cut roast in half; place in a 5-qt. slow cooker. Combine the water and seasonings; pour over roast. Cover and cook on

low for 10-12 hours or until the meat is very tender. Discard bay leaf. Remove meat and shred with a fork. Skim fat from cooking juices; return meat to slow cooker. Serve on rolls. **Yield:** 14 servings.

Nutritional Analysis: One serving (3 ounces cooked beef and 1/4 cup juice with roll) equals 386 calories, 11 g fat (5 g saturated fat), 80 mg cholesterol, 557 mg sodium, 36 g carbohydrate, 2 g fiber, 34 g protein.
Diabetic Exchanges: 3 lean meat, 2-1/2 starch.

Grilled Sirloin Steak

My husband and I and our four children are missionaries to Australia. We use this great-tasting marinade just about every time we barbecue, which is often in this sunny part of the world.
—*Jennie Sauvageot, Pialba, Queensland*

6 tablespoons reduced-sodium soy sauce
4-1/2 teaspoons brown sugar
4-1/2 teaspoons olive *or* canola oil
4 garlic cloves, minced
2 teaspoons ground cumin
2 teaspoons ground coriander
2 pounds boneless beef top sirloin steak

In a bowl, combine the first six ingredients; mix well. Pour a fourth of the marinade into a large resealable plastic bag; add steak. Seal bag and turn to coat; refrigerate for 8 hours or overnight. Cover and refrigerate remaining marinade for basting.

Coat grill rack with nonstick cooking spray before starting the grill. Drain and discard marinade from steak. Grill, covered, over medium-hot heat for 5-6 minutes on each side or until meat reaches desired doneness (for rare, a meat thermometer should read 140°; medium, 160°; well-done, 170°), basting occasionally with reserved marinade. **Yield:** 6 servings.

Nutritional Analysis: One serving (4 ounces cooked beef) equals 264 calories, 11 g fat (3 g saturated fat), 100 mg cholesterol, 480 mg sodium, 4 g carbohydrate, trace fiber, 35 g protein.
Diabetic Exchange: 4 lean meat.

Southwest Pasta Bake

(Pictured above right)

Fat-free cream cheese and reduced-fat cheddar make this creamy casserole lower in fat and calories. It's a good way to get our kids to eat spinach in "disguise".
—*Carol Lepak, Sheboygan, Wisconsin*

8 ounces uncooked penne *or* medium tube pasta
1 package (8 ounces) fat-free cream cheese, cubed
1/2 cup fat-free milk
1 package (10 ounces) frozen chopped spinach, thawed and squeezed dry

1 teaspoon dried oregano
1 pound lean ground beef
2 garlic cloves, minced
1 jar (16 ounces) picante sauce
1 can (8 ounces) tomato sauce
1 can (6 ounces) tomato paste
2 teaspoons chili powder
1 teaspoon ground cumin
1 cup (4 ounces) shredded reduced-fat cheddar cheese
1 can (2-1/4 ounces) sliced ripe olives, drained
1/4 cup sliced green onions

Cook pasta according to package directions. Meanwhile, in a small mixing bowl, beat cream cheese until smooth. Add milk; beat until smooth. Stir in spinach and oregano; set aside. In a nonstick skillet, cook beef and garlic over medium heat until meat is no longer pink; drain. Stir in the picante sauce, tomato sauce, tomato paste, chili powder and cumin; bring to a boil. Reduce heat; simmer, uncovered, for 5 minutes. Drain pasta; stir into meat mixture.

In a 13-in. x 9-in. x 2-in. baking dish coated with nonstick cooking spray, layer half of the meat mixture and all of the spinach mixture. Top with remaining meat mixture. Cover and bake at 350° for 30 minutes. Uncover; sprinkle with cheese. Bake 5 minutes longer or until cheese is melted. Sprinkle with olives and onions. Let stand for 10 minutes before serving. **Yield:** 8 servings.

Nutritional Analysis: One serving equals 333 calories, 10 g fat (4 g saturated fat), 41 mg cholesterol, 996 mg sodium, 38 g carbohydrate, 4 g fiber, 26 g protein.
Diabetic Exchanges: 3 lean meat, 3 vegetable, 1-1/2 starch.

Mexican-Style Stuffed Peppers

(Pictured below)

We've always liked stuffed peppers, but everyone is pleasantly surprised at this mildly spicy version. For convenience, you can assemble these pretty peppers ahead of time and bake them later.
—LaDonna Reed, Ponca City, Oklahoma

6 medium green *or* sweet red peppers
1 pound lean ground beef
1/3 cup chopped onion
1/3 cup chopped celery
3 cups cooked rice
1-1/4 cups salsa, *divided*
1 tablespoon chopped green chilies
2 teaspoons chili powder
1/4 teaspoon salt
1 cup (4 ounces) shredded reduced-fat Mexican blend cheese

Cut tops off peppers and discard; remove seeds. In a Dutch oven or large kettle, cook peppers in boiling water for 3-5 minutes. Drain and rinse in cold water; set aside. In a non-stick skillet, cook the beef, onion and celery over medium heat until meat is no longer pink; drain. Stir in the rice, 1 cup salsa, chilies, chili powder and salt. Spoon into peppers.

Place in a 13-in. x 9-in. x 2-in. baking dish coated with nonstick cooking spray. Add 1/4 cup water to dish. Cover and bake at 350° for 45-50 minutes or until heated through. Uncover; sprinkle with cheese and top with remaining salsa. Bake 2-3 minutes longer or until cheese is melted. **Yield:** 6 servings.

Nutritional Analysis: One stuffed pepper equals 334 calories, 9 g fat (4 g saturated fat), 44 mg cholesterol, 665 mg sodium, 41 g carbohydrate, 3 g fiber, 23 g protein.
Diabetic Exchanges: 3 lean meat, 3 vegetable, 1-1/2 starch.

Cooking with Ground Beef

- When cooking ground beef for spaghetti sauce, chili or similar dishes, I cook it in a microwave-safe colander in the microwave so the fat drains into a bowl underneath it. When it's completely cooked, I rinse the crumbled meat under hot running water to eliminate as much fat as possible. Then I use the meat in the dish as directed. I've reduced the fat by 50%...and no one can even tell!
—*Bunny Brooks, Oakville, Manitoba*
- To reduce some of the fat in your favorite dishes, our Test Kitchen home economists suggest you cut back on the amount of ground beef called for in recipes, and replace it with hearty and healthy oats, barley or bulgur.

Shredded Beef Barbecue

This beef roast simmers for hours in a homemade barbecue sauce, so it's very tender and easy to shred for sandwiches. The mixture freezes well, too.
—Lori Bergquist, Wilton, North Dakota

1 boneless beef sirloin tip roast (2-1/2 pounds)
1/2 teaspoon salt
1/4 teaspoon pepper
1 tablespoon canola oil
1 cup *each* ketchup and water
1/2 cup chopped onion
1/3 cup packed brown sugar
3 tablespoons Worcestershire sauce
2 tablespoons lemon juice
2 tablespoons cider vinegar
2 tablespoons Dijon mustard
2 teaspoons celery seed
2 teaspoons chili powder
12 kaiser rolls, split

Sprinkle roast with salt and pepper. In a nonstick skillet, brown roast in oil on all sides over medium-high heat; drain. Transfer roast to a 5-qt. slow cooker. Combine the ketchup, water, onion, brown sugar, Worcestershire sauce, lemon juice, vinegar, mustard, celery seed and chili powder; pour over roast. Cover and cook on low for 8-10 hours or until meat is tender. Remove meat; shred with two forks and return to slow cooker. Spoon 1/2 cup meat mixture onto each roll. **Yield:** 12 servings.

Nutritional Analysis: One sandwich equals 313 calories, 9 g fat (2 g saturated fat), 59 mg cholesterol, 688 mg sodium, 33 g carbohydrate, 2 g fiber, 26 g protein.
Diabetic Exchanges: 3 lean meat, 2 starch.

Chicken & Turkey Entrees

You don't have to eat like a bird—or forego flavor—in order to trim down on fat and calories. A simple solution is to choose chicken and turkey. Your family will flock to the table for these enticing entrees.

Tarragon Chicken with Apples (page 128)

Meanwhile, in a nonstick skillet, crumble and cook sausage over medium heat until no longer pink; drain. Press dough into a 13-in. x 9-in. x 2-in. baking pan coated with nonstick cooking spray. Bake at 425° for 12-14 minutes or until lightly browned. Combine tomatoes and Italian seasoning; spread over crust. Sprinkle with sausage, artichokes, olives and cheeses. Bake for 14-18 minutes or until crust is golden and cheeses are melted. **Yield:** 8 slices.

Nutritional Analysis: *One slice equals 300 calories, 12 g fat (5 g saturated fat), 27 mg cholesterol, 891 mg sodium, 33 g carbohydrate, 3 g fiber, 16 g protein.*
Diabetic Exchanges: *2 starch, 2 lean meat, 1 fat.*

Sage Turkey Thighs

(Pictured below)

I created this for my boys, who love dark meat. It's more convenient than cooking a whole turkey. It reminds me of our traditional Thanksgiving turkey and stuffing that's seasoned with sage.
—*Natalie Swanson, Catonsville, Maryland*

   4 **medium carrots, halved**
   1 **medium onion, chopped**
1/2 **cup water**
   2 **garlic cloves, minced**
1-1/2 **teaspoons rubbed sage, *divided***
   2 **turkey thighs *or* drumsticks (about 2 pounds), skin removed**
   1 **teaspoon browning sauce, optional**
1/4 **teaspoon salt**
1/8 **teaspoon pepper**
   1 **tablespoon cornstarch**
1/4 **cup cold water**

Sausage Artichoke Pizza

(Pictured above)

Turkey sausage, tomatoes and a host of tasty toppings crown this deep-dish pleaser. My husband and I re-created the Chicago-style pizza we'd always enjoyed in restaurants.
—*JoAnn Brass, Glendale, Arizona*

   1 **cup water (70° to 80°)**
4-1/2 **teaspoons olive *or* canola oil**
1/2 **teaspoon sugar**
   1 **teaspoon salt**
2-1/2 **cups bread flour**
1-3/4 **teaspoons active dry yeast**
   1 **turkey Italian sausage link (4 ounces), casing removed**
   1 **can (14-1/2 ounces) Italian diced tomatoes, drained**
   2 to 3 **teaspoons Italian seasoning**
   1 **jar (6-1/2 ounces) marinated artichokes, drained and chopped**
1/4 **cup sliced stuffed olives**
   1 **cup (4 ounces) shredded part-skim mozzarella cheese**
   1 **cup (4 ounces) shredded reduced-fat cheddar cheese**
1/4 **cup grated Parmesan cheese**

In bread machine pan, place the first six ingredients in order suggested by manufacturer. Select dough setting (check dough after 5 minutes of mixing; add 1 to 2 tablespoons of water or flour if needed). When the cycle is completed, turn dough onto a lightly floured surface. Punch down; cover and let stand for 10 minutes.

In a slow cooker, combine the carrots, onion, water, garlic and 1 teaspoon sage. Top with turkey. Sprinkle with remaining sage. Cover and cook on low for 6-8 hours or until a meat thermometer reads 180°.

Remove turkey and keep warm. Skim fat from cooking juices; strain and reserve vegetables. Place vegetables in a food processor; cover and process until smooth. Place in a saucepan; add cooking juices. Bring to a boil. Add browning sauce if desired, salt and pepper. Combine cornstarch and water until smooth; add to juices. Bring to a boil; cook and stir for 2 minutes or until thickened. Serve with the turkey. **Yield:** 4 servings.

Nutritional Analysis: One serving (4 ounces cooked turkey with 1/4 cup gravy) equals 277 calories, 8 g fat (3 g saturated fat), 96 mg cholesterol, 280 mg sodium, 15 g carbohydrate, 3 g fiber, 34 g protein.
Diabetic Exchanges: 4 lean meat, 3 vegetable.

Turkey Avocado Sandwiches

I like to jazz up a plain turkey sandwich with vegetables and fresh cilantro from my garden. I combine zesty taco sauce with fat-free cream cheese for the bread spread. A little hot pepper sauce quickly kicks the heat up a notch.
—Dave Bremson, Plantation, Florida

3 ounces fat-free cream cheese
2 teaspoons taco sauce
4 drops hot pepper sauce
4 slices whole wheat bread
4 ounces sliced cooked turkey breast
1/2 medium ripe avocado, peeled and sliced
1 medium ripe tomato, sliced
2 to 4 teaspoons chopped fresh cilantro *or* parsley
2 lettuce leaves

In a mixing bowl, beat cream cheese until smooth; beat in taco sauce and hot pepper sauce. Spread on each slice of bread. Layer turkey, avocado and tomato on two slices of bread; sprinkle with cilantro. Top with lettuce and remaining bread. **Yield:** 2 servings.

Nutritional Analysis: One serving (1 sandwich) equals 399 calories, 11 g fat (2 g saturated fat), 52 mg cholesterol, 617 mg sodium, 40 g carbohydrate, 7 g fiber, 33 g protein.
Diabetic Exchanges: 3 lean meat, 2 starch, 2 vegetable, 1/2 fat.

Pepperoni Ziti Casserole

(Pictured above right)

I took a traditional family recipe and put my own nutritious spin on it to create this casserole. The chopped spinach and turkey pepperoni add color and flair, pleasing both the eyes and the palate.
—Andrea Abrahamsen, Brentwood, California

1 package (1 pound) ziti *or* small tube pasta
1/2 pound lean ground turkey
2 cans (one 29 ounces, one 8 ounces) tomato sauce, *divided*
1-1/2 cups (6 ounces) shredded part-skim mozzarella cheese, *divided*
1 can (8 ounces) mushroom stems and pieces, drained
5 ounces frozen chopped spinach, thawed and squeezed dry
1/2 cup reduced-fat ricotta cheese
4 teaspoons Italian seasoning
2 garlic cloves, minced
1/2 teaspoon garlic powder
1/2 teaspoon crushed red pepper flakes
1/4 teaspoon pepper
1/2 cup water
1 tablespoon grated Parmesan cheese
1-1/2 ounces sliced turkey pepperoni

Cook pasta according to package directions. Meanwhile, in a large nonstick skillet, cook turkey over medium heat until no longer pink; drain. Transfer to a large bowl. Add the 29-oz. can of tomato sauce, 1 cup mozzarella cheese, mushrooms, spinach, ricotta cheese, Italian seasoning, garlic, garlic powder, red pepper flakes and pepper.

Drain pasta; fold into turkey mixture. Transfer to a 13-in. x 9-in. x 2-in. baking dish coated with nonstick cooking spray. Combine the water and remaining tomato sauce; pour over pasta mixture. Sprinkle with Parmesan cheese and remaining mozzarella cheese. Top with pepperoni. Cover and bake at 350° for 25-30 minutes or until bubbly. Uncover; bake 5 minutes longer or until cheese is melted. **Yield:** 10 servings.

Nutritional Analysis: One serving (1 cup) equals 306 calories, 7 g fat (3 g saturated fat), 37 mg cholesterol, 795 mg sodium, 42 g carbohydrate, 4 g fiber, 20 g protein.
Diabetic Exchanges: 2-1/2 starch, 2 lean meat, 1 vegetable.

Apricot Turkey Stir-Fry

(Pictured at right)

*Tender turkey, crunchy veggies and dried apricots
make this easy stir-fry a standout. Serve
it over rice or thin spaghetti.*
—*Robin Chamberlin, Los Costa, California*

      1 tablespoon cornstarch
  1/2 cup apricot nectar
      3 tablespoons reduced-sodium soy sauce
      2 tablespoons white vinegar
  1/4 teaspoon crushed red pepper flakes
  1/2 cup dried apricot halves, cut in half lengthwise
      1 pound turkey tenderloin, cut into thin slices
      1 teaspoon canola oil
      1 teaspoon sesame oil *or* additional canola oil
2-1/2 cups fresh snow peas
      1 medium onion, chopped
      1 medium sweet red *or* yellow pepper, cut into
          1-inch pieces
Hot cooked couscous, optional

In a small bowl, combine the cornstarch, apricot nectar, soy
sauce, vinegar and red pepper flakes until smooth. Add
apricots; set aside. In a large nonstick skillet or wok, stir-
fry turkey in canola and sesame oil until no longer pink. Add
the peas, onion and red pepper; stir-fry until crisp-tender.
Remove meat and vegetables with a slotted spoon; keep
warm.

Stir cornstarch mixture and add to the pan. Bring to a boil;
cook and stir for 1-2 minutes or until thickened. Return
meat and vegetables to the pan; toss to coat. Heat through.
Serve over couscous if desired. **Yield:** 4 servings.

*Nutritional Analysis: One serving (1-1/2 cups stir-fry mixture,
calculated without couscous) equals 270 calories, 3 g fat (1 g
saturated fat), 82 mg cholesterol, 512 mg sodium, 27 g carbohydrate, 4 g fiber, 33 g protein.*
*Diabetic Exchanges: 4 very lean meat, 2 vegetable, 1 fruit, 1/2
fat.*
    △ *Low-fat*

Southwestern Fried Rice

*This speedy skillet supper combines tender cubes of
chicken with a variety of vegetables, rice, salsa
and seasoning. Try pairing this entree with
refried beans or corn bread for fun fiesta fare.*
—*Marcia Lee, Dewitt, New York*

      1 pound boneless skinless chicken breasts,
          cubed
      1 package (10 ounces) frozen corn, thawed
      1 small green pepper, chopped
      1 small onion, chopped
      2 teaspoons canola *or* vegetable oil
      1 cup chicken broth
      1 cup salsa
      1 teaspoon chili powder
  1/4 teaspoon cayenne pepper
1-1/2 cups uncooked instant rice
  1/2 cup shredded reduced-fat cheddar cheese

In a large nonstick skillet, saute the chicken, corn, green
pepper and onion in oil until chicken juices run clear. Stir in
the broth, salsa, chili powder and cayenne; bring to a boil.
Add the rice. Cover and remove from the heat; let stand for
5 minutes. Fluff with a fork. Sprinkle with cheese; cover
and let stand for 2-3 minutes or until cheese is melted.
Yield: 6 servings.

*Nutritional Analysis: One serving (1 cup) equals 352 calories,
6 g fat (2 g saturated fat), 47 mg cholesterol, 445 mg sodium, 52
g carbohydrate, 3 g fiber, 24 g protein.*
Diabetic Exchanges: 3 starch, 2 lean meat.

Cabbage Roll Bake

*I love the foods of my grandparents' native Poland
but not the high calories and long preparation time.
So I adapted this easy recipe that tastes remarkably
like the cabbage rolls my mother learned to
make from her mother.*
—*Jill Bednarek, Madison Heights, Michigan*

      1 pound lean ground turkey
1-1/2 pounds chopped cabbage
      1 can (15 ounces) tomato sauce
      1 can (14-1/2 ounces) diced tomatoes, drained
      1 cup uncooked long grain rice
  3/4 cup chopped onion
      2 garlic cloves, minced
  1/4 teaspoon dried thyme
  1/4 teaspoon pepper
      1 can (14-1/2 ounces) beef broth

In a large nonstick skillet, cook turkey over medium heat until
no longer pink; drain. Transfer to a large bowl. Add the cabbage,
tomato sauce, tomatoes, rice, onion, garlic, thyme and pepper;
mix well.

Transfer to a 13-in. x 9-in. x 2-in. baking dish coated with
nonstick cooking spray. Pour broth over the mixture. Cover and
bake at 350° for 1 hour; stir. Bake, uncovered, 15-20 minutes
longer or until rice is tender. **Yield:** 8 servings.

*Nutritional Analysis: One serving (1 cup) equals 233 calories,
5 g fat (1 g saturated fat), 45 mg cholesterol, 558 mg sodium, 32
g carbohydrate, 4 g fiber, 15 g protein.*
Diabetic Exchanges: 2 lean meat, 1-1/2 starch, 1 vegetable.

Lentil Pepperoni Stew

Turkey pepperoni nicely spices this thick lentil stew with its rich tomato broth. This is a "stick-to-your-ribs" mainstay at our house.
—Diane Hixon, Niceville, Florida

6 cups water
1-1/2 cups lentils, rinsed
1 medium onion, chopped
4 ounces turkey pepperoni, quartered
1 can (6 ounces) tomato paste
1-1/2 teaspoons salt
1/4 teaspoon dried oregano
1/4 teaspoon rubbed sage
1/8 teaspoon cayenne pepper
2 medium tomatoes, chopped
1 celery rib with leaves, chopped
1 medium carrot, chopped

In a large saucepan or soup kettle, combine the first nine ingredients; bring to a boil. Reduce heat; cover and simmer for 30 minutes. Add the tomatoes, celery and carrot; cover and simmer 35-45 minutes longer or until vegetables are tender. **Yield:** 6 servings.

Nutritional Analysis: *One serving (1-1/2 cups) equals 244 calories, 3 g fat (1 g saturated fat), 23 mg cholesterol, 974 mg sodium, 37 g carbohydrate, 12 g fiber, 20 g protein.*
Diabetic Exchanges: *2 vegetable, 2 very lean meat, 1-1/2 starch.*
△ **Low-fat**

 ## Lively Lentils

LENTILS are richer in protein than any other legumes except soybeans. They are cholesterol-free and low in calories, fat and sodium, while packing plenty of vitamins and fiber. Here are some fun facts and cooking tips:

- Some archaeologists believe people started growing peas and lentils more than 20,000 years ago.
- Lentils are great served alone or added to soups and stews or dressed with vinaigrette and served as a salad.
- Store lentils in an airtight container for up to 1 year in a cool, dry place. For even longer storage, they can be frozen indefinitely.

Savory Roasted Chicken

(Pictured above right)

When you want an impressive centerpiece for Sunday dinner or a special-occasion meal, you can't go wrong with this golden chicken from our Test Kitchen. The moist, tender meat is enhanced with a hint of orange, savory and thyme.

1 roasting chicken (6 to 7 pounds)
1 teaspoon onion salt
1/2 teaspoon dried thyme
1/2 teaspoon dried savory

1/4 teaspoon grated orange peel
1/4 teaspoon pepper
1 teaspoon canola oil

Place chicken on a rack in a shallow roasting pan. Carefully loosen the skin above the breast meat. Combine the onion salt, thyme, savory, orange peel and pepper; rub half of the herb mixture under the loosened skin. Rub chicken skin with oil; sprinkle with remaining herb mixture.

Bake at 375° for 1-1/2 to 2 hours or until a meat thermometer reads 180°. Let stand for 10-15 minutes. Remove skin before carving. Skim fat and thicken pan juices for gravy if desired. **Yield:** 10 servings.

Nutritional Analysis: *One serving (4 ounces cooked chicken, skin removed, calculated without gravy) equals 197 calories, 8 g fat (2 g saturated fat), 86 mg cholesterol, 267 mg sodium, trace carbohydrate, trace fiber, 29 g protein.*
Diabetic Exchange: *4 lean meat.*

Turkey-Cheese Macaroni Bake

My family requests this casserole all year. It's a great way to use up leftover turkey, and it freezes well, too. I lightened up the original recipe by reducing the butter in the sauce and substituting reduced-fat cheese and fat-free milk.
—Doris Rector, Comanche, Oklahoma

1 cup uncooked elbow macaroni
1/4 cup finely chopped onion
2 tablespoons butter *or* stick margarine
1/4 cup all-purpose flour
1/2 teaspoon salt
1/4 teaspoon pepper

1/8 teaspoon dried thyme
2 cups fat-free milk
2 cups cubed cooked turkey breast
1 cup (4 ounces) reduced-fat shredded cheddar cheese, *divided*

TOPPING:
1/4 cup bread crumbs
1 tablespoon butter *or* stick margarine, melted
1 teaspoon minced fresh parsley

Cook macaroni according to package directions. Meanwhile, in a saucepan, saute the onion in butter. Add the flour, salt, pepper and thyme; stir until blended. Gradually add milk. Bring to a boil; cook and stir for 1-2 minutes or until thickened. Drain macaroni; add the white sauce, turkey and cheese. Transfer to a 2-qt. baking dish coated with nonstick cooking spray.

Combine the topping ingredients; sprinkle over casserole. Bake, uncovered, at 350° for 30-35 minutes or until heated through. Place under broiler for about 5 minutes or until golden brown. **Yield:** 6 servings.

Nutritional Analysis: *One serving equals 307 calories, 11 g fat (7 g saturated fat), 72 mg cholesterol, 363 mg sodium, 26 g carbohydrate, 1 g fiber, 25 g protein.*
Diabetic Exchanges: *3 lean meat, 1-1/2 starch, 1 fat.*

Almond Chicken Stir-Fry

Pineapple juice, ginger and soy sauce lend a slightly tangy flavor to the chicken strips and veggies in this pretty blend. A package of frozen vegetables speeds along the prep time, making this a quick meal for busy weeknights.
—Margaret Wilson, Hemet, California

1 pound boneless skinless chicken breasts, cut into thin strips
3/4 cup sliced almonds
1 tablespoon canola oil
1 package (16 ounces) frozen broccoli stir-fry vegetables
1 tablespoon cornstarch
1 tablespoon brown sugar
1/2 teaspoon ground ginger
1/3 cup unsweetened pineapple juice
1/3 cup reduced-sodium soy sauce
Hot cooked rice, optional

In a large nonstick skillet or wok, stir-fry chicken and almonds in hot oil for 2 minutes. Add vegetables. Reduce heat to low; cover and cook for 4 minutes or until vegetables are tender and chicken is no longer pink.

In a small bowl, combine the cornstarch, brown sugar and ginger. Stir in pineapple juice and soy sauce until smooth. Stir into chicken mixture. Bring to a boil; cook and stir for 2 minutes or until thickened. Serve with rice if desired. **Yield:** 5 servings.

Nutritional Analysis: *One serving (1 cup stir-fry mixture, calculated without rice) equals 278 calories, 11 g fat (1 g saturated fat), 54 mg cholesterol, 708 mg sodium, 17 g carbohydrate, 3 g fiber, 26 g protein.*
Diabetic Exchanges: *3 lean meat, 1 vegetable, 1/2 starch, 1/2 fat.*

Lemon Turkey Burgers

(Pictured below)

My mom used to cook these juicy burgers in butter or a little bacon fat. I do all of my sauteing in olive oil or nonstick cooking spray, yet my turkey burgers taste just as delicious as Mom's.
—Jane Harris, Framingham, Massachusetts

1 egg, lightly beaten
1/3 cup finely chopped onion
3 tablespoons minced fresh parsley
2 tablespoons lemon juice
1 tablespoon grated lemon peel
3 garlic cloves, minced
1 teaspoon caraway seeds, crushed
1 teaspoon salt
1/2 teaspoon pepper
1 pound lean ground turkey
1 tablespoon olive *or* canola oil
6 whole wheat sandwich rolls, split
6 lettuce leaves
6 thin tomato slices

In a bowl, combine the first nine ingredients. Crumble turkey over the mixture and mix well. Shape into six patties. In a large nonstick skillet, cook the patties in oil in two batches over medium heat until no longer pink and a meat thermometer reads 165°. Serve on rolls with lettuce and tomato. **Yield:** 6 servings.

Nutritional Analysis: *One sandwich equals 268 calories, 11 g fat (3 g saturated fat), 95 mg cholesterol, 680 mg sodium, 24 g carbohydrate, 4 g fiber, 18 g protein.*
Diabetic Exchanges: *2 lean meat, 1-1/2 starch, 1/2 fat.*

Smoked Sausage with Pasta

(Pictured above)

Chock-full of sausage, mushrooms, tomatoes and basil flavor, this quick recipe satisfies the toughest critics. It's one of my husband's favorite dishes, and he has no idea it's lower in fat. Add a green salad for a delicious meal.
—Ruth Ann Ruddell, Shelby, Michigan

    4 ounces uncooked angel hair pasta
  1/2 pound reduced-fat smoked turkey sausage, cut into 1/2-inch slices
    2 cups sliced fresh mushrooms
    2 garlic cloves, minced
4-1/2 teaspoons minced fresh basil *or* 1-1/2 teaspoons dried basil
    1 tablespoon olive *or* canola oil
    2 cups julienned seeded plum tomatoes
  1/8 teaspoon salt
  1/8 teaspoon pepper

Cook pasta according to package directions. Meanwhile, in a large nonstick skillet, saute the sausage, mushrooms, garlic and basil in oil until mushrooms are tender. Drain pasta; add to the sausage mixture. Add the tomatoes, salt and pepper; toss gently. Heat through. **Yield:** 4 servings.

Nutritional Analysis: One serving (1-1/4 cups) equals 258 calories, 9 g fat (1 g saturated fat), 0 cholesterol, 611 mg sodium, 30 g carbohydrate, 3 g fiber, 16 g protein.
Diabetic Exchanges: 2 lean meat, 1-1/2 starch, 1 vegetable, 1/2 fat.

Rosemary Chicken

A savory rosemary and garlic marinade enhances the chicken breasts in this easy skillet recipe. I like to garnish the chicken with fresh rosemary sprigs and serve it with rice.
—Veronica Snyder, Waterbury, Connecticut

1/4 cup white wine *or* 1/4 cup chicken broth and 1 tablespoon lemon juice
  2 tablespoons canola oil, *divided*
  1 tablespoon reduced-sodium soy sauce
  1 tablespoon minced fresh rosemary *or* 1 teaspoon dried rosemary, crushed
  3 garlic cloves, minced
  1 teaspoon sugar
1/2 teaspoon pepper
  6 boneless skinless chicken breast halves (4 ounces *each*)
1/4 teaspoon salt
Hot cooked rice and fresh rosemary, optional

In a large resealable plastic bag, combine the wine or broth plus lemon juice, 1 tablespoon oil, soy sauce, rosemary, garlic, sugar and pepper; add chicken. Seal bag and turn to coat; refrigerate for at least 1 hour.

Drain and discard marinade. Sprinkle chicken with salt. In a large nonstick skillet, cook chicken in remaining oil over medium-high heat for 15 minutes or until juices run clear. Serve over rice and garnish with rosemary if desired. **Yield:** 6 servings.

Nutritional Analysis: One serving (1 chicken breast half) equals 154 calories, 4 g fat (1 g saturated fat), 66 mg cholesterol, 197 mg sodium, trace carbohydrate, trace fiber, 26 g protein.
Diabetic Exchange: 3 lean meat.

Citrus Chicken Kabobs

I've been experimenting with lighter evening meals so we don't eat heavy right before bedtime. My family loves how fresh and light these appealing glazed kabobs taste.
—Suzi Sisson, San Diego, California

  1 pound fresh broccoli, broken into florets
  2 large navel oranges
  1 pound boneless skinless chicken breasts, cut into 1-inch cubes
  4 plum tomatoes, quartered
  1 large onion, cut into wedges
GLAZE:
1/4 cup barbecue sauce
  2 tablespoons lemon juice

2 tablespoons reduced-sodium soy sauce
2 tablespoons honey

Place 1 in. of water in a large saucepan; add broccoli. Bring to a boil. Reduce heat; cover and simmer for 3-4 minutes or until crisp-tender. Drain. Cut each orange into eight wedges. On eight metal or soaked wooden skewers, alternately thread chicken, vegetables and oranges. In a small bowl, combine the glaze ingredients.

If grilling the kabobs, coat grill rack with nonstick cooking spray before starting the grill. Grill kabobs, uncovered, over medium heat or broil 4-6 in. from the heat for 5-7 minutes on each side or until chicken juices run clear, turning once. Brush frequently with glaze. **Yield:** 4 servings.

Nutritional Analysis: One serving (2 kabobs) equals 278 calories, 3 g fat (1 g saturated fat), 63 mg cholesterol, 568 mg sodium, 38 g carbohydrate, 8 g fiber, 28 g protein.
Diabetic Exchanges: *3 very lean meat, 3 vegetable, 1-1/2 fruit.*
△ **Low-fat**

Stir-Fried Chicken Marinara

I'm always looking for ways to lighten up menus. This hearty dish is chock-full of chicken and vegetables.
—Bonnie Buckley, Kansas City, Missouri

1 can (14-1/2 ounces) diced tomatoes, undrained
1 tablespoon cornstarch
1 can (8 ounces) tomato sauce
1/4 cup reduced-sodium chicken broth
1/4 cup dry red wine *or* additional chicken broth
1/2 teaspoon *each* dried basil and thyme
1/4 teaspoon salt
1 pound boneless skinless chicken breasts, cut into 2-inch strips
2 garlic cloves, minced
1 tablespoon olive *or* canola oil
1 small onion, chopped
1 medium green *or* sweet yellow pepper, julienned
1 small eggplant, peeled and cut into 3/4-inch cubes (about 3 cups)
Hot cooked spaghetti
2 tablespoons grated Parmesan cheese

Drain tomatoes, reserving the juice. Set the tomatoes aside. In a bowl, combine the cornstarch, tomato sauce, chicken broth, wine or additional broth, seasonings and reserved juice until smooth. Set aside. In a large nonstick skillet or wok, stir-fry chicken and garlic in hot oil until no longer pink. Remove and keep warm.

In the same skillet, stir-fry the onion and pepper for 4 minutes. Add eggplant and stir-fry for 4-5 minutes or until tender. Stir sauce; add to the pan. Bring to a boil; cook and stir for 2 minutes or until thickened. Add the chicken and tomatoes; heat through. Serve over pasta. Top with cheese. **Yield:** 4 servings.

Nutritional Analysis: One serving (1 cup stir-fry, calculated without spaghetti) equals 251 calories, 6 g fat (1 g saturated fat), 68 mg cholesterol, 745 mg sodium, 17 g carbohydrate, 4 g fiber, 30 g protein.
Diabetic Exchanges: *3 lean meat, 3 vegetable.*

Turkey Gyros

(Pictured below)

Greek seasoning, feta cheese and dill-cucumber sauce make this gyro taste deliciously authentic. This was my family's introduction to how really good pita bread can be. Instead of feta cheese, they sometimes prefer cheddar or Monterey Jack.
—Donna Garvin, Glens Falls, New York

1/2 pound turkey tenderloin, cut into 1/4-inch slices
1 teaspoon olive *or* canola oil
1-1/2 teaspoons Greek seasoning
1 medium cucumber, peeled
2/3 cup reduced-fat sour cream
1/4 cup finely chopped onion
2 teaspoons dill weed
2 teaspoons lemon juice
1-1/2 cups shredded lettuce
8 thin tomato slices
2 tablespoons crumbled feta cheese
4 pita breads (6 inches), warmed

In a nonstick skillet, saute turkey in oil for 5-7 minutes or until no longer pink. Sprinkle with Greek seasoning; set aside. Cut two-thirds of the cucumber into thin slices; finely chop remaining cucumber. In a bowl, combine the chopped cucumber, sour cream, onion, dill and lemon juice. Place lettuce, tomato, sliced cucumber, turkey and feta cheese on top of pita breads. Top with cucumber sauce. Bring edges of pita over filling and secure with a toothpick. **Yield:** 4 servings.

Nutritional Analysis: One serving equals 328 calories, 7 g fat (4 g saturated fat), 53 mg cholesterol, 446 mg sodium, 42 g carbohydrate, 3 g fiber, 24 g protein.
Diabetic Exchanges: *2-1/2 starch, 2 lean meat, 1 vegetable.*

Garlic-Herb Roasted Chicken

Garlic and herbs roasting in and on the bird make this roasted chicken so flavorful you can even eliminate the salt from the recipe if you like. The aroma from the oven while it's baking is tantalizing.
—Cindy Steffen, Cedarburg, Wisconsin

- 1 roasting chicken (4 to 5 pounds)
- 2 teaspoons *each* chopped fresh parsley, rosemary, sage and thyme
- 3/4 teaspoon salt
- 1/4 teaspoon pepper
- 20 garlic cloves, peeled
- 1 medium lemon, halved
- 1 large whole garlic bulb
- 1 fresh sprig *each* parsley, rosemary, sage and thyme

Loosen skin around chicken breast, leg and thigh. Combine chopped parsley, rosemary, sage, thyme, salt and pepper; rub half under skin. Place whole garlic cloves under skin. Squeeze half of the lemon into the cavity and place the squeezed half in the cavity. Remove papery outer skin from garlic bulb (do not peel or separate cloves). Cut top off garlic bulb. Place garlic bulb and fresh herb sprigs in the cavity. Skewer openings; tie drumsticks together with kitchen string.

Place chicken breast side up on a rack in a roasting pan. Squeeze the remaining lemon over chicken; rub remaining herb mixture over chicken. Bake, uncovered, at 350° for 1-1/2 to 1-3/4 hours or until chicken juices run clear and a meat thermometer reads 180° (cover loosely with foil if browning too quickly). Baste with pan drippings if desired. Cover and let stand for 15 minutes. Remove and discard skin, garlic, lemon and herbs from cavity before carving. **Yield:** 8 servings.

Nutritional Analysis: One serving (3 ounces cooked chicken, skin removed) equals 163 calories, 6 g fat (2 g saturated fat), 67 mg cholesterol, 289 mg sodium, 3 g carbohydrate, trace fiber, 23 g protein.
Diabetic Exchange: 3 lean meat.

Tomato Sausage Ziti

This hearty pasta dish is a lifesaver for a busy mom like me—it allows me to put a tasty meal on the table quickly that my whole family will eat. I serve it with a green salad and crusty bread.
—Susan Pfeiffer, South Riding, Virginia

- 8 ounces uncooked ziti *or* small tube pasta
- 8 ounces turkey Italian sausage links, casings removed
- 1 small onion, chopped
- 1 garlic clove, minced
- 1 can (14-1/2 ounces) diced tomatoes, undrained
- 1/2 teaspoon dried oregano
- 1/2 teaspoon dried basil
- 1/4 teaspoon salt
- 1/4 teaspoon pepper
- 1/2 cup fat-free half-and-half
- 1/4 cup shredded Parmesan cheese

Cook pasta according to package directions. Meanwhile, crumble sausage into a nonstick skillet. Add onion and garlic; cook over medium heat until sausage is no longer pink. Drain. Add the tomatoes and seasonings; bring to a boil. Reduce heat; simmer, uncovered, for 10 minutes or until slightly thickened, stirring occasionally.

Stir in half-and-half; heat through (do not boil). Drain pasta; add sauce and toss to coat. Sprinkle with Parmesan cheese. **Yield:** 6 servings.

Nutritional Analysis: One serving (1 cup) equals 247 calories, 6 g fat (2 g saturated fat), 23 mg cholesterol, 503 mg sodium, 35 g carbohydrate, 3 g fiber, 14 g protein.
Diabetic Exchanges: 2 starch, 1 lean meat, 1 vegetable.

Italian Chicken and Penne

(Pictured at right)

This easy stir-fry combines chicken and pasta with green pepper, mushrooms and tomatoes in an Italian-style sauce. I made up this recipe one evening, and it was a big hit with my family.
—Janeen Longfellow, Wolcottville, Indiana

- 8 ounces uncooked penne *or* medium tube pasta
- 1 pound boneless skinless chicken breasts, cut into 1/2-inch pieces
- 1 small green pepper, julienned
- 1/2 cup chopped onion
- 1 garlic clove, minced
- 1 tablespoon olive *or* canola oil
- 1 cup sliced fresh mushrooms
- 1 cup halved cherry *or* grape tomatoes
- 1 can (8 ounces) pizza sauce
- 1/2 teaspoon Italian seasoning
- 1/3 cup shredded reduced-fat mozzarella cheese

Cook pasta according to package directions; drain. In a nonstick wok, stir-fry the chicken, pepper, onion and garlic in oil until chicken is no longer pink. Add the pasta, mushrooms, tomatoes, sauce and seasoning; heat through. Remove from heat. Sprinkle with cheese; let stand until melted. **Yield:** 6 servings.

Nutritional Analysis: One serving (1-1/3 cups) equals 288 calories, 5 g fat (1 g saturated fat), 47 mg cholesterol, 96 mg sodium, 36 g carbohydrate, 3 g fiber, 26 g protein.
Diabetic Exchanges: 3 very lean meat, 2 starch, 1 vegetable, 1/2 fat.
▲ **Low-sodium**

Tarragon Chicken with Apples

(Pictured on page 117)

When friends in Winnipeg served us this delicious chicken, I knew I had to have the recipe. It originally called for whipping cream, which is a little high in fat for me. I substituted 1% milk and found that it was just as good but not quite as rich.
—Karen Moffatt, Lake Cowichan, British Columbia

- **4 boneless skinless chicken breast halves (4 ounces *each*)**
- **2 tablespoons butter *or* stick margarine, *divided***
- 1/4 teaspoon salt
- 1/8 teaspoon pepper
- **2 medium tart apples, peeled and sliced**
- 1/2 cup apple juice
- 1/2 cup 1% milk
- 1 teaspoon cornstarch
- 1 tablespoon water
- 1 tablespoon minced fresh tarragon *or* 1 teaspoon dried tarragon
Hot cooked long grain and wild rice, optional

In a nonstick skillet, brown chicken in 1 tablespoon butter for 3-4 minutes on each side. Sprinkle with salt and pepper; remove and keep warm. In the same skillet, cook apples in remaining butter for 6-8 minutes or until tender; remove and keep warm.

Add apple juice to pan; cook and stir over medium heat for 4 minutes or until juice is reduced by half. Add milk. Return chicken to pan; cook for 3 minutes or until chicken juices run clear. Combine cornstarch and water until smooth; stir into pan juices. Bring to a boil; cook and stir for 2 minutes or until thickened. Add the apples and tarragon; heat through. Serve over rice if desired. **Yield:** 4 servings.

Nutritional Analysis: One serving (1 chicken breast half with apples, calculated without rice) equals 241 calories, 8 g fat (4 g saturated fat), 83 mg cholesterol, 296 mg sodium, 15 g carbohydrate, 1 g fiber, 28 g protein.
Diabetic Exchanges: 3 lean meat, 1 fruit.

 Tarragon Trivia

TO SPICE UP mealtime, try a touch of tarragon and share some of these herbal tidbits:

- Tarragon is known as the "king of herbs" in France. Its licorice-like flavor is a cornerstone of French cuisine.
- When colonists settled in America, they brought along tarragon for their kitchen gardens. Thomas Jefferson was an early distributor of tarragon in the U.S.
- The Roman scholar Pliny believed tarragon could prevent fatigue. Pilgrims in the Middle Ages placed tarragon sprigs in their shoes before beginning long journeys on foot.
- Due to the serpentine shape of its roots, tarragon was thought to cure snakebites. It was used by the ancient Greeks to relieve toothaches.

Turkey Lasagna Roll-Ups

(Pictured above)

When making traditional lasagna, my mother would always have leftover noodles, so she experimented and came up with this tasty way to use them up. You can substitute chicken for the ground turkey and use spinach instead of broccoli in the filling for these roll-ups.
—Renee Buck, Greenville, South Carolina

- **4 lasagna noodles**
- **6 ounces lean ground turkey**
- **1 small onion, chopped**
- **1 cup chopped fresh broccoli**
- 1/4 cup water
- **1 cup (8 ounces) reduced-fat ricotta cheese**
- **1 egg, beaten**
- **1 tablespoon fat-free milk**
- 1-1/2 teaspoons minced fresh thyme *or* 1/2 teaspoon dried thyme
- 1/4 teaspoon salt
- **2 cups meatless spaghetti sauce, *divided***
- 1/4 cup shredded Parmesan cheese

Cook the noodles according to package directions; rinse and drain. In a nonstick skillet, cook the turkey and onion over medium heat until turkey is no longer pink. Meanwhile, in a small saucepan, bring broccoli and water to a boil. Reduce heat; cover and simmer for 5 minutes or until crisp-tender; drain.

Add the broccoli, ricotta, egg, milk, thyme and salt to the turkey mixture. Spread over each noodle; drizzle each with 1/4 cup spaghetti sauce. Carefully roll up jelly-roll style. Place seam side down in an 8-in. square baking dish coated with nonstick cooking spray. Drizzle with remaining spaghetti sauce. Cover and bake at 375° for 45-50 minutes or until heated through. Sprinkle with Parmesan cheese. **Yield:** 4 servings.

Crispy Baked Chicken

I took a recipe off a box of baking mix and altered it to make it easier. The result was this moist oven-fried chicken with a thick golden coating that's a lot crispier than the original.
—*Angela Capettini, Boynton Beach, Florida*

 2 tablespoons butter *or* stick margarine, melted
 1 cup crushed cornflakes
 1 cup all-purpose flour
1-1/2 teaspoons seasoned salt
 4 chicken drumsticks (4 ounces *each*), skin removed
 4 chicken thighs (6 ounces *each*), skin removed
 3/4 cup egg substitute

Drizzle butter in a 13-in. x 9-in. x 2-in. baking dish. In a shallow bowl, combine cornflakes, flour and seasoned salt. Dip chicken in egg substitute, then roll in cornflake mixture. Dip again in egg substitute and roll in cornflake mixture.

Arrange chicken in prepared dish, meatier side down. Bake, uncovered, at 425° for 20 minutes. Turn chicken over; bake 10-15 minutes longer or until juices run clear and a meat thermometer reads 180°. **Yield:** 4 servings.

Nutritional Analysis: One serving (1 drumstick and 1 thigh) equals 237 calories, 10 g fat (4 g saturated fat), 71 mg cholesterol, 720 mg sodium, 15 g carbohydrate, trace fiber, 21 g protein.
Diabetic Exchanges: 3 lean meat, 1 starch.

White Chicken Enchiladas

(Pictured at right)

A thick and creamy sauce covers these corn tortillas that are filled with tender chunks of chicken. To suit our family's tastes, I usually leave out the red peppers and cumin.
—*Sharon Welsh, Onsted, Michigan*

 12 white *or* yellow corn tortillas (6 inches)
 4 ounces reduced-fat cream cheese
 1 tablespoon plus 1 cup fat-free milk, *divided*
 1 teaspoon ground cumin
 4 cups cubed cooked chicken breast
1/2 cup chopped green onions
1/2 cup chopped sweet red pepper

 1 can (10-3/4 ounces) reduced-fat reduced-sodium condensed cream of chicken soup, undiluted
 1 cup (8 ounces) fat-free sour cream
 2 jalapeno peppers, seeded and chopped*
1/4 teaspoon cayenne pepper
1/2 cup shredded reduced-fat cheddar cheese

Wrap tortillas in foil. Bake at 350° for 3-5 minutes or until softened. Meanwhile, in a large bowl, combine the cream cheese, 1 tablespoon milk and cumin until smooth. Stir in chicken. In a nonstick skillet coated with cooking spray, saute onions and red pepper until softened. Stir into chicken mixture.

In another bowl, combine the soup, sour cream, jalapenos, cayenne and remaining milk. Stir 2 tablespoons soup mixture into chicken mixture. Place 1/3 cup of chicken mixture down the center of each tortilla; roll up.

Place seam side down in a 13-in. x 9-in. x 2-in. baking dish coated with nonstick cooking spray. Top with the remaining soup mixture. Cover and bake at 350° for 30 minutes or until heated through. Uncover; sprinkle with the cheese. Bake 5 minutes longer or until cheese is melted. **Yield:** 6 servings.

*Editor's Note: When cutting or seeding hot peppers, use rubber or plastic gloves to protect your hands. Avoid touching your face.

Nutritional Analysis: One serving (2 enchiladas) equals 405 calories, 10 g fat (5 g saturated fat), 108 mg cholesterol, 435 mg sodium, 35 g carbohydrate, 3 g fiber, 40 g protein.
Diabetic Exchanges: 4 lean meat, 1 starch, 1 fat-free milk, 1/2 fat.

Kidney Bean Sausage Supper

I'm always looking for nutritious and tasty meals that do not take a lot of time to prepare. I created this bean and sausage dish by combining ingredients I happened to have on hand. It makes a filling and satisfying supper.
—*Carol Strong Battle, Heathsville, Virginia*

  1 **pound turkey Italian sausage links**
  1 **large green pepper, julienned**
  1 **medium onion, sliced**
1/2 **cup reduced-sodium chicken broth**
  1 **can (16 ounces) kidney beans, rinsed and drained**
  1 **can (14-1/2 ounces) diced tomatoes and green chilies, undrained**
Hot cooked rice

In a large nonstick skillet, cook sausage over medium heat until no longer pink; drain. Slice sausage and return to the pan. Add green pepper, onion and broth; cover and cook for 5 minutes or until vegetables are tender. Add beans and tomatoes; bring to a boil. Reduce heat; cover and simmer for 10 minutes or until vegetables are tender. Serve in bowls over rice. **Yield:** 4 servings.

Nutritional Analysis: One serving (1 cup sausage mixture, calculated without rice) equals 337 calories, 11 g fat (3 g saturated fat), 61 mg cholesterol, 1,564 mg sodium, 33 g carbohydrate, 10 g fiber, 27 g protein.
Diabetic Exchanges: 3 lean meat, 2 vegetable, 1-1/2 starch.

Montego Bay Chicken

(Pictured above)

You don't need high-fat ingredients to make this grilled chicken taste good. The marinade both flavors and tenderizes the meat.
—*Julie DeMatteo, Clementon, New Jersey*

1/4 **cup reduced-sodium soy sauce**
1/4 **cup orange juice**
  2 **tablespoons brown sugar**
  2 **garlic cloves, minced**
  1 **teaspoon hot pepper sauce**
  1 **teaspoon rum extract**
1/4 **teaspoon ground ginger** *or* 1 **teaspoon minced fresh gingerroot**
  4 **boneless skinless chicken breast halves (4 ounces** *each***)**

In a large resealable plastic bag, combine the first seven ingredients; add the chicken. Seal bag and turn to coat; refrigerate for at least 2 hours.

Drain and discard marinade. Coat grill rack with nonstick cooking spray before starting the grill. Grill chicken, uncovered, over indirect medium heat for 6-8 minutes on each side or until juices run clear. **Yield:** 4 servings.

Nutritional Analysis: One serving equals 138 calories, 1 g fat (trace saturated fat), 66 mg cholesterol, 379 mg sodium, 3 g carbohydrate, trace fiber, 27 g protein.
Diabetic Exchange: 3 lean meat.
△ *Low-fat*

Apple Chicken Quesadillas

My sister came up with this easy recipe. People are surprised by the combination of chicken, apples, tomatoes and corn inside the crispy tortillas, but they love it.
—*Stacia Slagle, Maysville, Missouri*

  2 **medium tart apples, sliced**
  1 **cup diced cooked chicken breast**
1/2 **cup shredded fat-free cheddar cheese**
1/2 **cup shredded part-skim mozzarella cheese**
1/2 **cup fresh** *or* **frozen corn, thawed**
1/2 **cup chopped fresh tomatoes**
1/2 **cup chopped onion**
1/4 **teaspoon salt**
  6 **flour tortillas (8 inches)**
3/4 **cup shredded lettuce**
3/4 **cup salsa**
  6 **tablespoons fat-free sour cream**

In a bowl, combine the first eight ingredients. Place about 3/4 cup on half of each tortilla. Fold tortilla in half over filling and secure with toothpicks. Place on a baking sheet coated with nonstick cooking spray. Bake at 400° for 8-10 minutes or until golden brown.

Carefully turn quesadillas over; bake 5-8 minutes longer or until golden. Discard toothpicks. Cut each quesadilla into three wedges; serve with lettuce, salsa and sour cream. **Yield:** 6 servings.

Homemade Italian Turkey Sausage

When I went to the library for some books on sausage-making, I was surprised to learn how easy it is! We use this sweet and spicy sausage on pizza, in spaghetti sauce, casseroles and breakfast patties.
—Joyce Haworth, Des Plaines, Illinois

1 pound lean ground turkey
2 teaspoons garlic powder
1-1/2 teaspoons fennel seed, crushed
1-1/2 teaspoons sugar
1 teaspoon salt
1 teaspoon dried oregano
1/2 teaspoon pepper

In a bowl, combine the turkey, garlic powder, fennel seed, sugar, salt, oregano and pepper. Cover and refrigerate for at least 8 hours or overnight. Shape into eight patties. Cook in a nonstick skillet coated with nonstick cooking spray for about 3 minutes on each side or until a meat thermometer reads 165°. Or crumble turkey into a nonstick skillet coated with nonstick cooking spray. Cook and stir for about 4 minutes or until meat is no longer pink. **Yield:** 8 servings.

Turkey with Orange Sauce

(Pictured at right)

I found this recipe in one of my mother's cookbooks. It's a quick way to fix turkey. My family likes it with rice and a tossed salad.
—Gaye O'Dell, Binghamton, New York

1 pound turkey breast tenderloins
1/2 teaspoon salt, *divided*
1/4 teaspoon pepper
2 teaspoons cornstarch
1 tablespoon brown sugar
1 cup orange juice
1-1/2 teaspoons lemon juice
2 teaspoons butter *or* stick margarine

Sprinkle turkey with 1/4 teaspoon salt and pepper; place in a microwave-safe 11-in. x 7-in. x 2-in. dish. Cover, venting one corner, and microwave on high for 4 minutes. Turn turkey over; cover and microwave 1-2 minutes longer or until turkey is no longer pink and a meat thermometer reads 170°.

In a microwave-safe bowl, combine the cornstarch, brown sugar, orange juice, lemon juice, butter and remaining salt. Microwave, uncovered, on high for 2 minutes or until thickened and smooth, stirring once. Serve with turkey. **Yield:** 4 servings.

Editor's Note: This recipe was tested in an 850-watt microwave.

Quick Turkey Chop Suey

Whenever I serve this chop suey to relatives or friends, I get asked for the recipe. Canned ingredients make it convenient to prepare.
—Anne Powers, Munford, Alabama

  1 pound lean ground turkey
1/2 cup chopped onion
  1 can (10-1/2 ounces) condensed chicken broth, undiluted, *divided*
  1 cup chopped celery
  1 can (8 ounces) sliced water chestnuts, drained
  1 jar (4-1/2 ounces) sliced mushrooms, drained
1/4 teaspoon ground ginger
  1 can (14 ounces) bean sprouts, drained
  2 tablespoons cornstarch
  2 tablespoons reduced-sodium soy sauce
Hot cooked white *or* brown rice, optional

In a nonstick skillet or wok, cook turkey and onion over medium heat until turkey is no longer pink; drain. Add 1 cup broth and next four ingredients. Bring to a boil. Reduce heat; cover and simmer for 10-15 minutes or until celery is tender.

Add bean sprouts. Combine the cornstarch, soy sauce and remaining broth; stir into turkey mixture. Bring to a boil; cook and stir for 2 minutes or until thickened. Serve over rice if desired. **Yield:** 5 servings.

Nutritional Analysis: One serving (1 cup chop suey, calculated without rice) equals 208 calories, 9 g fat (2 g saturated fat), 74 mg cholesterol, 850 mg sodium, 13 g carbohydrate, 4 g fiber, 19 g protein.
Diabetic Exchanges: 2 lean meat, 1 vegetable, 1/2 starch, 1/2 fat.

Southern Barbecue Spaghetti Sauce

(Pictured above right)

I revamped our favorite sloppy joe recipe into this thick spaghetti sauce that simmers in the slow cooker. The flavor is jazzy enough to be interesting to adults, yet mild enough to be enjoyed by children.
—Rhonda Melanson, Sarnia, Ontario

    1 pound lean ground turkey
    2 medium onions, chopped
1-1/2 cups sliced fresh mushrooms
    1 medium green pepper, chopped
    2 garlic cloves, minced
    1 can (14-1/2 ounces) diced tomatoes, undrained
    1 can (12 ounces) tomato paste
    1 can (8 ounces) tomato sauce
    1 cup ketchup
  1/2 cup beef broth
    2 tablespoons Worcestershire sauce
    2 tablespoons brown sugar
    1 tablespoon ground cumin
    2 teaspoons chili powder
   12 cups hot cooked spaghetti

In a large nonstick skillet, cook the turkey, onions, mushrooms, green pepper and garlic over medium heat until meat is no longer pink; drain. Transfer to a slow cooker. Stir in the tomatoes, tomato paste, tomato sauce, ketchup, broth, Worcestershire sauce, brown sugar, cumin and chili powder; mix well. Cover and cook on low for 4-5 hours. Serve over spaghetti. **Yield:** 12 servings.

Nutritional Analysis: One serving (2/3 cup sauce with 1 cup spaghetti) equals 342 calories, 4 g fat (1 g saturated fat), 30 mg cholesterol, 491 mg sodium, 60 g carbohydrate, 5 g fiber, 17 g protein.

Favorite Recipe Made Lighter

FOR an entree with plenty of comforting flavor, Four-Cheese Chicken Fettuccine from Rochelle Brownlee of Big Timber, Montana fits the bill.

Our Test Kitchen staff came up with Makeover Four-Cheese Chicken Fettuccine, which retains the rich flavor of the original yet fits into a healthier eating plan.

Four-Cheese Chicken Fettuccine

8 ounces uncooked fettuccine
1 can (10-3/4 ounces) condensed cream of mushroom soup, undiluted
1 package (8 ounces) cream cheese, cubed
1 jar (4-1/2 ounces) sliced mushrooms, drained
1 cup heavy whipping cream
1/2 cup butter *or* margarine
1/4 teaspoon garlic powder
3/4 cup grated Parmesan cheese
1/2 cup shredded mozzarella cheese
1/2 cup shredded Swiss cheese
2-1/2 cups cubed cooked chicken
TOPPING:
  1/3 cup seasoned bread crumbs
  2 tablespoons butter *or* margarine, melted
  1 to 2 tablespoons grated Parmesan cheese

Cook fettuccine according to package directions. Meanwhile, in a Dutch oven or large kettle, combine the soup, cream cheese, mushrooms, cream, butter and garlic powder. Cook and stir over medium heat until blended. Reduce heat to low; add cheeses and stir until melted. Add chicken; heat through. Drain fettuccine; add to the chicken mixture.

Transfer to a greased shallow 2-1/2-qt. baking dish. Combine topping ingredients; sprinkle over chicken mixture. Cover and bake at 350° for 30 minutes. Uncover; bake 5-10 minutes longer or until golden brown. **Yield:** 8 servings.

Nutritional Analysis: One serving (1 cup) equals 651 calories, 46 g fat (27 g saturated fat), 166 mg cholesterol, 952 mg sodium, 31 g carbohydrate, 1 g fiber, 29 g protein.

Makeover Four-Cheese Chicken Fettuccine

(Pictured at right)

8 ounces uncooked fettuccine
2 cups sliced fresh mushrooms
1 tablespoon butter *or* stick margarine

1 can (10-3/4 ounces) condensed reduced-fat reduced-sodium cream of mushroom soup, undiluted
1 package (8 ounces) fat-free cream cheese, cubed
2 cups fat-free milk
1/2 cup fat-free half-and-half
1/4 teaspoon garlic powder
2-1/2 cups cubed cooked chicken breast
3/4 cup grated Parmesan cheese
1/2 cup shredded part-skim mozzarella cheese
1/2 cup shredded reduced-fat Swiss cheese
TOPPING:
  1/3 cup seasoned bread crumbs
  1 tablespoon butter *or* stick margarine, melted
  1 tablespoon grated Parmesan cheese

Cook fettuccine according to package directions. Meanwhile, in a Dutch oven or large kettle, saute mushrooms in butter until tender. Add the soup, cream cheese, milk, half-and-half and garlic powder. Cook and stir over medium-low heat until smooth. Remove from the heat. Add chicken and cheeses; mix well. Drain fettuccine; add to chicken mixture and stir gently to coat.

Transfer to a shallow 2-1/2-qt. baking dish coated with nonstick cooking spray. Combine topping ingredients; sprinkle over chicken mixture. Cover and bake at 350° for 25 minutes. Uncover; bake 5-10 minutes longer or until golden brown. **Yield:** 8 servings.

Nutritional Analysis: One serving (1 cup) equals 377 calories, 10 g fat (5 g saturated fat), 65 mg cholesterol, 751 mg sodium, 36 g carbohydrate, 1 g fiber, 33 g protein.
Diabetic Exchanges: 3 lean meat, 2 starch, 1/2 fat-free milk.

Italian Turkey Cutlets

Because I'm watching my weight, I've used this recipe for years. Served with a flavorful tomato sauce, these cutlets taste so good that my son, who is thin and doesn't need to worry about his weight, requests them for his birthday dinner!
—Janet Bumb, Beallsville, Maryland

1 small onion, finely chopped
2 garlic cloves, minced
5 teaspoons olive *or* canola oil, *divided*
1 can (14-1/2 ounces) Italian stewed tomatoes
1 teaspoon dried basil
1 teaspoon dried oregano
1/2 teaspoon dried rosemary, crushed
1-1/4 pounds turkey breast cutlets
1/2 teaspoon salt
1/8 teaspoon pepper
2 tablespoons shredded Parmesan cheese

In a saucepan, saute onion and garlic in 2 teaspoons oil until tender. Stir in the tomatoes, basil, oregano and rosemary. Bring to a boil. Reduce heat; cook, uncovered, over medium heat for 15-20 minutes or until sauce thickens.

Meanwhile, sprinkle both sides of turkey cutlets with salt and pepper. In a large nonstick skillet over medium heat, cook turkey in batches in remaining oil until juices run clear. Serve with tomato sauce. Sprinkle with Parmesan cheese. **Yield:** 4 servings.

Nutritional Analysis: *One serving equals 263 calories, 7 g fat (2 g saturated fat), 90 mg cholesterol, 750 mg sodium, 11 g carbohydrate, 3 g fiber, 37 g protein.*
Diabetic Exchanges: *5 very lean meat, 2 vegetable, 1/2 fat.*

1-2 minutes or until thickened. Serve over rice if desired. **Yield:** 4 servings.

Nutritional Analysis: *One serving (1 cup stir-fry mixture, calculated without rice) equals 198 calories, 5 g fat (2 g saturated fat), 44 mg cholesterol, 1,164 mg sodium, 24 g carbohydrate, 2 g fiber, 14 g protein.*
Diabetic Exchanges: *2 lean meat, 1 starch, 1 vegetable.*

Sweet 'n' Sour Sausage Stir-Fry

(Pictured above right)

I am a product manager and home-school our two children. My family truly enjoys this quick meal. I can have it on the table in about 30 minutes with no thawing and no planning.
—Wendy Wendler, Satellite Beach, Florida

1 package (14 ounces) reduced-fat smoked
  turkey kielbasa, cut into 1/2-inch slices
2 small onions, quartered and separated
1 cup shredded carrots
1 can (8 ounces) unsweetened pineapple chunks
1 tablespoon cornstarch
1/2 to 1 teaspoon ground ginger
6 tablespoons water
2 tablespoons reduced-sodium soy sauce
Hot cooked rice, optional

In a large nonstick skillet, stir-fry sausage for 3-4 minutes or until lightly browned. Add onions and carrots; stir-fry until crisp-tender. Drain pineapple, reserving juice. Add pineapple to sausage mixture.

In a small bowl, combine cornstarch and ginger. Stir in the water, soy sauce and reserved pineapple juice until smooth. Add to the skillet. Bring to a boil; cook and stir for

Curried Chicken

A mild curry sauce complements the tender chicken and sweet apples in this speedy microwave main dish. This rapid recipe is perfect for the working gal. I like to serve it over aromatic basmati rice.
—Janet Boulger, Botwood, Newfoundland

2 tablespoons butter *or* stick margarine
2 to 3 teaspoons curry powder
1 medium onion, finely chopped
2 cups finely chopped peeled apple
1 can (10-3/4 ounces) reduced-fat reduced-
  sodium cream of mushroom soup, undiluted
1/2 cup fat-free milk
1-1/2 pounds boneless skinless chicken breasts,
  cubed
1 can (4 ounces) mushroom stems and pieces,
  drained
1 cup frozen peas
1/8 teaspoon paprika
Hot cooked noodles *or* rice, optional

Place butter in a 2-1/2-qt. microwave-safe dish. Cover and microwave on high for 40-50 seconds or until melted. Stir in curry powder. Add onion and apple; stir until coated. Cover and microwave on high for 2-3 minutes or until crisp-tender, stirring once.

Stir in the soup, milk, chicken and mushrooms; cover and microwave on high for 9-10 minutes or until chicken is no longer pink, stirring twice. Add peas; sprinkle with paprika. Cover and cook 3-4 minutes longer or until peas are tender. Serve over noodles if desired. **Yield:** 6 servings.

Editor's Note: This recipe was tested in an 850-watt microwave.

Nutritional Analysis: One serving (1 cup chicken mixture, calculated without noodles) equals 257 calories, 8 g fat (4 g saturated fat), 82 mg cholesterol, 399 mg sodium, 17 g carbohydrate, 3 g fiber, 29 g protein.
Diabetic Exchanges: 3 lean meat, 1/2 fruit, 1/2 starch, 1/2 fat.

Oriental Turkey Pitas

Tired of turkey sandwiches? Try this fresh-tasting adaptation—a warm spicy stir-fry tucked into pita bread. A neighbor gave me this quick-and-easy recipe years ago. It's been my most popular day-after-turkey dish ever since.
—Beverly Graml, Yorktown, Virginia

1 medium sweet red pepper, julienned
3 green onions, sliced
3 garlic cloves, minced
1 tablespoon canola oil
1/2 teaspoon cornstarch
1/2 to 1-1/2 teaspoons curry powder
1/4 teaspoon cayenne pepper
1/3 cup water
2 tablespoons reduced-sodium soy sauce
1 tablespoon honey
1 teaspoon sesame oil
3 cups shredded cooked turkey
4 whole wheat pita breads (6 inches), halved

In a nonstick skillet, saute the red pepper, onions and garlic in canola oil until vegetables are tender. Sprinkle with cornstarch, curry powder and cayenne; stir until blended. Add the water, soy sauce, honey and sesame oil; stir until blended. Add turkey. Bring to a boil; cook and stir for 1-2 minutes or until slightly thickened. Spoon into pita halves. **Yield:** 4 servings.

Nutritional Analysis: One serving (2 filled pita halves) equals 397 calories, 8 g fat (1 g saturated fat), 90 mg cholesterol, 705 mg sodium, 44 g carbohydrate, 6 g fiber, 39 g protein.
Diabetic Exchanges: 3 lean meat, 2-1/2 starch, 1 vegetable.

Tomato-Basil Chicken Spirals

(Pictured below)

After tasting a wonderful pasta dish at an Italian restaurant, I experimented until I came up with this recipe. It's become one of our favorite low-fat meals. The riper the tomatoes, the better it is!
—Sandra Giguere, Bremen, Maine

2 cups finely chopped sweet onion
1 cup chopped fresh basil
4 garlic cloves, minced
1 tablespoon olive *or* canola oil
5 cups chopped seeded tomatoes
1 can (6 ounces) tomato paste
1/2 teaspoon crushed red pepper flakes
1/2 teaspoon salt
1/4 teaspoon pepper
1 package (16 ounces) spiral pasta
3 cups cubed cooked chicken
1/2 cup shredded Parmesan cheese

In a large saucepan or Dutch oven, saute the onion, basil and garlic in oil until onion is tender. Stir in the tomatoes, tomato paste, red pepper flakes, salt and pepper. Bring to a boil. Reduce heat; cover and simmer for 30-45 minutes.

Meanwhile, cook pasta according to package directions. Add chicken to the tomato mixture; heat through. Drain pasta. Top with chicken mixture; sprinkle with Parmesan cheese. **Yield:** 8 servings.

Nutritional Analysis: One serving (1 cup chicken mixture with 1 cup pasta) equals 373 calories, 6 g fat (2 g saturated fat), 44 mg cholesterol, 291 mg sodium, 53 g carbohydrate, 5 g fiber, 27 g protein.
Diabetic Exchanges: 3 vegetable, 2-1/2 starch, 2 lean meat.

Cajun Stir-Fry

(Pictured below)

Cubes of chicken and chunks of smoked turkey kielbasa, plus plenty of herbs and veggies, make this a hearty stir-fry. I sometimes top off servings with shredded mozzarella cheese and minced basil and parsley.
—Sharon Clemens, Groveland, Illinois

3/4 pound boneless skinless chicken breasts, cut into 1-inch cubes
8 ounces reduced-fat smoked turkey kielbasa, cut into 1/4-inch slices
1 medium onion, chopped
3 garlic cloves, minced
1 tablespoon olive *or* canola oil
1 *each* medium green, sweet red and yellow pepper, coarsely chopped
1 pound fresh mushrooms, sliced
2 medium tomatoes, diced
1/4 cup *each* minced fresh basil, oregano and parsley *or* 4 teaspoons *each* dried basil, oregano and parsley
1-1/2 teaspoons Cajun seasoning
1/2 teaspoon salt
1/4 teaspoon pepper
1 tablespoon cornstarch
2 tablespoons cold water
Hot cooked spaghetti

In a large nonstick skillet, stir-fry the chicken, kielbasa, onion and garlic in oil until onion is tender. Add the peppers, mushrooms, tomatoes, herbs, Cajun seasoning, salt and pepper. Cook and stir until chicken juices run clear and vegetables are crisp-tender.

Sweet 'n' Sour Chicken

(Pictured above)

This entree was served at a special dinner hosted by my Sunday school teacher. The ingredients are simple, but the chicken is tender and tasty. I serve it to company and am often asked for the recipe.
—Christine McDonald, Riverdale, Utah

4 boneless skinless chicken breast halves (4 ounces *each*)
2/3 cup water
1/3 cup sugar
1/4 cup cider vinegar
1/4 cup reduced-sodium soy sauce
1 medium sweet red pepper, cut into 1-inch pieces
1 medium green pepper, cut into 1-inch pieces
2 tablespoons cornstarch
3 tablespoons cold water
Hot cooked rice

Place chicken in a 9-in. square baking dish; set aside. In a saucepan, bring the water, sugar, vinegar and soy sauce to a boil, stirring constantly. Add peppers; return to a boil. Combine cornstarch and cold water until smooth; gradually stir into pepper mixture. Bring to a boil; cook and stir for 1-2 minutes or until thickened. Pour over chicken.
Bake, uncovered, at 350° for 20-25 minutes or until chicken juices run clear, turning once. Serve with rice if desired. **Yield:** 4 servings.

Nutritional Analysis: One serving (1 chicken breast half with 1/2 cup sauce, calculated without rice) equals 231 calories, 2 g fat (trace saturated fat), 66 mg cholesterol, 683 mg sodium, 25 g carbohydrate, 1 g fiber, 28 g protein.
Diabetic Exchanges: 3 very lean meat, 1 starch, 1 vegetable.
△ *Low-fat*

Combine cornstarch and cold water until smooth; add to the skillet. Bring to a boil; cook and stir for 2 minutes or until thickened. Serve over spaghetti. **Yield:** 8 servings.

Nutritional Analysis: One serving (1 cup stir-fry mixture, calculated without spaghetti) equals 140 calories, 4 g fat (1 g saturated fat), 40 mg cholesterol, 555 mg sodium, 11 g carbohydrate, 2 g fiber, 17 g protein.
Diabetic Exchanges: 2 lean meat, 2 vegetable.

Garlic Chicken Kabobs

Tender and moist, these grilled kabobs are extra special when served with garlic dipping sauce. This is a lighter version of a dish my Lebanese mother-in-law taught me to make. I reduced the amount of oil and substituted yogurt for the mayonnaise.
—Sheri Jean Waked, Loveland, Ohio

  8 garlic cloves, minced
1/2 teaspoon salt
1/4 cup minced fresh cilantro *or* parsley
  1 teaspoon ground coriander
1/2 cup reduced-fat plain yogurt
  2 tablespoons lemon juice
1-1/2 teaspoons olive *or* canola oil
  2 pounds boneless skinless chicken breasts, cut into 1-inch cubes
GARLIC DIPPING SAUCE:
  4 garlic cloves, minced
1/4 teaspoon salt
  2 tablespoons olive *or* canola oil
  1 cup (8 ounces) reduced-fat plain yogurt

Place garlic and salt in a small bowl; crush with the back of a sturdy spoon. Add cilantro and coriander; crush together. Add the yogurt, lemon juice and oil; mix well. Pour into a large resealable plastic bag; add the chicken. Seal bag and turn to coat; refrigerate for 2 hours.

For dipping sauce, place garlic and salt in a small bowl; crush with the back of a sturdy spoon. Mix in oil. Stir in yogurt. Cover and refrigerate until serving.

If grilling the chicken, coat grill rack with nonstick cooking spray before starting the grill. Drain and discard marinade. Thread chicken on eight metal or soaked wooden skewers. Grill kabobs, covered, over medium heat or broil 4 in. from the heat for 3-4 minutes on each side or until juices run clear, turning once. Serve with dipping sauce. **Yield:** 8 servings.

Nutritional Analysis: One serving (1 kabob with 2 tablespoons dipping sauce) equals 186 calories, 6 g fat (1 g saturated fat), 68 mg cholesterol, 246 mg sodium, 4 g carbohydrate, trace fiber, 28 g protein.
Diabetic Exchanges: 3 lean meat, 1/2 fat.

Lemony Turkey Breast

(Pictured above)

Lemon and a hint of garlic add a lovely touch to these moist slices of slow-cooked turkey breast. I usually serve the gravy over a combination of white and brown rice, along with broccoli for a healthy meal.
—Lynn Laux, Ballwin, Missouri

  1 bone-in turkey breast (5 pounds), halved
  1 medium lemon, halved
  1 teaspoon salt-free lemon-pepper seasoning
  1 teaspoon garlic salt
  4 teaspoons cornstarch
1/2 cup reduced-sodium chicken broth

Remove skin from turkey. Pat turkey dry with paper towels; spray turkey with nonstick cooking spray. Place breast side up in a slow cooker. Squeeze half of the lemon over turkey; sprinkle with lemon-pepper and garlic salt. Place lemon halves under turkey. Cover and cook on low for 5-7 hours or until meat is no longer pink and a meat thermometer reads 170°. Remove turkey and keep warm. Discard lemon.

For gravy, pour cooking liquid into a measuring cup; skim fat. In a saucepan, combine cornstarch and broth until smooth. Gradually stir in cooking liquid. Bring to a boil; cook and stir for 2 minutes or until thickened. Serve with turkey. **Yield:** 14 servings.

Nutritional Analysis: One serving (4 ounces cooked turkey with 2 tablespoons gravy) equals 154 calories, 1 g fat (trace saturated fat), 92 mg cholesterol, 149 mg sodium, 1 g carbohydrate, trace fiber, 34 g protein.
Diabetic Exchange: 4 very lean meat.
△ *Low-fat*

Barbecued Turkey Sandwiches

These moist shredded turkey sandwiches are a welcome break from beef barbecue or sloppy joes. The turkey cooks in a tangy sauce made with ketchup, vinegar, Worcestershire sauce and mustard.
—Barbara Smith, Columbus, Ohio

1/4 cup chopped onion
1 tablespoon butter *or* stick margarine
3 cups shredded cooked turkey
1/2 cup water
1/2 cup ketchup
1/4 cup red wine vinegar *or* cider vinegar
1 tablespoon sugar
2 teaspoons Worcestershire sauce
1 teaspoon prepared mustard
1 teaspoon paprika
6 kaiser rolls, split

In a large nonstick skillet, saute onion in butter until tender. Add the turkey, water, ketchup, vinegar, sugar, Worcestershire sauce, mustard and paprika. Bring to a boil. Reduce heat; simmer, uncovered, for 15 minutes or until sauce is thickened. Serve on rolls. **Yield:** 6 servings.

Nutritional Analysis: One sandwich equals 340 calories, 8 g fat (3 g saturated fat), 56 mg cholesterol, 637 mg sodium, 39 g carbohydrate, 2 g fiber, 27 g protein.
Diabetic Exchanges: *3 lean meat, 2-1/2 starch.*

Cabbage and Brats

I make this simple stir-fried supper about every other week. Soy sauce and garlic powder add flavor to each bite of turkey bratwurst.
—Melanie Jones, Springfield, Illinois

1 small head cabbage (1-1/2 pounds)
1 large sweet onion
1 package (19-1/2 ounces) turkey bratwurst, casing removed and cut into 1-inch pieces
2 tablespoons reduced-sodium soy sauce
3/4 teaspoon garlic powder
1/2 teaspoon pepper

Cut cabbage in half through the core. Remove core and cut cabbage into 1/4-in. slices; set aside. Cut onion in half and cut into 1/4-in. slices; set aside. In a large nonstick skillet coated with nonstick cooking spray, cook and stir bratwurst over medium-high heat for 8 minutes or until browned on all sides. Drain and remove bratwurst; set aside and keep warm.

Add cabbage and onion to the same skillet; cook and stir for 6 minutes. Sprinkle with soy sauce, garlic powder and pepper. Cook and stir 4 minutes longer. Return bratwurst to skillet. Cook for 2 minutes. Cover; reduce heat and simmer for 5 minutes or until vegetables are tender and bratwurst is cooked through. Serve immediately. **Yield:** 5 servings.

Nutritional Analysis: One serving (1 bratwurst with 1 cup vegetables) equals 274 calories, 16 g fat (4 g saturated fat), 75 mg cholesterol, 929 mg sodium, 19 g carbohydrate, 4 g fiber, 18 g protein.
Diabetic Exchanges: *3 lean meat, 3 vegetable, 1 fat.*

Spicy Turkey Stir-Fry

(Pictured at right)

This is one of my husband's favorite recipes, and he doesn't even know it is good for him! The colorful broccoli and red pepper make it a perfect entree around the holidays.
—Alexandra Armitage, Nottingham, New Hampshire

1 tablespoon cornstarch
1 tablespoon sugar
1 cup reduced-sodium chicken broth
1/4 cup reduced-sodium soy sauce
2 tablespoons cider vinegar
1/8 to 1/4 teaspoon cayenne pepper
3 cups fresh broccoli florets
2 tablespoons water
1 pound boneless skinless turkey breast, cut into 3/4-inch pieces
2 teaspoons canola oil
1 medium sweet red pepper, cut into 3/4-inch pieces
1 garlic clove, minced
1/4 teaspoon ground ginger *or* 1 teaspoon minced fresh gingerroot
2 green onions, sliced
2 tablespoons dry roasted peanuts
Hot cooked rice

In a bowl, combine the first six ingredients until smooth; set aside. Place broccoli and water in a microwave-safe bowl; cover and cook on high for 2-3 minutes. Drain and set aside.

In a nonstick skillet coated with nonstick cooking spray, stir-fry turkey in hot oil for 2-3 minutes. Add sweet pepper, garlic, ginger and broccoli; stir-fry for 3-4 minutes or until vegetables are crisp-tender. Stir broth mixture; add to pan. Bring to a boil; cook and stir for 1-2 minutes or until thickened. Sprinkle with onions and peanuts. Serve with rice. **Yield:** 4 servings.

Nutritional Analysis: One serving (1 cup stir-fry, calculated without rice) equals 233 calories, 6 g fat (1 g saturated fat), 70 mg cholesterol, 866 mg sodium, 13 g carbohydrate, 3 g fiber, 33 g protein.
Diabetic Exchanges: *4 very lean meat, 2 vegetable, 1 fat.*

🍎 Flavorful "Unfried" Chicken

INSTEAD of frying chicken in oil on the stovetop, I place it in a casserole dish coated with nonstick cooking spray. I bake the chicken for 45-60 minutes at 375°. My family likes this healthier, less greasy version as much as regular fried chicken.
—Joy Beck, Cincinnati, Ohio

and bake at 350° for 30 minutes. Uncover; bake 10-15 minutes longer or until juices run clear. **Yield:** 8 servings.

Nutritional Analysis: One serving (1 chicken breast half) equals 207 calories, 7 g fat (2 g saturated fat), 89 mg cholesterol, 638 mg sodium, 1 g carbohydrate, trace fiber, 33 g protein. **Diabetic Exchange:** *4 lean meat.*

Crumb-Coated Chicken Thighs

These spicy roasted chicken thighs don't require a lot of prep time. I often put baking potatoes on the oven rack alongside the chicken. It's a simple satisfying meal.
—Kara De la vega, Suisun City, California

 1/4 cup dry bread crumbs
   1 teaspoon salt
   1 teaspoon ground cumin
   1 teaspoon paprika
   1 teaspoon chili powder
   1 teaspoon curry powder
 1/4 teaspoon pepper
   8 chicken thighs (about 5 ounces *each*), skin removed

In a large resealable plastic bag, combine the first seven ingredients. Add chicken, a few pieces at a time, and shake to coat. Place on a baking sheet coated with nonstick cooking spray. Bake, uncovered, at 400° for 20 minutes. Turn chicken pieces; bake 15-20 minutes longer or until a meat thermometer reads 180°. **Yield:** 4 servings.

Nutritional Analysis: One serving (2 chicken thighs) equals 323 calories, 16 g fat (4 g saturated fat), 131 mg cholesterol, 774 mg sodium, 6 g carbohydrate, 1 g fiber, 37 g protein. **Diabetic Exchanges:** *5 lean meat, 1/2 starch.*

Seasoned Lemon Chicken

(Pictured above)

This herbed chicken has been a family favorite since I clipped the recipe out of a newspaper some years ago. It has passed the supreme test—our teenage grandchildren love it. It's often on our dinner table, since chicken is a staple in my freezer. If I'm out of lemon, I substitute a sprinkling of lemon pepper.
—Mrs. Pat Miller, Joplin, Missouri

   2 tablespoons olive *or* canola oil
   2 bay leaves
   2 teaspoons seasoned salt
 1-1/2 teaspoons *each* garlic salt, pepper, dried basil, tarragon and thyme
 1-1/2 teaspoons dried rosemary, crushed
   8 bone-in chicken breast halves (7 ounces *each*), skin removed
   1 large lemon, thinly sliced
 1/4 cup lemon juice

In a large resealable plastic bag, combine the oil, bay leaves and seasonings. Add chicken. Seal bag and turn to coat; refrigerate for 1 hour.

Discard bay leaves. Place chicken in a 13-in. x 9-in. x 2-in. baking dish coated with nonstick cooking spray. Arrange lemon slices over chicken. Drizzle with lemon juice. Cover

Turkey Casserole

Turkey teams up temptingly with pretty green peas and crunchy water chestnuts in this yummy casserole. Its creamy sauce combined with melted cheese and a golden crouton topping is sure to win you compliments.
—Beth Struble, Bryan, Ohio

   2 cups cubed cooked turkey breast
   1 package (10 ounces) frozen peas, thawed
   1 cup chopped celery
   1 can (8 ounces) sliced water chestnuts, drained
   2 tablespoons chopped green pepper
   1 tablespoon chopped onion
   1 can (10-3/4 ounces) reduced-fat reduced-sodium condensed cream of chicken soup, undiluted
 1/2 cup fat-free milk
   1 cup (4 ounces) shredded reduced-fat cheddar cheese, *divided*
   2 tablespoons white wine *or* chicken broth
   1 tablespoon lemon juice
 1/2 teaspoon salt
   2 slices white bread, cubed

In a large bowl, combine the first six ingredients. In a small saucepan, combine the soup, milk, 1/2 cup cheese, wine or broth, lemon juice and salt. Cook and stir over low heat until smooth and heated through. Pour over turkey mixture; toss to coat.

Transfer to a 2-qt. baking dish coated with nonstick cooking spray. Top with bread cubes. Bake, uncovered, at 375° for 25 minutes. Sprinkle with remaining cheese; bake 5 minutes longer or until cheese is melted. **Yield:** 6 servings.

Nutritional Analysis: One serving (3/4 cup) equals 248 calories, 7 g fat (4 g saturated fat), 48 mg cholesterol, 713 mg sodium, 22 g carbohydrate, 5 g fiber, 24 g protein.
Diabetic Exchanges: 3 lean meat, 1-1/2 starch.

Spicy Honey-Mustard Chicken Stir-Fry

Peanut butter, lime juice, Dijon mustard and cayenne pepper boost the flavor in this tangy chicken dish from our Test Kitchen. Served with or without rice, it's a satisfying supper.

2 teaspoons cornstarch
1/2 cup reduced-sodium chicken broth
2 tablespoons reduced-fat peanut butter
4 teaspoons lime juice
1 tablespoon Dijon mustard
1 tablespoon honey
2 teaspoons reduced-sodium soy sauce
2 teaspoons sesame oil
1/4 teaspoon hot pepper sauce
1/8 teaspoon cayenne pepper
1 pound boneless skinless chicken breasts, cut into thin strips
2 teaspoons canola oil, *divided*
2 small zucchini, sliced
1 medium sweet red pepper, julienned
Hot cooked rice, optional

In a blender or food processor, combine the first 10 ingredients; cover and process until smooth. In a large nonstick skillet, stir-fry chicken in 1 teaspoon hot oil for 5-7 minutes or until juices run clear. Remove chicken and keep warm. In the same skillet, stir-fry vegetables in remaining hot oil until crisp-tender. Return chicken to pan. Stir sauce and add to the pan. Bring to a boil; cook and stir for 1-2 minutes or until thickened. Serve over rice if desired. **Yield:** 4 servings.

Nutritional Analysis: One serving (1 cup stir-fry, calculated without rice) equals 258 calories, 9 g fat (1 g saturated fat), 66 mg cholesterol, 398 mg sodium, 14 g carbohydrate, 2 g fiber, 30 g protein.
Diabetic Exchanges: 4 lean meat, 1 vegetable, 1/2 starch.

Oven Barbecued Chicken

(Pictured below)

A friend made this moist chicken for us when we had our first child. I pared down the recipe to make it lower in fat and calories. It is now a family favorite, and even the kids ask for it.
—Marge Wagner, Roselle, Illinois

6 bone-in skinless chicken breast halves (8 ounces *each*)
1/3 cup chopped onion
3/4 cup ketchup
1/2 cup water
1/3 cup white vinegar
3 tablespoons brown sugar
1 tablespoon Worcestershire sauce
1 teaspoon ground mustard
1/4 teaspoon salt
1/8 teaspoon pepper

In a nonstick skillet coated with nonstick cooking spray, brown chicken over medium heat. Transfer to a 13-in. x 9-in. x 2-in. baking dish coated with nonstick cooking spray.

Recoat skillet with nonstick cooking spray; cook onion over medium heat until tender. Stir in the remaining ingredients. Bring to a boil. Reduce heat; simmer, uncovered, for 15 minutes. Pour over chicken. Bake, uncovered, at 350° for 45-55 minutes or until chicken juices run clear and a meat thermometer reads 170°. **Yield:** 6 servings.

Nutritional Analysis: One serving (1 chicken breast half) equals 241 calories, 4 g fat (1 g saturated fat), 90 mg cholesterol, 563 mg sodium, 17 g carbohydrate, 1 g fiber, 34 g protein.
Diabetic Exchanges: 4 very lean meat, 1 starch.

Cranberry-Orange Turkey Cutlets

(Pictured at right)

Every time I make this, my husband suggests it would be a great company dish. It is easy to prepare, but looks elegant.
—Joan Tweed, Irmo, South Carolina

1 pound turkey breast cutlets
1 cup dry bread crumbs
1 egg white
1 tablespoon fat-free milk
1/2 teaspoon salt
3/4 cup cranberry-orange sauce* *or* **whole-berry cranberry sauce**
1 tablespoon olive *or* **canola oil**

Flatten turkey to 1/4-in. thickness. Place bread crumbs in a shallow bowl. In another bowl, beat the egg white, milk and salt. Dip turkey into egg white mixture, then coat with crumbs. Refrigerate turkey, uncovered, for 10 minutes.

Meanwhile, in a small saucepan, heat cranberry-orange sauce. In a large nonstick skillet, brown turkey in oil for 3-4 minutes on each side or until juices run clear. Serve sauce over turkey. **Yield:** 4 servings.

*Editor's Note: This recipe was tested with Ocean Spray Cranberry-Orange sauce. Look for it in the canned fruit section of your grocery store.

Nutritional Analysis: One serving (4 ounces turkey with 3 tablespoons sauce) equals 399 calories, 9 g fat (1 g saturated fat), 82 mg cholesterol, 609 mg sodium, 44 g carbohydrate, 1 g fiber, 34 g protein.
Diabetic Exchanges: 3 lean meat, 1-1/2 starch, 1-1/2 fruit.

Chicken and Herbs

This recipe is for moist and tender chicken. Nicely seasoned with a variety of herbs, it's easy to prepare...but seems special enough for company.
—Judy Sargent, Rome, New York

4 bone-in chicken breast halves (2 pounds)
2 tablespoons olive *or* **canola oil**
1 tablespoon grated onion
2 garlic cloves, minced
1 teaspoon dried thyme

1/2 teaspoon salt
1/2 teaspoon dried rosemary, crushed
1/2 teaspoon coarsely ground pepper
1/4 teaspoon rubbed sage
1/8 teaspoon dried marjoram
1/8 teaspoon hot pepper sauce
4-1/2 teaspoons minced fresh parsley

Arrange chicken in an 11-in. x 7-in. x 2-in. baking dish coated with nonstick cooking spray. Whisk together the oil, onion, garlic, thyme, salt, rosemary, pepper, sage, marjoram and hot pepper sauce. Pour over chicken. Bake, uncovered, at 425° for 30-40 minutes or until juices run clear and a meat thermometer reads 170°, basting occasionally. Remove and discard skin from chicken. Sprinkle with parsley. Drizzle with juices. **Yield:** 4 servings.

Nutritional Analysis: One serving (1 chicken breast half with 1 tablespoon juice) equals 240 calories, 11 g fat (2 g saturated fat), 90 mg cholesterol, 373 mg sodium, 1 g carbohydrate, trace fiber, 33 g protein.
Diabetic Exchanges: 4 lean meat, 1 fat.

Favorite Chicken Recipe Made Lighter

FOR MOST families across the country, chicken is a tried-and-true main dish that makes a regular appearance on dinner tables. That is certainly true for Helen Copeland of Greenback, Tennessee. And her finger-licking good Butter Roasted Chicken is a family favorite.

"We love this recipe," she says. "The chicken is always juicy and flavorful. But I don't like all the butter that's used to make it, because I know it's fattening and not heart-healthy. Is there a way to cut the fat and calories from this dish, but not all the flavor and juiciness?"

Our Test Kitchen staff was eager to tackle the challenge. For starters, they removed the skin from the chicken. This not only lowered the fat, it allowed the meat to pick up more flavor from the lemony basting sauce.

The sauce itself was lightened by decreasing the butter from 1/2 cup to 1 tablespoon and by adding chicken broth to make up for the loss of moisture. To keep the flavor of the sauce balanced, both the lemon juice and the salt were reduced.

Those changes slashed the fat by 70% and saturated fat by 80%, cut calories and sodium by about half and reduced cholesterol by more than a third. Yet the buttery-tasting makeover version is sure to please Helen's family and yours.

Butter Roasted Chicken

1 broiler/fryer chicken (2-1/2 pounds), cut up
1/2 cup butter *or* margarine
1/3 cup lemon juice
1 tablespoon paprika
2 teaspoons salt
1 teaspoon brown sugar
1 teaspoon pepper
1/2 teaspoon dried rosemary, crushed
1/8 teaspoon ground nutmeg
1/8 teaspoon cayenne pepper

Place chicken in an ungreased 13-in. x 9-in. x 2-in. baking dish. Combine the remaining ingredients in a small saucepan; bring to a boil. Remove from the heat and pour over chicken. Bake, uncovered, at 325° for 1 to 1-1/4 hours or until juices run clear, basting occasionally. **Yield:** 4 servings.

Nutritional Analysis: One serving (5 ounces cooked chicken) equals 547 calories, 43 g fat (20 g saturated fat), 174 mg cholesterol, 1,516 mg sodium, 4 g carbohydrate, 1 g fiber, 36 g protein.

Makeover Butter Roasted Chicken

(Pictured below)

1 broiler/fryer chicken (2-1/2 pounds), cut up and skin removed
1/2 cup reduced-sodium chicken broth
1/4 cup lemon juice
1 tablespoon butter *or* stick margarine
1 tablespoon paprika
1 teaspoon salt
1 teaspoon brown sugar
1/2 teaspoon pepper
1/2 teaspoon dried rosemary, crushed
1/8 teaspoon ground nutmeg
1/8 teaspoon cayenne pepper

Place chicken in an ungreased 13-in. x 9-in. x 2-in. baking dish. Combine the remaining ingredients in a small saucepan; bring to a boil. Remove from the heat and pour over chicken. Cover and bake at 325° for 1 to 1-1/4 hours or until juices run clear, basting occasionally. **Yield:** 4 servings.

Nutritional Analysis: One serving (5 ounces cooked skinless chicken) equals 281 calories, 13 g fat (4 g saturated fat), 115 mg cholesterol, 802 mg sodium, 4 g carbohydrate, 1 g fiber, 37 g protein.
Diabetic Exchange: 5 lean meat.

hour. Add pasta; heat through. Top each serving with 1 tablespoon mozzarella cheese. **Yield:** 8 servings.

Nutritional Analysis: One serving (1-1/2 cups) equals 300 calories, 12 g fat (4 g saturated fat), 65 mg cholesterol, 1,237 mg sodium, 22 g carbohydrate, 3 g fiber, 25 g protein.
Diabetic Exchanges: 3 lean meat, 2 vegetable, 1 starch.

Pineapple Chicken with Spaghetti

The recipe for this stir-fry is full of crisp-tender veggies.
Chunks of pineapple add a colorful burst
of fruity goodness to every forkful.
—Cheryl Harris, Canton, Ohio

    8 ounces uncooked spaghetti, broken in half
    1 can (20 ounces) unsweetened pineapple chunks
    1 large green pepper, julienned
    2 medium carrots, thinly sliced
    3 green onions, chopped
3/4 teaspoon ground ginger *or* 1 tablespoon minced fresh gingerroot
    1 tablespoon canola oil
    1 pound boneless skinless chicken breasts, cut into 1-inch strips
    1 garlic clove, minced
    4 teaspoons cornstarch
1/4 cup reduced-sodium soy sauce

Cook spaghetti according to package directions; drain. Drain pineapple, reserving juice; set aside. In a large nonstick skillet or wok, stir-fry green pepper, carrots, onions and ginger in oil for 3 minutes. Add chicken and garlic; stir-fry for 5 minutes or until chicken is no longer pink. Add the spaghetti and pineapple; stir-fry for 1 minute.

In a small bowl, combine the cornstarch, soy sauce and reserved pineapple juice until smooth; pour over chicken mixture. Bring to a boil; cook and stir for 2 minutes or until thickened. **Yield:** 6 servings.

Italian Stew

(Pictured above)

Spice up autumn evenings with this zippy stew,
a blend of Italian turkey sausage, seasoned tomato
broth, pasta and veggies. This reheats well
and tastes even better the next day.
—Nancy Cox, Martinsville, Indiana

    2 pounds turkey Italian sausage links, casings removed
    1 cup chopped onion
3/4 cup chopped green pepper
    3 garlic cloves, minced
    1 can (28 ounces) diced tomatoes, undrained
    1 can (15 ounces) Italian-seasoned tomato sauce
1/2 pound fresh mushrooms, sliced
    1 cup water
1/2 cup beef broth
1/2 cup red wine *or* additional beef broth
1-1/2 cups cooked spiral pasta
1/2 cup reduced-fat shredded mozzarella cheese

In a large nonstick saucepan coated with nonstick cooking spray, cook the sausage, onion, green pepper and garlic until meat is no longer pink; drain. Add the tomatoes, tomato sauce, mushrooms, water, broth and wine or additional broth. Bring to a boil. Reduce heat; cover and simmer for 1

Using Leftover Turkey

SOME FOLKS look forward to leftover turkey as much as they enjoy the main meal itself. So the next time you have a bit of the bird left in your refrigerator, consider the following:

- The majority of turkey's fat can be found in its skin. Be sure to remove the skin from leftover turkey before adding the meat to the dish you're preparing.
- Think beyond sandwiches. Slice cooked turkey breast into strips and reheat it with some salsa. Wrap the mixture in a tortilla with reduced-fat cheese. Or, cube last night's turkey, stir-fry it with veggies in low-sodium soy sauce and serve over rice.

Nutritional Analysis: One serving (1-1/3 cups) equals 346 calories, 5 g fat (1 g saturated fat), 45 mg cholesterol, 464 mg sodium, 50 g carbohydrate, 4 g fiber, 23 g protein.
Diabetic Exchanges: 3 very lean meat, 2 starch, 1 fruit, 1 vegetable.

Mexican Pizza

I impressed my wife-to-be with this homemade pizza on our very first date...and we've been cooking together ever since. Since Angela's family is Mexican-American, and I'm from the Midwest, I combined flavors from both backgrounds in this pizza.
—Patrick Conyers, Iowa City, Iowa

1-1/4 to 1-1/2 cups all-purpose flour
1/3 cup cornmeal
1 package (1/4 ounce) active dry yeast
1 teaspoon salt
1/8 teaspoon sugar
1/4 cup water
1/4 cup fat-free milk
2 tablespoons olive *or* canola oil
TOPPING:
1 cup salsa
3/4 cup canned black beans, rinsed and drained
2 cups cubed cooked chicken breast
1 small onion, thinly sliced
1 can (4 ounces) chopped green chilies
2 cups (8 ounces) shredded reduced-fat Mexican cheese blend
1 medium tomato, seeded and chopped
1 jalapeno pepper, seeded and chopped*
1 tablespoon minced fresh cilantro *or* parsley

In a mixing bowl, combine 1/2 cup flour, cornmeal, yeast, salt and sugar. In a saucepan, heat water, milk and oil to 120°-130°. Add to dry ingredients; beat until smooth. Beat in enough remaining flour to form a soft dough. Turn onto a floured surface; knead until smooth and elastic, about 6-8 minutes. Place in a bowl coated with nonstick cooking spray, turning once to coat top. Cover and let rise in a warm place until doubled, about 1 hour.

Punch dough down. On a floured surface, roll dough into a 13-in. circle. Transfer to a 14-in. pizza pan coated with nonstick cooking spray; build up edges slightly. Prick dough several times with a fork. Bake at 400° for 8-10 minutes or until lightly browned. Spread salsa over crust. Top with the beans, chicken, onion, chilies, cheese, tomato, jalapeno and cilantro. Bake 12-15 minutes longer or until crust is golden brown and cheese is melted. **Yield:** 8 slices.

*Editor's Note: When cutting or seeding hot peppers, use rubber or plastic gloves to protect your hands. Avoid touching your face.

Nutritional Analysis: One slice equals 302 calories, 10 g fat (4 g saturated fat), 40 mg cholesterol, 877 mg sodium, 30 g carbohydrate, 3 g fiber, 24 g protein.
Diabetic Exchanges: 3 lean meat, 2 starch.

Baked Chicken Fajitas

(Pictured below)

I can't remember when or where I found this recipe, but I've used it nearly every week since. We like it with hot sauce for added spice.
—Amy Trinkle, Milwaukee, Wisconsin

1 pound boneless skinless chicken breasts, cut into thin strips
1 can (14-1/2 ounces) diced tomatoes with green chilies, drained
1 medium onion, cut into thin strips
1 medium green pepper, cut into thin strips
1 medium sweet red pepper, cut into thin strips
2 tablespoons canola oil
2 teaspoons chili powder
2 teaspoons ground cumin
1/4 teaspoon salt
12 flour tortillas (6 inches), warmed

In a 13-in. x 9-in. x 2-in. baking dish coated with nonstick cooking spray, combine the chicken, tomatoes, onion and peppers. Combine the oil, chili powder, cumin and salt. Drizzle over chicken mixture; toss to coat. Bake, uncovered, at 400° for 20-25 minutes or until chicken is no longer pink and vegetables are tender. Spoon onto tortillas; fold in sides. **Yield:** 6 servings.

Nutritional Analysis: Two fajitas equals 340 calories, 8 g fat (1 g saturated fat), 44 mg cholesterol, 330 mg sodium, 41 g carbohydrate, 5 g fiber, 27 g protein.
Diabetic Exchanges: 2 starch, 2 lean meat, 2 vegetable, 1/2 fat.

Sprinkle with salt and pepper. Bake, uncovered, at 350° for 55-65 minutes or until juices run clear, basting occasionally with reserved marinade. **Yield:** 6 servings.

Nutritional Analysis: One serving (1 chicken breast half) equals 200 calories, 6 g fat (1 g saturated fat), 79 mg cholesterol, 462 mg sodium, 7 g carbohydrate, trace fiber, 29 g protein. Diabetic Exchanges: 4 very lean meat, 1/2 starch, 1/2 fat.

Honey Rosemary Chicken

(Pictured above)

I never get tired of finding new ways to cook with herbs! A rosemary marinade sweetened with honey gives this moist chicken wonderful flavor and a pretty golden sheen.
—Elsie Barton, Hoover, Alabama

1/4 cup honey
1/4 cup balsamic vinegar
1/4 cup minced fresh rosemary
  2 tablespoons olive *or* canola oil
  6 bone-in skinless chicken breast halves (7 ounces *each*)
  1 teaspoon salt
1/4 teaspoon pepper

In a bowl, combine the honey, vinegar, rosemary and oil; mix well. Pour half of the marinade into a large resealable plastic bag; add the chicken. Seal bag and turn to coat; refrigerate for 2 hours. Cover and refrigerate remaining marinade.

Drain and discard marinade from chicken. Place chicken bone side down in a 13-in. x 9-in. x 2-in. baking pan.

🍎 Harvesting Herbs from the Garden

COOKING with appealing herbs is an ideal way to get mouths watering—whether family members are on special diets or not. Keep the following in mind the next time you're growing, purchasing or cooking with one of your fragrant favorites.

● Harvest homegrown herbs before the plants begin to flower. Picking leaves regularly encourages herb plants to grow.

● If you purchase fresh herbs from a farmer's market or grocery store, select those that have firm stalks with leaves that are not yellowing, bruised or wilted.

● Remember that dried herbs are much stronger than fresh herbs. To substitute dried herbs when fresh herbs are called for in a recipe, use 1 teaspoon of crumbled dried leaves for every tablespoon of finely chopped fresh herbs.

● If you'd like to add herbs to a recipe but aren't sure which would best complement your dish, consider a small amount of basil, parsley or thyme. These versatile herbs work well with many flavors.

Pork & Lamb Favorites

Lean cuts of pork and lamb
are ideal for people who are
eating a little lighter. Plus, with
a quick cooking time, versatile pork
and lamb are mealtime mainstays.

Jamaican Pork Tenderloin (page 151)

Easy Barbecued Pork Chops

This is my favorite "penny pincher" skillet supper. Sweet red peppers add color and flavor to this main dish, but when I'm watching our budget, I use less expensive green peppers.
—Jorie Welch, Acworth, Georgia

   4 bone-in pork loin chops (6 ounces *each*)
   2 teaspoons canola oil
   1 medium green pepper, chopped
2/3 cup chopped celery
1/3 cup chopped onion
   1 cup ketchup
1/4 cup packed brown sugar
1/4 cup reduced-sodium chicken broth
   2 tablespoons chili powder

In a large nonstick skillet, brown pork chops in oil over medium-high heat. Remove chops and keep warm. Add green pepper, celery and onion to the skillet; cook and stir until vegetables begin to soften.

Return chops to the pan. In a bowl, combine ketchup, brown sugar, broth and chili powder. Pour over chops and vegetables. Bring to a boil. Reduce heat; cover and simmer for 30 minutes or until meat is tender. **Yield:** 4 servings.

Nutritional Analysis: *One serving (1 pork chop with 1/3 cup sauce) equals 312 calories, 9 g fat (2 g saturated fat), 66 mg cholesterol, 867 mg sodium, 35 g carbohydrate, 3 g fiber, 24 g protein.*
Diabetic Exchanges: *3 lean meat, 2 starch.*

Pork Cabbage Stir-Fry

(Pictured above)

The ginger comes through nicely in this colorful stir-fry that is lower in fat and sodium than many. It's great served over steamed rice or cooked noodles.
—Marcie Nor, Macungie, Pennsylvania

      4 teaspoons cornstarch
1-1/2 teaspoons sugar
   1/4 cup white wine *or* chicken broth
      3 tablespoons reduced-sodium soy sauce
      1 pound boneless pork loin, cut into 2-inch strips
      4 teaspoons canola oil
      1 cup thinly sliced carrots
      2 garlic cloves, minced
      1 teaspoon ground ginger
1-1/2 pounds Chinese *or* napa cabbage, thinly sliced
Hot cooked rice

In a bowl, combine the cornstarch and sugar. Stir in wine or broth and soy sauce until smooth; set aside. In a large nonstick skillet or wok, stir-fry pork in oil until lightly browned. Add carrots, garlic and ginger; stir-fry for 2 minutes. Add cabbage; stir-fry until cabbage is wilted. Stir soy sauce mixture; add to skillet. Bring to a boil; cook and stir for 2 minutes or until thickened. Serve with rice. **Yield:** 4 servings.

Nutritional Analysis: *One serving (1 cup stir-fry mixture, calculated without rice) equals 312 calories, 12 g fat (3 g saturated fat), 63 mg cholesterol, 550 mg sodium, 19 g carbohydrate, 6 g fiber, 30 g protein.*
Diabetic Exchanges: *3 lean meat, 3 vegetable, 1 fat.*

Rosemary Seasoned Lamb

I most often use this pleasant rosemary spice blend on lamb. But the versatile rub also tastes terrific on pork, chicken and firm fish.
—Caroline Layton, Brevard, North Carolina

   2 tablespoons chopped fresh rosemary
   1 teaspoon coarsely ground pepper
3/4 teaspoon salt
1/2 teaspoon ground mustard
1/2 teaspoon dried oregano
1/2 teaspoon garlic powder
1/4 teaspoon white pepper
1/8 teaspoon cayenne pepper
   1 boneless leg of lamb (about 4 pounds)

In a blender or spice mill, combine the first eight ingredients; cover and process until coarsely ground. Untie leg of lamb and unroll. Rub spice blend over both sides of meat. Reroll and tie with kitchen string.

Place on a rack in a shallow roasting pan. Bake, uncovered, at 350° for 1-3/4 to 2-1/4 hours or until meat reaches desired doneness (for rare, a meat thermometer should read 140°; medium, 160°; well-done, 170°). Transfer to a serving platter. Let stand for 10-15 minutes before slicing. **Yield:** 12 servings.

Nutritional Analysis: *One serving (3 ounces cooked seasoned lamb) equals 181 calories, 8 g fat (3 g saturated fat), 81 mg cholesterol, 209 mg sodium, trace carbohydrate, trace fiber, 25 g protein.*
Diabetic Exchange: *3 lean meat.*

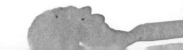

Foil Fixin's

GRILLING foods in aluminum foil makes cleanup a snap. Try one of these ideas from the Reynolds Kitchens:

- For steamed vegetables, wrap a combination of your favorite fresh sliced veggies and one to two ice cubes in heavy-duty aluminum foil and cook on a covered grill about 20 minutes.
- To heat baked beans or sauces on the grill, mold a stack of three sheets of heavy-duty foil around a coffee can to form a saucepan shape. Remove the can and fill the foil pan with the beans or sauce.
- Shape foil around delicate fish to form a "boat" to keep the fish from falling through the grill rack.
- For fajitas, wrap slices of onion and green pepper in a foil packet and grill just until tender. Grill steak or chicken alongside on the rack. Wrap tortillas in foil and heat on the grill just before filling and serving the fajitas.

Pork with Sugar Snap Peas

Tender pork slices are paired with pretty peas in this fast-to-fix stovetop supper. Molasses adds a slightly sweet flavor to the saucy mixture.
—*Erin Anderson, Far Hills, New Jersey*

     1 pound pork tenderloin, cut into 1/4-inch slices
     2 garlic cloves, minced
     2 teaspoons olive *or* canola oil
    10 ounces fresh *or* frozen sugar snap peas
     3 tablespoons reduced-sodium soy sauce
     2 tablespoons white wine vinegar *or* white vinegar
     1 tablespoon molasses
   3/4 teaspoon ground ginger *or* 1 tablespoon minced fresh gingerroot
   1/4 teaspoon crushed red pepper flakes
Hot cooked rice

In a nonstick skillet, stir-fry pork and garlic in hot oil for 6 minutes or until meat is no longer pink. Remove from skillet. In same pan, cook the peas in soy sauce, vinegar, molasses, ginger and red pepper flakes for 4 minutes or until peas are crisp-tender. Return pork to pan; cook for 3 minutes or until glazed. Serve over rice. **Yield:** 4 servings.

Nutritional Analysis: One serving (1 cup stir-fry, calculated without rice) equals 226 calories, 6 g fat (2 g saturated fat), 67 mg cholesterol, 513 mg sodium, 10 g carbohydrate, 2 g fiber, 27 g protein.
Diabetic Exchanges: 3 lean meat, 1 vegetable, 1/2 starch.

Pork 'n' Veggie Packets

(Pictured below)

I love the flavor of grilled food, especially these no-mess pork packets with their delicious sesame and ginger sauce. Since the doctor put my husband on a low-fat diet, this all-in-one meal has become a favorite of ours.
—*Andrea Bolden, Unionville, Tennessee*

     1 pound pork tenderloin, sliced
     2 cups broccoli florets
     2 cups sliced carrots
     1 can (8 ounces) sliced water chestnuts, drained
     1 medium green pepper, julienned
     2 green onions, sliced
   1/4 cup reduced-sodium soy sauce
     4 teaspoons sesame oil
     1 teaspoon ground ginger
Hot cooked rice, optional

Divide pork, broccoli, carrots, water chestnuts, green pepper and onions evenly among four pieces of double-layered heavy-duty foil (about 18 in. x 12 in.). Combine the soy sauce, sesame oil and ginger; drizzle over pork and vegetables. Fold foil around filling and seal tightly.

Grill, covered, over medium heat for 8-10 minutes or until vegetables are tender and pork is no longer pink. Serve with rice if desired. **Yield:** 4 servings.

Nutritional Analysis: One serving (one packet, calculated without rice) equals 265 calories, 9 g fat (2 g saturated fat), 67 mg cholesterol, 621 mg sodium, 19 g carbohydrate, 7 g fiber, 27 g protein.
Diabetic Exchanges: 3 lean meat, 2 vegetable, 1/2 starch.

Fruited Pork

I came across this saucy stir-fry many years ago when I was a working mother and my mealtime preparation was limited.
—Vaunda Box, American Fork, Utah

  1 can (20 ounces) pineapple tidbits
3/4 cup water, *divided*
1/2 cup fat-free Catalina salad dressing
  2 tablespoons reduced-sodium soy sauce
  1 teaspoon white vinegar
  2 tablespoons cornstarch
1-1/2 pounds boneless pork loin chops, cut into thin strips
  1 tablespoon canola oil
  1 medium green pepper, chopped
1/2 cup sliced onion
Hot cooked rice, optional

Drain pineapple, reserving juice; set pineapple aside. In a bowl, combine 1/2 cup water, salad dressing, soy sauce, vinegar and reserved pineapple juice; set aside. In a small bowl, combine cornstarch and remaining water until smooth; set aside.

In a large nonstick skillet or wok, stir-fry pork in oil until no longer pink. Add the green pepper, onion and pineapple; stir-fry for 5 minutes or until vegetables begin to soften. Stir in salad dressing mixture; bring to a boil. Reduce heat; simmer, uncovered, for 5-7 minutes or until vegetables are crisp-tender. Stir cornstarch mixture and add to the pan. Bring to a boil; cook and stir for 2 minutes or until thickened. Serve over rice if desired. **Yield:** 6 servings.

Nutritional Analysis: One serving (1 cup stir-fry mixture, calculated without rice) equals 273 calories, 8 g fat (2 g saturated fat), 62 mg cholesterol, 462 mg sodium, 26 g carbohydrate, 2 g fiber, 25 g protein.
Diabetic Exchanges: 3 lean meat, 1 fruit, 1/2 starch.

Pork Paprika

A nicely spiced sauce with tomatoes seasons pork in this hearty entree. I often scramble to put a meal on the table, but this comes together quickly.
—Monette Johnson, San Antonio, Texas

  1 pork tenderloin (1 pound), cut into cubes
  1 tablespoon canola oil
  1 large onion, chopped
  1 medium green pepper, chopped
  2 garlic cloves, minced
  1 can (14-1/2 ounces) diced tomatoes, undrained
1/2 cup dry white wine *or* chicken broth
  4 teaspoons paprika
  1 teaspoon sugar
  1 teaspoon grated lemon peel, optional
1/2 teaspoon caraway seeds
1/2 teaspoon dried marjoram
1/4 teaspoon salt
1/4 teaspoon pepper
Hot cooked noodles, optional
1/4 cup reduced-fat sour cream

In a large nonstick skillet, cook pork in oil until no longer pink; remove and keep warm. Add the onion, green pepper and garlic to pan; cook and stir until crisp-tender. Add the next nine ingredients; bring to a boil. Reduce heat; cover and simmer for 10-15 minutes or until slightly thickened. Stir in pork. Serve over noodles if desired. Dollop with sour cream. **Yield:** 4 servings.

Nutritional Analysis: One serving (1 cup pork mixture with 1 tablespoon sour cream, calculated without noodles) equals 255 calories, 10 g fat (3 g saturated fat), 73 mg cholesterol, 380 mg sodium, 13 g carbohydrate, 3 g fiber, 27 g protein.
Diabetic Exchanges: 3 lean meat, 2 vegetable, 1 fat.

Braised Pork Chops

(Pictured below)

I'm always looking for recipes that are low-calorie and sugar- and salt-free to fix for my husband—he's diabetic and prone to high blood pressure.
—Shirley Antaya, Arab, Alabama

1/2 teaspoon dried marjoram
1/8 teaspoon onion powder
1/8 teaspoon garlic powder
1/8 teaspoon pepper
  4 bone-in pork loin chops (6 ounces *each* and 3/4 inch thick)
  1 teaspoon olive *or* canola oil
1/2 cup water
  2 teaspoons cornstarch
1/4 cup reduced-sodium chicken broth

Combine seasonings; sprinkle over pork chops. In a non-stick skillet, cook chops in oil until browned on both sides. Add water. Bring to a boil. Reduce heat; cover and simmer for 45-60 minutes or until tender. Remove meat and keep warm. Combine cornstarch and broth until smooth; stir into cooking juices. Bring to a boil; cook and stir for 2 minutes or until thickened. Serve over pork chops. **Yield:** 4 servings.

Nutritional Analysis: One serving (1 pork chop with 2 tablespoons gravy) equals 180 calories, 9 g fat (3 g saturated fat), 67 mg cholesterol, 83 mg sodium, 1 g carbohydrate, trace fiber, 23 g protein.
Diabetic Exchange: 3 lean meat.
▲ *Low-sodium*

Jamaican Pork Tenderloin

(Pictured on page 147)

A spicy citrus marinade adds plenty of flavor to the tenderloin overnight. Then you can grill the meat in just minutes the next day.
—Rosetta Hockett, Colorado Springs, Colorado

1/3 cup orange juice
1/3 cup reduced-sodium soy sauce
3 tablespoons lemon juice
2 tablespoons olive *or* canola oil
1 large onion, chopped
1 cup chopped green onions
1 jalapeno pepper*
3 tablespoons minced fresh thyme *or* 2 teaspoons dried thyme
3/4 teaspoon salt
3/4 teaspoon *each* ground allspice, cinnamon and nutmeg
1/4 teaspoon ground ginger *or* 2 teaspoons minced fresh gingerroot
1/4 teaspoon pepper
2 pork tenderloins (1 pound *each*)

In a food processor, combine the orange juice, soy sauce, lemon juice, oil, onion, green onions, jalapeno, thyme, salt, allspice, cinnamon, nutmeg, ginger and pepper. Cover and process until smooth. Pour into a large resealable plastic bag; add the pork. Seal bag and turn to coat; refrigerate overnight.

Coat grill rack with nonstick cooking spray before starting the grill. Drain and discard marinade from pork. Grill, covered, over indirect medium heat for 20-25 minutes or until a meat thermometer reads 160°. Let stand for 5 minutes before slicing. **Yield:** 6 servings.

***Editor's Note:** For a milder marinade, remove the seeds from the jalapeno. While seeding, use rubber or plastic gloves to protect your hands; avoid touching your face.

Nutritional Analysis: One serving (4 ounces cooked pork) equals 225 calories, 8 g fat (2 g saturated fat), 90 mg cholesterol, 481 mg sodium, 4 g carbohydrate, 1 g fiber, 33 g protein.
Diabetic Exchange: 4 lean meat.

Ham and Noodle Casserole

(Pictured above)

Cottage cheese is the secret to this creamy pasta casserole that has lots of colorful frozen veggies and ham. Add a green salad and fruit for dessert for a complete meal.
—Ruth Hastings, Louisville, Illinois

6 ounces uncooked yolk-free fine noodles
1-1/2 cups (12 ounces) 1% small-curd cottage cheese
1 package (10 ounces) frozen mixed vegetables, thawed and drained
1 cup cubed fully cooked lean ham
3/4 cup reduced-fat sour cream
1/4 cup fat-free milk
3 tablespoons grated Parmesan cheese
2 teaspoons all-purpose flour
1 teaspoon dill weed *or* 1 tablespoon snipped fresh dill
1/4 teaspoon salt

Cook noodles according to package directions; drain. In a large bowl, combine the remaining ingredients. Add noodles and toss to coat. Transfer to a 2-qt. baking dish coated with nonstick cooking spray. Cover and bake at 350° for 30 minutes. Uncover; bake 5-10 minutes longer or until heated through. Let stand for 5 minutes before serving. **Yield:** 4 servings.

Nutritional Analysis: One serving (1-1/2 cups) equals 266 calories, 5 g fat (3 g saturated fat), 21 mg cholesterol, 702 mg sodium, 32 g carbohydrate, 3 g fiber, 21 g protein.
Diabetic Exchanges: 2 lean meat, 1-1/2 starch, 1 vegetable.

Savory Pork Roast

(Pictured above)

Seasoned with a flavorful rub of sage, oregano, thyme and nutmeg, this mouth-watering roast is perfect for special occasions. The impressive entree will have guests asking for seconds.
—Edith Fisher, Leyden, Massachusetts

      2 teaspoons dried rosemary, crushed
      2 teaspoons salt
1-1/2 teaspoons dried oregano
1-1/2 teaspoons dried thyme
1-1/2 teaspoons rubbed sage
   1/4 teaspoon ground nutmeg
   1/4 teaspoon pepper
      1 bone-in pork loin roast (5 pounds)
      1 cup sliced onion
      1 cup sliced carrots

In a small bowl, combine the first seven ingredients. With a sharp knife, cut 1/2-in.-deep slits in fat side of roast. Rub spice mixture into slits and over roast. Place roast fat side up in a shallow roasting pan. Place onion and carrots around roast. Bake, uncovered, at 350° for 1-3/4 to 2-1/4 hours or until a meat thermometer reads 160°. Let stand for 10 minutes before carving. **Yield:** 12 servings.

Nutritional Analysis: *One serving (4 ounces cooked pork) equals 219 calories, 10 g fat (4 g saturated fat), 83 mg cholesterol, 459 mg sodium, 1 g carbohydrate, 1 g fiber, 29 g protein.*
Diabetic Exchange: *4 lean meat.*

Teriyaki Pork

Season tender pork loin and an assortment of crisp-tender vegetables with a soy sauce and garlic marinade for this savory stir-fry.
—Molly Gee, Plainwell, Michigan

3/4 cup reduced-sodium chicken broth, *divided*
1/3 cup reduced-sodium soy sauce
   2 tablespoons red wine vinegar *or* cider vinegar
   2 teaspoons honey
   2 teaspoons garlic powder
   1 pound boneless pork loin chops, cut into thin strips
   1 tablespoon canola oil
   2 cups broccoli florets
   3 medium carrots, sliced
   3 celery ribs, sliced
   4 cups shredded cabbage
   6 green onions, sliced
   1 tablespoon cornstarch
Hot cooked rice, optional

In a bowl, combine 1/4 cup broth, soy sauce, vinegar, honey and garlic powder; mix well. Pour 1/3 cup marinade into a large resealable plastic bag; add the pork. Seal bag and turn to coat; refrigerate for 1 hour. Cover and refrigerate remaining marinade.

Drain and discard marinade from pork. In a large non-stick skillet or wok, stir-fry pork in oil for 2-3 minutes or until no longer pink. Remove and keep warm. In the same pan, stir-fry broccoli and carrots in reserved marinade for 2 minutes. Add celery; stir-fry for 2 minutes. Add cabbage and green onions; stir-fry 2-3 minutes longer or until vegetables are crisp-tender.

Combine cornstarch and remaining broth until smooth; stir into vegetable mixture. Bring to a boil; cook and stir until thickened. Return pork to the pan; heat through. Serve over rice if desired. **Yield:** 4 servings.

Nutritional Analysis: *One serving (1-1/2 cups stir-fry mixture, calculated without rice) equals 302 calories, 11 g fat (3 g saturated fat), 63 mg cholesterol, 802 mg sodium, 20 g carbohydrate, 5 g fiber, 30 g protein.*
Diabetic Exchanges: *3 lean meat, 3 vegetable, 1/2 starch, 1/2 fat.*

Light Linguine Carbonara

(Pictured below)

We're a busy family. When we need to rush off to an evening sporting event or meeting, I prepare this pasta toss along with breadsticks or garlic toast for a quick light dinner.
—Mary Jo Nikolaus, Mansfield, Ohio

    8 ounces uncooked linguine
    1 egg, lightly beaten
    1 cup fat-free evaporated milk
    1/4 cup finely chopped sweet red pepper
    1/8 teaspoon crushed red pepper flakes
    1/8 teaspoon pepper
    1/2 cup grated Parmesan cheese, *divided*
    1/2 cup frozen peas, thawed
    2 bacon strips, cooked and crumbled

Cook linguine according to package directions. Meanwhile, in a small saucepan, combine the next five ingredients. Cook and stir over medium-low heat until mixture reaches 160° and coats the back of a metal spoon. Stir in 1/4 cup Parmesan cheese, peas and bacon; heat through. Drain linguine; toss with sauce. Sprinkle with the remaining Parmesan cheese. **Yield:** 4 servings.

Nutritional Analysis: One serving (1 cup) equals 352 calories, 7 g fat (3 g saturated fat), 66 mg cholesterol, 349 mg sodium, 52 g carbohydrate, 3 g fiber, 20 g protein.
Diabetic Exchanges: 3 starch, 1 lean meat, 1 fat, 1/2 fat-free milk.

Curtail Your Use of Cream

AS a replacement for heavy cream, I thicken low-fat milk with flour and use it in cooked dishes, such as soups, sauces and casseroles.

Generally, I blend 1 tablespoon flour into 1 cup milk, which provides the consistency of heavy cream without the fat. I adjust the amount depending on the desired end result. With most of my recipes, there are so many other great flavors involved that no one notices whether I've used real cream or not.
—Suzanne Appleyard
Queensbury, New York

Herb-Stuffed Pork Loin

I serve this pork roast often when I'm entertaining company. It's especially good with garden-fresh herbs, but dried work nicely as well. It makes a stunning presentation.
—Michele Montgomery, Lethbridge, Alberta

    1 boneless pork loin roast (3 pounds)
    1/4 cup Dijon mustard
    4 garlic cloves, minced
    1/3 cup minced chives
    1/4 cup minced fresh sage *or* 4 teaspoons rubbed
       sage
    2 tablespoons minced fresh thyme *or* 2
       teaspoons dried thyme
    1 tablespoon minced fresh rosemary *or* 1
       teaspoon dried rosemary, crushed
 2-3/4 teaspoons pepper, *divided*
    1 teaspoon salt, *divided*
    1 tablespoon olive *or* canola oil

Starting about a third in from one side, make a lengthwise slit down the roast to within 1/2 in. of the bottom. Turn roast over and make another lengthwise slit starting about a third in from the opposite side. Open roast so it lies flat; cover with plastic wrap. Flatten to 3/4-in. thickness; remove plastic wrap.

Combine mustard and garlic; rub two-thirds of the mustard mixture over roast. Combine the chives, sage, thyme, rosemary, 3/4 teaspoon pepper and 1/2 teaspoon salt. Sprinkle two-thirds of the herb mixture over roast. Roll up jelly-roll style, starting with a long side; tie several times with kitchen string. Rub oil over roast; sprinkle with remaining salt and pepper.

Coat grill rack with nonstick cooking spray before starting the grill. Grill, covered, over indirect medium heat or bake, uncovered, at 350° for 1 hour. Brush roast with remaining mustard mixture and sprinkle with remaining herbs. Grill or bake 20-25 minutes longer or until a meat thermometer reads 160°. Let stand for 10 minutes before slicing. **Yield:** 12 servings.

Nutritional Analysis: One serving (3 ounces cooked pork) equals 199 calories, 10 g fat (3 g saturated fat), 69 mg cholesterol, 372 mg sodium, 2 g carbohydrate, trace fiber, 25 g protein.
Diabetic Exchange: 3 lean meat.

Dijon Grilled Pork Chops

(Pictured above)

My mom gave me the recipe for these savory chops with a sweet and tangy marinade. The apple juice and Dijon mustard complement the pork nicely. With a vegetable and some rice or pasta, you have a meal.
—Babette Watterson, Atglen, Pennsylvania

6 tablespoons Dijon mustard
6 tablespoons brown sugar
3 tablespoons unsweetened apple juice
3 tablespoons Worcestershire sauce
4 bone-in pork loin chops (8 ounces *each*)

In a bowl, combine the first four ingredients; mix well. Pour 2/3 cup marinade into a large resealable plastic bag; add the pork chops. Seal bag and turn to coat. Refrigerate for 8 hours or overnight. Cover and refrigerate remaining marinade for basting.

Coat grill rack with nonstick cooking spray before starting the grill. Drain marinade from pork. Grill, covered, over medium heat for 6-10 minutes on each side or until a meat thermometer reads 160°, basting occasionally with reserved marinade. **Yield:** 4 servings.

Nutritional Analysis: One pork chop equals 252 calories, 9 g fat (3 g saturated fat), 78 mg cholesterol, 413 mg sodium, 13 g carbohydrate, trace fiber, 29 g protein.
Diabetic Exchanges: 4 lean meat, 1 fruit.

Pork Chops with Red Cabbage

Add pineapple and sweet-and-sour cabbage to these tender chops to give them tangy flavor.
—Steve Rose, Mesa, Arizona

5 boneless lean pork loin chops (4 ounces *each*)
1 tablespoon olive *or* canola oil
1 jar (16 ounces) shredded sweet-and-sour red cabbage, undrained

1 can (8 ounces) unsweetened pineapple chunks, drained
1 tablespoon minced fresh parsley
1 teaspoon dried minced onion
1 teaspoon dried oregano
1/4 teaspoon coarsely ground pepper
Dash celery seed
1 small onion, peeled and halved

In a large nonstick skillet, brown pork chops on both sides in oil. In a bowl, combine the cabbage, pineapple, parsley, dried onion, oregano, pepper and celery seed. Cut each onion half into eight wedges; place over pork chops. Top with cabbage mixture. Bring to a boil. Reduce heat; cover and simmer for 15-20 minutes or until meat juices run clear and onions are tender. **Yield:** 5 servings.

Nutritional Analysis: One serving (1 pork chop with 1/2 cup cabbage mixture) equals 336 calories, 8 g fat (2 g saturated fat), 57 mg cholesterol, 67 mg sodium, 43 g carbohydrate, 1 g fiber, 23 g protein.
Diabetic Exchanges: 3 lean meat, 2 vegetable, 1-1/2 starch, 1/2 fruit.
▲ *Low-sodium*

Favorite Recipe Made Lighter

CREAMY, cheesy and comforting...Ranch Ham 'n' Cheese Pasta is all of these things and more! "I adapted this recipe from *Taste of Home* a long time ago," says Kathy Heller of Colorado Springs, Colorado. "We love it, but I cringe at all the calories and fat.

"I've lightened it up as well as I know how, but it's still so fattening that I rarely make it. My husband and kids would love it if you could come up with a light version of it!"

Our *Light & Tasty* home economists also enjoyed the down-home taste of this rich pasta bake, so they jumped at the chance to slim it down for Kathy's family and their own families, too.

To cut the fat, they reduced the amount of butter from 1/4 cup to 1 tablespoon, switched the cheese to a reduced-fat Mexican cheese blend and chose lean ham over regular.

They greatly reduced the sodium by eliminating both the saltine crackers and the salad dressing mix...and substituted a blend of herbs and seasonings to keep the dish's great ranch flavor.

These changes cut the calories by nearly a third and reduced the fat, saturated fat, cholesterol and sodium by more than half.

Ranch Ham 'n' Cheese Pasta

  1 package (16 ounces) penne *or* medium tube pasta
  1 cup fat-free milk
1/4 cup butter *or* margarine
  2 envelopes (1 ounce *each*) ranch salad dressing mix
  1 teaspoon garlic salt
  1 teaspoon lemon-pepper seasoning
  1 teaspoon garlic pepper*
  2 cups (8 ounces) shredded Colby-Monterey Jack cheese
  1 cup (8 ounces) reduced-fat sour cream
  2 cups cubed fully cooked ham
1/2 cup crushed saltines (about 15 crackers)
1/4 cup shredded Parmesan cheese

Cook pasta according to package directions; drain. In a Dutch oven, combine the next seven ingredients. Cook and stir over medium heat until cheese is melted and mixture begins to thicken. Reduce heat; fold in sour cream until blended. Add the ham, cracker crumbs and pasta; cook and stir until heated through. Sprinkle with Parmesan cheese. **Yield:** 10 servings.

  *Editor's Note: This recipe was tested with McCormick garlic pepper.

  Nutritional Analysis: One serving (1 cup) equals 440 calories, 21 g fat (12 g saturated fat), 64 mg cholesterol, 1,337 mg sodium, 42 g carbohydrate, 2 g fiber, 21 g protein.

Makeover Ranch Ham 'n' Cheese Pasta

(Pictured below)

  1 package (16 ounces) penne *or* medium tube pasta
  1 tablespoon butter *or* stick margarine
  1 tablespoon all-purpose flour
  1 cup fat-free milk
  2 teaspoons dried parsley flakes
  1 teaspoon garlic salt
  1 teaspoon salt-free lemon-pepper seasoning
1/2 teaspoon garlic powder
1/2 teaspoon dried minced onion
1/2 teaspoon dill weed
1/4 teaspoon onion powder
1/8 teaspoon pepper
  1 cup (8 ounces) reduced-fat sour cream
  2 cups cubed fully cooked lean ham
1-1/2 cups (6 ounces) shredded reduced-fat Mexican cheese blend
1/4 cup shredded Parmesan cheese

Cook pasta according to package directions; drain. In a Dutch oven, melt butter; whisk in flour until smooth. Gradually add milk and seasonings. Bring to a boil; cook and stir for 2 minutes or until thickened. Reduce heat; fold in sour cream until blended. Add ham and pasta; cook and stir until heated through. Remove from the heat; stir in Mexican cheese blend until melted. Sprinkle with Parmesan cheese. **Yield:** 10 servings.

  Nutritional Analysis: One serving (1 cup) equals 306 calories, 9 g fat (5 g saturated fat), 27 mg cholesterol, 612 mg sodium, 38 g carbohydrate, 2 g fiber, 20 g protein.
  Diabetic Exchanges: 2-1/2 starch, 2 lean meat.

Ham-Stuffed Jumbo Shells

(Pictured below)

This is a good way to use up leftover ham. I made it for a family reunion, and the dish came back empty. I also received a lot of requests for the recipe.
—*Leona Reuer, Medina, North Dakota*

24 jumbo pasta shells
3 tablespoons all-purpose flour
2 cups 1% milk
1/2 pound fresh mushrooms, halved and sliced
1/2 cup chopped onion
1/2 cup chopped green pepper
1 tablespoon canola oil
3 cups cubed fully cooked lean ham
1 cup (4 ounces) shredded reduced-fat Swiss cheese, *divided*
3 tablespoons grated Parmesan cheese
2 tablespoons minced fresh parsley
1/4 teaspoon paprika

Cook pasta shells according to package directions. Meanwhile, in a small saucepan, combine flour and milk until smooth. Bring to a boil; cook and stir for 2 minutes or until thickened. Remove from the heat; set aside.

In a large nonstick skillet, saute the mushrooms, onion and green pepper in oil until tender. Reduce heat; add the ham, 1/2 cup Swiss cheese and Parmesan cheese. Cook and stir until cheese is melted. Remove from the heat. Stir in 1/2 cup of the reserved sauce.

Drain pasta; stuff each shell with about 3 tablespoons of filling. Place in a 13-in. x 9-in. x 2-in. baking dish coated with nonstick cooking spray. Top with remaining sauce. Cover and bake at 350° for 30 minutes or until heated through. Sprinkle with parsley, paprika and remaining Swiss cheese. **Yield:** 8 servings.

Nutritional Analysis: *One serving (3 stuffed shells) equals 274 calories, 7 g fat (2 g saturated fat), 26 mg cholesterol, 703 mg sodium, 30 g carbohydrate, 2 g fiber, 23 g protein.*
Diabetic Exchanges: *2 lean meat, 2 starch.*

Pork Soft-Shell Tacos

(Pictured above)

It's hard to find recipes that have enough flavor to satisfy my husband without overwhelming our kids. This Southwestern take on pork tenderloin earned a thumbs-up from them all!
—*Margaret Steele, North Vancouver, British Columbia*

1 pork tenderloin (1 pound), cut into 1-inch strips
1 small onion, chopped
1 teaspoon canola oil
MOLE SAUCE:
2/3 cup enchilada sauce
1 tablespoon dry roasted peanuts
1 tablespoon semisweet chocolate chips
1 tablespoon raisins
1 garlic clove, minced
1 teaspoon ground cumin
1/4 teaspoon crushed red pepper flakes
1/2 cup frozen corn, thawed
8 corn tortillas (6 inches), warmed

1 cup shredded lettuce
1/4 cup reduced-fat sour cream
1/4 cup sliced green onions

In a large nonstick skillet or wok, stir-fry pork and onion in oil for 3 minutes or until pork is no longer pink; drain and keep warm.

In the same skillet, combine the enchilada sauce, peanuts, chocolate chips, raisins, garlic, cumin and red pepper flakes. Cook and stir over medium heat for 2-3 minutes or until chocolate is melted. Pour into a blender or food processor; cover and process until smooth. Return to skillet. Stir in corn and pork mixture; heat through. Spoon onto tortillas. Serve with lettuce, sour cream and green onions. **Yield:** 4 servings.

Nutritional Analysis: One serving (2 tacos) equals 370 calories, 10 g fat (3 g saturated fat), 67 mg cholesterol, 263 mg sodium, 41 g carbohydrate, 5 g fiber, 30 g protein.
Diabetic Exchanges: 3 lean meat, 2-1/2 starch.

Sweet 'n' Tangy Pork Chops

Even our toddler will eat this dish. The tender chops covered in a flavorful sauce are quick to fix. I like to serve them on a bed of no-yolk noodles.
—*Michelle Bishop, Peru, Indiana*

1/4 cup sherry *or* chicken broth
2 tablespoons brown sugar
2 tablespoons reduced-sodium soy sauce
1/4 teaspoon crushed red pepper flakes
4 boneless pork loin chops (4 ounces *each*)
1 teaspoon olive *or* canola oil
2 teaspoons cornstarch
2 tablespoons water
1/4 cup diced green pepper
1/4 cup diced sweet red pepper

In a bowl, combine the sherry or broth, brown sugar, soy sauce and red pepper flakes; set aside. In a large nonstick skillet, brown pork chops in oil. Pour sauce over pork chops. Reduce heat; cover and simmer for 10-12 minutes or until meat juices run clear. Combine the cornstarch and water until smooth; add to the skillet. Bring to a boil; cook and stir for 1-2 minutes or until thickened. Garnish with diced peppers. **Yield:** 4 servings.

Nutritional Analysis: One serving (1 pork chop with 2 tablespoons sauce) equals 229 calories, 9 g fat (3 g saturated fat), 63 mg cholesterol, 342 mg sodium, 10 g carbohydrate, trace fiber, 26 g protein.
Diabetic Exchanges: 3 lean meat, 1/2 starch.

Barbecued Country Ribs

(Pictured at right)

I created this sauce over 45 years ago when I adapted a recipe I saw in a magazine. The original called for much more oil. I usually triple the sauce and keep some in my freezer to use on chicken, beef or pork.
—*Barbara Gerriets, Topeka, Kansas*

2-1/2 pounds boneless country-style pork ribs
2 teaspoons Liquid Smoke, optional
1/2 teaspoon salt
1 cup water
BARBECUE SAUCE:
2/3 cup chopped onion
1 tablespoon canola oil
3/4 cup *each* water and ketchup
1/3 cup lemon juice
3 tablespoons sugar
3 tablespoons Worcestershire sauce
2 tablespoons prepared mustard
1/2 teaspoon salt
1/2 teaspoon pepper
1/4 teaspoon Liquid Smoke, optional

Place ribs in an 11-in. x 7-in. x 2-in. baking dish coated with nonstick cooking spray. Sprinkle with Liquid Smoke if desired and salt. Pour water over ribs. Cover and bake at 350° for 1 hour. Meanwhile, in a saucepan, saute onion in oil until tender. Add the remaining sauce ingredients; bring to a boil. Reduce heat; simmer, uncovered, for 15 minutes or until slightly thickened.

Drain the ribs; top with half of the barbecue sauce. Cover and bake 1 hour longer or until the meat is tender, basting every 20 minutes. Serve with remaining sauce. **Yield:** 8 servings.

Nutritional Analysis: One serving (4 ounces cooked pork with 2 tablespoons sauce) equals 292 calories, 14 g fat (4 g saturated fat), 91 mg cholesterol, 668 mg sodium, 14 g carbohydrate, 1 g fiber, 28 g protein.
Diabetic Exchanges: 4 lean meat, 1 starch, 1/2 fat.

Pork Chops with Apple Stuffing

(Pictured above)

Here's an easy way to dress up plain old pork chops—top them with a moist apple stuffing! Apples and pork always seem to go together so well... this makes a wonderful fall meal.
—Alta Looney, Howard, Ohio

1/2 cup all-purpose flour
1-1/2 teaspoons salt, *divided*
6 lean boneless pork loin chops (5 ounces *each*)
3 cups day-old bread cubes, toasted
1-1/2 cups chopped peeled tart apples
1/2 cup chopped celery
1/2 cup chopped onion
1 teaspoon poultry seasoning
1/4 teaspoon pepper
1/3 cup boiling water
1 teaspoon butter *or* stick margarine, melted

In a large resealable plastic bag, combine flour and 1/2 teaspoon salt. Add pork chops and toss to coat. In a nonstick skillet coated with nonstick cooking spray, brown chops for about 3 minutes on each side. Transfer to a shallow 2-1/2-qt. baking dish.

In a bowl, combine the bread cubes, apples, celery, onion, poultry seasoning, pepper and remaining salt; toss to coat evenly. Add water and butter; toss to coat. Place 1/2 cup of stuffing on each pork chop. Cover and bake at 350° for 30 minutes. Uncover; bake 5-10 minutes longer or until a meat thermometer reads 160° and stuffing is lightly browned. **Yield:** 6 servings.

Nutritional Analysis: One serving (1 pork chop with stuffing) equals 345 calories, 11 g fat (4 g saturated fat), 88 mg cholesterol, 787 mg sodium, 25 g carbohydrate, 2 g fiber, 35 g protein.
Diabetic Exchanges: 4 lean meat, 1 starch, 1/2 fruit.

Pork Picante

Lots of outdoor activity on our farm stimulates the appetites of my husband and three teenagers. This meal always satisfies them.
—Susan Miller, Marion, Illinois

1/3 cup all-purpose flour
1 teaspoon chili powder
1/2 teaspoon ground cumin
1/4 teaspoon garlic powder
1/4 teaspoon cayenne pepper
1-1/2 pounds pork tenderloin, cut into 3/4-inch cubes
1 tablespoon canola oil
1 cup salsa
1/3 cup peach preserves
Hot cooked rice, optional

In a large resealable plastic bag, combine the first five ingredients. Add the pork, a few pieces at a time, and shake to coat. In a large nonstick skillet or wok, brown pork in oil. Add salsa and peach preserves; cover and simmer for 10-15 minutes or until meat is no longer pink. Serve over rice if desired. **Yield:** 6 servings.

Nutritional Analysis: One serving (2/3 cup meat mixture, calculated without rice) equals 241 calories, 7 g fat (2 g saturated fat), 74 mg cholesterol, 258 mg sodium, 21 g carbohydrate, 1 g fiber, 25 g protein.
Diabetic Exchanges: 3 lean meat, 1 vegetable, 1/2 fruit, 1/2 starch.

Caramelized Pork Slices

This easy treatment for pork caught my eye when I was paging through a cookbook and saw the word "caramelized". The slightly sweet glaze is yummy. I like to serve this over noodles or rice...or with mashed sweet potatoes.
—Elisa Lochridge, Aloha, Oregon

1 pork tenderloin (1 pound), cut into 1-inch slices
2 teaspoons canola oil
2 garlic cloves, minced

2 tablespoons brown sugar
1 tablespoon orange juice
1 tablespoon molasses
1/2 teaspoon salt
1/4 teaspoon pepper

Flatten pork to 1/2-in. thickness. In a nonstick skillet, brown pork in oil over medium-high heat. Remove and keep warm. In the same skillet, saute garlic for 1 minute; stir in the brown sugar, orange juice, molasses, salt and pepper. Return pork to pan; cook, uncovered, for 3-4 minutes or until pork is no longer pink. **Yield:** 4 servings.

Nutritional Analysis: One serving (3 ounces glazed cooked meat) equals 200 calories, 6 g fat (2 g saturated fat), 74 mg cholesterol, 355 mg sodium, 11 g carbohydrate, trace fiber, 24 g protein.
Diabetic Exchanges: 3 lean meat, 1/2 starch.

Irish Stew

(Pictured below)

This satisfying stew is chock-full of potatoes, turnips, carrots and lamb. Served with Irish soda bread, it makes a hearty St. Patrick's Day meal.
—Lois Gelzer, Cape Elizabeth, Maine

1-1/2 pounds lamb stew meat
2 teaspoons olive *or* canola oil
4 cups water
2 cups sliced peeled potatoes
1 medium onion, sliced

1/2 cup sliced carrot
1/2 cup cubed turnip
1 teaspoon salt
1/2 teaspoon *each* dried marjoram, thyme and rosemary, crushed
1/8 teaspoon pepper
2 tablespoons all-purpose flour
2 tablespoons fat-free milk
1/2 teaspoon browning sauce, optional
3 tablespoons minced fresh parsley

In a Dutch oven, brown lamb in oil over medium-high heat. Add water; bring to a boil. Reduce heat; cover and simmer for 1 hour.

Add the potatoes, onion, carrot, turnip and seasonings. Bring to a boil. Reduce heat; cover and simmer for 30 minutes or until the vegetables are tender. In a small bowl, combine the flour, milk and browning sauce if desired until smooth; stir into stew. Add parsley. Bring to a boil; cook and stir for 2 minutes or until thickened. **Yield:** 6 servings.

Nutritional Analysis: One serving (1-1/2 cups) equals 279 calories, 9 g fat (3 g saturated fat), 92 mg cholesterol, 469 mg sodium, 17 g carbohydrate, 2 g fiber, 31 g protein.
Diabetic Exchanges: 3 lean meat, 1 starch, 1 vegetable.

Pork Loin with Currant Sauce

I serve this roast often to family and friends...and someone at the table always asks for the recipe. To complete the meal, I make stir-fried green beans and a lightened-up version of twice-baked potatoes.
—Edie Urso, Spokane, Washington

3/4 cup sherry *or* apple juice
3/4 cup reduced-sodium soy sauce
6 garlic cloves, minced
4 teaspoons ground mustard
1-1/2 teaspoons ground ginger
1-1/2 teaspoons dried thyme
1 bone-in pork loin roast (5 pounds)
SAUCE:
2/3 cup currant jelly
1 tablespoon sherry *or* apple juice
1-1/2 teaspoons reduced-sodium soy sauce

In a bowl, combine the first six ingredients; mix well. Pour 1-1/4 cups marinade into a 2-gal. resealable plastic bag; add the pork roast. Seal bag and turn to coat; refrigerate overnight. Cover and refrigerate remaining marinade.

Drain and discard marinade from roast. Place on a rack in a shallow roasting pan. Bake, uncovered, at 325° for 2-1/2 to 3 hours or until a meat thermometer reads 160°, basting every 30 minutes with reserved marinade. Let stand for 10 minutes before slicing. In a small saucepan, combine sauce ingredients; bring to a boil over medium heat. Serve with the pork. **Yield:** 10 servings.

Nutritional Analysis: One serving (4 ounces cooked pork with 1 tablespoon sauce) equals 298 calories, 11 g fat (4 g saturated fat), 91 mg cholesterol, 481 mg sodium, 15 g carbohydrate, trace fiber, 33 g protein.
Diabetic Exchanges: 4 lean meat, 1 starch.

Rio Grande Pork Roast

(Pictured below)

Years ago, I used this recipe many times during in-store promotions when I was the Nebraska Pork Industry Queen. It is still a family favorite and one I like to make when we have company.
—Konnie McKown, Ringgold, Georgia

1 garlic clove, minced
1/2 teaspoon salt
1 teaspoon chili powder, *divided*
1 lean boneless top loin pork roast (3 pounds)
1/2 cup apple jelly
1/2 cup barbecue sauce

Rub garlic, salt and 1/2 teaspoon chili powder over roast. Place on a rack in a shallow roasting pan. Bake, uncovered, at 350° for 30 minutes. In a small saucepan, combine the apple jelly, barbecue sauce and remaining chili powder; bring to a boil. Reduce heat; simmer, uncovered, for 2 minutes. Pour over roast. Bake 40-50 minutes longer or until a meat thermometer reads 160°, basting occasionally. Remove roast and keep warm.

Stir drippings in pan to loosen browned bits; pour into a 2-cup measuring cup. Skim fat. Add enough water to measure 1-1/4 cups. Transfer to a small saucepan; bring to a boil. Remove from heat; serve with roast. **Yield:** 10 servings.

Nutritional Analysis: *One serving (4 ounces cooked pork with 2 tablespoons pan juices) equals 286 calories, 8 g fat (3 g saturated fat), 89 mg cholesterol, 346 mg sodium, 15 g carbohydrate, trace fiber, 35 g protein.*
Diabetic Exchanges: *4 lean meat, 1 fruit.*

Apricot-Glazed Ham

(Pictured above)

This delicious ham from our Test Kitchen gets a spicy-sweet tang from its glaze, which also adds a sumptuous sheen to the meat. The zip from the mustard and subtle apricot flavor permeate every tender juicy slice. Count on this ham to entice company to the table and make a great impression with your dinner guests.

1/2 boneless fully cooked lean ham (4 pounds)
Whole cloves
2 cups ginger ale
2/3 cup 100% apricot spreadable fruit
1/4 cup packed brown sugar
3 tablespoons Dijon mustard
1/2 teaspoon ground ginger

Score surface of ham, making diamond shapes 1/4 in. deep. Insert a clove in each diamond. Place ham on a rack in a shallow roasting pan; pour ginger ale into pan. Loosely cover with foil. Bake at 325° for 1 hour.

In a small bowl, combine the spreadable fruit, brown sugar, mustard and ginger; brush some over ham. Bake, uncovered, for 1-1/2 to 2 hours or until a meat thermometer reads 140° and ham is heated through, brushing occasionally with glaze. Serve with remaining glaze. **Yield:** 16 servings.

Nutritional Analysis: *One serving (3 ounces cooked ham with 1-1/2 teaspoons additional glaze) equals 182 calories, 5 g fat (2 g saturated fat), 47 mg cholesterol, 1,200 mg sodium, 12 g carbohydrate, trace fiber, 21 g protein.*
Diabetic Exchanges: *3 lean meat, 1 fruit.*

Fruited Pork Chops

Here's one of my best slow-cooker recipes. I often prepare these tender chops with pineapple sauce for guests. I like to serve them with brown rice.
—Cindy Ragan, North Huntingdon, Pennsylvania

    3 tablespoons all-purpose flour
1-1/2 teaspoons dried oregano
    3/4 teaspoon salt
    1/4 teaspoon garlic powder
    1/4 teaspoon pepper
     6 lean boneless pork loin chops (5 ounces *each*)
     1 tablespoon olive *or* canola oil
     1 can (20 ounces) unsweetened pineapple
        chunks
    3/4 cup unsweetened pineapple juice
    1/4 cup water
     2 tablespoons brown sugar
     2 tablespoons dried minced onion
     2 tablespoons tomato paste
    1/4 cup raisins

In a large resealable plastic bag, combine the flour, oregano, salt, garlic powder and pepper; add the pork chops, one at a time, and shake to coat. In a nonstick skillet, brown chops on both sides in oil. Transfer to a slow cooker.

Drain pineapple, reserving juice; set pineapple aside. In a bowl, combine the 3/4 cup pineapple juice with reserved pineapple juice. Stir in the water, brown sugar, onion and tomato paste; pour over chops. Sprinkle with raisins. Cover and cook on high for 3 to 3-1/2 hours or until meat is tender and a meat thermometer reads 160°. Stir in reserved pineapple. Cover and cook 10 minutes longer or until heated through. **Yield:** 6 servings.

Nutritional Analysis: One serving (1 pork chop with 2/3 cup fruit) equals 366 calories, 12 g fat (4 g saturated fat), 79 mg cholesterol, 353 mg sodium, 31 g carbohydrate, 2 g fiber, 32 g protein.
Diabetic Exchanges: 4 lean meat, 2 fruit.

Grilled Lamb Kabobs

(Pictured at right)

My sister-in-law, who lives in Florida, sends fresh fruit every year at Christmas. I've invented various recipes for using it. We get plenty of snow here, but our grill is always put to good use!
—Kathleen Boulanger, Williston, Vermont

1-1/4 cups grapefruit juice
1/3 cup honey

     2 tablespoons minced fresh mint
    3/4 teaspoon salt
    3/4 teaspoon ground coriander
    3/4 teaspoon pepper
     1 pound boneless lamb, cut into 1-inch cubes
CITRUS SALSA:
     4 medium navel oranges, *divided*
     2 medium pink grapefruit
    1/2 cup mango chutney
     1 to 2 tablespoons minced fresh mint
     2 medium onions, cut into wedges
     1 large sweet red pepper, cut into 1-inch pieces

In a bowl, combine the first six ingredients; mix well. Pour 1 cup into a large resealable plastic bag; add the lamb. Seal bag and turn to coat; refrigerate for 1-4 hours. Cover and refrigerate remaining marinade.

For salsa, peel and section two oranges and grapefruit, then coarsely chop fruit. In a bowl, combine the chopped fruit, chutney and mint. Cover and refrigerate.

Coat grill rack with nonstick cooking spray before starting the grill. Peel remaining oranges; cut each into eight wedges. Drain and discard marinade from lamb. On eight metal or wooden soaked skewers, alternately thread onions, orange wedges, red pepper and lamb. Grill, uncovered, over medium heat for 4-5 minutes on each side or until meat reaches desired doneness and vegetables are tender, basting occasionally with reserved marinade. Serve kabobs with salsa. **Yield:** 4 servings.

Nutritional Analysis: One serving (2 kabobs with 1/2 cup salsa) equals 367 calories, 7 g fat (2 g saturated fat), 65 mg cholesterol, 282 mg sodium, 56 g carbohydrate, 7 g fiber, 24 g protein.

🍎 Pointers on Pork

THE NEXT TIME you decide to take advantage of pork's bountiful benefits, keep the following tips in mind:

- Unlike beef, cuts of pork vary little in tenderness. The cooking method, however, can make a difference. Pan-broil, grill or stir-fry pork when you want a firmer texture. Braising pork (browning it in a skillet and then simmering it in a little water) will yield fork-tender results. Oven roasting is often recommended for large cuts such as tenderloin and loin roasts.
- Pork should be cooked to at least 160°. At this temperature, the internal color of boneless roasts may still be a faint pink...and bone-in roasts may also remain slightly pink near the bone. Use a meat thermometer to be sure pork is thoroughly cooked.
- Pork offers lots of convenience for healthy cooks on the go. Light marinades can add flavor to pork overnight without a lot of fuss on the cook's part ...and herbal rubs help season the meat without adding many calories or fat. Leftover pork also freezes well for last-minute meals and speedy sandwiches.

Ham 'n' Swiss-Topped Potatoes

(Pictured above right)

This is one of my husband's favorite light recipes. I often double the sauce to make sure I have some left over. It can easily be reheated to put over a microwaved potato for a quick lunch.
—*Jill Hayes, Westerville, Ohio*

  3 medium baking potatoes (12 ounces *each*)
  2 tablespoons cornstarch
  2 cups fat-free milk
  1 tablespoon Dijon mustard
1/2 teaspoon pepper
1/2 cup reduced-fat shredded Swiss cheese
  2 cups cubed fully cooked lean ham
  2 cups steamed cut fresh asparagus

Bake potatoes at 375° for 1 hour or until tender. Meanwhile, in a saucepan, combine cornstarch and milk until smooth. Bring to a boil over medium heat; cook and stir for 2 minutes or until thickened. Reduce heat; stir in the mustard, pepper and Swiss cheese. Cook and stir until the cheese is melted. Stir in ham and asparagus. Cook for 5 minutes or until heated through. Cut potatoes in half lengthwise; place cut side up and fluff the pulp with a fork. Spoon 2/3 cup sauce over each half. **Yield:** 6 servings.

Nutritional Analysis: One stuffed potato half equals 285 calories, 3 g fat (1 g saturated fat), 19 mg cholesterol, 673 mg sodium, 44 g carbohydrate, 4 g fiber, 20 g protein.
Diabetic Exchanges: 2 starch, 1 vegetable, 1 lean meat, 1/2 fat-free milk.

Fish & Seafood Fare

Fabulous fish dinners and sensational seafood entrees can add appetizing variety to any cook's healthy menu planning. You'll quickly get hooked on these from-the-sea favorites swimming in fantastic flavor!

Citrus Orange Roughy and Seafood Pasta Delight (page 174)

Chinese Fish

A Chinese friend gave me the recipe for this flavorful fish. She didn't know U.S. measurements, so I'd hold up a plastic teaspoon and ask, "How much?" for each ingredient she used. It took some time to record, but it was worth it!
—Ruth Solyntjes, Waterville, Minnesota

4 fresh *or* frozen orange roughy fillets (6 ounces *each*), thawed
1 tablespoon canola oil
1 cup water
1/3 cup sliced green onions
2 teaspoons cider vinegar
2 teaspoons reduced-sodium soy sauce
2 garlic cloves, minced
1/2 teaspoon Chinese five-spice powder
1/8 teaspoon crushed red pepper flakes
1/4 teaspoon salt
1/4 teaspoon ground ginger *or* 1 teaspoon minced fresh gingerroot
1/2 teaspoon sesame oil

In a large nonstick skillet, cook fish in canola oil for 2 minutes. Turn and cook 2 minutes longer. Add the next nine ingredients. Cover and simmer for 4 minutes or until fish flakes easily with a fork. Sprinkle with sesame oil. **Yield:** 4 servings.

Nutritional Analysis: One serving equals 160 calories, 5 g fat (trace saturated fat), 34 mg cholesterol, 355 mg sodium, 2 g carbohydrate, trace fiber, 25 g protein.
Diabetic Exchange: *3 lean meat.*

Crab Cakes

(Pictured at right)

My family really likes crab cakes but always thought they had too much breading and not enough crab. So I experimented until I found the right light combination. This recipe is so good, you can serve it as an appetizer or a main dish.
—Kathy Buchanan, Hartsville, South Carolina

1 egg, lightly beaten
1/4 cup fat-free mayonnaise
1/2 cup soft bread crumbs
2 green onions, finely chopped
1 tablespoon minced fresh parsley
1 teaspoon ground mustard
1/4 teaspoon salt
1/4 teaspoon pepper
4 cans (6 ounces *each*) crabmeat, drained, flaked and cartilage removed
1 tablespoon butter *or* stick margarine
1 tablespoon canola oil
6 tablespoons seafood sauce

In a bowl, combine the first eight ingredients. Add crab; mix gently. Shape rounded tablespoonfuls into 2-in. patties. In a large nonstick skillet, cook patties in butter and oil over medium heat for 3-4 minutes on each side or until golden brown. Serve with seafood sauce. **Yield:** 9 servings.

Nutritional Analysis: One serving (3 crab cakes with 2 teaspoons seafood sauce) equals 139 calories, 5 g fat (1 g saturated fat), 94 mg cholesterol, 547 mg sodium, 7 g carbohydrate, 1 g fiber, 17 g protein.
Diabetic Exchanges: *2 very lean meat, 1/2 starch, 1/2 fat.*

Italian Catfish Fillets

(Pictured at right)

A tangy red sauce adds pizzazz to the catfish fillets in this easy entree. I've been preparing this recipe for years, and my family loves it.
—Cheri Lefkowitch, Norwalk, Connecticut

1 can (8 ounces) tomato sauce
2 teaspoons olive *or* canola oil
1 teaspoon zesty Italian salad dressing mix
1/4 teaspoon salt
1/8 teaspoon pepper
4 catfish fillets (6 ounces *each*)
3 tablespoons shredded Romano cheese

In a bowl, combine the first five ingredients. Pour half of the sauce into an 11-in. x 7-in. x 2-in. baking dish coated with nonstick cooking spray. Arrange fish over sauce. Top with remaining sauce. Bake, uncovered, at 375° for 20 minutes. Sprinkle with cheese. Bake 5 minutes longer or until fish flakes easily with a fork and cheese is melted. **Yield:** 4 servings.

Nutritional Analysis: One serving (1 fillet with 1/4 cup sauce) equals 292 calories, 17 g fat (4 g saturated fat), 85 mg cholesterol, 911 mg sodium, 6 g carbohydrate, 1 g fiber, 29 g protein.
Diabetic Exchanges: *4 lean meat, 1 vegetable, 1 fat.*

🍎 Frozen Fish Facts

FOLLOW these tips to get the best flavor from frozen fish you buy at the grocery store:

• Make sure the fish is solidly frozen and the wrapping is not damaged. There should be no odor or icy spots.

• It takes about 24 hours to thaw a pound of frozen fish. To quick-thaw, place the fish in its packaging in cold water. Allow about an hour for 1 pound of fish.

  Or use the defrost feature on your microwave to thaw the fish.

• After it has thawed, pat the fish dry with paper towels before preparing.

• Leftovers? Cut them into chunks for a salad...or use them in a fish chowder, along with diced potatoes, onions, celery and herbs.

DATE	DESCRIPTION	
03/10/04	LIGHT & TASTY ANNUAL RECIPES 2004	
	SHIPPING AND HANDLING GST	
	TOTAL BALANCE DUE (PAYABLE IN CANADIAN FUNDS)	$ 38.5

Paid Nov 16/04,
Visa

Taste of Home • BOOKS

ACCT # DZ21 0298-2102

Dear Ms. Diane James,

Just as we promised, the enclosed copy of LIGHT & TASTY ANNUAL RECIPES 2004 was reserved in your name. I hope you have an easy chair nearby, because once you start browsing through the 518 mouth-watering recipes that are all lower in fat, sugar or salt, you're going to be sitting a spell!

As a Preferred Customer, you have 30 days to savor this new cookbook before deciding whether to send payment for the amount above or return the book with no obligation to pay anything. But that's not all...you'll also save $5 off the regular price!

If you decide to keep this healthy, taste-tempting recipe book, please detach the invoice and return it with your payment in the enclosed pre-addressed envelope. You may write a check payable to Taste of Home Books, or use your credit card.

Thank you for agreeing to preview LIGHT & TASTY ANNUAL RECIPES 2004. After you peruse and use it for 30 days, we think you and your family will want its hundreds of delicious recipes in your kitchen for keeps.

Sincerely,

Brenda Tweed

Brenda Tweed
Test Group Coordinator

P.S. If you have any questions about your book order, or if you'd like to order additional copies as gifts, please call us at 1-800/344-2560.

Correspondence to: *Taste of Home Books*, PO Box 2090 Stn Main, Niagara Falls, ON L2E 7L9
Payment to: *Taste of Home Books*, PO Box 2150 Stn Main, Niagara Falls, ON L2E 7L5
Book Returns to: *Taste of Home Books*, PO Box 1015, Niagara Falls, ON L2E 6V9

BK-OF4

Customer Service Guide
Welcome to Reiman Publications

Taste of Home · BOOKS   **Country** · BOOKS

Reminisce · BOOKS   **BIRDS & BLOOMS** • **BOOKS**

Thank you for placing your order with us. Your complete satisfaction is our first priority. That's why all the products we publish come with a free preview period during which you have no obligation to buy. You can taste-test our recipes in your own kitchen, review the ideas we provide for craft projects, home decoration or holiday entertaining, or just kick back and enjoy our upbeat true-life stories all before you decide whether or not you even want to keep the product.

Satisfaction Guaranteed

If you are not 100% satisfied with any purchase you've made, simply return the product and we'll refund 100% of your payment, no questions asked.

We hope you enjoy our products and the convenience of ordering by mail from Reiman Publications. To help you know us, we've included a sampling of commonly asked questions and answers that you might find helpful.

What if I decide to buy the product I'm previewing?

Simply turn this form over, detach the invoice located at the top, and then write a check (made payable to the name shown) for the amount now due, or total amount due. Or, if you prefer to pay by credit card, complete necessary information in the space indicated. Then return the invoice, with your check or credit card information, in the envelope provided. It's that easy.

How do I handle returns?

During your free-preview period, if you decide the product is not for you, simply return it to us at the address shown on the bottom of the other side of this form. It's clearly marked for returns.

To insure that we properly adjust your account, include the top portion of this form with the returned shipment, and please allow 4 to 6 weeks for the returned product to reach us, be processed, and be posted to your account. You may call and request a reimbursement for your postal charges or a postage-paid return label.

What if I have questions about my account?

You may have billing questions related to the timing of bills and payments as they move through the mail. Should you receive a bill after you've already paid for a product, please disregard it. Occasionally another bill will be mailed before your account has been credited. We do our best to adjust your account accurately and quickly to avoid billing problems.

If ever you have questions about your account, feel free to call or write us and we'll be happy to help. Our toll-free number and correspondence address are on the other side of this form. If you choose to call us, the best times to call are on Wednesday, Thursday or Friday between 7:30 a.m. and 5:00 p.m. Central Time. And please tell us your account number, which is clearly marked on the other side of this form.

What if I have questions about the editorial content?

Please direct questions about recipes or projects to: Editor (name of product), Reiman Publications, PO Box 989, Greendale, WI 53129-0989. We'll do our best to respond right away.

What should I do if I'm moving?

When you know you'll be moving, please contact us with your new address. If possible, we'd like to know at least six weeks before you change addresses. That way you won't miss a single Reiman product, and you'll avoid shipping delays.

What should I know about mailing lists?

Occasionally we make our customer lists available to other carefully selected companies who offer products or services we think might interest you. If you would prefer to be left off these lists, simply let us know in writing, and we'll honor your request.

Can I give Reiman products as gifts?

You bet! Simply call the toll-free number on the other side of this form to arrange details. Products sent will acknowledge you as the sender and you will be sent a convenient single invoice.

Baked Flounder

I fix this fish frequently because my husband is on a low-calorie diet, and my whole family enjoys it. The flounder is baked on a bed of mushrooms and green onions and topped with bread crumbs and reduced-fat cheese.
—*Brenda Taylor, Benton, Kentucky*

2/3 cup sliced green onions
1/2 cup sliced fresh mushrooms
2 pounds flounder *or* sole fillets
1 teaspoon dried marjoram
1/2 teaspoon salt
1/8 teaspoon pepper
2 tablespoons dry white wine *or* chicken broth
2 teaspoons lemon juice
1/4 cup shredded reduced-fat Mexican cheese blend
1/4 cup soft whole wheat bread crumbs
2 tablespoons butter *or* stick margarine, melted

Sprinkle green onions and mushrooms in a 13-in. x 9-in. x 2-in. baking dish coated with nonstick cooking spray. Arrange fish over vegetables, overlapping the thickest end of fish over the thin end. Season with marjoram, salt and pepper. Pour wine or broth and lemon juice over fish. Cover with cheese and bread crumbs; drizzle with butter. Bake, uncovered, at 400° for 10-12 minutes or until fish flakes easily with a fork. **Yield:** 6 servings.

Nutritional Analysis: One serving equals 212 calories, 7 g fat (4 g saturated fat), 86 mg cholesterol, 438 mg sodium, 5 g carbohydrate, 1 g fiber, 31 g protein.
***Diabetic Exchanges:** 4 very lean meat, 1 fat, 1/2 starch.*

Salmon-Stuffed Potatoes

(Pictured at right)

Here's a tasty twist on twice-baked potatoes. The spuds are stuffed with a rich mixture of potato, sour cream and smoked salmon, then sprinkled with chives. They're hearty enough to be served as a main dish alongside a salad or bowl of soup.
—*Carolyn Schmeling, Brookfield, Wisconsin*

4 medium baking potatoes (about 8 ounces *each*)
1/2 cup reduced-fat sour cream
1/2 cup 1% buttermilk

1 tablespoon butter *or* stick margarine
1/4 teaspoon salt
1/8 teaspoon pepper
4 ounces smoked salmon, cut into 1/2-inch pieces
4 teaspoons snipped chives

Scrub and pierce potatoes. Bake at 400° for 40-60 minutes or until tender. Cool until easy to handle. Cut a thin slice off the top of each potato and discard. Scoop out the pulp, leaving a thin shell.

In a bowl, mash the pulp with sour cream. Stir in the buttermilk, butter, salt and pepper. Gently fold in the salmon. Spoon into potato shells. Sprinkle with the chives. **Yield:** 4 servings.

Nutritional Analysis: One serving (1 stuffed potato) equals 307 calories, 7 g fat (4 g saturated fat), 26 mg cholesterol, 820 mg sodium, 52 g carbohydrate, 4 g fiber, 11 g protein.
***Diabetic Exchanges:** 3 starch, 1 lean meat, 1/2 fat.*

Spanish Fish

(Pictured at right)

These flaky fish fillets get fresh flavor from onions and tomato, plus a little zip from cayenne pepper. This recipe is a particular favorite of my family's. The fish doesn't get dry...it's moist and delicious.
—*Pix Stidham, Exeter, California*

1 tablespoon olive *or* canola oil
1 large onion, thinly sliced
2 tablespoons diced pimientos
6 sea bass *or* halibut fillets (6 ounces *each*)
1-1/4 teaspoons salt
1/4 teaspoon ground mace
1/4 teaspoon cayenne pepper
1/4 teaspoon pepper
6 thick slices tomato
1 cup thinly sliced fresh mushrooms
3 tablespoons chopped green onions
1/4 cup white wine *or* chicken broth
4-1/2 teaspoons butter *or* stick margarine
1/2 cup dry bread crumbs

Brush oil onto bottom of a 13-in. x 9-in. x 2-in. baking dish; top with onion and pimientos. Pat fish dry. Combine the salt, mace, cayenne and pepper; sprinkle over both sides of fish. Arrange fish over onions and pimientos. Top each fillet with a tomato slice; sprinkle with mushrooms and green onions. Pour wine or broth over fish and vegetables.

In a nonstick skillet, melt butter; add bread crumbs. Cook and stir over medium heat until lightly browned. Sprinkle over fish. Cover and bake at 350° for 20 minutes. Uncover and bake 20-25 minutes longer or until fish flakes easily with a fork. **Yield:** 6 servings.

Nutritional Analysis: One serving equals 251 calories, 9 g fat (3 g saturated fat), 68 mg cholesterol, 700 mg sodium, 11 g carbohydrate, 1 g fiber, 29 g protein.
***Diabetic Exchanges:** 4 very lean meat, 1 vegetable, 1 fat, 1/2 starch.*

Fish & Seafood Fare

Pirate's Delight

You'll get hooked on this quick-to-fix dish. The flaky baked cod is enhanced by a delicately seasoned golden coating and a sprinkling of Parmesan cheese.
—Susan Kaye, Olivet, Michigan

> 4 teaspoons dry white wine *or* chicken broth
> 12 ounces fresh *or* frozen cod, thawed and cut into 1-inch pieces
> 1/3 cup crushed saltines (about 8 crackers)
> 1/2 teaspoon Italian seasoning
> 1/8 teaspoon garlic powder
> 1/8 teaspoon paprika
> 2 teaspoons olive *or* canola oil
> 2 teaspoons grated Parmesan cheese

Pour wine or broth into a 13-in. x 9-in. x 2-in. baking dish coated with nonstick cooking spray. Place fish on top. Combine cracker crumbs, Italian seasoning, garlic powder and paprika; sprinkle over fish. Drizzle with oil. Top with cheese. Bake, uncovered, at 400° for 12-15 minutes or until lightly browned and fish flakes easily with a fork. **Yield:** 4 servings.

Nutritional Analysis: One serving equals 125 calories, 4 g fat (1 g saturated fat), 37 mg cholesterol, 144 mg sodium, 5 g carbohydrate, trace fiber, 16 g protein.
Diabetic Exchanges: 2 very lean meat, 1/2 starch, 1/2 fat.

Citrus Tuna Steaks

(Pictured at right)

This grilled fish is a summertime favorite my family requests often. I adapted it from a traditional Jamaican jerk recipe.
—Shannon Edwards, Arlington, Texas

> 1 medium pink grapefruit
> 1/4 cup lemon juice
> 1/4 cup lime juice
> 2 tablespoons honey
> 1 tablespoon snipped fresh dill *or* 1 teaspoon dill weed
> 1 teaspoon crushed red pepper flakes
> 1/2 teaspoon ground ginger *or* 2 teaspoons minced fresh gingerroot
> 4 tuna steaks *or* fillets (6 ounces *each*)

Peel and section grapefruit over a bowl, reserving juice. Refrigerate half of the grapefruit sections. Add remaining grapefruit to the reserved grapefruit juice. Add the lemon juice, lime juice, honey, dill, red pepper flakes and ginger. Remove 1/4 cup for basting; cover and refrigerate. Pour remaining marinade into a large resealable plastic bag; add the tuna steaks. Seal bag and turn to coat; refrigerate for 30 minutes, turning once.

Drain and discard marinade. Coat grill rack with nonstick cooking spray before starting the grill. Grill tuna, uncovered, over medium heat for 6-7 minutes on each side, basting frequently with reserved marinade. Top tuna steaks with reserved grapefruit sections. Cover and cook for 5 minutes or until fish flakes easily with a fork. **Yield:** 4 servings.

Nutritional Analysis: One serving (1 tuna steak) equals 224 calories, 2 g fat (trace saturated fat), 77 mg cholesterol, 63 mg sodium, 11 g carbohydrate, 3 g fiber, 40 g protein.
Diabetic Exchanges: 5 very lean meat, 1 fruit.
△ **Low-fat**
▲ **Low-sodium**

Peanut-Crusted Orange Roughy

(Pictured at right)

I rely on this nutty treatment when having fish for dinner. Even kids are likely to go for the flavorful fillets crowned with a golden topping of roasted peanuts. Colorful corn salsa makes a zippy accompaniment.
—Michelle Smith, Sykesville, Maryland

> 4 fresh *or* frozen orange roughy fillets (6 ounces *each*), thawed
> 2 tablespoons reduced-fat mayonnaise
> 1/3 cup unsalted dry roasted peanuts, finely chopped
> 1/8 teaspoon pepper
> **CORN SALSA:**
> 1 cup fresh *or* frozen corn, thawed
> 1/2 cup chopped green pepper
> 1/4 cup chopped red onion
> 2 tablespoons minced fresh cilantro *or* parsley
> 1 tablespoon lime juice
> 1 garlic clove, minced
> 1/8 teaspoon salt
> 1/8 teaspoon cayenne pepper

Arrange fish fillets in a 13-in. x 9-in. x 2-in. baking dish coated with nonstick cooking spray. Brush the top of each fillet with mayonnaise. Sprinkle with peanuts and pepper. Bake, uncovered, at 450° for 10-15 minutes or until fish flakes easily with a fork. Meanwhile, combine the salsa ingredients in a bowl. Serve with the fish. **Yield:** 4 servings.

Nutritional Analysis: One serving (1 fillet with 1/3 cup salsa) equals 261 calories, 10 g fat (1 g saturated fat), 37 mg cholesterol, 244 mg sodium, 15 g carbohydrate, 3 g fiber, 30 g protein.
Diabetic Exchanges: 4 very lean meat, 1 starch, 1 fat.

🍎 Improve the Flavor of Fish

HERE'S a trick I use with most any type of fish. I cover the fish in milk and let it soak for 30 minutes to 1-1/2 hours in the fridge. Then I pour off the milk and prepare the fish as my recipe directs. This seems to get rid of some of the fishy taste. —*Sandy Fank Olivia, Minnesota*

Salmon with Garlic and Ginger

A citrus marinade sparked with garlic and ginger perks up these salmon fillets. I rely on my microwave to cook the fish in minutes.
—*Patricia Cohen, Floral City, Florida*

  3/4 cup minced fresh parsley
1-1/4 teaspoons ground ginger *or* 4 teaspoons
     minced fresh gingerroot
    6 garlic cloves, minced
    1 to 2 tablespoons lemon juice
    1 to 2 tablespoons lime juice
  1/2 teaspoon salt
  1/4 teaspoon dried tarragon
  1/8 teaspoon pepper
    1 tablespoon olive *or* canola oil
    4 salmon fillets (6 ounces *each*)

In a food processor, combine the parsley, ginger and garlic; cover and process until minced. Add the lemon juice, lime juice, salt, tarragon and pepper; cover and process until blended. While processing, gradually add oil in a steady stream. Spread mixture over salmon fillets. Place in a shallow 2-qt. microwave-safe dish, positioning the thickest portion of fish toward the outside edges. Cover and chill for 30 minutes.

Cover and microwave on high for 4-5 minutes or until fish flakes easily with a fork. Let stand, covered, for 2 minutes before serving. **Yield:** 4 servings.

Editor's Note: This recipe was tested in an 850-watt microwave.

Nutritional Analysis: One serving (1 salmon fillet) equals 292 calories, 14 g fat (2 g saturated fat), 96 mg cholesterol, 375 mg sodium, 4 g carbohydrate, trace fiber, 35 g protein.
Diabetic Exchanges: *5 lean meat, 1/2 fat.*

Pineapple Shrimp Kabobs

(Pictured at right)

I like to fire up the grill to cook these easy kabobs. Try them at your next backyard gathering!
—*Isabel Fowler, Fairbanks, Alaska*

  1/4 cup *each* reduced-sodium soy sauce, balsamic
     vinegar and honey
    1 garlic clove, minced
    1 pound uncooked medium shrimp, peeled and
     deveined
    1 large green pepper, cut into 1-inch pieces
    1 can (8 ounces) pineapple chunks, drained

In a bowl, combine the soy sauce, vinegar, honey and garlic. Set aside 1/3 cup. On eight metal or soaked wooden skewers, thread the shrimp, green pepper and pineapple. Place in a shallow dish; pour remaining marinade over kabobs. Cover and chill for 1 hour. Cover and chill reserved marinade.

Coat grill rack with nonstick cooking spray before starting the grill. Drain and discard marinade from kabobs. Grill, uncovered, over medium heat for 3 minutes, turning once. Baste with reserved marinade. Grill 3-4 minutes longer or until shrimp turn pink, turning and basting frequently. **Yield:** 4 servings.

Nutritional Analysis: One serving (2 kabobs) equals 154 calories, 1 g fat (trace saturated fat), 135 mg cholesterol, 429 mg sodium, 21 g carbohydrate, 1 g fiber, 15 g protein.
Diabetic Exchanges: *2 very lean meat, 1 vegetable, 1 fruit.*
△ **Low-fat**

Grilled Citrus Salmon Fillet

(Pictured at right)

My family is thrilled when I serve salmon with a creamy orange yogurt sauce. It gives each bite a zesty citrus boost.
—*Heidi Farrar, Sierra Vista, Arizona*

  1/3 cup orange juice
  1/4 cup lemon juice
    1 tablespoon grated orange peel
1-1/2 teaspoons sugar
    1 teaspoon grated lemon peel
    1 teaspoon olive *or* canola oil
1-1/2 teaspoons minced fresh rosemary *or* 1/2
     teaspoon dried rosemary, crushed
  3/4 teaspoon minced fresh basil *or* 1/4 teaspoon
     dried basil
  1/2 teaspoon salt
  1/4 teaspoon pepper
  1/4 teaspoon cayenne pepper
    1 salmon fillet (1-1/4 pounds), cut into 4 pieces
ORANGE YOGURT SAUCE:
    1 cup (8 ounces) reduced-fat plain yogurt
    1 to 2 tablespoons orange juice
    1 tablespoon sugar
    1 tablespoon grated orange peel

In a bowl, combine the first 11 ingredients; mix well. Set aside 1/4 cup. Pour remaining marinade into a large resealable plastic bag; add salmon. Turn to coat. Refrigerate for 30 minutes; turn once or twice. Cover and chill reserved marinade.

Coat grill rack with nonstick cooking spray before starting the grill. Drain and discard marinade from salmon. Place skin side down on grill. Grill, covered, over medium-hot heat for 5 minutes. Baste with reserved marinade. Grill 5-10 minutes longer or until fish flakes easily with a fork, basting frequently.

For sauce, in a small bowl, combine all the sauce ingredients. Serve with the salmon. **Yield:** 4 servings.

Nutritional Analysis: One serving (1 piece of salmon with 1/4 cup sauce) equals 329 calories, 17 g fat (4 g saturated fat), 87 mg cholesterol, 273 mg sodium, 11 g carbohydrate, trace fiber, 32 g protein.
Diabetic Exchanges: *4 lean meat, 1 fat, 1/2 reduced-fat milk.*

Parmesan Catfish

(Pictured at right)

This moist baked fish has a slightly crunchy coating with a mild Parmesan flavor. Even my kids love this delicious, easy-to-fix recipe.
—*Lettie Simon, Baton Rouge, Louisiana*

1/2 cup all-purpose flour
1/4 cup grated Parmesan cheese
3 tablespoons cornmeal
1 teaspoon paprika
1/4 teaspoon salt
1/4 teaspoon pepper
1 egg white
1/4 cup fat-free milk
4 catfish fillets (6 ounces *each*)

In a shallow dish, combine the flour, Parmesan cheese, cornmeal, paprika, salt and pepper; set aside. In another shallow dish, beat egg white and milk. Dip fillets in milk mixture, then in flour mixture. Place in a 13-in. x 9-in. x 2-in. baking dish coated with nonstick cooking spray. Bake, uncovered, at 350° for 35-40 minutes or until fish flakes easily with a fork. **Yield:** 4 servings.

Nutritional Analysis: One serving (1 fillet) equals 342 calories, 15 g fat (4 g saturated fat), 84 mg cholesterol, 355 mg sodium, 18 g carbohydrate, 1 g fiber, 32 g protein.
Diabetic Exchanges: 4 lean meat, 1 starch, 1/2 fat.

Getting the Jump on Catfish

IT'S NO FISH STORY! Aquaculture is the fastest-growing segment of agriculture in the U.S., with catfish being the leader in farm-raised fish and seafood.

- According to The Catfish Institute, nearly 450 million pounds of catfish were produced in man-made ponds as of 1995. Catfish farms cover more than 144,000 acres in the Mississippi delta area alone.
- A 3.5-ounce serving of farm-raised catfish contains 15 grams of protein, 7 grams of fat, 33 milligrams of cholesterol, 33 milligrams of sodium and 128 calories.

Rotini with Shrimp

(Pictured at right)

A lovely lemon-dill sauce coats this colorful blend of shrimp, rotini pasta and minced green onions. It's attractive enough to serve guests, and no one will guess the creamy sauce is low-fat.
—*Janice Mitchell, Aurora, Colorado*

4 quarts water
8 ounces uncooked spiral pasta
1-1/2 pounds uncooked medium shrimp, peeled and deveined
CREAMY LEMON SAUCE:
1 tablespoon butter *or* stick margarine
2 tablespoons all-purpose flour
1-1/2 cups 2% milk
1/3 cup dry white wine *or* chicken broth
1 tablespoon grated lemon peel
1 teaspoon dill weed
1 garlic clove, minced
3/4 teaspoon salt
1/8 teaspoon white pepper
1/4 cup finely chopped green onions

In a Dutch oven, bring water to a boil. Stir in pasta; return to a boil. Boil, uncovered, for 5 minutes. Add shrimp; boil 3 minutes longer or until pasta is tender and shrimp turn pink.

In a saucepan, melt butter. Stir in flour until smooth; gradually add milk. Bring to a boil; cook and stir for 1-2 minutes or until thickened. Stir in the wine or broth, lemon peel, dill, garlic, salt and pepper. Drain pasta and shrimp; place in a serving bowl. Add sauce and toss to coat. Sprinkle with onions. **Yield:** 4 servings.

Nutritional Analysis: One serving (1-1/2 cups) equals 420 calories, 7 g fat (3 g saturated fat), 257 mg cholesterol, 797 mg sodium, 48 g carbohydrate, 2 g fiber, 36 g protein.
Diabetic Exchanges: 4 very lean meat, 3 starch, 1 fat.

Walleye Veracruz

Living in Minnesota lake country, we've naturally had to come up with a variety of recipes for fresh walleye. This is a family favorite of ours that has Mexican flair. We sprinkle the fish with lemon-pepper, then top it with slices of onion, green pepper and tomato.
—*Robert and Linda Nagle, Park Rapids, Minnesota*

4 walleye *or* catfish fillets (6 ounces *each*)
2 teaspoons lemon-pepper seasoning
1 medium red onion, sliced and separated into rings
1 medium green pepper, sliced into rings
1 large tomato, sliced
1/4 cup sliced ripe olives

Place the fillets in a 13-in. x 9-in. x 2-in. baking dish coated with nonstick cooking spray. Sprinkle with lemon-pepper. Layer with the onion, green pepper, tomato and olives. Cover and bake at 350° for 25-30 minutes or until fish flakes easily with a fork. **Yield:** 4 servings.

Nutritional Analysis: One serving equals 197 calories, 3 g fat (1 g saturated fat), 146 mg cholesterol, 396 mg sodium, 7 g carbohydrate, 2 g fiber, 34 g protein.
Diabetic Exchanges: 5 very lean meat, 1 vegetable.
△ *Low-fat*

Citrus Orange Roughy

(Pictured at right and on page 163)

I hope you enjoy this wonderful recipe sent in by a total "non-fish" person. I love this baked orange roughy with crumb topping...and I love to serve it, too—to rave reviews! It's also quick and ultra-easy to prepare.
—Janet Escovitz, Pittsburgh, Pennsylvania

```
1/2 cup dry bread crumbs
3/4 teaspoon salt
1/2 cup orange juice
  2 tablespoons reduced-sodium soy sauce
  1 tablespoon butter or stick margarine, melted
  1 tablespoon olive or canola oil
1/2 teaspoon lemon juice
  4 orange roughy fillets (6 ounces each)
```

In a shallow bowl, combine bread crumbs and salt. In another shallow bowl, combine the orange juice, soy sauce, butter, oil and lemon juice. Dip the fillets into orange juice mixture, then coat with crumb mixture. Place in a 13-in. x 9-in. x 2-in. baking dish coated with nonstick cooking spray. Bake, uncovered, at 450° for 15-18 minutes or until fish flakes easily with a fork. **Yield:** 4 servings.

Nutritional Analysis: One serving equals 244 calories, 8 g fat (2 g saturated fat), 42 mg cholesterol, 996 mg sodium, 13 g carbohydrate, trace fiber, 27 g protein.
Diabetic Exchanges: 3 lean meat, 1 starch.

Seafood Pasta Delight

(Pictured at right and on page 163)

I concocted this appetizing recipe shortly after my husband gave me a pasta maker for Christmas—and it's been a big hit ever since. When I visit friends each summer, I take my wok along with me and prepare this shrimp and scallops dinner for the whole family.
—Debbi Campbell, Dartmouth, Nova Scotia

```
  8 ounces uncooked vermicelli
  2 tablespoons cornstarch
  1 teaspoon sugar
3/4 teaspoon salt
Dash pepper
1/2 cup chicken broth
1/2 cup dry white wine or additional chicken broth
1/4 cup reduced-sodium soy sauce
  1 medium sweet red pepper, julienned
  1 medium sweet yellow pepper, julienned
  1 cup fresh or frozen sugar snap peas
  2 to 3 garlic cloves, minced
1/4 teaspoon ground ginger or 1 teaspoon minced
    fresh gingerroot
  1 tablespoon olive or canola oil
  1 pound uncooked sea scallops, halved
  1 pound uncooked medium shrimp, peeled and
    deveined
  2 teaspoons sesame oil
```

Cook pasta according to package directions. In a bowl, combine the cornstarch, sugar, salt and pepper; stir in the broth, wine or additional broth and soy sauce until smooth; set aside.

In a large nonstick skillet or wok, stir-fry the peppers, peas, garlic and ginger in oil for 2-4 minutes or until crisp-tender. Add the scallops and shrimp; stir-fry 2 minutes longer. Stir cornstarch mixture and add to the pan. Bring to a boil; cook and stir for 2 minutes or until thickened. Drain the pasta; add to skillet. Heat until the scallops are firm and opaque and shrimp turn pink. Sprinkle with sesame oil. **Yield:** 8 servings.

Nutritional Analysis: One serving (1 cup) equals 288 calories, 5 g fat (1 g saturated fat), 105 mg cholesterol, 741 mg sodium, 31 g carbohydrate, 2 g fiber, 26 g protein.
Diabetic Exchanges: 3 very lean meat, 1-1/2 starch, 1 vegetable, 1 fat.

Poached Halibut

This recipe proves that even busy cooks can offer their family an unforgettable dinner. By using your microwave, you can get delicious whitefish on the table in no time.
—Rosadene Herold, Lakeville, Indiana

```
  4 halibut or cod fillets (1-1/2 pounds)
  1 teaspoon chicken bouillon granules
1/2 cup water
  1 tablespoon lemon juice
  1 teaspoon minced fresh parsley
3/4 teaspoon minced chives
1/4 teaspoon salt
  4 whole peppercorns
  1 bay leaf
  1 medium lemon, sliced
THYME WINE SAUCE:
  2 tablespoons butter or stick margarine
  1 garlic clove, minced
1/4 cup dry white wine or chicken broth
  1 teaspoon lemon juice
1/4 teaspoon each dried thyme and salt
```

Place the fillets in a microwave-safe dish; sprinkle with bouillon. In a bowl, combine the next seven ingredients. Pour over fish. Place lemon over fillets. Cover and microwave on high for 5 minutes or until fish flakes easily with a fork. Remove fish and keep warm. Strain cooking liquid; reserve 2 tablespoons.

For sauce, place butter and garlic in a microwave-safe dish. Microwave, uncovered, on high for 1 minute. Add the remaining ingredients and reserved cooking liquid. Cook 30 seconds longer or until bubbly. Serve over fish. **Yield:** 4 servings.

Editor's Note: This recipe was tested in an 850-watt microwave.

Nutritional Analysis: One serving equals 256 calories, 10 g fat (4 g saturated fat), 70 mg cholesterol, 733 mg sodium, 2 g carbohydrate, trace fiber, 36 g protein.
Diabetic Exchange: 5 lean meat.

Halibut with Kiwi Salsa

(Pictured on front cover)

Angling for a healthy way to prepare seafood, our Test Kitchen came up with a recipe for halibut with a tropical twist. Grilled to tender perfection, the fillets stay moist with a light coating of lemon and oil. They're topped with a fruity salsa of emerald kiwifruit, golden mango and red peppers for an eye-catching presentation.

 2 medium mangoes *or* 4 medium peaches, peeled and cubed (about 1-1/3 cups)
 3 kiwifruit, peeled and cubed (about 1 cup)
1/2 cup diced sweet red pepper
1/2 cup diced onion
 1 jalapeno pepper, seeded and minced*
 2 tablespoons lemon juice, *divided*
 1 tablespoon lime juice
 2 teaspoons minced fresh mint *or* 3/4 teaspoon dried mint
 1 teaspoon honey
1/2 teaspoon salt, *divided*
 1 tablespoon olive *or* canola oil
 4 halibut fillets *or* tuna steaks (6 ounces *each*)
1/4 teaspoon chili powder

For salsa, in a bowl, combine the mangoes, kiwi, red pepper, onion, jalapeno, 1 tablespoon lemon juice, lime juice, mint, honey and 1/4 teaspoon salt. Cover and refrigerate until serving.

In a small bowl, combine the oil and remaining lemon juice; brush over both sides of fish. Sprinkle with chili powder and remaining salt. If grilling the fish, coat grill rack with nonstick cooking spray before starting the grill. Grill fillets, covered, over medium heat or broil 6 in. from the heat for 5-7 minutes on each side or until fish flakes easily with a fork. Serve with salsa. **Yield:** 4 servings.

*Editor's Note: When cutting or seeding hot peppers, use rubber or plastic gloves to protect your hands. Avoid touching your face.

Nutritional Analysis: One serving (1 fillet with 1/2 cup salsa) equals 301 calories, 8 g fat (1 g saturated fat), 54 mg cholesterol, 391 mg sodium, 21 g carbohydrate, 3 g fiber, 37 g protein.
Diabetic Exchanges: 5 very lean meat, 1 fruit, 1 vegetable, 1 fat.

Shrimp Stir-Fry

(Pictured above)

In the 15 years I've been making this stir-fry, I've shared the recipe many times. When our children were still at home, they offered to wash the pan after dinner to encourage me to make it!
—*Delia Kennedy, Deer Park, Washington*

1-1/2 pounds medium uncooked shrimp, peeled and deveined
1/2 teaspoon salt
1/4 teaspoon pepper
 2 tablespoons canola oil
 1 cup fresh broccoli florets
 1 cup julienned sweet red pepper
 4 tablespoons reduced-sodium chicken broth, *divided*
 1 cup sliced fresh mushrooms
1-1/2 cups fresh sugar snap peas
3/4 cup sliced green onions
 3 garlic cloves, minced

Sprinkle shrimp with salt and pepper. In a large nonstick skillet or wok, stir-fry shrimp in hot oil until shrimp turn pink. Remove with a slotted spoon and keep warm.

In the same pan, stir-fry the broccoli and red pepper in 2 tablespoons broth for 5 minutes. Add mushrooms; stir-fry for 2 minutes. Add the peas, onions, garlic and remaining broth; stir-fry for 3-4 minutes or until vegetables are crisp-tender. Return shrimp to the pan; stir-fry for 1-2 minutes or until heated through. **Yield:** 4 servings.

Nutritional Analysis: One serving (1-1/2 cups) equals 226 calories, 8 g fat (1 g saturated fat), 202 mg cholesterol, 581 mg sodium, 12 g carbohydrate, 4 g fiber, 25 g protein.
Diabetic Exchanges: 3 lean meat, 2 vegetable.

Open-Face Tuna Melts

I created this recipe when I got married 20 years ago and have served it countless times since then. Sometimes I add a little chili powder, heap the tuna mixture over tortilla chips instead and microwave for hearty nachos.
—Marilyn Smelser, Albany, Oregon

- 2 cans (6 ounces *each*) light water-packed tuna, drained and flaked
- 3/4 cup chopped sweet red pepper
- 1/2 cup chopped fresh mushrooms
- 1/2 cup shredded reduced-fat cheddar cheese
- 1/4 cup sliced stuffed olives
- 4-1/2 teaspoons reduced-fat mayonnaise *or* salad dressing
- 4 English muffins, split and toasted
- 8 thin slices tomato

In a bowl, combine the tuna, red pepper, mushrooms, cheese and olives. Fold in mayonnaise. Spread over English muffin halves. Top each with a tomato slice. Broil 6 in. from the heat for 7-9 minutes or until lightly browned. Serve immediately. **Yield:** 8 servings.

Nutritional Analysis: *One serving equals 165 calories, 5 g fat (2 g saturated fat), 24 mg cholesterol, 413 mg sodium, 16 g carbohydrate, 2 g fiber, 14 g protein.*
Diabetic Exchanges: *2 lean meat, 1 starch.*

Salsa Fish Skillet

Zucchini and yellow summer squash add seasonal flair to this colorful fish dish from our Test Kitchen.

- 1 pound halibut steaks *or* other firm whitefish, cut into 1-inch pieces
- 3 teaspoons canola oil, *divided*
- 1 medium yellow summer squash, julienned
- 1 medium zucchini, julienned
- 1 cup sliced fresh mushrooms
- 2 garlic cloves, minced
- 1/4 to 1/2 teaspoon ground cumin
- 1-1/2 cups chunky salsa
- 4 teaspoons minced fresh cilantro *or* parsley

In a large nonstick skillet or wok, stir-fry fish in 2 teaspoons hot oil for 3-4 minutes or until fish flakes easily with a fork; remove and keep warm. Add vegetables, garlic, cumin and remaining oil to the skillet. Stir-fry for 2-3 minutes or until vegetables are crisp-tender. Return fish to the pan. Add salsa; heat through. Sprinkle with cilantro. **Yield:** 4 servings.

Nutritional Analysis: *One serving (1 cup) equals 207 calories, 6 g fat (1 g saturated fat), 36 mg cholesterol, 486 mg sodium, 11 g carbohydrate, 3 g fiber, 27 g protein.*
Diabetic Exchanges: *3 lean meat, 2 vegetable.*

Spicy Salmon Patties

(Pictured below)

Made with canned salmon, these patties are good hot or cold. I usually serve them on buns with slices of ripe tomato, sweet red onion, and red and green bell pepper.
—Barbara Coston, Little Rock, Arkansas

- 2 slices whole wheat bread
- 12 fat-free pretzel twists
- 2 teaspoons Italian seasoning
- 2 teaspoons salt-free spicy seasoning blend
- 1/2 teaspoon pepper
- 1/2 cup egg substitute
- 1 can (14-3/4 ounces) salmon, drained, bones and skin removed
- 1/2 cup finely chopped onion
- 1/3 cup finely chopped green pepper
- 1 tablespoon finely chopped jalapeno pepper*
- 2 garlic cloves, minced
- 2 tablespoons olive *or* canola oil

Place the first five ingredients in a blender or food processor; cover and process until mixture resembles fine crumbs. In a bowl, combine the egg substitute, salmon, onion, green pepper, jalapeno, garlic and 1/2 cup crumb mixture. Shape into eight 1/2-in.-thick patties. Coat with remaining crumb mixture.

In a large nonstick skillet over medium heat, cook patties in oil for 4-5 minutes on each side or until lightly browned. **Yield:** 4 servings.

***Editor's Note:** When cutting or seeding hot peppers, use rubber or plastic gloves to protect your hands. Avoid touching your face.

Nutritional Analysis: *One serving (2 patties) equals 304 calories, 14 g fat (2 g saturated fat), 58 mg cholesterol, 870 mg sodium, 18 g carbohydrate, 2 g fiber, 26 g protein.*
Diabetic Exchanges: *3 lean meat, 1-1/2 fat, 1 starch.*

1 tablespoon butter *or* stick margarine
1 small onion, thinly sliced
4 fresh *or* frozen cod *or* haddock fillets (6 ounces *each*), thawed
1 teaspoon seasoned salt
1/2 teaspoon dill weed
1/4 teaspoon pepper
1/4 cup grated Parmesan cheese
1/4 cup fat-free mayonnaise
1 tablespoon minced fresh parsley
1 tablespoon lemon juice
2 tablespoons sliced almonds, toasted

Place butter in a 13-in. x 9-in. x 2-in. baking dish; place in a 400° oven until melted. Spread butter over bottom of dish; cover with onion. Arrange fish over onion; sprinkle with salt, dill and pepper. Combine the Parmesan cheese, mayonnaise, parsley and lemon juice; spread over fish. Bake, uncovered, at 400° for 18-20 minutes or until fish flakes easily with a fork. Sprinkle with almonds. **Yield:** 4 servings.

Nutritional Analysis: One serving (1 fillet) equals 223 calories, 7 g fat (3 g saturated fat), 86 mg cholesterol, 716 mg sodium, 4 g carbohydrate, 1 g fiber, 33 g protein.
Diabetic Exchanges: 4 very lean meat, 1 fat, 1/2 starch.

Coriander Salmon

(Pictured above)

This pleasant salmon is good hot or cold. For a hot meal, I serve it with rice or pierogies. For a cold meal in the summer, I serve it with a salad and some crusty bread.
—*Nancy Deans, Rochester, New York*

1/2 teaspoon salt
1/8 teaspoon pepper
1/2 teaspoon ground coriander
4 salmon fillets (6 ounces *each*)
2 teaspoons olive *or* canola oil
2 garlic cloves, minced
2 teaspoons lime juice
1/4 to 1/2 teaspoon hot pepper sauce

In a small dish, combine the salt, pepper and coriander. Sprinkle over salmon. In a nonstick skillet, cook salmon in oil over medium heat for 4 minutes on each side. Add the garlic, lime juice and hot pepper sauce. Reduce heat; cover and cook 3-4 minutes longer or until fish flakes easily with a fork. **Yield:** 4 servings.

Nutritional Analysis: One fillet equals 335 calories, 21 g fat (4 g saturated fat), 100 mg cholesterol, 396 mg sodium, 1 g carbohydrate, trace fiber, 34 g protein.
Diabetic Exchanges: 5 lean meat, 1 fat.

Almond-Topped Fish

A co-worker gave me this recipe, but I didn't try it until recently. What a mistake it was to wait! It's easier than dipping, coating and frying...and the flavor is outstanding. Once you've tried this tender fish, you'll never go back to fried.
—*Heidi Kirsch, Waterloo, Iowa*

Stir-Fried Scallops

Scallops add interest to this mild tomato-based stovetop supper. Try serving the saucy mixture over rice or angel hair pasta...and garnish with cilantro if you like.
—*Stephany Gocobachi, Novato, California*

1 small onion, chopped
3 garlic cloves, minced
1 tablespoon olive *or* canola oil
3/4 pound sea scallops, halved
2 medium plum tomatoes, chopped
2 tablespoons lemon juice
1/4 teaspoon salt
1/8 teaspoon pepper
Hot cooked pasta *or* rice, optional

In a small nonstick skillet or wok, stir-fry onion and garlic in hot oil until tender. Add scallops; stir-fry until scallops turn opaque. Add tomatoes; cook and stir 1-2 minutes longer or until heated through. Stir in lemon juice, salt and pepper. Serve over pasta or rice if desired. **Yield:** 2 servings.

Nutritional Analysis: One serving (1 cup stir-fry mixture, calculated without pasta or rice) equals 246 calories, 8 g fat (1 g saturated fat), 56 mg cholesterol, 575 mg sodium, 13 g carbohydrate, 1 g fiber, 30 g protein.
Diabetic Exchanges: 4 very lean meat, 2 vegetable, 1-1/2 fat.

Meatless Main Dishes

You won't find any meat in these main dishes
…but you won't miss it, either. This hearty
vegetarian fare is so delightfully satisfying,
even your most ardent meat-and-potatoes
lovers will give it rave reviews.

Mushroom Zucchini Lasagna (page 180)

Penne with Veggies 'n' Black Beans

(Pictured below)

Chock-full of zucchini, tomatoes, sweet pepper and carrots, this hearty pasta dish puts your garden harvest to good use. For variety, I sometimes add one-half cup of salsa or one-half cup of thickened teriyaki sauce. I'm always asked for the recipe.
—Vickie Spoerle, Carmel, Indiana

10 ounces uncooked penne *or* medium tube pasta
1 cup sliced zucchini
1 cup sliced carrots
1/2 cup sliced fresh mushrooms
1/2 cup julienned green *or* sweet red pepper
1 small onion, thinly sliced
1 garlic clove, minced
1 tablespoon *each* minced fresh basil, oregano and thyme *or* 1 teaspoon *each* dried basil, oregano and thyme
1/2 teaspoon salt
1/4 teaspoon pepper
2 tablespoons olive *or* canola oil, *divided*
1 can (15 ounces) black beans, rinsed and drained
2/3 cup chopped seeded tomatoes
1/3 cup shredded Parmesan cheese
2 tablespoons minced fresh parsley

Cook pasta according to package directions. Meanwhile, in a large nonstick skillet, saute the zucchini, carrots, mushrooms, green pepper, onion, garlic and seasonings in 1 tablespoon oil until crisp-tender. Stir in the beans.

Drain pasta; add to vegetable mixture. Add tomatoes and remaining olive oil; toss gently. Sprinkle with Parmesan cheese and parsley. **Yield:** 6 servings.

Nutritional Analysis: One serving (1-1/3 cups) equals 315 calories, 8 g fat (2 g saturated fat), 3 mg cholesterol, 502 mg sodium, 50 g carbohydrate, 7 g fiber, 13 g protein.
Diabetic Exchanges: 3 starch, 1 vegetable, 1 fat.
▲ **Meatless**

Spaghetti Pie

Pasta shows its versatility as a "pie crust" in this family-pleasing main dish. This is a combination of several recipes. I came up with it when I didn't have all the ingredients to make any one of them. This nice alternative to lasagna doesn't taste light.
—Carol Beyerl, Ellensburg, Washington

6 ounces uncooked spaghetti
1/2 cup egg substitute
1/2 cup grated Parmesan cheese, *divided*
3 ounces reduced-fat cream cheese
1/2 cup reduced-fat sour cream
1/2 cup chopped green pepper
1/2 pound fresh mushrooms, sliced
4 garlic cloves, minced
2 tablespoons butter *or* stick margarine
2 cups meatless spaghetti sauce
1/2 cup shredded part-skim mozzarella cheese

Cook spaghetti according to package directions; drain. Add the egg substitute and 1/4 cup Parmesan cheese. Press onto the bottom and up the sides of a 9-in. deep-dish pie plate coated with nonstick cooking spray. In a mixing bowl, beat the cream cheese, sour cream, green pepper and remaining Parmesan cheese. Spread over spaghetti crust.

In a nonstick skillet, saute mushrooms and garlic in butter until tender. Spoon over cheese mixture. Spread with spaghetti sauce. Bake, uncovered, at 350° for 20 minutes. Sprinkle with mozzarella cheese; bake 5 minutes longer or until cheese is melted. Let stand for 10-15 minutes before cutting. **Yield:** 6 servings.

Nutritional Analysis: One serving equals 326 calories, 13 g fat (8 g saturated fat), 37 mg cholesterol, 707 mg sodium, 36 g carbohydrate, 3 g fiber, 17 g protein.
Diabetic Exchanges: 2 starch, 2 lean meat, 1 vegetable, 1 fat.
▲ **Meatless**

Mushroom Zucchini Lasagna

(Pictured on page 179)

A homemade zucchini tomato sauce gives this entree its fresh-tasting flair. I know you'll enjoy the recipe for this creamy meatless lasagna.
—Billie Moss, El Sobrante, California

1-1/4 pounds zucchini, *divided*
1/2 pound fresh mushrooms, sliced
1 large onion, finely chopped
3 garlic cloves, minced
1 tablespoon olive *or* canola oil
1 can (28 ounces) crushed tomatoes

6 tablespoons minced fresh parsley, *divided*
2 tablespoons sugar
1/2 teaspoon salt, *divided*
1/4 teaspoon pepper, *divided*
3 eggs
2 cups (8 ounces) shredded part-skim mozzarella cheese
1-1/2 cups reduced-fat ricotta cheese
1 package (8 ounces) reduced-fat cream cheese
1/2 cup grated Parmesan cheese
1/4 teaspoon onion powder
9 lasagna noodles, cooked, rinsed and drained
2 tablespoons shredded Parmesan cheese

Finely dice 1/2 cup zucchini; set aside. Slice the remaining zucchini. In a large saucepan, saute the sliced zucchini, mushrooms, onion and garlic in oil until tender. Stir in the tomatoes, 3 tablespoons parsley, sugar, 1/4 teaspoon salt and 1/8 teaspoon pepper. Bring to a boil. Reduce heat; simmer, uncovered, for 12-15 minutes.

In a mixing bowl, combine the eggs, mozzarella, ricotta, cream cheese, grated Parmesan, onion powder and remaining parsley, salt and pepper. Spread 1 cup of the tomato sauce in a 13-in. x 9-in. x 2-in. baking dish coated with nonstick cooking spray. Layer with three noodles, half of the cheese mixture and a third of the remaining sauce. Repeat layers once. Top with remaining noodles and sauce.

Cover and bake at 350° for 35 minutes. Uncover; sprinkle with diced zucchini and shredded Parmesan. Bake 10-15 minutes longer or until bubbly. Let stand for 15 minutes before cutting. **Yield:** 12 servings.

Nutritional Analysis: One serving equals 263 calories, 13 g fat (7 g saturated fat), 87 mg cholesterol, 551 mg sodium, 20 g carbohydrate, 2 g fiber, 17 g protein.
Diabetic Exchanges: 2 lean meat, 1 starch, 1 vegetable, 1 fat.
▲ *Meatless*

Mexican Vegetable Pizza

(Pictured above right)

Hold the pepperoni! Try this change-of-pace pizza that's big on veggie flavor. Topped with black beans, red tomato, golden corn and green pepper, it's as colorful as it is tasty. Why not spice up your next party, light lunch or dinner with zesty slices?
—Barbara Nowakowski, North Tonawanda, New York

1/2 small onion, chopped
1 teaspoon chili powder
1/2 teaspoon ground cumin
1/4 teaspoon ground cinnamon
1 tablespoon water
1 can (15 ounces) black beans, rinsed and drained
1/4 cup canned diced green chilies
1 package (16 ounces) prebaked Italian bread shell crust
1 cup salsa
1 cup (4 ounces) shredded reduced-fat cheddar cheese, *divided*
3/4 cup chopped fresh tomato
1/2 cup frozen corn, thawed
1/2 cup chopped green pepper
3 tablespoons sliced ripe olives, drained
1/2 cup reduced-fat sour cream

In a nonstick skillet coated with nonstick cooking spray, combine the onion, chili powder, cumin, cinnamon and water. Cover and cook for 3-4 minutes. Remove from the heat; stir in beans and chilies. Transfer half of the bean mixture to a food processor; cover and process until almost smooth.

Spread pureed bean mixture over the crust. Spread with salsa. Top with half of the cheese and remaining bean mixture. Sprinkle with tomato, corn, green pepper, olives and remaining cheese. Bake at 450° for 10-12 minutes or until crust is golden brown. Serve with sour cream. **Yield:** 8 servings.

Nutritional Analysis: One slice with 1 tablespoon sour cream equals 281 calories, 8 g fat (3 g saturated fat), 13 mg cholesterol, 767 mg sodium, 40 g carbohydrate, 4 g fiber, 15 g protein.
Diabetic Exchanges: 2 starch, 1 lean meat, 1 vegetable, 1 fat.
▲ *Meatless*

and pepper; stir in vegetables. Pour over crust. Sprinkle with cheese. Bake, uncovered, at 375° for 25-30 minutes or until a knife inserted near the center comes out clean. **Yield:** 6 servings.

Nutritional Analysis: One serving equals 226 calories, 7 g fat (5 g saturated fat), 24 mg cholesterol, 527 mg sodium, 23 g carbohydrate, 2 g fiber, 19 g protein.
Diabetic Exchanges: 2 lean meat, 1 starch, 1 vegetable.
▲ *Meatless*

Broccoli Rice Hot Dish 6PP

(Pictured above)

With green broccoli, golden cheese and sweet red peppers, this bountiful bake has plenty of eye appeal...and it makes a tasty and satisfying meatless entree or side dish.
—Gretchen Widner, Sun City West, Arizona

   2 cups hot cooked rice
3/4 cup shredded reduced-fat cheddar cheese
1/2 cup egg substitute
3/4 teaspoon garlic salt
FILLING:
   1 package (10 ounces) frozen chopped broccoli, thawed
   4 ounces chopped fresh mushrooms
1/2 cup chopped sweet red pepper
1/2 medium onion, chopped
   1 cup egg substitute
1/2 cup fat-free milk
1/2 teaspoon onion salt
1/2 teaspoon pepper
   1 cup (4 ounces) shredded reduced-fat cheddar cheese

In a bowl, combine rice, cheese, egg substitute and garlic salt. Press firmly into a 2-qt. baking dish coated with nonstick cooking spray. Bake at 375° for 10 minutes. Meanwhile, place broccoli, mushrooms, red pepper and onion in a steamer basket over 1 in. boiling water in a saucepan. Bring to a boil; cover and steam for 5 minutes or until crisp-tender.
   In a bowl, combine the egg substitute, milk, onion salt

Stir-Fried Asparagus

This saucy dish, with crisp-tender asparagus and crunchy water chestnuts, can be served as a meatless entree or side.
—Rochelle Higgins, Woodbridge, Virginia

   1 tablespoon cornstarch
3/4 cup reduced-sodium chicken broth *or* vegetable broth
   2 tablespoons reduced-sodium soy sauce
3/4 pound fresh asparagus, trimmed and cut into 2-inch pieces
1/2 medium green pepper, cut into julienned strips
1/4 cup sliced green onions
   1 garlic clove, minced
   1 tablespoon canola oil
   1 cup sliced fresh mushrooms
   1 can (8 ounces) water chestnuts, drained

In a small bowl, combine the cornstarch, broth and soy sauce until smooth; set aside. In a large nonstick skillet or wok, stir-fry the asparagus, green pepper, onions and garlic in hot oil for 2-3 minutes. Add the mushrooms; stir-fry for 1-2 minutes. Add water chestnuts; stir-fry 1-2 minutes longer. Stir broth mixture; add to the vegetables. Bring to a boil; cook and stir for 2 minutes or until thickened. **Yield:** 3 servings.

 ## Selecting Asparagus Spears

• Fresh asparagus is generally available February through late June.
• Look for firm, bright green spears with closed tips that may have a lavender tint. Thinner spears are more tender. Choose spears that are approximately the same size—they'll cook more evenly.
• Store asparagus in a sealed plastic bag in the refrigerator for up to 4 days. Wash it just before using.
• To prepare, snap off the woody ends. When bent, a fresh asparagus spear will break off naturally at the point where it becomes tough. If the outer layer of the stalk is fibrous, use a vegetable peeler to remove it.
• Fresh asparagus can be steamed on the stovetop, cooked in the microwave or roasted in the oven. Cook only until stalks are crisp-tender.

Nutritional Analysis: One serving (1 cup) equals 133 calories, 5 g fat (trace saturated fat), 0 cholesterol, 567 mg sodium, 17 g carbohydrate, 6 g fiber, 5 g protein.
Diabetic Exchanges: *2 vegetable, 1 fat, 1/2 starch.*
▲ *Meatless*

Spinach-Stuffed Pizza

(Pictured below)

I had my first stuffed pizza when I attended college near Chicago. I was amazed to see pizza well over an inch thick, with toppings on the inside! When I serve this version to my family, there are no leftovers.
—*Nancy Gilmour, Sumner, Iowa*

1 loaf (1 pound) frozen bread dough, thawed
1 package (10 ounces) frozen chopped spinach, thawed and squeezed dry
1 cup chopped fresh mushrooms
1/2 cup chopped onion
1/4 teaspoon salt
1/8 teaspoon pepper
2 cups (8 ounces) shredded part-skim mozzarella cheese
1/2 cup pizza sauce
2 tablespoons shredded Parmesan cheese

Place dough in a greased bowl, turning once to grease top. Cover and let rise in a warm place until doubled, about 1 hour. Punch dough down; divide into thirds. On a lightly floured surface, roll one portion of dough into a 10-in. circle. Transfer to a 9-in. springform pan coated with nonstick cooking spray. Press dough onto bottom and up sides of pan.

In a bowl, combine the spinach, mushrooms, onion, salt and pepper. Sprinkle half of the mozzarella cheese over crust. Cover with spinach mixture; sprinkle with remaining mozzarella. On a lightly floured surface, roll out a second portion of dough into a 10-in. circle; place over cheese layer. Pinch together top and bottom crust. (Save remaining dough for another use.)

Bake at 400° for 25-30 minutes or until lightly browned. Spread pizza sauce over top crust; sprinkle with Parmesan cheese. Bake 5-6 minutes longer or until cheese is melted. Let stand for 5 minutes before cutting. **Yield:** 6 servings.

Nutritional Analysis: One serving (one piece) equals 285 calories, 9 g fat (4 g saturated fat), 23 mg cholesterol, 712 mg sodium, 35 g carbohydrate, 4 g fiber, 18 g protein.
Diabetic Exchanges: *2 starch, 1 lean meat, 1 vegetable, 1 fat.*
▲ *Meatless*

Sweet Potato Lentil Stew

Years ago, I fell in love with the spicy flavor and wonderful aroma of this hearty slow-cooker recipe. You can serve the stew alone or as a topper for meat and poultry. It's great either way!
—*Heather Gray, Little Rock, Arkansas*

4 cups vegetable broth
3 cups sweet potatoes, peeled and cubed (about 1-1/4 pounds)
1-1/2 cups lentils, rinsed
3 medium carrots, cut into 1-inch pieces
1 medium onion, chopped
4 garlic cloves, minced
1/2 teaspoon ground cumin
1/4 teaspoon ground ginger
1/4 teaspoon cayenne pepper
1/4 cup minced fresh cilantro *or* parsley
1/4 teaspoon salt

In a slow cooker, combine the first nine ingredients. Cover and cook on low for 5-6 hours or until vegetables are tender. Stir in the cilantro and salt. **Yield:** 6 servings.

Nutritional Analysis: One serving (1-1/3 cups) equals 247 calories, 1 g fat (trace saturated fat), 0 cholesterol, 785 mg sodium, 48 g carbohydrate, 13 g fiber, 14 g protein.
Diabetic Exchanges: *2-1/2 starch, 1 very lean meat, 1 vegetable.*
△ *Low-fat*
▲ *Meatless*

Unfried Refried Beans

Refried beans were a staple in our home when I was growing up, but the dish my dad made called for crisp bacon and bacon fat. Being health-conscious, I lightened up the recipe and found that it remained as tasty as I remember from my childhood.
—Michele Martinez, Albany, New York

8 ounces dried pinto beans, sorted and rinsed
2 quarts water
2 tablespoons chili powder
2 garlic cloves, slightly crushed
2 teaspoons ground cumin, *divided*
1 teaspoon pepper
1 teaspoon salt, *divided*
1/8 to 1/4 teaspoon crushed red pepper flakes
Tostada shells, optional
Toppings of your choice, optional

Place beans in a soup kettle or Dutch oven; add water to cover by 2 in. Bring to a boil; boil for 2 minutes. Remove from the heat; cover and let stand for 1 hour. Drain and rinse beans, discarding liquid.

Return the beans to Dutch oven; add the 2 quarts of water. Add the chili powder, garlic, 1-3/4 teaspoons cumin, pepper, 3/4 teaspoon salt and pepper flakes. Bring to a boil. Reduce heat; cover and simmer for 2-3 hours or until the beans are tender.

Drain beans, reserving 3/4 cup liquid. Place bean mixture in a bowl; coarsely mash. Gradually stir in reserved cooking liquid until mixture reaches desired consistency. Stir in the remaining cumin and salt. Serve on tostada shells with toppings of your choice if desired. **Yield:** 5 servings.

Nutritional Analysis: One serving (1/2 cup) equals 165 calories, 1 g fat (trace saturated fat), 0 cholesterol, 505 mg sodium, 31 g carbohydrate, 11 g fiber, 10 g protein.
Diabetic Exchanges: *1-1/2 starch, 1 very lean meat.*
△ **Low-fat**
▲ **Meatless**

Roasted Veggie Sandwiches

Looking for a delicious way to use a variety of veggies? Our Test Kitchen home economists recommend tucking your garden harvest into this hearty sandwich. The pleasant flavor of eggplant, red pepper, onion, zucchini and yellow summer squash is enhanced by a creamy basil yogurt spread. The bright blend of colors is sure to perk appetites, too!

3 tablespoons balsamic vinegar
2 teaspoons olive *or* canola oil
1/4 cup minced fresh basil *or* 1 tablespoon dried basil
1 small eggplant, peeled and sliced lengthwise
1 medium sweet red pepper, sliced
1 small red onion, sliced and separated into rings
1 small zucchini, thinly sliced
1 small yellow summer squash, thinly sliced
BASIL YOGURT SPREAD:
1/4 cup fat-free plain yogurt
2 tablespoons reduced-fat mayonnaise

1 tablespoon minced fresh basil *or* 1 teaspoon dried basil
1 teaspoon lemon juice
4 French rolls, warmed

In a large bowl, combine the vinegar, oil and basil. Add the eggplant, red pepper, onion, zucchini and yellow squash; toss to coat. Place vegetables in a single layer in a large roasting pan. Roast, uncovered, at 450° for 20-30 minutes or until tender, stirring occasionally.

Meanwhile, in a small bowl, combine the yogurt, mayonnaise, basil and lemon juice. Hollow out rolls if necessary. Serve roasted vegetables on rolls with yogurt spread. **Yield:** 4 servings.

Nutritional Analysis: One sandwich equals 275 calories, 7 g fat (1 g saturated fat), 3 mg cholesterol, 421 mg sodium, 47 g carbohydrate, 8 g fiber, 9 g protein.
Diabetic Exchanges: *3 vegetable, 2 starch, 1 fat.*
▲ **Meatless**

Broccoli 'n' Tomato Pasta

(Pictured below)

Fresh tomatoes and broccoli add pretty color to this hearty spaghetti dish. You're guaranteed to not miss the meat.
—Lillian Justis, Woodbine, New Jersey

8 ounces uncooked spaghetti
2 cups fresh broccoli florets
2 large tomatoes, peeled, seeded and coarsely chopped
2 garlic cloves, minced
1/4 to 1/2 teaspoon crushed red pepper flakes
2 tablespoons olive *or* canola oil
1/2 cup sliced ripe olives

1/2 cup minced fresh parsley
1/4 cup grated Romano cheese
3/4 teaspoon salt
1/8 teaspoon pepper

In a large kettle or Dutch oven, bring 3 quarts water to a boil. Add spaghetti; boil, uncovered, for 5 minutes. Add broccoli; boil 3-4 minutes longer or until pasta and broccoli are tender.

Meanwhile, in a nonstick skillet, saute the tomatoes, garlic and pepper flakes in oil for 2 minutes. Drain pasta mixture; add to the skillet. Add remaining ingredients and toss to coat. **Yield:** 4 servings.

Nutritional Analysis: One serving (1 cup) equals 348 calories, 12 g fat (2 g saturated fat), 7 mg cholesterol, 688 mg sodium, 51 g carbohydrate, 4 g fiber, 12 g protein.
Diabetic Exchanges: 3 starch, 2 fat, 1 vegetable.
▲ *Meatless*

Mostaccioli Bake

This homey lasagna-style casserole will appeal to the whole family. There's plenty of spaghetti sauce to keep the layers of tender pasta and spinach-cheese mixture moist. It's a hearty main dish that can be made early in the day, refrigerated and baked at dinnertime.
—Dorothy Bateman, Carver, Massachusetts

8 ounces uncooked mostaccioli *or* medium tube pasta
1 egg
1 egg white
1 carton (16 ounces) 1% cottage cheese
1 package (10 ounces) frozen chopped spinach, thawed and squeezed dry
1 cup (4 ounces) shredded part-skim mozzarella cheese, *divided*
2/3 cup shredded Parmesan cheese, *divided*
1/3 cup minced fresh parsley
1/4 teaspoon salt
1/4 teaspoon pepper
2-1/2 cups meatless spaghetti sauce, *divided*

Cook pasta according to package directions. Meanwhile, in a large bowl, combine the egg, egg white, cottage cheese, spinach, 2/3 cup mozzarella cheese, 1/3 cup Parmesan cheese, parsley, salt and pepper; set aside. Drain pasta; stir in 2 cups spaghetti sauce.

Layer half of the pasta mixture in an 11-in. x 7-in. x 2-in. baking dish coated with nonstick cooking spray. Top with spinach mixture, remaining pasta mixture and remaining spaghetti sauce. Cover and bake at 350° for 35-40 minutes or until bubbly. Uncover; sprinkle with remaining mozzarella and Parmesan cheeses. Bake 5 minutes longer or until cheese is melted. **Yield:** 8 servings.

Nutritional Analysis: One serving equals 286 calories, 7 g fat (4 g saturated fat), 42 mg cholesterol, 837 mg sodium, 35 g carbohydrate, 4 g fiber, 21 g protein.
Diabetic Exchanges: 2 lean meat, 2 vegetable, 1-1/2 starch.
▲ *Meatless*

Veggie Brown Rice Wraps

(Pictured above)

Salsa gives a bit of zip to the brown rice and bean filling in these meatless tortilla wraps.
—Lisa Sullivan, St. Marys, Ohio

1 medium sweet red *or* green pepper, diced
1 cup sliced fresh mushrooms
2 garlic cloves, minced
1 tablespoon olive *or* canola oil
2 cups cooked brown rice
1 can (16 ounces) kidney beans, rinsed and drained
1 cup frozen corn, thawed
1/4 cup chopped green onions
1/2 teaspoon ground cumin
1/2 teaspoon pepper
1/4 teaspoon salt
6 flour tortillas (8 inches), warmed
1/2 cup shredded reduced-fat cheddar cheese
3/4 cup salsa

In a large nonstick skillet, saute the red pepper, mushrooms and garlic in oil until tender. Add the rice, beans, corn, green onions, cumin, pepper and salt. Cook and stir for 4-6 minutes or until heated through. Spoon 3/4 cup onto each tortilla. Sprinkle with cheese; drizzle with salsa. Fold sides of tortilla over filling; serve immediately. **Yield:** 6 servings.

Nutritional Analysis: One wrap equals 371 calories, 8 g fat (2 g saturated fat), 7 mg cholesterol, 816 mg sodium, 63 g carbohydrate, 5 g fiber, 14 g protein.
▲ *Meatless*

Greek Hero

(Pictured above)

With plenty of garden-fresh flavors and a hearty bean spread that packs protein, this stacked submarine makes a satisfying meal-in-one.
—Margaret Wilson, Hemet, California

2 tablespoons lemon juice
1 tablespoon olive *or* canola oil
1 can (15 ounces) garbanzo beans *or* chickpeas, rinsed and drained
2 garlic cloves, minced
1 teaspoon dried oregano
1/4 teaspoon salt
1/8 teaspoon pepper
SANDWICH:
   1 unsliced loaf (8 ounces) French bread
   2 medium sweet red peppers, cut into thin strips
1/2 medium cucumber, sliced
   2 small tomatoes, sliced
1/4 cup thinly sliced red onion
1/4 cup chopped ripe olives
1/4 cup chopped stuffed olives
1/2 cup crumbled feta cheese
   4 lettuce leaves

For hummus, place the lemon juice, oil and beans in a food processor; cover and process until smooth. Add garlic, oregano, salt and pepper; mix well.

Slice bread in half horizontally. Carefully hollow out bottom half, leaving a 1/2-in. shell. Spread hummus into shell. Layer with the red peppers, cucumber, tomatoes, onion, olives, cheese and lettuce. Replace bread top. Cut into four portions. **Yield:** 4 servings.

Nutritional Analysis: One serving equals 350 calories, 12 g fat (4 g saturated fat), 17 mg cholesterol, 1,219 mg sodium, 50 g carbohydrate, 9 g fiber, 12 g protein.
Diabetic Exchanges: 2-1/2 starch, 2 vegetable, 1-1/2 fat, 1 lean meat.
▲ *Meatless*

Four-Cheese Spinach Pizza

I adapted this recipe from one given to me by my Aunt Rosemary. I especially like to make this pizza in summer when fresh spinach and basil are plentiful—they are key to the wonderful taste.
—Barbra Robinson, Hamburg, Pennsylvania

   2 packages (10 ounces *each*) fresh spinach
3/4 cup shredded part-skim mozzarella cheese, *divided*
1/2 cup fat-free cottage cheese
1/3 cup grated Parmesan cheese
1/4 teaspoon salt
1/8 teaspoon pepper
   1 prebaked Italian bread shell crust (10 ounces)
   1 medium tomato, chopped
1/4 cup chopped green onions
1/4 cup sliced ripe olives
   1 teaspoon minced fresh basil
   1 teaspoon olive *or* canola oil
   1 teaspoon balsamic vinegar
   1 garlic clove, minced
1/2 cup crumbled feta cheese

In a large nonstick skillet coated with nonstick cooking spray, saute spinach for 2-3 minutes or until limp; remove from the skillet. Cool slightly; chop. In a bowl, combine 1/4 cup mozzarella cheese, cottage cheese and Parmesan cheese. Stir in the spinach, salt and pepper. Spread over crust to within 1/2 in. of edge.

In a bowl, combine the tomato, onions, olives, basil, oil, vinegar and garlic; sprinkle over spinach mixture. Top with the feta cheese and remaining mozzarella cheese. Bake at 400° for 12-14 minutes or until cheese softens and is lightly browned. **Yield:** 6 servings.

Nutritional Analysis: One slice equals 270 calories, 11 g fat (4 g saturated fat), 24 mg cholesterol, 823 mg sodium, 28 g carbohydrate, 1 g fiber, 17 g protein.
Diabetic Exchanges: 1-1/2 starch, 1-1/2 fat, 1 lean meat, 1 vegetable.
▲ *Meatless*

Sweet-Sour Kidney Beans

(Pictured at right)

You can substitute a variety of beans—such as soybeans, pinto or navy beans—in this versatile dish. It's a healthy and tasty alternative to sweet-and-sour pork or chicken. I like to serve it over brown rice.
—Elizabeth Bowen, Harbor Beach, Michigan

1 can (8 ounces) unsweetened pineapple chunks
1/4 cup packed brown sugar
1 tablespoon cornstarch
1/4 teaspoon ground ginger
1/4 cup white vinegar
2 tablespoons reduced-sodium soy sauce
1 medium onion, cut into wedges
1 large green pepper, cut into 1-inch pieces
1/2 medium sweet red pepper, cut into 1-inch pieces
1/2 cup sliced carrot
1 garlic clove, minced
2 cans (16 ounces *each*) kidney beans, rinsed and drained
1 medium tomato, cut into 1-inch cubes
Hot cooked rice, optional

Drain pineapple, reserving juice. Set pineapple aside. In a bowl, combine the brown sugar, cornstarch and ginger. Add enough water to reserved juice to measure 1/2 cup; stir into cornstarch mixture until smooth. Add vinegar and soy sauce; set aside.

In a large nonstick skillet or wok coated with nonstick cooking spray, stir-fry the onion, peppers and carrot until crisp-tender. Add garlic; stir-fry 1 minute longer. Add the beans, tomato and reserved pineapple. Cook and stir for 2-3 minutes or until heated through. Stir soy sauce mixture and add to bean mixture. Bring to a boil; cook and stir for 1-2 minutes or until thickened. Serve with rice if desired. **Yield:** 4 servings.

Nutritional Analysis: One serving (1-1/4 cups stir-fry mixture, calculated without rice) equals 336 calories, trace fat (trace saturated fat), 0 cholesterol, 688 mg sodium, 70 g carbohydrate, 14 g fiber, 16 g protein.
△ *Low-fat*
▲ *Meatless*

🍎 Spinach Savvy

ARE YOU GREEN when it comes to cooking with spinach? If so, review the following and you'll be making the vibrant veggie a mainstay in no time.

- You can buy spinach loose at farmers markets or already bagged at the grocery store. When buying it loose, look for small crisp deep-green leaves. When buying bagged spinach, gently squeeze it to make sure the leaves are springy.

- The thicker the spinach stems, the more likely it is to be overgrown and bitter. Before you begin preparing a recipe, pinch off any stems that are not delicate enough to eat raw.

- It's often necessary to remove as much liquid as possible from frozen chopped spinach that has been thawed. To "squeeze dry" thawed spinach, place the greens in a colander. Press on the spinach with the back of a clean spoon or saucer, or simply use your hands to gently squeeze out the liquid.

Potato Spinach Pie

I combined two recipes to come up with this dish, which is terrific for either brunch or dinner. Reduced-fat cheese, egg whites and a shredded-potato crust help lighten it up.
—Lola Kauffmann, Goshen, Indiana

3 cups coarsely shredded peeled potatoes
2 tablespoons olive *or* canola oil, *divided*
1 teaspoon salt, *divided*
1/3 cup chopped onion
1 package (10 ounces) frozen chopped spinach, thawed and squeezed dry
1 cup (4 ounces) shredded reduced-fat Swiss cheese
1/2 cup fat-free evaporated milk
2 eggs, lightly beaten
2 egg whites, lightly beaten
1/2 to 1 teaspoon dried oregano
1/4 teaspoon ground nutmeg

In a bowl, combine the potatoes, 4 teaspoons oil and 1/2 teaspoon salt. Press onto the bottom and up the sides of a 9-in. pie plate coated with nonstick cooking spray. Bake at 425° for 20-25 minutes or until crust is lightly browned. Cool on a wire rack. Reduce temperature to 350°.

In a nonstick skillet, saute onion in remaining oil until tender. In a bowl, combine the spinach, Swiss cheese, milk, eggs, egg whites, oregano, nutmeg, onion and remaining salt. Pour into crust. Bake for 25-30 minutes or until top begins to brown and a knife inserted near the center comes out clean. Let stand for 10 minutes before cutting. **Yield:** 6 servings.

Nutritional Analysis: One piece equals 251 calories, 12 g fat (4 g saturated fat), 84 mg cholesterol, 555 mg sodium, 24 g carbohydrate, 3 g fiber, 14 g protein.
Diabetic Exchanges: 2 lean meat, 1-1/2 starch, 1 fat.
▲ *Meatless*

Black-Eyed Peas 'n' Pasta

Tradition has it that if you eat black-eyed peas on New Year's Day, you'll enjoy prosperity all year through, but I serve this tasty combination of pasta, peas and tangy tomato sauce anytime.
—Marie Malsch, Bridgman, Michigan

1 cup chopped green pepper
1/2 cup chopped onion
1 jalapeno pepper, seeded and chopped*
3 garlic cloves, minced
1 tablespoon olive *or* canola oil
1 can (28 ounces) crushed tomatoes
1 can (15-1/2 ounces) black-eyed peas, rinsed and drained
1 to 3 tablespoons minced fresh cilantro *or* parsley
1 teaspoon cider vinegar
1 teaspoon sugar
1 teaspoon salt
1/8 teaspoon pepper
5 cups hot cooked bow tie pasta

In a large skillet, saute green pepper, onion, jalapeno and garlic in oil for 5 minutes or until tender. Add tomatoes; bring to a boil. Simmer, uncovered, for 10 minutes. Stir in peas, cilantro, vinegar, sugar, salt and pepper; simmer 10 minutes longer. Toss with pasta and serve immediately. **Yield:** 6 servings.

*Editor's Note: When cutting or seeding hot peppers, use rubber or plastic gloves to protect your hands. Avoid touching your face.

Nutritional Analysis: One serving (1 cup) equals 266 calories, 3 g fat (trace saturated fat), 0 cholesterol, 866 mg sodium, 49 g carbohydrate, 6 g fiber, 11 g protein.
Diabetic Exchanges: 2-1/2 starch, 2 vegetable, 1 very lean meat.
△ **Low-fat**
▲ **Meatless**

Herbed Lentils and Rice

Looking for dishes that are both healthy and yummy, I latched on to lentils. I'm trying to incorporate more legumes and whole grains into our diet, so this blend of lentils and rice is perfect.
—Judy Manbeck, Chanute, Kansas

2-2/3 cups reduced-sodium chicken broth *or* vegetable broth
3/4 cup dry lentils
3/4 cup chopped onion
1/2 cup uncooked brown rice
1/4 cup dry white wine *or* additional broth
1/2 teaspoon dried basil
1/4 teaspoon salt
1/4 teaspoon dried oregano
1/4 teaspoon dried thyme
1/8 teaspoon garlic powder

1/8 teaspoon pepper
1 cup (4 ounces) shredded reduced-fat Swiss cheese, *divided*

In a bowl, combine the first 11 ingredients; stir in 1/2 cup cheese. Transfer to a 1-1/2-qt. baking dish coated with nonstick cooking spray. Cover and bake at 350° for 1-1/2 to 2 hours or until lentils and rice are tender and liquid is absorbed, stirring twice. Uncover; sprinkle with remaining cheese. Bake 2-3 minutes longer or until cheese is melted. **Yield:** 4 servings.

Nutritional Analysis: One serving (1 cup) equals 329 calories, 7 g fat (4 g saturated fat), 20 mg cholesterol, 601 mg sodium, 43 g carbohydrate, 12 g fiber, 22 g protein.
Diabetic Exchanges: 3 very lean meat, 2 starch, 1 fat.
▲ **Meatless**

Spinach Lentil Stew

(Pictured below)

When my children requested more vegetarian dishes, this chunky stew became a favorite. Red wine vinegar perks up the flavor and carrots add color. We like to ladle helpings over cooked rice.
—Alice McEachern, Surrey, British Columbia

1/2 cup chopped onion
2 garlic cloves, minced
1 tablespoon canola oil
5 cups water
1 cup lentils, rinsed
4 teaspoons vegetable *or* chicken bouillon granules
3 teaspoons Worcestershire sauce
1/2 teaspoon salt

1/2 teaspoon dried thyme
1/4 teaspoon pepper
1 bay leaf
1 cup chopped carrots
1 can (14-1/2 ounces) diced tomatoes, undrained
1 package (10 ounces) frozen chopped spinach, thawed and squeezed dry
1 tablespoon red wine vinegar *or* cider vinegar

In a large saucepan, saute onion and garlic in oil until tender. Add the water, lentils, bouillon, Worcestershire sauce, salt, thyme, pepper and bay leaf; bring to a boil. Reduce heat; cover and simmer for 20 minutes.

Add carrots, tomatoes and spinach; return to a boil. Reduce heat; cover and simmer 15-20 minutes longer or until lentils are tender. Stir in vinegar. Discard bay leaf before serving. **Yield:** 6 servings.

Nutritional Analysis: One serving (1-1/4 cups) equals 168 calories, 3 g fat (trace saturated fat), trace cholesterol, 1,123 mg sodium, 27 g carbohydrate, 10 g fiber, 10 g protein.
Diabetic Exchanges: *2 vegetable, 1 lean meat, 1 starch.*
△ *Low-fat*
▲ *Meatless*

Italian Zucchini Bake

Kids of all ages are sure to like this fun vegetarian spin on pizza! You can't even tell there's zucchini in this dish. If you have meat eaters in your family, try adding turkey pepperoni or sausage.
—*Carol Mieske, Red Bluff, California*

3-1/2 cups shredded zucchini
1/2 teaspoon salt
3/4 cup egg substitute
1/2 cup dry bread crumbs
1/4 cup all-purpose flour
2 teaspoons Italian seasoning
1/2 pound fresh mushrooms, sliced
2 teaspoons olive *or* canola oil
1 can (15 ounces) pizza sauce, *divided*
3/4 cup chopped green pepper
1/4 cup sliced ripe olives, drained
1-1/2 cups (6 ounces) shredded part-skim mozzarella cheese, *divided*

Place zucchini in a colander over a plate; sprinkle with salt and toss. Let stand for 15 minutes. Rinse and drain well. In a bowl, combine the zucchini, egg substitute, bread crumbs, flour and Italian seasoning. Spread in an 11-in. x 7-in. x 2-in. baking dish coated with nonstick cooking spray. Bake, uncovered, at 350° for 25 minutes.

In a nonstick skillet, saute mushrooms in oil. Spread half of the pizza sauce over zucchini mixture; sprinkle with the mushrooms, green pepper, olives and half of the cheese. Top with remaining pizza sauce and cheese. Bake 15 minutes longer or until hot and bubbly. **Yield:** 6 servings.

Nutritional Analysis: One serving equals 226 calories, 8 g fat (4 g saturated fat), 17 mg cholesterol, 818 mg sodium, 24 g carbohydrate, 3 g fiber, 16 g protein.
Diabetic Exchanges: *2 vegetable, 1 starch, 1 lean meat, 1 fat.*
▲ *Meatless*

Spinach Ricotta Tart

(Pictured above)

Topped with tomato slices and crumbled blue cheese, this tart is a great way to get spinach into your diet.
—*Cindy Kelly, Amston, Connecticut*

2 pounds fresh spinach, torn
3 eggs, lightly beaten
1 carton (15 ounces) part-skim ricotta cheese
1 medium onion, chopped
2 tablespoons minced fresh basil
1 teaspoon salt
1/8 teaspoon pepper
Dash ground nutmeg
4 sheets phyllo dough (14 inches x 9 inches)
3 medium tomatoes, halved, seeded and sliced
2 tablespoons crumbled blue cheese

Place spinach in a steamer basket. Place in a saucepan over 1 in. of water; bring to a boil. Cover and steam for 2-3 minutes or until wilted; drain well. Chop spinach; squeeze dry and set aside. In a large bowl, combine the eggs, ricotta cheese, onion, basil, salt, pepper and nutmeg; mix well. Add the spinach.

Place one sheet of phyllo dough in a 9-in. pie plate coated with nonstick cooking spray; spray phyllo dough with nonstick cooking spray. Place another sheet of phyllo across first sheet; spray with nonstick cooking spray. Repeat with remaining phyllo. Pour spinach mixture into phyllo crust. Fold excess dough under crust to form a rim; spray rim with nonstick cooking spray. Arrange tomato slices over tart. Bake at 400° for 35-40 minutes or until set. Sprinkle with blue cheese. Let stand for 10 minutes before cutting. **Yield:** 6 servings.

Nutritional Analysis: One slice equals 221 calories, 10 g fat (5 g saturated fat), 130 mg cholesterol, 706 mg sodium, 19 g carbohydrate, 5 g fiber, 18 g protein.
Diabetic Exchanges: *2 lean meat, 2 vegetable, 1/2 starch, 1/2 fat.*
▲ *Meatless*

cheeses. Bake, uncovered, at 350° for 40-45 minutes or until heated through. **Yield:** 7 servings.

Nutritional Analysis: One serving (2 stuffed shells) equals 423 calories, 13 g fat (7 g saturated fat), 37 mg cholesterol, 1,128 mg sodium, 51 g carbohydrate, 6 g fiber, 24 g protein.
Diabetic Exchanges: 2-1/2 starch, 2 lean meat, 2 vegetable, 1 fat.
▲ *Meatless*

Veggie Quesadillas

*I got the idea for this recipe from a restaurant
I used to frequent when I was in school. The tortillas
are packed full of vegetables, cheese and seasonings,
then baked to a golden brown.*
—Shari Johnson, Green Bay, Wisconsin

1/2 **pound fresh mushrooms, sliced**
1 **medium zucchini, sliced**
1/2 **cup sliced green onions**
2 **cans (15-1/4 ounces** *each***) whole kernel corn, drained**
2 **medium tomatoes, seeded and diced**
1 **teaspoon dried basil**
3/4 **teaspoon salt**
1/4 **teaspoon pepper**
6 **flour tortillas (8 inches)**
2 **cups (8 ounces) shredded reduced-fat Mexican cheese blend**
3/4 **cup salsa**
6 **tablespoons reduced-fat sour cream**

In a large nonstick skillet coated with nonstick cooking spray, saute the mushrooms, zucchini and onions until tender. Add the corn, tomatoes, basil, salt and pepper; cook 2-3 minutes longer or until heated through. Using a slotted spoon, spoon filling on half of each tortilla. Sprinkle vegetable mixture with cheese and fold over tortilla. Lightly spray top of tortillas with nonstick cooking spray. Bake, uncovered, at 400° for 10-12 minutes or until golden brown. Serve with salsa and sour cream. **Yield:** 6 servings.

Nutritional Analysis: One serving (1 quesadilla with 2 tablespoons salsa and 1 tablespoon sour cream) equals 374 calories, 12 g fat (6 g saturated fat), 18 mg cholesterol, 1,061 mg sodium, 53 g carbohydrate, 7 g fiber, 23 g protein.
▲ *Meatless*

Overnight Spinach Manicotti

(Pictured above)

*A friend gave me an awesome recipe for
manicotti…and I set out to make it a little
healthier. Now, whenever we have company,
my husband asks me to serve this.*
—Tonya Fitzgerald, West Monroe, Louisiana

1 **carton (15 ounces) reduced-fat ricotta cheese**
1 **package (10 ounces) frozen chopped spinach, thawed and squeezed dry**
1-1/2 **cups (6 ounces) shredded part-skim mozzarella cheese,** *divided*
1/2 **cup grated Parmesan cheese,** *divided*
2 **egg whites**
2 **teaspoons minced fresh parsley**
1/2 **teaspoon salt**
1/2 **teaspoon onion powder**
1/2 **teaspoon pepper**
1/4 **teaspoon garlic powder**
4-1/2 **cups meatless spaghetti sauce**
3/4 **cup water**
1 **package (8 ounces) manicotti shells**

In a large bowl, combine the ricotta cheese, spinach, 1 cup mozzarella cheese, 1/4 cup Parmesan cheese, egg whites, parsley, salt, onion powder, pepper and garlic powder. Combine spaghetti sauce and water; spread 1 cup in an ungreased 13-in. x 9-in. x 2-in. baking dish. Stuff uncooked manicotti shells with ricotta mixture; arrange over tomato sauce. Top with remaining sauce. Cover and refrigerate overnight.

Remove from the refrigerator 30 minutes before baking. Sprinkle with remaining mozzarella and Parmesan

From the Bread Basket

Is your family getting enough grains?
It's easy to ingrain the goodness of wheat,
oats, rye and more into your meal plans
when you present an incredible assortment
of breads, rolls and muffins.

Almond Rhurbarb Coffee Cake (page 195)

Spinach Pinwheel Rolls

(Pictured below)

I often serve these tasty morsels alongside a Greek salad at a ladies luncheon. Whether they're eaten warm or cold, the tender rolls with their tasty filling are always a hit!
—Maryalice Wood, Langley, British Columbia

    4 to 5 cups all-purpose flour
    1 tablespoon sugar
    3 teaspoons active dry yeast
    1 teaspoon grated lemon peel
1-1/2 teaspoons salt, *divided*
    3/4 cup water
    3/4 cup plus 2 tablespoons fat-free milk, *divided*
    1 tablespoon canola oil
    4 teaspoons lemon juice, *divided*
    1 package (10 ounces) fresh spinach, torn
    4 ounces reduced-fat cream cheese
    2 tablespoons reduced-fat mayonnaise
    1 teaspoon salt-free lemon-pepper seasoning
    3 tablespoons cornmeal

In a large mixing bowl, combine 2 cups flour, sugar, yeast, lemon peel and 1 teaspoon salt. In a saucepan, heat water, 3/4 cup milk, oil and 3 teaspoons lemon juice to 120°-130°. Add to dry ingredients; beat just until moistened. Stir in enough remaining flour to form a soft dough (dough will be sticky). Turn onto a floured surface; knead until smooth and elastic, about 6-8 minutes. Place in a bowl coated with nonstick cooking spray, turning once to coat top. Cover and let rise until doubled, about 1 hour.

Place spinach in a steamer basket in a saucepan over 1 in. of water; bring to a boil. Cover and steam until wilted; drain. Combine the cream cheese, mayonnaise, lemon-pepper and remaining lemon juice and salt. Stir in spinach; cool.

Punch dough down. Roll into a 24-in. x 14-in. rectangle. Spread filling to within 1/2 in. of edges. Roll up jelly-roll style, starting with a long side; pinch seams to seal and tuck ends under. Cut into 20 slices. Coat baking sheets with nonstick cooking spray and sprinkle with cornmeal. Place slices cut side up on pans. Cover and let rise until doubled, about 30 minutes. Brush remaining milk over rolls. Bake at 325° for 30-35 minutes or until golden brown. **Yield:** 20 rolls.

Nutritional Analysis: One roll equals 130 calories, 3 g fat (1 g saturated fat), 4 mg cholesterol, 244 mg sodium, 22 g carbohydrate, 1 g fiber, 4 g protein.
Diabetic Exchange: 1-1/2 starch.
△ *Low-fat*
▲ *Meatless*

Lentil Bread

Lentils pack a little extra protein and fiber into this fragrant and flavorful bread. I grew up on a farm where bread was baked weekly...and have been making my own bread for over 20 years. I like to experiment with all types of grains and flours to make very hearty loaves. This is a favorite.
—Mike Buescher, Ft. Wayne, Indiana

    3/4 cup lentils, rinsed
1-1/2 cups water
4-1/2 teaspoons finely chopped onion
    1 garlic clove, minced
    2 packages (1/4 ounce *each*) active dry yeast
    1 cup warm water (110° to 115°)
1-1/2 cups warm fat-free milk (110° to 115°)
    1/4 cup olive *or* canola oil
    1/4 cup sugar
    1 tablespoon grated Parmesan cheese
    1 tablespoon salt
    1 cup whole wheat flour
    6 to 7 cups bread flour

In a saucepan, combine the lentils, water, onion and garlic; bring to a boil. Reduce heat; cover and simmer for about 30 minutes or until lentils are tender. Cool slightly. Transfer mixture to a blender or food processor; cover and process until smooth. Cool to 110°-115°.

In a mixing bowl, dissolve yeast in warm water. Add the milk, lentil mixture, oil, sugar, Parmesan cheese, salt, whole wheat flour and 3 cups bread flour. Beat until smooth. Stir in enough remaining bread flour to form a soft dough. Turn onto a floured surface; knead until smooth and elastic, about 6-8 minutes. Place in a greased bowl, turning once to grease top. Cover and let rise in a warm place until doubled, about 1 hour.

Punch dough down. Turn onto a lightly floured surface. Divide into thirds; shape into loaves. Place in three greased 9-in. x 5-in. x 3-in. loaf pans. Cover and let rise until doubled, about 30-40 minutes. Bake at 375° for 35-45 minutes or until golden brown. Remove from pans to wire racks to cool. **Yield:** 3 loaves (12 slices each).

Nutritional Analysis: One slice equals 118 calories, 2 g fat (trace saturated fat), trace cholesterol, 205 mg sodium, 22 g carbohydrate, 2 g fiber, 5 g protein.
Diabetic Exchange: 1-1/2 starch.
△ *Low-fat*
▲ *Meatless*

Lemon-Blueberry Oat Muffins

(Pictured above)

*These yummy oatmeal muffins showcase
juicy blueberries and zesty lemon flavor.*
—*Jamie Brown, Walden, Colorado*

1 cup quick-cooking oats
1 cup all-purpose flour
1/2 cup sugar
3 teaspoons baking powder
1/4 teaspoon salt
1 egg
1 egg white
1 cup fat-free milk
2 tablespoons butter *or* stick margarine, melted
1 teaspoon grated lemon peel
1 teaspoon vanilla extract
1 cup fresh *or* frozen blueberries*
TOPPING:
1/2 cup quick-cooking oats
2 tablespoons brown sugar
1 tablespoon butter *or* stick margarine, softened

In a bowl, combine the first five ingredients. In another bowl, combine the egg, egg white, milk, butter, lemon peel and vanilla; mix well. Add to dry ingredients just until moistened. Fold in berries. Coat muffin cups with nonstick cooking spray or use paper liners; fill two-thirds full with batter. Combine topping ingredients; sprinkle over batter. Bake at 400° for 20-22 minutes or until top is lightly browned and springs back when lightly touched. Cool 5 minutes; remove to a wire rack. **Yield:** 1 dozen.

*Editor's Note: If using frozen blueberries, do not thaw before adding to the batter.

Nutritional Analysis: One muffin equals 166 calories, 4 g fat (2 g saturated fat), 26 mg cholesterol, 158 mg sodium, 28 g car-

bohydrate, 2 g fiber, 4 g protein.
Diabetic Exchanges: 1-1/2 starch, 1 fat.
▲ *Meatless*

Orange Pecan Muffins

(Pictured above)

*My sister-in-law graciously shared the recipe
for these delicious muffins.*
—*Maya McLane, Valdosta, Georgia*

2 cups reduced-fat biscuit/baking mix
1/4 cup sugar
1 egg
1/2 cup orange juice
2 tablespoons canola oil
1/2 cup chopped pecans
1/2 cup orange marmalade
TOPPING:
2 tablespoons sugar
2 teaspoons all-purpose flour
1/4 teaspoon ground cinnamon
Dash ground nutmeg

In a bowl, combine biscuit mix and sugar. In a small bowl, beat the egg, orange juice and oil; stir into dry ingredients just until moistened. Fold in pecans and marmalade. Coat muffin cups with nonstick cooking spray or use paper liners; fill two-thirds full with batter. Combine topping ingredients; sprinkle over batter. Bake at 400° for 15-18 minutes or until a toothpick comes out clean. Cool 5 minutes; remove to a wire rack. **Yield:** 1 dozen.

Nutritional Analysis: One muffin equals 200 calories, 8 g fat (1 g saturated fat), 18 mg cholesterol, 245 mg sodium, 31 g carbohydrate, 1 g fiber, 3 g protein.
Diabetic Exchanges: 2 starch, 1-1/2 fat.
▲ *Meatless*

Corn Bread Squares

My husband doesn't like traditional Texas corn bread, so I came up with this recipe. This is the only kind he'll eat! Yogurt makes this variation different from most.
—Amanda Andrews, Mansfield, Texas

    1 cup yellow cornmeal
1/4 cup all-purpose flour
    2 teaspoons baking powder
1/2 teaspoon salt
1/4 teaspoon baking soda
    1 egg, lightly beaten
    1 carton (8 ounces) fat-free plain yogurt
1/2 cup fat-free milk
1/4 cup canola oil
    1 tablespoon honey

In a large bowl, combine the first five ingredients. In another bowl, combine the egg, yogurt, milk, oil and honey. Stir into dry ingredients just until moistened. Pour into an 8-in. square baking dish coated with nonstick cooking spray. Bake at 425° for 16-20 minutes or until a toothpick comes out clean. **Yield:** 9 servings.

Nutritional Analysis: One piece equals 157 calories, 7 g fat (1 g saturated fat), 24 mg cholesterol, 349 mg sodium, 20 g carbohydrate, 1 g fiber, 4 g protein.
***Diabetic Exchanges:** 1-1/2 starch, 1 fat.*
▲ **Meatless**

Irish Soda Bread

(Pictured above)

I'm allergic to yeast, so I appreciate recipes for quick breads, biscuits and soda breads. This tender loaf that's dotted with golden raisins is great. It's one way I can enjoy toast for breakfast.
—Carol Fritz, Fulton, Illinois

    4 cups all-purpose flour
    1 tablespoon sugar
1-1/2 teaspoons baking soda
    1 teaspoon baking powder
1/2 teaspoon salt
1/4 cup cold butter *or* stick margarine
    1 cup golden raisins
1-3/4 cups 1% buttermilk

In a large bowl, combine the flour, sugar, baking soda, baking powder and salt. Cut in butter until mixture resembles coarse crumbs. Add raisins. Stir in buttermilk just until moistened. Turn onto a lightly floured surface; gently knead 6-8 times.

Place on an ungreased baking sheet; pat into a 7-in. round loaf. Using a sharp knife, cut a 1-in. cross about 1/4 in. deep on top of the loaf. Bake at 375° for 40-45 minutes or until golden brown. **Yield:** 1 loaf (16 slices).

Nutritional Analysis: One slice equals 181 calories, 3 g fat (2 g saturated fat), 9 mg cholesterol, 265 mg sodium, 33 g carbohydrate, 1 g fiber, 4 g protein.
***Diabetic Exchanges:** 1-1/2 starch, 1/2 fruit, 1/2 fat.*
△ **Low-fat**
▲ **Meatless**

Buttermilk Biscuits

I scribbled down this recipe when our family visited the Cooperstown Farm Museum more than 25 years ago. I must have gotten it right, because these biscuits turn out great every time.
—Patricia Kile, Greentown, Pennsylvania

    2 cups all-purpose flour
    3 teaspoons baking powder
1/2 teaspoon baking soda
1/4 teaspoon salt
    3 tablespoons cold butter *or* stick margarine
3/4 to 1 cup 1% buttermilk
    1 tablespoon fat-free milk

In a bowl, combine the flour, baking powder, baking soda and salt; cut in butter until mixture resembles coarse crumbs. Stir in enough buttermilk just to moisten dough. Turn onto a lightly floured surface; knead 3-4 times.

Pat or roll to 3/4-in. thickness. Cut with a floured 2-1/2-in. biscuit cutter. Place on a baking sheet coated with nonstick cooking spray. Brush with milk. Bake at 450° for 12-15 minutes or until golden brown. **Yield:** 8 biscuits.

Nutritional Analysis: One biscuit equals 164 calories, 5 g fat (3 g saturated fat), 13 mg cholesterol, 382 mg sodium, 25 g carbohydrate, 1 g fiber, 4 g protein.
***Diabetic Exchanges:** 1-1/2 starch, 1 fat.*
▲ **Meatless**

Favorite Coffee Cake Recipe Made Lighter

ELIZABETH Studley of Cheyenne, Wyoming has enjoyed Almond Rhubarb Coffee Cake since it was published in a *Taste of Home* cookbook years ago.

"This is a wonderful cake," she says, "but it's too high in calories and fat to fit my current weight-loss program. I would hate to stop making it. Can you slim it down and still retain the great taste?"

Our Test Kitchen staff took on her challenge! They reduced the amount of oil called for in the recipe and used canola rather than vegetable oil since it is lower in saturated fat.

To further cut back on fat, they substituted a smaller amount of 1% buttermilk for the whole milk…and added an egg white to help keep the cake texture tender.

Our home economists also cut back on almonds (to lower the fat even more), but added almond extract to retain the original nutty flavor. Plus, they slightly reduced the amount of butter in the tasty topping.

Each piece of Makeover Almond Rhubarb Coffee Cake has less than half the fat and just a third of the saturated fat of the original. Plus, the calories have been cut by a quarter. But the flavor is still terrific!

Almond Rhubarb Coffee Cake

    1 egg
1-1/2 cups packed brown sugar
    2/3 cup vegetable oil
    1 teaspoon vanilla extract
2-1/2 cups all-purpose flour
    1 teaspoon salt
    1 teaspoon baking soda
    1 cup milk
1-1/2 cups sliced fresh *or* frozen rhubarb
    3/4 cup sliced almonds, *divided*
    1/3 cup sugar
    1 tablespoon butter *or* margarine, melted

In a mixing bowl, beat the egg, brown sugar, oil and vanilla until smooth. Combine the flour, salt and baking soda; add to sugar mixture alternately with milk. Fold in the rhubarb and 1/2 cup almonds. Pour into two greased 9-in. round baking pans.

In a small bowl, combine sugar and butter; stir in the remaining almonds. Sprinkle over batter. Bake at 350° for 25-30 minutes or until a toothpick comes out clean. Cool on wire racks. **Yield:** 14 servings.

Nutritional Analysis: One piece equals 337 calories, 15 g fat (3 g saturated fat), 20 mg cholesterol, 289 mg sodium, 47 g carbohydrate, 1 g fiber, 5 g protein.

Makeover Almond Rhubarb Coffee Cake

(Pictured below and on page 179)

2-1/2 cups all-purpose flour
1-1/2 cups packed brown sugar
    1 teaspoon baking soda
    1 teaspoon salt
    1 egg
    1 egg white
    3/4 cup 1% buttermilk
    1/4 cup canola oil
    1 teaspoon vanilla extract
    1/4 teaspoon almond extract
1-1/2 cups sliced fresh *or* frozen rhubarb
    1/2 cup sliced almonds, toasted, *divided*
    1/3 cup sugar
    2 teaspoons butter *or* stick margarine, melted

In a large bowl, combine the flour, brown sugar, baking soda and salt. In a mixing bowl, beat the egg, egg white, buttermilk, oil and extracts. Stir into dry ingredients just until moistened. Fold in rhubarb and 1/4 cup almonds. Pour into two 9-in. round baking pans coated with nonstick cooking spray.

In a small bowl, combine sugar and butter; stir in the remaining almonds. Sprinkle over batter. Bake at 350° for 25-30 minutes or until a toothpick comes out clean. Cool on wire racks. **Yield:** 14 servings.

Nutritional Analysis: One piece equals 264 calories, 7 g fat (1 g saturated fat), 17 mg cholesterol, 295 mg sodium, 47 g carbohydrate, 1 g fiber, 4 g protein.
Diabetic Exchanges: 3 starch, 1 fat.

🍎 A More Healthy Homemade Bread

MY HUSBAND loves bread made in our bread machine, but he generally only likes plain white bread or sourdough bread. I wanted us to get more fiber in our diets, so I tossed a cup of high-fiber cereal into the dough one day. It was great and he loved it.

I've often found that whole-grain breads are not fluffy and light, but my version was still soft and yummy...and it had the added fiber and flavor from the whole-grain cereal. I've used Grape Nuts, Oatmeal Squares and even a couple of flaked cereals with nuts and fruit. Each has been wonderful, so don't be afraid to experiment!

—*Cheryl Norwood, Canton, Georgia*

Sausage-Seafood Mini Corn Muffins

I pack big seafood taste into these bite-size appetizers. Turkey Italian sausage provides a little kick.
—*Melissa Jane Robinson, Indianapolis, Indiana*

- 1 package (16 ounces) corn bread stuffing mix
- 4 ounces turkey Italian sausage, casings removed
- 2 cups finely chopped onion
- 1/2 cup finely chopped celery
- 2 tablespoons olive *or* canola oil
- 1 can (10-1/2 ounces) condensed chicken broth, undiluted
- 1-1/3 cups water
- 1 can (6 ounces) crabmeat, drained, flaked and cartilage removed
- 1 can (6 ounces) small shrimp, rinsed and drained
- 6 egg whites
- 2 eggs
- 1/8 teaspoon garlic powder
- 2-3/4 cups reduced-fat shredded cheddar cheese, *divided*

In a food processor, process the stuffing mix until finely crushed; set aside. Crumble sausage into a large nonstick skillet; add the onion, celery and oil. Cook over medium heat until sausage is no longer pink and vegetables are crisp-tender; drain. Remove from the heat; stir in the next seven ingredients and crushed stuffing. Fold in 2 cups cheese.

Spoon 2 tablespoonfuls into miniature muffin cups coated with nonstick cooking spray. Sprinkle with remaining cheese. Bake at 350° for 20-22 minutes or until a toothpick comes out clean. Cool 5 minutes; remove to wire racks. **Yield:** 6 dozen.

Nutritional Analysis: One serving (3 mini muffins) equals 156 calories, 6 g fat (3 g saturated fat), 51 mg cholesterol, 589 mg sodium, 16 g carbohydrate, 1 g fiber, 11 g protein.
Diabetic Exchanges: 1 starch, 1 lean meat, 1/2 fat.

Vegetable Focaccia

(Pictured below)

This popular recipe began as herb focaccia but gradually came to include vegetables. There's no cheese because my husband can't have dairy products.
—*Michele Fairchok, Grove City, Ohio*

- 2 to 2-1/4 cups bread flour
- 1 package (1/4 ounce) quick-rise yeast
- 1 teaspoon salt
- 1 cup warm water (120° to 130°)
- 1 tablespoon olive *or* canola oil

TOPPING:
- 3 plum tomatoes, chopped
- 5 medium fresh mushrooms, sliced
- 1/2 cup chopped green pepper
- 1/2 cup sliced ripe olives
- 1/4 cup chopped onion
- 3 tablespoons olive *or* canola oil
- 2 teaspoons red wine vinegar *or* cider vinegar
- 3/4 teaspoon salt
- 1/4 teaspoon garlic powder
- 1/4 teaspoon dried oregano
- 1/4 teaspoon pepper
- 2 teaspoons cornmeal

In a mixing bowl, combine 2 cups flour, yeast and salt. Add water and oil; beat until smooth. Stir in enough remaining flour to form a soft dough. Turn onto a floured surface; knead until smooth and elastic, about 4 minutes. Cover and let rest for 15 minutes. Meanwhile, in a bowl, combine tomatoes, mushrooms, green pepper, olives, onion, oil, vinegar and seasonings.

Coat a 15-in. x 10-in. x 1-in. baking pan with nonstick cooking spray; sprinkle with cornmeal. Press dough into pan. Prick dough generously with a fork. Bake at 475° for 5 minutes or until lightly browned. Cover with vegetable mix-

ture. Bake 8-10 minutes longer or until edges of crust are golden. **Yield:** 12 servings.

Nutritional Analysis: One piece equals 121 calories, 5 g fat (1 g saturated fat), 0 cholesterol, 376 mg sodium, 17 g carbohydrate, 1 g fiber, 3 g protein.
Diabetic Exchanges: 1 starch, 1 fat.
▲ *Meatless*

Carrot Bread

This lovely moist quick bread is flecked with crunchy walnuts and colorful shredded carrot. For variety, I sometimes substitute a cup of shredded raw zucchini for the carrot or add a half cup of drained crushed pineapple.
—Connie Simon, Reed City, Michigan

1 cup sugar
1 cup all-purpose flour
1/2 cup whole wheat flour
1 teaspoon baking powder
1 teaspoon baking soda
1 teaspoon salt
1 teaspoon ground cinnamon
3/4 cup unsweetened applesauce
1/2 cup egg substitute
1 teaspoon vanilla extract
1 cup shredded carrots
1/4 cup chopped walnuts

Coat an 8-in. x 4-in. x 2-in. loaf pan with nonstick cooking spray and dust with flour; set aside. In a bowl, combine the sugar, flours, baking powder, baking soda, salt and cinnamon. In another bowl, combine the applesauce, egg substitute and vanilla; stir into dry ingredients until just moistened. Fold in carrots and walnuts.

Pour into prepared pan. Bake at 350° for 50-55 minutes or until a toothpick comes out clean. Cool for 10 minutes before removing from pan to a wire rack. **Yield:** 1 loaf (10 slices).

Nutritional Analysis: One slice equals 182 calories, 2 g fat (trace saturated fat), 0 cholesterol, 439 mg sodium, 38 g carbohydrate, 2 g fiber, 4 g protein.
Diabetic Exchanges: 2 starch, 1 vegetable.
△ *Low-fat*
▲ *Meatless*

Rustic Round Herb Bread

(Pictured above)

I've had this bread recipe for at least 10 years. It takes only 10 minutes to stir together. Wedges are marvelous served warm and are great with soup.
—Patricia Vatta, Norwood, Ontario

2 cups all-purpose flour
1 cup (4 ounces) shredded reduced-fat cheddar cheese
1 tablespoon sugar
2 teaspoons baking powder
1/2 teaspoon baking soda
1/2 teaspoon salt
1/2 teaspoon rubbed sage
1/2 teaspoon dried thyme
1/2 teaspoon dill weed
3 tablespoons cold butter *or* stick margarine
1 egg
1/2 cup fat-free plain yogurt
1/2 cup fat-free milk
1/2 teaspoon poppy seeds

In a large bowl, combine the first nine ingredients; mix well. Cut in butter until mixture resembles fine crumbs. In another bowl, whisk the egg, yogurt and milk. Stir into dry ingredients until just moistened.

Spoon into a 9-in. round baking pan coated with nonstick cooking spray. Sprinkle with poppy seeds. Bake at 400° for 20-25 minutes or until golden brown. Cool in pan on a wire rack. Cut into wedges. **Yield:** 10 servings.

Nutritional Analysis: One wedge equals 185 calories, 7 g fat (4 g saturated fat), 39 mg cholesterol, 379 mg sodium, 23 g carbohydrate, 1 g fiber, 7 g protein.
Diabetic Exchanges: 1-1/2 starch, 1 fat.
▲ *Meatless*

Cinnamon Breadsticks

(Pictured above)

I think this is the best sweet breadstick you'll find. I love to snack on these while drinking my morning coffee. Each twist has just 1 gram of fat and is quite satisfying.
—Carol Birkemeier, Nashville, Indiana

    1 package (16 ounces) hot roll mix
    1 cup warm water (120° to 130°)
    2 tablespoons canola oil
    1 egg white, lightly beaten
    1/2 cup sugar
    1-1/2 teaspoons ground cinnamon
Refrigerated butter-flavored spray

In a bowl, combine roll mix and contents of yeast package. Add the water, oil and egg white; beat until smooth. Turn dough onto a lightly floured surface; knead until smooth and elastic, about 5 minutes. Cover and let rest for 10 minutes.

Roll into a 16-in. x 12-in. rectangle. Cut widthwise into sixteen 1-in. strips. Cut strips in half widthwise, forming 32 strips. Twist each strip 5-6 times; place on a baking sheet coated with nonstick cooking spray.

Combine the sugar and cinnamon. Spray dough sticks generously with refrigerated butter-flavored spray; sprinkle with the cinnamon-sugar. Cover and let rise in a warm place until doubled, about 25 minutes. Bake at 375° for 10-12 minutes or until golden brown. Serve warm. **Yield:** 32 breadsticks.

Nutritional Analysis: One breadstick equals 72 calories, 1 g fat (trace saturated fat), 0 cholesterol, 96 mg sodium, 13 g carbohydrate, trace fiber, 2 g protein.
  Diabetic Exchange: 1 starch.
  △ **Low-fat**
  ▲ **Low-sodium**
  ▲ **Meatless**

Cranberry Sauce Muffins

I created this recipe because I'm always watching my weight. These muffins are easy to make and have less fat and calories than many others. Occasionally, I'll substitute canned pumpkin for the cranberry sauce, which is also good!
—Glenda Cameron, Landenberg, Pennsylvania

    2 cups All-Bran
1-1/4 cups fat-free milk
    1/4 cup egg substitute
    2 tablespoons canola oil
    3/4 cup whole wheat flour
    1/2 cup all-purpose flour
Sugar substitute equivalent to 1/2 cup sugar*
    3 teaspoons baking powder
    1/4 teaspoon salt
    1 cup whole-berry cranberry sauce

In a bowl, combine cereal and milk; let stand for 5 minutes. Add egg substitute and oil; mix well. Combine the next five ingredients; stir into cereal mixture just until moistened. Fold in cranberry sauce. Coat muffin cups with nonstick cooking spray; fill two-thirds full with batter. Bake at 400° for 15-20 minutes or until a toothpick comes out clean. Cool 5 minutes; remove from pan to a wire rack. **Yield:** 1 dozen.

*Editor's Note: This recipe was tested with Splenda No Calorie Sweetener. Look for it in the baking aisle of your grocery store.

Nutritional Analysis: One muffin equals 145 calories, 3 g fat (trace saturated fat), 1 mg cholesterol, 156 mg sodium, 29 g carbohydrate, 5 g fiber, 4 g protein.
  Diabetic Exchanges: 1-1/2 starch, 1/2 fat.
  △ **Low-fat**
  ▲ **Meatless**

Favorite Quick Bread Recipe Made Lighter

THE RECIPE for Holiday Pumpkin Bread has been in Gale Spross' family for about 30 years. "We are not big pumpkin eaters, but no one turns down a slice of this bread," says the Wills Point, Texas cook. "Can you help us cut down on the fat and sugar?"

To reduce the fat and calories, our Test Kitchen staff eliminated an egg, used half the amount of oil and just a third of the nuts called for in the original recipe.

They also reduced the sugar by nearly 1 cup, using a combination of white and brown sugar to retain the sweetness of the original bread. They added some whole wheat flour for a nutrition boost...and to keep the volume of the dough similar to the original so that it would have the same yield (two loaves).

Holiday Pumpkin Bread

3 cups sugar
2 cups all-purpose flour
1 teaspoon *each* ground cinnamon, nutmeg and
  allspice
1/2 teaspoon baking powder
1/2 teaspoon baking soda
1/2 teaspoon salt
3 eggs
1 can (15 ounces) solid-pack pumpkin
1 cup vegetable oil
1 teaspoon vanilla extract
1-1/2 cups chopped pecans

In a bowl, combine the sugar, flour, spices, baking powder, baking soda and salt. In another bowl, combine the eggs, pumpkin, oil and vanilla; mix well. Stir into dry ingredients just until moistened. Fold in pecans.

Spoon into two greased and floured 8-in. x 4-in. x 2-in. baking pans. Bake at 350° for 65-75 minutes or until a toothpick inserted near the center comes out clean. Cool for 15 minutes before removing from pans to wire racks. **Yield:** 2 loaves (12 slices each).

Nutritional Analysis: One slice equals 283 calories, 15 g fat (2 g saturated fat), 27 mg cholesterol, 94 mg sodium, 35 g carbohydrate, 2 g fiber, 3 g protein.
  ▲ *Low-sodium*
  ▲ *Meatless*

Makeover Holiday Pumpkin Bread

(Pictured at right)

2 cups all-purpose flour
1-1/2 cups plus 4 teaspoons sugar, *divided*
1 cup whole wheat flour
1/2 cup packed brown sugar
2 teaspoons baking powder
1 teaspoon ground cinnamon
1 teaspoon ground allspice
1/2 teaspoon baking soda
1/2 teaspoon salt
1/2 teaspoon ground nutmeg
2 eggs
1 can (15 ounces) solid-pack pumpkin
1/2 cup canola oil
1/2 cup water
1 teaspoon vanilla extract
1/2 cup chopped pecans

In a bowl, combine the all-purpose flour, 1-1/2 cups sugar, whole wheat flour, brown sugar, baking powder, cinnamon, allspice, baking soda, salt and nutmeg. Combine the eggs, pumpkin, oil, water and vanilla; mix well. Stir into dry ingredients just until moistened. Fold in pecans.

Spoon into two 8-in. x 4-in. x 2-in. baking pans coated with nonstick cooking spray. Sprinkle with remaining sugar. Bake at 350° for 50-60 minutes or until a toothpick inserted near the center comes out clean. Cool for 15 minutes before removing from pans to wire racks. **Yield:** 2 loaves (12 slices each).

Nutritional Analysis: One slice equals 197 calories, 7 g fat (1 g saturated fat), 18 mg cholesterol, 124 mg sodium, 31 g carbohydrate, 2 g fiber, 3 g protein.
  Diabetic Exchanges: 2 starch, 1 fat.
  ▲ *Low-sodium*
  ▲ *Meatless*

Apple Zucchini Loaf

(Pictured below)

I save time, use less oil and have moister results when I add jars of baby food fruit to my quick breads. This recipe is a big help if company is coming and you want to make bread for dinner or to have with coffee.
—JoAnn Lee, Accord, New York

1-1/2 cups all-purpose flour
    1 cup sugar
    1 teaspoon ground cinnamon
    1/2 teaspoon baking soda
    1/4 teaspoon baking powder
    1/4 teaspoon salt
    1 jar (4-1/2 ounces) diced apple baby food
    1 egg
    1 tablespoon canola oil
    1 cup finely shredded zucchini
TOPPING:
    1/4 cup quick-cooking oats
    1/4 cup flaked coconut
    1/4 cup packed brown sugar
    2 tablespoons butter *or* stick margarine, melted
Dash ground cinnamon

In a large bowl, combine the flour, sugar, cinnamon, baking soda, baking powder and salt. Drain apples, reserving juice. In another bowl, beat the egg, oil and reserved juice. Stir into the dry ingredients just until blended. Fold in zucchini and apples until moistened.

Pour into an 8-in. x 4-in. x 2-in. loaf pan coated with nonstick cooking spray. Combine topping ingredients; sprinkle over top. Bake at 350° for 50-55 minutes or until a toothpick comes out clean. Cool for 10 minutes before removing from pan to a wire rack. **Yield:** 1 loaf (12 slices).

Nutritional Analysis: One slice equals 193 calories, 4 g fat (2 g saturated fat), 23 mg cholesterol, 139 mg sodium, 37 g carbohydrate, 1 g fiber, 3 g protein.
    Diabetic Exchanges: 1-1/2 starch, 1 fruit, 1 fat.
   ▲ **Low-sodium**
   ▲ **Meatless**

Holiday Cranberry Yeast Bread

Wonderful aromas permeate the house while this bread is baking! My family loves it hot from the oven. The cranberries give each slice a yummy hint of sweet-tart flavor…and the whole wheat flour adds a healthy touch to our holiday menu.
—Joan Hallford, North Richland Hills, Texas

1-1/2 cups fresh *or* frozen cranberries, halved
    1/3 cup packed brown sugar
    1/3 cup molasses
1-1/4 cups warm water (110° to 115°), *divided*
    1 tablespoon active dry yeast
    1 tablespoon honey
    2 tablespoons butter *or* stick margarine, melted
    1 teaspoon salt
    1/4 teaspoon ground allspice
2-1/2 cups whole wheat flour
1-1/2 to 2 cups all-purpose flour

In a bowl, combine the cranberries, brown sugar and molasses; let stand for 1 hour. Stir in 1 cup warm water. In a mixing bowl, dissolve yeast in remaining warm water. Add honey; let stand for 5 minutes. Add the butter, salt, allspice, whole wheat flour, 1 cup all-purpose flour and cranberry mixture. Beat until smooth. Stir in enough remaining all-purpose flour to form a soft dough. Turn onto a floured surface; knead until smooth and elastic, about 6-8 minutes. Place in a bowl coated with nonstick cooking spray, turning once to coat top. Cover and let rise in a warm place until doubled, about 1 hour.

Punch dough down and turn onto a floured surface; shape into a loaf. Place in a 9-in. x 5-in. x 3-in. loaf pan coated with nonstick cooking spray. Cover and let rise until doubled, about 30 minutes. Bake at 350° for 50-60 minutes or until golden brown. Remove from pan to wire rack to cool. **Yield:** 1 loaf (16 slices).

Nutritional Analysis: One slice equals 163 calories, 2 g fat (1 g saturated fat), 4 mg cholesterol, 167 mg sodium, 34 g carbohydrate, 3 g fiber, 4 g protein.
    Diabetic Exchange: 2 starch.
   △ **Low-fat**
   ▲ **Meatless**

Peaches Have Appeal

WHILE making zucchini bread, I ran out of the fat replacement I usually use in my recipe. Since I had fresh peaches on hand, I peeled several, blended them in my food processor and added a pinch of ginger. I used an equal amount of the peach mixture to make the bread, which turned out moist and delicious.
—*Rosella Simmons, Muncie, Indiana*

Bake at 350° for 30-35 minutes or until golden brown. Remove from pan to wire rack. Melt remaining butter; brush over loaf. **Yield:** 1 loaf (16 slices).

Editor's Note: If your bread machine has a time-delay feature, we recommend you do not use it for this recipe.

Nutritional Analysis: One slice equals 109 calories, 2 g fat (1 g saturated fat), 17 mg cholesterol, 174 mg sodium, 19 g carbohydrate, 2 g fiber, 4 g protein.
Diabetic Exchanges: 1 starch, 1/2 fat.
△ **Low-fat**
▲ **Meatless**

Pumpkin Chocolate Chip Muffins

When I was trying to modify my mom's pumpkin bread recipe to cut down on the fat and cholesterol, I came up with these moist sweet muffins. My kids love them…and they get a healthy dose of vitamin A from the pumpkin without even knowing it!
—Kathy Fannoun, Brooklyn Park, Minnesota

2-1/2 cups all-purpose flour
   2 cups sugar
1/2 cup whole wheat flour
1-1/2 teaspoons baking powder
1-1/2 teaspoons ground cinnamon
   1 teaspoon salt
1/2 teaspoon baking soda
1/2 teaspoon ground nutmeg
   1 egg
3/4 cup egg substitute
   1 can (15 ounces) solid-pack pumpkin
1/2 cup unsweetened applesauce
1/4 cup canola oil
   1 cup (6 ounces) semisweet chocolate chips

In a mixing bowl, combine the first eight ingredients. In another bowl, combine the egg, egg substitute, pumpkin, applesauce and oil; stir into dry ingredients just until moistened. Stir in chocolate chips. Coat muffin cups with nonstick cooking spray; fill two-thirds full with batter. Bake at 400° for 18-22 minutes or until a toothpick comes out clean. Cool for 5 minutes before removing from pans to wire racks. **Yield:** 2 dozen.

Nutritional Analysis: One muffin equals 193 calories, 5 g fat (2 g saturated fat), 9 mg cholesterol, 242 mg sodium, 35 g carbohydrate, 2 g fiber, 3 g protein.
Diabetic Exchanges: 2 starch, 1 fat.
▲ **Meatless**

Superb Herb Bread

(Pictured above)

Caraway, poppy seed, sage and nutmeg give this tender bread its superb flavor. I received a blue ribbon at our fall festival for this recipe. My bread machine makes it convenient to prepare the dough for this loaf—it's light, delicious and the wheat flour makes it extra nutritious.
—Doris White, De Land, Illinois

   1 cup warm fat-free milk (70° to 80°)
   1 egg
   2 tablespoons butter *or* stick margarine, softened, *divided*
   2 tablespoons sugar
   1 teaspoon salt
   2 teaspoons caraway seeds
1-1/2 teaspoons poppy seeds
1-1/2 teaspoons dried minced onion
   1 teaspoon rubbed sage
1/2 teaspoon ground nutmeg
   2 cups bread flour
   1 cup whole wheat flour
1-1/2 teaspoons active dry yeast

In bread machine pan, place the milk, egg, 1 tablespoon butter, sugar, salt, caraway seeds, poppy seeds, onion, sage, nutmeg, flours and yeast in the order suggested by manufacturer. Select dough setting (check dough after 5 minutes of mixing; add 1 to 2 tablespoons of water or flour if needed).

When the cycle is completed, turn dough onto a lightly floured surface. Punch down; shape into a loaf. Place in a 9-in. x 5-in. x 3-in. loaf pan coated with nonstick cooking spray. Cover and let rise until doubled, about 45 minutes.

Three-Grain Pan Rolls

(Pictured above)

The first time I made these rolls, I was a little worried that my husband wouldn't like them. But he loved them! The seeds on top add flavor and fun crunch.
—Montserrat Wadsworth, Fallon, Nevada

```
  2 cups water
1/2 cup bulgur*
  1 package (1/4 ounce) active dry yeast
  1 cup warm milk (110° to 115°)
1/2 cup quick-cooking oats
1/3 cup honey
  2 eggs
  2 teaspoons salt
3/4 teaspoon pepper
1-1/2 cups whole wheat flour
2-1/2 to 3-1/2 cups all-purpose flour
  2 tablespoons olive or canola oil
  2 teaspoons each celery seed, fennel seed and
    sesame seeds
  1 teaspoon poppy seeds
```

In a saucepan, bring water to a boil. Stir in bulgur. Reduce heat; cover and simmer for 15 minutes or until tender. Drain. In a large mixing bowl, dissolve yeast in warm milk. Add the oats, honey, eggs, salt, pepper, cooked bulgur and whole wheat flour. Beat until smooth. Stir in enough all-purpose flour to form a soft dough. Turn onto a lightly floured surface; knead until elastic, about 6-8 minutes (mixture will be lumpy). Place in a bowl coated with nonstick cooking spray, turning once to coat top. Cover and let rise in a warm place until doubled, about 1-1/4 hours.

Punch dough down. Turn onto a lightly floured surface; divide into 22 pieces. Roll into balls. Brush two 9-in. round baking pans with some of the oil. Arrange 11 balls in each pan; brush tops with remaining oil. In a bowl, combine the seeds; sprinkle over rolls. Cover and let rise in a warm place until doubled, about 40 minutes. Bake at 375° for 18-22 minutes or until golden brown. Remove from pans to wire racks to cool. **Yield:** 22 rolls.

*Editor's Note: Look for bulgur in the cereal, rice or organic food aisle of your grocery store.

Nutritional Analysis: One roll equals 157 calories, 3 g fat (1 g saturated fat), 21 mg cholesterol, 227 mg sodium, 29 g carbohydrate, 2 g fiber, 5 g protein.
Diabetic Exchanges: 2 starch, 1/2 fat.
△ *Low-fat*
▲ *Meatless*

Flavorful Herb Bread

This lovely low-sodium loaf gets its delicious flavor from a handful of fragrant herbs.
—Nancy Zimmerman
Cape May Court House, New Jersey

```
  1 package (1/4 ounce) active dry yeast
  1 cup warm water (110° to 115°)
  3 tablespoons sugar
  2 tablespoons butter or stick margarine, melted
  1 tablespoon dried parsley flakes
1-1/2 teaspoons dried basil
1/2 teaspoon each dried oregano and thyme
1/4 teaspoon garlic powder
2-1/2 to 3 cups all-purpose flour
```

In a large mixing bowl, dissolve yeast in water. Stir in the sugar, butter, parsley, basil, oregano, thyme, garlic powder and 1 cup flour. Beat until smooth. Stir in enough remaining flour to form a soft dough. Turn onto a lightly floured surface; knead until smooth and elastic, about 5-6 minutes. Place in a bowl coated with nonstick cooking spray, turning once to coat top. Cover and let rise in a warm place until doubled, about 1 hour.

Punch dough down; turn onto a lightly floured surface. Shape into a loaf. Place in a 9-in. x 5-in. x 3-in. loaf pan coated with nonstick cooking spray. Cover and let rise in a warm place until doubled, about 30 minutes. Bake at 375° for 30-35 minutes or until golden brown. Remove from pan to a wire rack to cool. **Yield:** 1 loaf (16 slices).

Nutritional Analysis: One slice equals 103 calories, 2 g fat (1 g saturated fat), 4 mg cholesterol, 16 mg sodium, 19 g carbohydrate, 1 g fiber, 2 g protein.
Diabetic Exchanges: 1 starch, 1/2 fat.
△ *Low-fat*
▲ *Low-sodium*
▲ *Meatless*

Favorite Scone Recipe Made Lighter

CRANBERRIES add festive color and fun flavor to baked goods and other dishes. In Sandy Ferrario's Ione, California home, Cranberry Pecan Scones are a favorite treat for breakfast or a snack. "I would just love it if you could lower their calorie and fat content," says Sandy.

Our home economists were happy to lighten up the moist golden-brown scones. To reduce the fat, they cut the amount of butter and eggs in half. To replace some of the lost moisture, they doubled the amount of orange juice. They also increased the sugar slightly to maintain the scones' tender texture.

Increasing the orange juice added acidity to the recipe, so our Test Kitchen staff had to adjust the leavening, decreasing some of the baking powder and adding a little baking soda.

They also reduced the amount of nuts to further cut the fat, but they toasted them to boost the flavor.

These changes cut the calories by a quarter and the fat, saturated fat and cholesterol by half. But the makeover scones still have a tender texture, an appealing orange flavor and tart bursts of cranberry goodness.

Cranberry Pecan Scones

  2 cups all-purpose flour
1/3 cup sugar
  2 teaspoons baking powder
1/2 teaspoon salt
1/2 cup cold butter *or* margarine
  2 eggs
  3 tablespoons orange juice
  1 teaspoon vanilla extract
1/2 teaspoon grated orange peel
1/2 cup chopped fresh *or* frozen cranberries, thawed
1/2 cup chopped pecans
  1 egg white
1/2 teaspoon water

In a large bowl, combine the flour, sugar, baking powder and salt; cut in butter until mixture resembles coarse crumbs. In another bowl, beat the eggs, orange juice, vanilla and orange peel. Add to flour mixture along with cranberries and pecans; stir just until moistened.

Pat dough into a 6-1/2-in. circle on a greased baking sheet. Combine egg white and water; brush over dough. Cut into eight wedges (do not separate). Bake at 400° for 20-25 minutes or until golden brown. Cool on a wire rack. **Yield:** 8 servings.

Nutritional Analysis: One scone equals 323 calories, 19 g fat (8 g saturated fat), 84 mg cholesterol, 409 mg sodium, 34 g carbohydrate, 2 g fiber, 6 g protein.
▲ *Meatless*

Makeover Cranberry Pecan Scones

(Pictured below)

  2 cups all-purpose flour
1/2 cup sugar
  1 teaspoon baking powder
1/2 teaspoon salt
1/4 teaspoon baking soda
1/4 cup cold butter *or* stick margarine
  1 egg
  6 tablespoons orange juice
  1 teaspoon vanilla extract
1/2 teaspoon grated orange peel
1/2 cup chopped fresh *or* frozen cranberries, thawed
  3 tablespoons chopped pecans, toasted
  1 egg white
1/2 teaspoon water

In a large bowl, combine the flour, sugar, baking powder, salt and baking soda; cut in butter until mixture resembles coarse crumbs. Beat the egg, orange juice, vanilla and orange peel. Add to flour mixture along with cranberries and pecans; stir just until moistened.

Pat dough into a 6-1/2-in. circle on a baking sheet coated with nonstick cooking spray. Combine egg white and water; brush over dough. Cut into eight wedges (do not separate). Bake at 400° for 20-25 minutes or until golden brown. Cool on a wire rack. **Yield:** 8 servings.

Nutritional Analysis: One scone equals 250 calories, 9 g fat (4 g saturated fat), 42 mg cholesterol, 321 mg sodium, 38 g carbohydrate, 2 g fiber, 5 g protein.
Diabetic Exchanges: 2 starch, 1-1/2 fat, 1/2 fruit.
▲ *Meatless*

Herbed Swirl Bread

This yeast bread is so pretty, with a swirl of herbs in each slice! Try it with whatever herbs are growing in your garden.
—*Laura Dennison, Pensacola, Florida*

3 packages (1/4 ounce *each*) active dry yeast
2-1/2 cups warm water (110° to 115°), *divided*
1 teaspoon sugar
3-1/4 cups whole wheat flour
1 tablespoon salt
2-3/4 to 3-1/2 cups bread flour
6 green onions, finely chopped
1 garlic clove, minced
1 cup minced fresh parsley
2 tablespoons minced fresh rosemary
1 tablespoon *each* minced fresh basil and oregano
1 teaspoon minced fresh thyme
1/4 teaspoon pepper
2 tablespoons butter *or* stick margarine
1 egg, beaten

In a large mixing bowl, dissolve yeast in 3/4 cup warm water. Add sugar; let stand for 5 minutes. Add the whole wheat flour, salt and remaining water; beat until smooth. Stir in enough bread flour to form a soft dough (dough will be sticky).

Turn onto a floured surface; knead until smooth and elastic, about 6-8 minutes. Place in a bowl coated with nonstick cooking spray; turn once to coat top. Cover and let rise in a warm place until doubled, about 1 hour. In a nonstick skillet, saute onions, garlic, herbs and pepper in butter until tender. Set aside.

Punch dough down and turn onto a floured surface; divide in half. Roll each piece into a 14-in. x 9-in. rectangle. Brush with some of the egg; refrigerate rest of egg. Spread herb mixture over dough to within 1/2 in. of edges. Roll up jelly-roll style, starting with a short side; pinch seams to seal and tuck ends under. Place seam side down in two 9-in. x 5-in. x 3-in. loaf pans coated with nonstick cooking spray. Cover; let rise until doubled, about 45 minutes.

Brush with reserved egg. Bake at 375° for 40-50 minutes or until bread sounds hollow when tapped. Remove from pans to wire racks. **Yield:** 2 loaves (12 slices each).

Nutritional Analysis: One slice equals 134 calories, 2 g fat (1 g saturated fat), 11 mg cholesterol, 309 mg sodium, 25 g carbohydrate, 3 g fiber, 5 g protein.
Diabetic Exchange: 1-1/2 starch.
△ *Low-fat*
▲ *Meatless*

Raisin Wheat Bread

(Pictured below)

My husband likes dense, hearty breads with a little crunch. I took a basic wheat bread recipe and added crunchy sunflower seeds plus raisins and honey for sweetness. It's moist and tender but filling, too.
—*Lorraine Darocha, Mountain City, Tennessee*

1-1/4 cups plus 1 tablespoon water (70° to 80°)
2 tablespoons olive *or* canola oil
2 tablespoons honey
2 tablespoons molasses
1-1/2 teaspoons salt
1/3 cup unsalted sunflower kernels
2/3 cup raisins
2 cups whole wheat flour
1-1/3 cups bread flour
2-1/2 teaspoons active dry yeast

In bread machine pan, place all ingredients in order suggested by manufacturer. Select wheat bread setting*. Choose crust color and loaf size if available. Bake according to bread machine directions (check dough after 5 minutes of mixing; add 1 to 2 tablespoons of water or flour if needed). **Yield:** 1 loaf (16 slices).

***Editor's Note:** If your bread machine does not have a wheat setting, follow the manufacturer's directions using the basic setting.

Nutritional Analysis: One slice equals 164 calories, 4 g fat (trace saturated fat), 0 cholesterol, 223 mg sodium, 29 g carbohydrate, 3 g fiber, 5 g protein.
Diabetic Exchanges: 2 starch, 1/2 fat.
▲ *Meatless*

Dazzling Desserts

It used to be the words "rich", "creamy" and "yummy" were never spoken in the same sentence as "low fat", especially when the conversation turned to desserts. But now you can have your cake and eat it, too!

No-Bake Chocolate Cheesecake (page 206)

Almond-Coated Chocolate Truffles

(Pictured below)

Using baking fat replacement trims a third of the fat from these wonderful chocolate bites created by our Test Kitchen home economists. The rich candies make a perfect gift for Valentine's Day or another special occasion.

6 ounces semisweet chocolate, coarsely chopped
3 tablespoons confectioners' sugar
1/3 cup baking fat replacement*
1 tablespoon butter (no substitutes)
1 tablespoon half-and-half cream
2 tablespoons ground almonds

Place chocolate and confectioners' sugar in a food processor or blender; cover and process until finely chopped. In a microwave-safe bowl, combine baking fat replacement, butter and cream. Microwave on high for 50-60 seconds or until hot.

With blender or food processor running, gradually add hot cream mixture to chocolate mixture in a steady stream. Blend until smooth. Transfer to a bowl; cover and refrigerate for 1-2 hours or until easy to handle.

Shape chilled mixture into 1-in. balls; roll in almonds. Place on waxed paper-lined baking sheets. Chill for 1-2 hours or until firm. **Yield:** 16 truffles.

***Editor's Note:** This recipe was tested with Sunsweet Lighter Bake. Look for it in the baking aisle of your grocery store.

Nutritional Analysis: *One truffle equals 80 calories, 5 g fat (3 g saturated fat), 2 mg cholesterol, 10 mg sodium, 9 g carbohydrate, 1 g fiber, 1 g protein.*
Diabetic Exchanges: *1 fat, 1/2 starch.*
△ *Low-sodium*

Peanut Butter Pudding

Dress up sugar-free instant pudding with peanut butter for this simply yummy dessert. I came up with the idea one day when I was looking for something fast for dessert. It's delicious.
—Joyce Crouse, Chambersburg, Pennsylvania

1-3/4 cups fat-free milk
2 tablespoons reduced-fat creamy peanut butter
1 package (1 ounce) sugar-free instant vanilla pudding mix
1/4 cup reduced-fat whipped topping
4 teaspoons chocolate syrup

In a bowl, whisk the milk and peanut butter until blended. Add pudding mix; whisk for 2 minutes or until slightly thickened. Spoon into dessert dishes. Refrigerate for at least 5 minutes or until set. Just before serving, dollop with whipped topping and drizzle with chocolate syrup. **Yield:** 4 servings.

Nutritional Analysis: *One serving equals 112 calories, 3 g fat (1 g saturated fat), 2 mg cholesterol, 186 mg sodium, 14 g carbohydrate, 1 g fiber, 6 g protein.*
Diabetic Exchanges: *1/2 starch, 1/2 fat-free milk, 1/2 fat.*
△ *Low-fat*

No-Bake Chocolate Cheesecake

(Pictured on page 205)

Your valentine will fall in love with this sweet treat from our Test Kitchen. Each silky smooth slice is topped with juicy raspberries and a drizzle of white chocolate, making it an attractive finish to a special meal.

3/4 cup graham cracker crumbs (about 12 squares)
2 tablespoons reduced-fat margarine, melted
1 envelope unflavored gelatin
1 cup cold water
4 squares (1 ounce *each*) semisweet chocolate, coarsely chopped
4 packages (8 ounces *each*) fat-free cream cheese
Sugar substitute equivalent to 1 cup sugar*
1/2 cup sugar
1/4 cup baking cocoa
2 teaspoons vanilla extract
TOPPING:
2 cups fresh raspberries
1 ounce white candy coating

In a bowl, combine cracker crumbs and margarine; press onto the bottom of a 9-in. springform pan. Bake at 375° for 8-10 minutes or until lightly browned. Cool on a wire rack.

For filling, in a small saucepan, sprinkle gelatin over cold water; let stand for 1 minute. Heat over low heat, stirring until gelatin is completely dissolved. Add the semisweet chocolate; stir until melted. In a mixing bowl, beat the cream cheese, sugar substitute and sugar until smooth. Gradually add the chocolate mixture and cocoa. Beat in vanilla. Pour into crust; refrigerate for 2-3 hours or until firm.

Arrange raspberries on top of cheesecake. In a heavy saucepan or microwave, melt white candy coating; stir until smooth. Drizzle or pipe over berries. Carefully run a knife around edge of pan to loosen. Remove sides of pan. Refrigerate leftovers. **Yield:** 12 servings.

*Editor's Note: This recipe was tested with Splenda No Calorie Sweetener. Look for it in the baking aisle of your grocery store.

Nutritional Analysis: One slice equals 227 calories, 7 g fat (4 g saturated fat), 7 mg cholesterol, 457 mg sodium, 30 g carbohydrate, 2 g fiber, 13 g protein.
Diabetic Exchanges: 2 starch, 1 very lean meat, 1 fat.

Chocolate-Cherry Mousse Delight

(Pictured above)

I concocted this for a ladies get-together because several of us were watching our weight. I topped each slice of cherry cake with homemade mousse and chocolate covered cherries—sure to delight!
—Teressa Gilbreth, Columbia, Missouri

1 jar (10 ounces) maraschino cherries with stems
1 package (16 ounces) one-step angel food cake mix
2/3 cup semisweet chocolate chips
1-1/2 cups cold fat-free milk
1 package (1.4 ounces) sugar-free instant chocolate pudding mix
1 carton (8 ounces) frozen reduced-fat whipped topping, thawed

Drain cherries, reserving juice; set cherries aside. Add enough cold water to cherry juice to measure 1-1/4 cups. In a mixing bowl, beat cake mix and cherry juice mixture on low speed until moistened. Beat on medium for 1 minute. Gently spoon into an ungreased 10-in. tube pan. Cut through batter with a knife to remove air pockets.

Bake on the lowest oven rack at 350° for 40-50 minutes or until dark golden brown and cracks feel very dry. Immediately invert pan onto a wire rack; cool completely, about 1 hour. Run a knife around sides of cake and remove from pan.

In a microwave or heavy saucepan, melt chocolate chips; stir until smooth. Pat cherries dry with paper towels. Holding cherries by the stem, dip in chocolate and place on waxed paper. Refrigerate until set.

In a bowl, whisk milk and pudding mix until thickened, about 2 minutes. Let stand for 15 minutes; whisk for 1 minute or until smooth. Fold in whipped topping. Slice cake; serve with mousse and dipped cherries. **Yield:** 12 servings.

Nutritional Analysis: One serving (one piece with 1/3 cup chocolate mousse and 2 cherries) equals 280 calories, 5 g fat (4 g saturated fat), 1 mg cholesterol, 392 mg sodium, 54 g carbohydrate, 1 g fiber, 5 g protein.

Fresh Pear Crisp

This comforting fruit crisp is a pared-down version of one my mother used to fix. I made it healthier by using reduced-fat margarine, fresh pears instead of canned and oats for some of the flour.
—Mildred Sherrer, Fort Worth, Texas

1/3 cup all-purpose flour
1/3 cup quick-cooking oats
1/3 cup packed brown sugar
1 teaspoon ground cinnamon, *divided*
3 tablespoons cold reduced-fat stick margarine,* cut into pieces
4 cups sliced peeled pears (about 2 pounds)
2 tablespoons sugar
1 tablespoon lemon juice
1 teaspoon grated lemon peel
1/2 teaspoon ground ginger

In a bowl, combine the flour, oats, brown sugar and 1/2 teaspoon cinnamon. Cut in margarine until coarse crumbs form; set aside. Place pears in a large bowl. Sprinkle with sugar, lemon juice, lemon peel, ginger and remaining cinnamon; toss to coat. Transfer to an 8-in. square baking dish coated with nonstick cooking spray. Sprinkle with crumb mixture. Bake at 350° for 45-50 minutes or until pears are tender. **Yield:** 9 servings.

*Editor's Note: This recipe was tested with Parkay Light margarine.

Nutritional Analysis: One serving equals 130 calories, 3 g fat (trace saturated fat), 0 cholesterol, 43 mg sodium, 28 g carbohydrate, 2 g fiber, 1 g protein.
Diabetic Exchanges: 1 starch, 1 fruit.
△ *Low-fat*
▲ *Low-sodium*

LIKE other fruits, pears are packed with pluses. Check out these tasty tidbits from USA Pears:
- Pears are loaded with dietary fiber and are a good source of potassium. An average-size pear weighs in at only 100 calories.
- Pears have no cholesterol, sodium or saturated fat.
- Pears are one of the few fruits that ripen best off the tree. Bartletts change color as they ripen. Other varieties don't change color, so to test for ripeness, gently press near the stem. If it gives in to gentle pressure, the pear is sweet, juicy and ready to eat.

Baked Ginger Pears

These dressed-up canned pears are a nice alternative to baked apples. Sweetened with a little brown sugar and sprinkled with pecans and ginger, they're wonderful served warm or cold.
—Shirley Glaab, Hattiesburg, Mississippi

2 cans (14-1/2 ounces *each***) reduced-sugar pear halves**
1/3 cup packed brown sugar
1/4 cup chopped pecans
1 teaspoon lemon juice
1/2 teaspoon ground ginger
4 gingersnap cookies, crumbled

Drain pears, reserving juice; set aside eight pear halves and 1/4 cup juice (save remaining pears and juice for another use). Arrange pear halves cut side up in an ungreased 5-cup baking dish. Combine the brown sugar, pecans, lemon juice and ginger; sprinkle over pears. Spoon reserved pear juice around pears. Bake, uncovered, at 350° for 20-25 minutes or until bubbly. Garnish with cookie crumbs. **Yield:** 4 servings.

Nutritional Analysis: One serving equals 114 calories, 3 g fat (trace saturated fat), trace cholesterol, 18 mg sodium, 22 g carbohydrate, 2 g fiber, 1 g protein.
Diabetic Exchanges: *1-1/2 fruit, 1/2 fat.*
△ *Low-fat*
▲ *Low-sodium*

Eggless Chocolate Cake

(Pictured at right)

This dense moist cake is sure to satisfy anyone's chocolate cravings. Drizzled with semi-sweet chocolate, the rich cake is special enough for company... if your family doesn't get to it first!
—Peggy Weed, Cheshire, Connecticut

1 tablespoon plus 1/2 cup baking cocoa, *divided*
3 cups all-purpose flour
2 cups sugar
2 teaspoons baking soda
1 teaspoon salt
1/4 teaspoon ground cinnamon
2 cups cold brewed coffee
1/3 cup canola oil
2 tablespoons white vinegar
2 teaspoons vanilla extract
1/2 cup semisweet chocolate chips
1/2 teaspoon shortening

Coat a 10-in. fluted tube pan with nonstick cooking spray and dust with 1 tablespoon cocoa; set aside. In a large bowl, combine the flour, sugar, baking soda, salt, cinnamon and remaining cocoa. In another bowl, combine the coffee, oil, vinegar and vanilla. Stir into dry ingredients just until combined. Pour into prepared pan.

Bake at 350° for 40-50 minutes or until a toothpick inserted near the center comes out clean. Cool for 10 minutes before removing from pan to a wire rack to cool completely. In a microwave or heavy saucepan, melt chocolate chips and shortening; stir until smooth. Drizzle over cake. **Yield:** 14 servings.

Nutritional Analysis: One piece equals 295 calories, 8 g fat (2 g saturated fat), 1 mg cholesterol, 355 mg sodium, 55 g carbohydrate, 2 g fiber, 4 g protein.

Cranberry Cheesecake Bars

(Pictured at right)

I came across this recipe several years ago, and it's become a family favorite. A crumbly oat topping and crust sandwich the smooth cream cheese and sweet-tart cranberry fillings.
—Rhonda Lund, Laramie, Wyoming

2 cups plus 2 tablespoons all-purpose flour, *divided*
1 cup quick-cooking oats
3/4 cup packed brown sugar
1/2 cup butter *or* **stick margarine, melted**
1 package (8 ounces) reduced-fat cream cheese
1 can (14 ounces) fat-free sweetened condensed milk
4 egg whites
1 teaspoon vanilla extract
1 can (16 ounces) whole-berry cranberry sauce
2 tablespoons cornstarch

In a bowl, combine 2 cups flour, oats, brown sugar and butter; mix until crumbly. Press 2-1/2 cups of the crumb mixture into a greased 13-in. x 9-in. x 2-in. baking dish. Bake at 350° for 10 minutes.

In a mixing bowl, beat the cream cheese until smooth. Add the milk, egg whites, vanilla and remaining flour; mix well. Spoon over prepared crust. In a bowl, combine the cranberry sauce and cornstarch; mix well. Spoon over cream cheese mixture. Sprinkle with the remaining crumb mixture. Bake at 350° for 30-35 minutes or until center is almost set. Cool on a wire rack before cutting. **Yield:** 3 dozen.

Nutritional Analysis: One bar equals 142 calories, 4 g fat (2 g saturated fat), 11 mg cholesterol, 67 mg sodium, 24 g carbohydrate, 1 g fiber, 3 g protein.
Diabetic Exchanges: *1-1/2 starch, 1/2 fat.*
▲ *Low-sodium*

Strawberry Cheesecake Torte

(Pictured at right)

After I tasted this dessert at a party, a friend shared the recipe. It originally called for pound cake...and I decided to lighten it up by substituting angel food. The result was this delicious light torte.
—Kathy Martinez, Tucson, Arizona

1 package (16 ounces) one-step angel food cake mix
1 tablespoon confectioners' sugar
1 package (.3 ounce) sugar-free strawberry gelatin
1/2 cup boiling water
1/4 cup seedless strawberry jam
1 package (8 ounces) reduced-fat cream cheese, cubed
1/3 cup fat-free milk
2 tablespoons lemon juice
3 cups reduced-fat whipped topping
1 package (3.4 ounces) instant cheesecake *or* vanilla pudding mix
1 cup sliced fresh strawberries
1 kiwifruit, peeled, halved and sliced
1-1/2 teaspoons grated lemon peel

Line a 15-in. x 10-in. x 1-in. baking pan with ungreased parchment paper. Prepare cake mix according to package directions. Spread batter evenly in prepared pan. Bake at 350° for 24-26 minutes or until top is lightly browned. Sprinkle sugar over a waxed paper-lined baking sheet. Immediately invert cake onto baking sheet. Gently peel off parchment paper; cool completely.

Dissolve gelatin in boiling water. Stir in jam until melted. With a fork, poke cake at 1/2-in. intervals. Brush with gelatin mixture; chill for 10 minutes.

In a bowl, beat cream cheese, milk and lemon juice. Add whipped topping and pudding mix; whisk well. Reserve 1 cup. Place remaining pudding mixture in a pastry bag with a large star tip.

Trim edges of cake. Cut widthwise into three equal rectangles; place one on serving plate. Spread 1/2 cup reserved pudding mixture in center. Pipe pudding mixture around top edge of cake. Repeat with second cake layer. Top with remaining cake layer. Pipe pudding mixture along top edges. Fill center with fruit. Sprinkle with lemon peel. Store in refrigerator. **Yield:** 12 servings.

Nutritional Analysis: One piece equals 284 calories, 6 g fat (4 g saturated fat), 11 mg cholesterol, 427 mg sodium, 51 g carbohydrate, 1 g fiber, 6 g protein.

🍎 Clues for Light and Airy Cakes

CAN'T WAIT to bake an angel food or sponge cake? Keep the following in mind for sweet success:

- If a recipe calls for egg whites only, separate *cold* eggs carefully so there are no specks of yolk in the whites. For maximum volume, let the egg whites stand for 30 minutes at room temperature before beating.
- For a golden crust, use aluminum baking pans with dull rather than shiny or dark finishes. If using a tube pan, do not grease or flour it. If a recipe calls for a 15-in. x 10-in. x 1-in. baking pan, line it with parchment paper.
- Cake is done when the top springs back when touched. Cakes baked in tube pans should cool completely before being removed from the pans.
- Cut angel food and sponge cakes with a serrated knife or an electric knife, using a sawing motion.

Fluffy Cherry Frosting

Try topping your favorite cake with this creamy cooked frosting from our Test Kitchen. A pink tint and a hint of cherry flavor make it extra special.

1-1/2 cups sugar
4 egg whites
1/4 cup water
1/4 cup maraschino cherry juice
1/2 teaspoon cream of tartar
1 teaspoon vanilla extract
1/2 teaspoon cherry extract *or* 1/4 teaspoon almond extract

In a heavy saucepan, combine the sugar, egg whites, water, cherry juice and cream of tartar. With a portable mixer, beat on low speed for 1 minute. Continue beating on low over low heat until frosting reaches 160° on a candy thermometer, about 10 minutes. Pour into a large mixing bowl; add extracts. Beat on high until frosting forms stiff peaks, about 7 minutes. **Yield:** 8 cups.

Editor's Note: A stand mixer is recommended for beating the frosting after it reaches 160°. We recommend that you test your candy thermometer before each use by bringing water to a boil; the thermometer should read 212°. Adjust your recipe temperature up or down based on your test.

Nutritional Analysis: One serving (2/3 cup) equals 107 calories, 0 fat (0 saturated fat), 0 cholesterol, 19 mg sodium, 26 g carbohydrate, 0 fiber, 1 g protein.
△ **Low-fat**
▲ **Low-sodium**

Pumpkin Angel Food Cake

(Pictured below)

Here's an easy way to jazz up an angel food cake mix using canned pumpkin, nutmeg and other spices. I like to serve pieces with a dollop of whipped topping and a sprinkling of cinnamon.
—Pamela Overton, Charleston, Illinois

1 cup canned pumpkin
1 teaspoon vanilla extract
1/2 teaspoon ground cinnamon
1/2 teaspoon ground nutmeg
1/4 teaspoon ground cloves
1/8 teaspoon ground ginger
1 package (16 ounces) one-step angel food cake mix
14 tablespoons reduced-fat whipped topping
Additional ground cinnamon, optional

In a large bowl, combine the pumpkin, vanilla, cinnamon, nutmeg, cloves and ginger. Prepare cake mix according to package directions. Fold a fourth of the batter into pumpkin mixture. Gently fold in the remaining batter. Gently spoon into an ungreased 10-in. tube pan. Cut through batter with a knife to remove air pockets.
Bake on the lowest oven rack at 350° for 38-44 minutes

or until top is golden brown and cake springs back when lightly touched. Immediately invert pan onto a wire rack; cool completely, about 1 hour. Run a knife around sides of cake and remove to a serving plate. Garnish each slice with whipped topping; sprinkle with cinnamon if desired. **Yield:** 14 servings.

Nutritional Analysis: One piece with 1 tablespoon whipped topping equals 151 calories, 1 g fat (1 g saturated fat), 0 cholesterol, 264 mg sodium, 33 g carbohydrate, 1 g fiber, 3 g protein. **Diabetic Exchange:** *2 starch.*
△ **Low-fat**

Rhubarb Custard Pie

Rhubarb adds a slightly tart flavor and a fruity touch of spring to this homemade custard pie. Our Test Kitchen staff cooked up this lighter variation on that classic favorite.

1 sheet refrigerated pie pastry
1-1/4 cups sugar, *divided*
1/4 cup all-purpose flour
1/4 teaspoon salt
3 tablespoons orange juice concentrate
2 egg yolks
1 tablespoon butter *or* stick margarine, melted
3 cups sliced fresh *or* frozen rhubarb, thawed and drained
3 egg whites
1/4 cup chopped walnuts

Roll out pastry to fit a 9-in. pie plate. Transfer to pie plate coated with nonstick cooking spray; trim and flute edges. In a large bowl, combine 1 cup sugar, flour and salt. Stir in the juice concentrate, yolks and butter; mix well. Add rhubarb.
In a mixing bowl, beat egg whites until soft peaks form. Gradually beat in remaining sugar until stiff peaks form. Fold into rhubarb mixture. Pour into pie shell. Sprinkle with nuts.
Bake at 375° for 15 minutes. Reduce heat to 325°; bake 40-45 minutes longer or until golden. Cover loosely with foil during the last 10 minutes if crust is browning too quickly. Cool on a wire rack for 1 hour. Store in the refrigerator. **Yield:** 8 servings.

Nutritional Analysis: One piece equals 333 calories, 12 g fat (5 g saturated fat), 62 mg cholesterol, 213 mg sodium, 53 g carbohydrate, 1 g fiber, 5 g protein.

Warm Blackberry Cobbler

*Fat-free yogurt and egg whites in the biscuit topping
make the classic favorite a little healthier.*
—*Pat Patty, Spring, Texas*

    5 cups fresh *or* frozen blackberries
    3/4 cup sugar
      2 tablespoons all-purpose flour
      1 tablespoon lemon juice
      1 teaspoon grated lemon peel
      1 teaspoon vanilla extract
    TOPPING:
      1 cup all-purpose flour
      1/2 teaspoon baking powder
      1/2 teaspoon baking soda
      2 egg whites
      1/2 cup fat-free plain yogurt
      2 tablespoons butter *or* stick margarine, melted
      2 tablespoons lemon juice
      1 teaspoon vanilla extract
      1/2 cup reduced-fat whipped topping

In a bowl, combine the blackberries, sugar, flour, lemon juice, lemon peel and vanilla. Spoon into an 11-in. x 7-in. x 2-in. baking dish coated with nonstick cooking spray; set aside.

For topping, in a bowl, combine the flour, baking powder and baking soda. In another bowl, combine the egg whites, yogurt, butter, lemon juice and vanilla; stir into dry ingredients just until moistened. Drop by tablespoonfuls over blackberry mixture. Bake at 400° for 30 minutes or until filling is bubbly and topping is golden. Serve with whipped topping. **Yield:** 8 servings.

Nutritional Analysis: One serving (3/4 cup cobbler with 1 tablespoon whipped topping) equals 232 calories, 4 g fat (2 g saturated fat), 8 mg cholesterol, 145 mg sodium, 47 g carbohydrate, 5 g fiber, 4 g protein.
Diabetic Exchanges: 2 starch, 1 fruit, 1/2 fat.

Ladyfinger Lemon Dessert

(Pictured at right)

*For an elegant ending to dinner,
make this light, airy dessert.*
—*Tawana Flowers, El Macero, California*

      1 can (12 ounces) evaporated milk
      1 package (3 ounces) ladyfingers, split
      1 package (3 ounces) lemon gelatin
      1 cup boiling orange juice

      1/2 cup sugar
      1/3 cup lemon juice
        2 teaspoons grated lemon peel
        1 cup reduced-fat whipped topping

Pour milk into a small metal mixing bowl; place mixer beaters in the bowl. Cover and refrigerate for at least 2 hours or overnight. Line the sides of a 9-in. springform pan with ladyfingers; set aside. In a large bowl, dissolve gelatin in orange juice. Stir in the sugar, lemon juice and peel; cool to room temperature.

Beat chilled milk until soft peaks form; fold into gelatin mixture. Pour into prepared pan. Refrigerate for at least 3 hours or until firm. Spread with whipped topping. Remove sides of pan. Refrigerate leftovers. **Yield:** 10 servings.

Nutritional Analysis: One serving equals 221 calories, 5 g fat (2 g saturated fat), 98 mg cholesterol, 100 mg sodium, 40 g carbohydrate, trace fiber, 6 g protein.
Diabetic Exchanges: 1-1/2 starch, 1 fruit, 1 fat.
▲ **Low-sodium**

14-Karat Cake

(Pictured at right)

*When I served this carrot cake to my family
one Easter, everyone loved it…and they couldn't
tell I had lightened it up!*
—*Ellen Schub, Sherwood, Wisconsin*

    1-1/3 cups sugar
        2 eggs
        2 egg whites
      1/2 cup unsweetened applesauce
      1/3 cup canola oil
        1 cup all-purpose flour
        1 cup whole wheat flour
    1-1/2 teaspoons baking soda
        1 teaspoon salt
        1 teaspoon ground cinnamon
      1/2 teaspoon ground allspice
      1/4 teaspoon ground cloves
        3 cups shredded carrots
      1/2 cup golden raisins
        6 ounces reduced-fat cream cheese
        1 tablespoon butter *or* stick margarine, softened
      1/2 teaspoon vanilla extract
        3 cups confectioners' sugar
      1/4 cup chopped walnuts
        3 tablespoons flaked coconut, toasted

In a mixing bowl, combine the first five ingredients until smooth. Combine the flours, baking soda, salt and spices; add to the egg mixture and mix well. Stir in carrots and raisins. Pour into a 13-in. x 9-in. x 2-in. baking pan coated with nonstick cooking spray. Bake at 350° for 30-35 minutes or until a toothpick inserted near the center comes out clean. Cool on a wire rack.

For frosting, in a mixing bowl, beat the cream cheese, butter and vanilla until smooth. Beat in sugar. Frost the cake. Sprinkle with walnuts and coconut. Refrigerate. **Yield:** 18 servings.

Nutritional Analysis: One piece equals 286 calories, 9 g fat (3 g saturated fat), 33 mg cholesterol, 304 mg sodium, 49 g carbohydrate, 2 g fiber, 4 g protein.

Orange Tea Cake

(Pictured below)

This from-scratch sponge cake has a hint of orange in every bite...and is wonderful served with a cup of hot tea or coffee. It doesn't need frosting—just dust a little confectioners' sugar on top.
—Beth Duerr, North Tonawanda, New York

7 eggs, *separated*
1-1/2 cups sugar, *divided*
6 tablespoons orange juice
4-1/2 teaspoons grated orange peel
1-3/4 cups all-purpose flour
1/2 teaspoon salt
3/4 teaspoon confectioners' sugar

In a large mixing bowl, beat egg yolks until slightly thickened. Gradually add 1/2 cup sugar, beating until thick and lemon-colored. Beat in orange juice and peel. Sift together flour and salt; add to egg mixture. Beat until smooth.

In another mixing bowl, beat egg whites until soft peaks form. Add the remaining granulated sugar, 1 tablespoon at a time, beating until stiff peaks form. Fold a fourth of the egg whites into the batter; fold in remaining whites. Gently spoon into an ungreased 10-in. tube pan. Cut through batter with a knife to remove air pockets.

Bake on the lowest oven rack at 350° for 30-35 minutes or until cake springs back when lightly touched. Immediately invert pan onto a wire rack; cool completely, about 1 hour. Run a knife around sides of cake and remove to a serving plate. Dust with confectioners' sugar. **Yield:** 12 servings.

Nutritional Analysis: One piece equals 211 calories, 3 g fat (1 g saturated fat), 124 mg cholesterol, 135 mg sodium, 40 g carbohydrate, 1 g fiber, 6 g protein.
Diabetic Exchange: *2-1/2 starch.*
△ **Low-fat**
▲ **Low-sodium**

Warm Chocolate Almond Pudding

When I get the urge for something creamy and chocolaty, I whip up this old-fashioned pudding.
—Darlene Markel, Salem, Oregon

1/2 cup sugar
1/3 cup baking cocoa
2 tablespoons cornstarch
2 cups fat-free milk
1 egg, lightly beaten
1/4 teaspoon vanilla extract
1/4 to 1/2 teaspoon almond extract
1/4 cup reduced-fat whipped topping

In a saucepan, combine sugar, cocoa and cornstarch. Whisk in milk and egg. Cook and stir over medium heat until mixture comes to a boil. Boil for 1 minute. Remove from the heat; stir in extracts. Serve warm. Garnish with whipped topping. **Yield:** 8 servings.

Nutritional Analysis: One serving (1/2 cup) equals 205 calories, 3 g fat (1 g saturated fat), 56 mg cholesterol, 83 mg sodium, 40 g carbohydrate, 2 g fiber, 7 g protein.
Diabetic Exchanges: *2 starch, 1/2 reduced-fat milk.*
△ **Low-fat**
▲ **Low-sodium**

Jewish Apple Cake

My family loves this low-fat version of Jewish Apple Cake, with two layers of cinnamon-seasoned apples.
—Kylene Konosky, Jermyn, Pennsylvania

2 tablespoons reduced-fat cream cheese, cubed
1 cup plus 3 tablespoons sugar, *divided*
1 cup packed brown sugar
2 eggs
3 egg whites
1/2 cup unsweetened applesauce
1/2 cup orange juice
1/3 cup canola oil
2-1/2 teaspoons vanilla extract
3 cups all-purpose flour
3 teaspoons baking powder
3-1/2 cups sliced peeled apples
2 tablespoons chopped walnuts
1 tablespoon ground cinnamon
2 teaspoons confectioners' sugar

In a mixing bowl, beat the cream cheese, 1 cup sugar and brown sugar until blended. Add eggs and egg whites, one at a time, beating well after each addition. Add the applesauce, orange juice, oil and vanilla; beat until smooth. Combine flour and baking powder; add to egg mixture and mix well. In a bowl, toss the apples, walnuts, cinnamon and remaining sugar.

Coat a 10-in. fluted tube pan with nonstick cooking spray and dust with flour. Spoon a third of the batter into prepared pan. Top with half of the apple mixture. Top with another third of the batter and the remaining apple mixture. Top with remaining batter. Bake at 350° for 70-80 minutes or until a toothpick inserted near the center comes out clean. Cool for

10 minutes before removing from pan to a wire rack to cool completely. Dust with confectioners' sugar. **Yield:** 16 servings.

Nutritional Analysis: One piece equals 285 calories, 7 g fat (1 g saturated fat), 28 mg cholesterol, 73 mg sodium, 53 g carbohydrate, 2 g fiber, 4 g protein.
▲ *Low-sodium*

🍎 Secrets to a Successful Meringue

THE NEXT TIME you make meringue, keep these tips in mind:

- Separate eggs carefully. Make sure no yolk gets into the whites. Even a speck can hold down the peaks as you beat the egg whites.
- Egg whites expand 6 to 8 times their volume when beaten. Your mixing bowl should be deep enough so that beaters come in contact with as much egg white as possible. Use a grease-free metal or glass bowl.
- For optimum volume when making meringues, add the sugar *gradually* once soft peaks form.
- Sugar absorbs water on a humid day or in a steamy kitchen, which can result in a limp, sticky meringue. If possible, make meringue on days when humidity is low.

Spiced Pear Cake

Although I took a shortcut by using a convenient mix, I didn't shortchange cake lovers with the results!
—*Becky Vaughn Coleman*
Desert Hot Springs, California

    1 can (15 ounces) reduced-sugar pear halves
    1 package (18-1/4 ounces) white cake mix
    1 egg
    2 egg whites
 1/4 cup reduced-fat sour cream
 1/4 cup packed brown sugar
 1/4 teaspoon ground cinnamon
 1/8 teaspoon ground nutmeg
    2 teaspoons confectioners' sugar

Coat a 10-in. fluted tube pan with nonstick cooking spray and dust with flour; set aside. Drain pears, reserving juice. Chop pears; place in a large mixing bowl. Add reserved pear juice. Add the next seven ingredients. Beat on low speed until moistened. Beat on high for 2 minutes. Pour into prepared pan.

Bake at 350° for 60-65 minutes or until a toothpick inserted near the center comes out clean. Cool for 10 minutes before removing from pan to a wire rack to cool completely. Dust with confectioners' sugar. **Yield:** 14 servings.

Nutritional Analysis: One piece equals 207 calories, 4 g fat (1 g saturated fat), 16 mg cholesterol, 268 mg sodium, 40 g carbohydrate, 1 g fiber, 3 g protein.
Diabetic Exchanges: 1-1/2 starch, 1 fat, 1/2 fruit.

Cocoa-Almond Meringue Cookies

(Pictured above)

Our Test Kitchen dreamed up these yummy chocolate, almond and coconut treats that taste just like a popular candy bar.

    4 egg whites
 1/4 teaspoon cream of tartar
 1/2 teaspoon coconut extract
 1/4 teaspoon almond extract
 1/4 teaspoon vanilla extract
 1/8 teaspoon salt
    1 cup sugar
 1/4 cup plus 1 tablespoon baking cocoa, *divided*

In a mixing bowl, beat the egg whites, cream of tartar, extracts and salt on medium speed until soft peaks form. Gradually beat in sugar, 1 tablespoon at a time, on high until stiff peaks form, about 6 minutes. Sift 1/4 cup cocoa over egg whites; fold in. Place mixture in a pastry or heavy-duty resealable plastic bag; cut a small hole in a corner of bag.

Pipe meringue in 2-in. circles onto parchment paper-lined baking sheets. Bake at 250° for 50-60 minutes or until set and dry. Turn off oven; leave cookies in oven for 1-1/2 hours. Dust with remaining cocoa. Carefully remove from parchment paper. Store in an airtight container. **Yield:** 3 dozen.

Nutritional Analysis: One cookie equals 26 calories, trace fat (0 saturated fat), 0 cholesterol, 14 mg sodium, 6 g carbohydrate, trace fiber, 1 g protein.
Diabetic Exchange: 1/2 starch.
▲ *Low-fat*
▲ *Low-sodium*

Orange Rosemary Sorbet

(Pictured above)

Add a refreshing finish to any meal with this smooth icy dessert. The subtle hint of fresh rosemary lends a delightfully different flavor to the citrusy sorbet.
—Bonnie Kinzler, New York, New York

1-1/2 cups water
1-1/2 cups sugar
   2 to 3 fresh rosemary sprigs
   3 cups orange juice
1/3 cup lemon juice

In a large saucepan, bring water, sugar and rosemary to a boil. Reduce heat; simmer, uncovered, for 10 minutes. Cool. Strain, discarding rosemary. Stir in orange juice and lemon juice. Fill cylinder of ice cream freezer two-thirds full; freeze according to manufacturer's directions. Allow to ripen in ice cream freezer or firm up in the refrigerator freezer for 2-4 hours before serving. **Yield:** 8 servings.

Nutritional Analysis: One serving (3/4 cup) equals 190 calories, trace fat (0 saturated fat), 0 cholesterol, 1 mg sodium, 48 g carbohydrate, trace fiber, trace protein.

Pineapple Pudding

My husband and I have cut down considerably on fat and sugar, so I'm always on the lookout for dessert recipes like this one. With only four ingredients, the pudding is quick to prepare, too.
—Ruth Vauthrin, Costa Mesa, California

   2 cups (16 ounces) fat-free sour cream
   2 cans (8 ounces *each*) unsweetened crushed pineapple, undrained
   1 package (1 ounce) sugar-free instant vanilla pudding mix
   6 vanilla wafers

In a bowl, whisk the sour cream, pineapple and pudding mix until blended and thickened. Serve immediately with vanilla wafers. Refrigerate leftovers. **Yield:** 6 servings.

Nutritional Analysis: One serving (2/3 cup pudding with 1 wafer) equals 159 calories, 1 g fat (trace saturated fat), trace cholesterol, 274 mg sodium, 31 g carbohydrate, 1 g fiber, 5 g protein.
Diabetic Exchanges: *1 fat-free milk, 1 fruit.*
△ **Low-fat**

Fudgy Brownie Cookies

Our Test Kitchen used baking cocoa and miniature chocolate chips to help keep down the fat and calories in these treats.

   1 egg
   1 egg white
   1 cup sugar
   2 teaspoons instant coffee granules
   1 tablespoon boiling water
1/4 cup butter *or* stick margarine, melted
   1 tablespoon light corn syrup
1/2 cup all-purpose flour
1/2 cup baking cocoa
1/4 teaspoon baking powder
1/4 teaspoon salt
1/4 cup miniature semisweet chocolate chips
1/4 cup chopped walnuts

In a mixing bowl, beat egg, egg white and sugar. In a small bowl, dissolve coffee granules in boiling water. Add the coffee, butter and corn syrup to egg mixture; mix well. Combine the flour, cocoa, baking powder and salt; gradually add to egg mixture. Stir in chocolate chips and nuts.

Line baking sheets with parchment paper and lightly coat with nonstick cooking spray. Drop batter by tablespoonfuls onto prepared baking sheets. Bake at 350° for 10-12 minutes or until set. Cool for 2 minutes before removing to wire racks to cool completely. **Yield:** 2-1/2 dozen.

Nutritional Analysis: One serving (2 cookies) equals 139 calories, 6 g fat (3 g saturated fat), 22 mg cholesterol, 89 mg sodium, 21 g carbohydrate, 1 g fiber, 2 g protein.
Diabetic Exchanges: *1-1/2 starch, 1 fat.*
▲ **Low-sodium**

Favorite Recipe Made Lighter

FOR Stephanie Malszycki of Ft. Myers, Florida, Crispy Oat Cookies are a family favorite. "My mother-in-law, Cindy Malszycki, shared this recipe with me," Stephanie says. "Can you make it lighter?"

After several attempts, *Light & Tasty* home economists came up with Makeover Crispy Oat Cookies, a lower-fat version that still has the original cookie's wonderful shortbread-like texture.

First, they reduced the amount of butter, oil, coconut and nuts to trim fat and calories. Then they stirred in additional crisp rice cereal to replace some of the lost crunch from fewer nuts. Finally, they used a combination of flour and cornstarch instead of flour alone to create the cookie's tender texture.

The revised recipe makes a smaller batch, but yields cookies the same size as the original. The trimmed-down treats have 40% fewer calories and just half the fat and saturated fat of the original. So nibble one of these cookies anytime.

Crispy Oat Cookies

1 cup butter *or* margarine, softened
1 cup vegetable oil
1-1/3 cups sugar, *divided*
1 egg
1 teaspoon vanilla extract
3-1/2 cups all-purpose flour
1 teaspoon baking soda
1 teaspoon cream of tartar
1 teaspoon salt
1 cup crisp rice cereal
1 cup quick-cooking oats
1 cup flaked coconut
1 cup chopped walnuts

In a mixing bowl, beat the butter, oil and 1 cup sugar. Beat in egg and vanilla. Combine the flour, baking soda, cream of tartar and salt; gradually add to the butter mixture. Stir in the cereal, oats, coconut and nuts.

Roll into 1-in. balls; roll in some of the remaining sugar. Place 2 in. apart on ungreased baking sheets. Flatten with a glass dipped in remaining sugar. Bake at 350° for 10-12 minutes or until lightly browned. Remove to wire racks to cool. **Yield:** 8 dozen.

Nutritional Analysis: One cookie equals 82 calories, 5 g fat (2 g saturated fat), 7 mg cholesterol, 72 mg sodium, 8 g carbohydrate, trace fiber, 1 g protein.
▲ *Low-sodium*

Makeover Crispy Oat Cookies

(Pictured at right)

1/4 cup butter *or* stick margarine, softened
1/4 cup canola oil

1 cup sugar, *divided*
1 tablespoon water
1 egg
1 teaspoon vanilla extract
3/4 cup all-purpose flour
1/4 cup cornstarch
1 teaspoon baking soda
1 teaspoon cream of tartar
1/2 teaspoon salt
1-1/2 cups crisp rice cereal
1 cup quick-cooking oats
1/3 cup flaked coconut
1/4 cup chopped walnuts

In a mixing bowl, beat the butter, oil, 3/4 cup sugar and water. Beat in egg and vanilla. Combine the flour, cornstarch, baking soda, cream of tartar and salt; gradually add to the butter mixture. Stir in the cereal, oats, coconut and nuts (dough will be sticky).

Shape into 1-in. balls; roll in some of the remaining sugar. Place dough 2 in. apart on baking sheets coated with nonstick cooking spray. Flatten with a glass dipped in remaining sugar. Bake at 350° for 10-12 minutes or until lightly browned. Remove to wire racks to cool. **Yield:** 5 dozen.

Nutritional Analysis: One cookie equals 50 calories, 2 g fat (1 g saturated fat), 6 mg cholesterol, 58 mg sodium, 7 g carbohydrate, trace fiber, 1 g protein.
Diabetic Exchanges: 1/2 starch, 1/2 fat.
△ *Low-fat*
▲ *Low-sodium*

Rhubarb-Orange Angel Food Torte

(Pictured at right)

This pretty torte is the perfect dessert for when company comes! And it's so simple—just spread a fruity sauce between layers of a prepared angel food cake, then frost and garnish with berries.
—*Sheila Long, Elmwood, Ontario*

1 package (16 ounces) one-step angel food cake mix
1-1/2 cups sliced fresh *or* frozen rhubarb
3/4 cup frozen unsweetened raspberries, thawed
6 tablespoons sugar
5 tablespoons orange juice, *divided*
1/2 teaspoon grated orange peel
1/4 teaspoon ground ginger *or* 1 teaspoon minced fresh gingerroot
2 teaspoons cornstarch
1 carton (8 ounces) frozen reduced-fat whipped topping, thawed
Fresh raspberries, optional

Prepare cake mix according to package directions. Gently spoon batter into an ungreased 10-in. tube pan. Cut through batter with a knife to remove air pockets. Bake according to package directions. Immediately invert pan onto a wire rack; cool completely, about 1 hour. Run a knife around sides of cake and remove from pan.

In a saucepan, combine the rhubarb, raspberries, sugar, 4 tablespoons orange juice, orange peel and ginger. Cook, uncovered, over medium heat until rhubarb is tender, about 7 minutes. In a small bowl, combine cornstarch and remaining orange juice until smooth; stir into the fruit mixture. Bring to a boil; cook and stir for 2 minutes or until thickened. Remove from the heat; cool completely.

Split cake into three horizontal layers. Place the bottom layer on a serving plate; spread half of the rhubarb mixture evenly to within 1/2 in. of edges. Top with second cake layer; spread remaining rhubarb mixture to within 1/2 in. of edges. Replace cake top. Frost top and sides with whipped topping. Garnish with raspberries if desired. Refrigerate leftovers. **Yield:** 12 servings.

Nutritional Analysis: One piece equals 215 calories, 2 g fat (2 g saturated fat), 0 cholesterol, 224 mg sodium, 44 g carbohydrate, trace fiber, 4 g protein.
△ **Low-fat**

1 teaspoon coconut extract
1-1/2 cups reduced-fat whipped topping

In a mixing bowl, beat the dry cake mix, egg whites, water and 1/3 cup coconut on low speed for 2 minutes. Transfer to a 13-in. x 9-in. x 2-in. baking pan coated with nonstick cooking spray. Bake at 350° for 20-25 minutes or until a toothpick comes out clean. Cool on a wire rack for 10 minutes.

Meanwhile, combine milk and extract. Using a large meat fork, punch holes in cake. Gently spread half of the milk mixture over cake. Let stand for 3 minutes. Spread remaining milk mixture over cake. Cool for 30 minutes. Toast the remaining coconut. Spread whipped topping over cake; sprinkle with coconut. Cover and chill for at least 4 hours. Refrigerate leftovers. **Yield:** 15 servings.

Nutritional Analysis: One piece equals 255 calories, 6 g fat (2 g saturated fat), 2 mg cholesterol, 276 mg sodium, 46 g carbohydrate, trace fiber, 5 g protein.
Diabetic Exchanges: 3 starch, 1 fat.

Coconut Cream Cake

Have the urge to splurge? Try this moist and mouth-watering cake. No one who's ever eaten a piece can believe it's lower in fat.
—*Deborah Protzman, Bloomington, Illinois*

1 package (18-1/4 ounces) white cake mix
3 egg whites
1-1/4 cups water
2/3 cup flaked coconut, *divided*
1 can (14 ounces) fat-free sweetened condensed milk

Raspberry Whip

The original recipe for this attractive dessert called for regular gelatin and yogurt. I substituted sugar-free gelatin and reduced-fat yogurt, and it tastes just as good. It's especially nice after a large meal.
—*Gale Lalmond, Deering, New Hampshire*

1 package (.3 ounce) sugar-free raspberry gelatin
1 cup boiling water
2/3 cup cold water
1 cup (8 ounces) reduced-fat vanilla yogurt
1 cup fresh *or* frozen unsweetened raspberries, drained, *divided*

In a mixing bowl, dissolve gelatin in boiling water. Stir in cold water. Cover and refrigerate until partially set, about 30-45 minutes. Add yogurt. Beat on medium speed until light and foamy, about 2-3 minutes. Refrigerate for 15 minutes.

Divide 2/3 cup raspberries among six dessert dishes. Top each with about 1/2 cup gelatin mixture and remaining raspberries. Refrigerate until serving. **Yield:** 6 servings.

Nutritional Analysis: One serving equals 48 calories, 1 g fat (trace saturated fat), 2 mg cholesterol, 65 mg sodium, 8 g carbohydrate, 1 g fiber, 3 g protein.
Diabetic Exchange: 1/2 reduced-fat milk.
△ **Low-fat**
▲ **Low-sodium**

Mocha Dream Cake

(Pictured below)

This lovely layered cake looks like you fussed, but it's easy to make. Baking cocoa gives the angel food cake a chocolaty boost without adding a lot of fat...and the rich, creamy mocha frosting is yummy!
—*Shirley Seltzer, Nanaimo, British Columbia*

3/4 cup baking cocoa
1/2 cup boiling water
1/4 cup sugar
1 package (16 ounces) one-step angel food cake mix
1-1/4 cups cold water
1 tablespoon instant coffee granules
1-1/2 cups cold fat-free milk
1 envelope whipped topping mix
1 package (1.4 ounces) sugar-free instant chocolate pudding mix

Line a 15-in. x 10-in. x 1-in. baking pan with parchment paper; set aside. In a bowl, combine the cocoa, boiling water and sugar; stir until cocoa and sugar are dissolved. Cool. In a mixing bowl, beat cake mix, cold water and cocoa

mixture on low speed until moistened. Beat on medium for 1 minute. Gently spoon batter into prepared pan. Cut through batter with a knife to remove air pockets.

Bake at 350° for 18-20 minutes or until cake springs back when lightly touched. Immediately invert pan onto a wire rack. Remove cake from pan and gently peel off parchment paper. Cool.

In a small mixing bowl, dissolve coffee granules in milk; add whipped topping and pudding mixes. Beat on low speed until moistened; beat on high until smooth and soft peaks form. Refrigerate for 5 minutes. Cut cake widthwise into three equal rectangles. Place one piece on a serving plate; spread with a third of the pudding mixture. Repeat layers twice. **Yield:** 12 servings.

Nutritional Analysis: One piece equals 210 calories, 2 g fat (1 g saturated fat), 1 mg cholesterol, 392 mg sodium, 46 g carbohydrate, 2 g fiber, 6 g protein.
△ **Low-fat**

Coconut Banana Chocolate Cream Pie

What's not to like about this pleasing pie? It's easy to prepare and chock-full of delicious ingredients.
—*Mary Jones, St. Louis, Missouri*

1-1/3 cups cold water
2/3 cup nonfat dry milk powder
1 package (1.4 ounces) sugar-free instant chocolate pudding mix
1 cup reduced-fat whipped topping, *divided*
1/2 teaspoon coconut extract, *divided*
2 medium ripe bananas, cut into 1/4-inch slices
1 chocolate crumb crust (9 inches)
1 tablespoon flaked coconut, toasted

In a bowl, combine water and dry milk powder; stir until milk powder is dissolved. Add pudding mix; whisk for 1-2 minutes or until thickened. Fold in 1/4 cup whipped topping and 1/4 teaspoon extract. Layer banana slices in pie crust; top with pudding mixture. Cover and refrigerate.

Meanwhile, combine remaining whipped topping and extract. Spread over pudding. Sprinkle with coconut. Cover and refrigerate for at least 1 hour. **Yield:** 8 servings.

Nutritional Analysis: One slice equals 172 calories, 5 g fat (2 g saturated fat), 1 mg cholesterol, 172 mg sodium, 28 g carbohydrate, 2 g fiber, 4 g protein.
Diabetic Exchanges: 1-1/2 starch, 1 fat, 1/2 fruit.

Cranberry Almond Biscotti

*A fellow stay-at-home mom gave me this recipe
so we could enjoy our latte breaks more affordably
with homemade biscotti. I modified the original version
by using a sugar substitute and reducing the
carbohydrates and fat. Tangy dried cranberries
and spices give it delicious flavor.*
—Evelyn Bethards Wohlers, Columbia, Maryland

> 2 eggs
> 3 egg whites
> 2 tablespoons molasses
> 3/4 teaspoon almond extract
> Sugar substitute equivalent to 1 cup sugar*
> 2-1/4 cups all-purpose flour
> 1 teaspoon baking powder
> 1 teaspoon ground cinnamon
> 1/2 teaspoon baking soda
> 1/2 teaspoon ground nutmeg
> 3/4 cup slivered almonds
> 1/2 cup dried cranberries
> 1/2 cup chopped white candy coating

In a mixing bowl, beat the eggs, egg whites, molasses and
extract. Beat in sugar substitute. Combine the flour, baking
powder, cinnamon, baking soda and nutmeg; gradually add
to egg mixture (dough will be sticky). Turn onto a floured surface. Knead in almonds and cranberries. Divide dough in
half; shape each half into a 12-in. x 3-in. rectangle. Transfer to a baking sheet coated with nonstick cooking spray.

Bake at 325° for 15-20 minutes or until lightly browned.
Cool for 5 minutes. Transfer to a cutting board; cut each loaf
with a serrated knife into 16 slices. Place each slice cut side
down on baking sheets coated with nonstick cooking spray.
Bake at 325° for 25-35 minutes or until firm, turning once.
Remove to wire racks to cool.

In a microwave or heavy saucepan, melt candy coating;
stir until smooth. Drizzle over biscotti. Store in an airtight
container. **Yield:** 32 cookies.

*Editor's Note: This recipe was tested with Splenda
No Calorie Sweetener. Look for it in the baking aisle of
your grocery store.

Nutritional Analysis: One cookie equals 84 calories, 3 g fat (1
g saturated fat), 14 mg cholesterol, 39 mg sodium, 13 g carbohy-
drate, 1 g fiber, 2 g protein.
Diabetic Exchange: 1 starch.
△ **Low-fat**
▲ **Low-sodium**

Pineapple Almond Bars

(Pictured at right)

*Oats and almonds are a nice crunchy complement
to the sweet pineapple filling in these
yummy bar cookies.*
—Janice Smith, Cynthiana, Kentucky

> 3/4 cup all-purpose flour
> 3/4 cup quick-cooking oats
> 1/3 cup packed brown sugar
> 5 tablespoons cold reduced-fat stick margarine*
> 1/2 teaspoon almond extract

> 3 tablespoons sliced almonds
> 1 cup pineapple preserves

In a food processor, combine the flour, oats and brown sugar; cover and process until blended. Add margarine and extract; cover and pulse until crumbly. Remove 1/2 cup
crumb mixture to a bowl; stir in sliced almonds. Press remaining crumb mixture into a 9-in. square baking pan
coated with nonstick cooking spray. Spread preserves
over crust. Sprinkle with reserved crumb mixture. Bake at
350° for 25-30 minutes or until golden. Cool on a wire
rack. **Yield:** 1 dozen.

*Editor's Note: This recipe was tested with Parkay Light
stick margarine.

Nutritional Analysis: One bar equals 166 calories, 4 g fat (1
g saturated fat), 0 cholesterol, 39 mg sodium, 34 g carbohydrate,
1 g fiber, 2 g protein.
Diabetic Exchanges: 1 fruit, 1 starch, 1/2 fat.
▲ **Low-sodium**

Red, White and Blueberry Pie

(Pictured at right)

*This is a wonderful light dessert for a Fourth
of July party or other summer get-together.*
—Kimberly McFarland, Broken Arrow, Oklahoma

> 4 squares (1 ounce *each*) white baking chocolate
> 8 whole fresh strawberries, halved lengthwise
> 1 reduced-fat graham cracker crust (8 inches)
> 3/4 cup sliced fresh strawberries
> 1 package (8 ounces) reduced-fat cream cheese,
>   cubed
> 3/4 cup confectioners' sugar
> 3/4 cup cold fat-free milk
> 1 package (3.4 ounces) instant vanilla pudding
>   mix
> 1 cup fresh *or* frozen blueberries
> 1 cup reduced-fat whipped topping

In a microwave or heavy saucepan, melt white chocolate;
stir until smooth. Dip the halved strawberries halfway in
chocolate. Place cut side down on a waxed paper-lined baking sheet. Refrigerate for 15 minutes or until set. Spread the
remaining melted chocolate over the bottom and sides of
crust. Arrange sliced strawberries in crust.

In a mixing bowl, beat cream cheese and confectioners' sugar until smooth. Gradually add milk; mix well. Beat
in pudding mix on low speed for 2 minutes or until thickened;
spread evenly over sliced strawberries. Place blueberries in
center of pie. Arrange dipped strawberries around the edge.
Pipe whipped topping between the strawberries and blueberries. Refrigerate until serving. **Yield:** 8 servings.

Nutritional Analysis: One piece equals 342 calories, 14 g fat
(8 g saturated fat), 19 mg cholesterol, 238 mg sodium, 46 g carbohydrate, 1 g fiber, 6 g protein.

Chocolate-Coconut Angel Cupcakes

(Pictured below)

These cupcakes don't taste light at all. In fact, my guests are never satisfied with just one. The meringue-like tops make them different, but the chocolate and coconut make them memorable.
—Bernice Janowski, Stevens Point, Wisconsin

6 egg whites
1-1/3 cups sugar, *divided*
2/3 cup all-purpose flour
1/4 cup baking cocoa
1/2 teaspoon baking powder
1 teaspoon almond extract
1/2 teaspoon cream of tartar
1/4 teaspoon salt
1 cup flaked coconut

Place egg whites in a mixing bowl; let stand at room temperature for 30 minutes. Combine 1 cup sugar, flour, cocoa and baking powder. Sift together twice; set aside.

Add almond extract, cream of tartar and salt to egg whites; beat on medium speed until soft peaks form. Gradually add the remaining sugar, about 2 tablespoons at a time, beating on high until stiff glossy peaks form. Gradually fold in cocoa mixture, about 1/2 cup at a time. Gently fold in coconut.

Fill paper-lined muffin cups two-thirds full. Bake at 350° for 30-35 minutes or until golden brown and top appears dry. Cool for 10 minutes before removing from pans to wire racks. **Yield:** 1-1/2 dozen.

Nutritional Analysis: One cupcake equals 103 calories, 2 g fat (1 g saturated fat), 0 cholesterol, 68 mg sodium, 21 g carbohydrate, 1 g fiber, 2 g protein.
Diabetic Exchange: 1-1/2 starch.
△ *Low-fat*
▲ *Low-sodium*

Frosted Pumpkin Bars

My health-conscious granddaughter, Jennifer, gave me the recipe for these nicely spiced bars.
—Dovie Sears, Shepherdsville, Kentucky

1 cup all-purpose flour
1 cup sugar
1 teaspoon ground cinnamon
1 teaspoon baking powder
1/2 teaspoon salt
1/2 teaspoon ground cloves
1 egg
2 egg whites
1 cup canned pumpkin
1/4 cup canola oil
2 tablespoons water
4 ounces reduced-fat cream cheese
1-1/2 cups confectioners' sugar
1 teaspoon vanilla extract
1/4 teaspoon grated lemon peel

In a mixing bowl, combine the first six ingredients. Add egg, egg whites, pumpkin, oil and water; mix well. Transfer to an 11-in. x 7-in. x 2-in. baking pan coated with nonstick cooking spray. Bake at 350° for 25-30 minutes or until a toothpick inserted near the center comes out clean. Cool on a wire rack.

In a mixing bowl, beat cream cheese. Beat in confectioners' sugar, then vanilla and lemon peel. Frost bars. Chill for 15 minutes, then cut. Refrigerate leftovers. **Yield:** 15 servings.

Nutritional Analysis: One bar equals 185 calories, 6 g fat (1 g saturated fat), 18 mg cholesterol, 146 mg sodium, 32 g carbohydrate, 1 g fiber, 3 g protein.
Diabetic Exchanges: 2 starch, 1 fat.

Carrot Cake Cookies

These yummy cookies taste just like bite-size carrot cakes! I fill my irresistible treats with grated carrots, raisins and chopped pecans.
—Michelle Nichols, Joplin, Missouri

6 tablespoons butter *or* stick margarine, softened
3/4 cup packed brown sugar
1 egg
1/2 teaspoon vanilla extract
1-1/2 cups all-purpose flour
1 teaspoon baking powder
1/4 teaspoon *each* baking soda, salt and ground cinnamon
1 cup grated carrots
1/2 cup *each* raisins and chopped pecans

In a mixing bowl, cream butter and sugar. Add egg and vanilla; mix well. Combine the flour, baking powder, baking soda, salt and cinnamon. Gradually add to creamed mixture until blended. Stir in carrots, raisins and pecans.

Drop by rounded tablespoonfuls 2 in. apart on ungreased baking sheets. Bake at 325° for 12-15 minutes or until edges are lightly browned and cookies are set. Cool for 2 minutes before removing to wire racks. **Yield:** 28 cookies.

Nutritional Analysis: One cookie equals 95 calories, 4 g fat (2 g saturated fat), 14 mg cholesterol, 72 mg sodium, 14 g carbohydrate, 1 g fiber, 1 g protein.
  Diabetic Exchanges: 1 fat, 1/2 starch, 1/2 fruit.
  ▲ *Low-sodium*

Luscious Lime Angel Squares

(Pictured above)

A creamy lime topping turns angel food cake into these yummy squares that are perfect for potlucks or picnics. You can eat a piece of this light and airy dessert without feeling one bit guilty. I adapted this luscious treat from another recipe. It is super-easy to make.
—Beverly Marshall, Orting, Washington

  1 package (.3 ounce) sugar-free lime gelatin
  1 cup boiling water
  1 prepared angel food cake (8 inches), cut into
    1-inch cubes
  1 package (8 ounces) reduced-fat cream cheese,
    cubed
1/2 cup sugar
  2 teaspoons lemon juice
1-1/2 teaspoons grated lemon peel
  1 carton (8 ounces) reduced-fat whipped topping,
    thawed, *divided*

In a bowl, dissolve gelatin in boiling water. Refrigerate until mixture just begins to thicken, about 35 minutes. Place cake cubes in a 13-in. x 9-in. x 2-in. dish coated with nonstick cooking spray; set aside.
  In a small mixing bowl, beat cream cheese until smooth. Beat in sugar, lemon juice and peel. Add gelatin mixture;

beat until combined. Fold in 1-1/2 cups whipped topping. Spread over cake, covering completely. Refrigerate for at least 2 hours or until firm. Cut into squares; top with remaining whipped topping. **Yield:** 15 servings.

Nutritional Analysis: One piece equals 139 calories, 4 g fat (3 g saturated fat), 8 mg cholesterol, 145 mg sodium, 21 g carbohydrate, trace fiber, 3 g protein.
  Diabetic Exchanges: 1-1/2 starch, 1 fat.

Grape Nectarine Dessert Cups

(Pictured below)

This summery dessert is so refreshing after a heavy meal. Lemon-lime soda coats the fun fruit medley that's topped with a yummy scoop of pineapple sherbet. In winter, you can substitute frozen peaches for the nectarines.
—Jeanette Oberholtzer, Manheim, Pennsylvania

  7 medium nectarines, peeled and sliced
  2 cups green grapes
  1 cup chilled lemon-lime soda
2-1/2 cups pineapple sherbet

In a large bowl, combine nectarines and grapes; cover and refrigerate until chilled. Just before serving, pour soda over fruit. Spoon into dessert dishes; top with sherbet. **Yield:** 10 servings.

Nutritional Analysis: One serving (1/2 cup fruit with 1/4 cup sherbet) equals 122 calories, 1 g fat (trace saturated fat), 2 mg cholesterol, 20 mg sodium, 28 g carbohydrate, 2 g fiber, 1 g protein.
  Diabetic Exchanges: 1 fruit, 1 starch.
  △ *Low-fat*
  ▲ *Low-sodium*

Lemonade Icebox Pie

I first made this easy freezer dessert for visitors at our local art museum. It's rich and sweet, with just the right touch of tartness.
—Jeannie Brown, Overland Park, Kansas

1 can (12 ounces) fat-free evaporated milk
3/4 cup pink lemonade concentrate
1-1/2 cups reduced-fat whipped topping
1 reduced-fat graham cracker crust (8 inches)
1 medium lemon, sliced

In a bowl, combine milk and lemonade concentrate; fold in whipped topping. Pour into crust. Freeze for 3 hours. Garnish with lemon slices. **Yield:** 8 servings.

Nutritional Analysis: *One piece equals 202 calories, 5 g fat (3 g saturated fat), 2 mg cholesterol, 145 mg sodium, 34 g carbohydrate, trace fiber, 4 g protein.*
Diabetic Exchanges: *2 starch, 1 fat.*

Angel Berry Trifle

(Pictured above)

I usually serve this in summer when fresh berries are bountiful, but I recently prepared it with frozen cherries and light cherry pie filling instead. It was a delicious glimpse of summer-to-come!
—Brenda Paine, North Syracuse, New York

1-1/2 cups cold fat-free milk
1 package (1 ounce) sugar-free instant vanilla pudding mix
1 cup (8 ounces) fat-free vanilla yogurt
6 ounces reduced-fat cream cheese, cubed
1/2 cup reduced-fat sour cream
2 teaspoons vanilla extract
1 carton (12 ounces) reduced-fat frozen whipped topping, thawed, *divided*
1 prepared angel food cake (8 inches), cut into 1-inch cubes
1 pint *each* blackberries, raspberries and blueberries

In a small bowl, whisk the milk and pudding mix for 2 minutes or until thickened. In a mixing bowl, beat the yogurt, cream cheese, sour cream and vanilla until smooth. Fold in pudding mixture and 1 cup whipped topping.

Place a third of the cake cubes in a 4-qt. trifle bowl. Top with a third of the pudding mixture, a third of the berries and half of the remaining whipped topping. Repeat layers once. Top with remaining cake, pudding and berries. Serve immediately or refrigerate. **Yield:** 14 servings.

Nutritional Analysis: *One serving (3/4 cup) equals 209 calories, 6 g fat (5 g saturated fat), 10 mg cholesterol, 330 mg sodium, 32 g carbohydrate, 3 g fiber, 5 g protein.*
Diabetic Exchanges: *1 starch, 1 fat, 1/2 fruit, 1/2 reduced-fat milk.*

Chocolate Layer Cake

(Pictured on front cover)

No one will suspect this decadent layered chocolate cake is light! Our Test Kitchen staff concocted the eye-catching dessert.

1 package (18-1/4 ounces) chocolate cake mix
1-1/4 cups 1% buttermilk
1 egg
4 egg whites
ORANGE FILLING:
1 cup cold fat-free milk
1 package (3.3 *or* 3.4 ounces) instant white chocolate *or* vanilla pudding mix
1/4 teaspoon grated orange peel
1/8 teaspoon orange extract
1/2 cup heavy whipping cream, whipped
CHOCOLATE GLAZE:
3 squares (1 ounce *each*) semisweet chocolate, chopped
1 tablespoon fat-free milk
1-1/2 teaspoons butter *or* stick margarine

Coat three 9-in. round baking pans with nonstick cooking spray and line with waxed paper. Coat waxed paper with nonstick cooking spray and dust with flour; set aside. In a mixing bowl, beat first four ingredients on low speed for 2 minutes. Pour into prepared pans. Bake at 350° for 20-25 minutes or until a toothpick comes out clean. Cool for 10 minutes before removing to wire racks to cool. Gently peel off waxed paper.

In a bowl, whisk the first four filling ingredients for 2 minutes; fold in whipped cream. Place one cake layer on a serving plate; top with half of the filling. Repeat layers. Top with the third cake layer. In a microwave-safe bowl, microwave the glaze ingredients, uncovered, at 30% power for 45 seconds; stir until smooth. Spread over top of the cake. **Yield:** 12 servings.

Nutritional Analysis: *One slice equals 316 calories, 13 g fat (6 g saturated fat), 66 mg cholesterol, 559 mg sodium, 44 g carbohydrate, 1 g fiber, 8 g protein.*
Diabetic Exchanges: *3 starch, 2 fat.*

Favorite Recipe Made Lighter

FROM Louisville, Kentucky, Amy Olson asks, "Can you reduce the sugar and fat in Strawberry Pretzel Dessert without altering the wonderful flavor in this family favorite?"

The trimmed-down treat has just half the fat, a quarter of the cholesterol and a third fewer calories and carbohydrates, but it still tastes terrific. Why not make it for your family today?

Strawberry Pretzel Dessert

2-2/3 cups crushed pretzels (10 ounces)
1 cup butter *or* margarine, melted
1 package (8 ounces) cream cheese, softened
1 cup sugar
1 carton (8 ounces) frozen whipped topping, thawed
1 can (20 ounces) crushed pineapple
2 packages (3 ounces *each*) strawberry gelatin
2 packages (10 ounces *each*) frozen sliced sweetened strawberries, thawed

In a bowl, combine the pretzels and butter. Press onto the bottom of a greased 13-in. x 9-in. x 2-in. baking dish. Bake at 350° for 8-10 minutes or until set. Cool on a wire rack. In a mixing bowl, beat cream cheese and sugar until smooth. Fold in whipped topping. Spread over cooled crust. Refrigerate until chilled.

Drain pineapple, reserving juice; set pineapple aside. Add water to pineapple juice if necessary to measure 1 cup; pour into a saucepan. Bring to a boil. Pour into a large bowl; stir in gelatin until dissolved.

Drain strawberries, reserving juice; set strawberries aside. Add water to strawberry juice if necessary to measure 1 cup; stir into gelatin mixture. Refrigerate until partially set. Stir in reserved pineapple and strawberries. Carefully spoon over filling. Cover and refrigerate for 3-4 hours or until firm. **Yield:** 18 servings.

Nutritional Analysis: One serving equals 363 calories, 18 g fat (11 g saturated fat), 41 mg cholesterol, 592 mg sodium, 49 g carbohydrate, 1 g fiber, 4 g protein.

Makeover Strawberry Pretzel Dessert

(Pictured at right)

2 cups crushed pretzels (8 ounces)
3/4 cup reduced-fat stick margarine, melted
3 tablespoons plus 1/2 cup sugar, *divided*
1 package (8 ounces) reduced-fat cream cheese
Sugar substitute equivalent to 1/2 cup sugar
1 carton (8 ounces) reduced-fat frozen whipped topping, thawed
1 can (20 ounces) unsweetened crushed pineapple
2 packages (.3 ounce *each*) sugar-free strawberry gelatin
2 packages (10 ounces *each*) frozen sliced sweetened strawberries, thawed

In a bowl, combine the pretzels, margarine and 3 tablespoons sugar. Press onto the bottom of a 13-in. x 9-in. x 2-in. baking dish coated with nonstick cooking spray. Bake at 400° for 18-20 minutes or until set. Cool on a wire rack. In a small mixing bowl, beat cream cheese, sugar substitute and remaining sugar until smooth. Fold in whipped topping. Spread over cooled crust. Refrigerate until chilled.

Drain pineapple, reserving juice; set pineapple aside. Add water to pineapple juice if necessary to measure 1 cup; pour into a saucepan. Bring to a boil. Pour into a large bowl; stir in gelatin until dissolved.

Drain strawberries, reserving juice; set strawberries aside. Add water to strawberry juice if necessary to measure 1-1/2 cups; stir into gelatin mixture. Refrigerate until partially set. Stir in reserved pineapple and strawberries. Carefully spoon over filling. Cover and refrigerate for 3-4 hours or until firm. **Yield:** 18 servings.

Editor's Note: This recipe was tested with Parkay Light stick margarine and Splenda No Calorie Sweetener. Look for Splenda in the baking aisle of your grocery store.

Nutritional Analysis: One serving equals 230 calories, 9 g fat (4 g saturated fat), 10 mg cholesterol, 466 mg sodium, 34 g carbohydrate, 1 g fiber, 3 g protein.
Diabetic Exchanges: 2 fat, 1 starch, 1 fruit.

Strawberry Pie

(Pictured below)

There's plenty of sweet berry flavor in this refreshing dessert. Made with sugar-free gelatin and a graham cracker crust, the summery pie is easy to fix and attractive enough to serve to guests. I sometimes substitute fresh peaches and peach gelatin.
—D. Smith, Feasterville-Trevose, Pennsylvania

  2 pints fresh strawberries, hulled
  2 tablespoons cornstarch
1-1/2 cups cold water
  1 package (.3 ounce) sugar-free strawberry gelatin
  3 tablespoons sugar
  1 reduced-fat graham cracker crust (8 inches)
  2 cups reduced-fat whipped topping

Set aside four whole berries for garnish. Slice remaining strawberries and set aside. In a saucepan, combine cornstarch and water until smooth. Bring to a boil; cook and stir for 2 minutes or until thickened. Remove from the heat; stir in gelatin and sugar until dissolved. Stir in sliced strawberries. Pour into the crust. Cover and refrigerate for 2 hours or until firm.

Cut reserved strawberries in half. Garnish each serving with whipped topping and a berry half. **Yield:** 8 servings.

Nutritional Analysis: *One serving (1 piece with 1/4 cup whipped topping) equals 197 calories, 5 g fat (3 g saturated fat), trace cholesterol, 125 mg sodium, 33 g carbohydrate, 2 g fiber, 2 g protein.*
  Diabetic Exchanges: *1 starch, 1 fruit, 1 fat.*
  ▲ ***Low-sodium***

Mazurka

Raisins, walnuts and dried plums fill this fruitcake-like dessert. When I have leftover egg whites, I like to make this old Russian family recipe.
—Kera Bredin, Vancouver, British Columbia

  1 cup all-purpose flour
3/4 cup sugar
  1 teaspoon baking powder
1/4 teaspoon salt
  1 cup raisins
  1 cup chopped dried plums
  1 cup chopped walnuts
  4 egg whites
  1 teaspoon vanilla extract

In a bowl, combine flour, sugar, baking powder and salt. Stir in raisins, plums and walnuts; toss to coat evenly. In a mixing bowl, beat egg whites on high speed until stiff peaks form. Stir about a third of the egg whites and vanilla into flour mixture. Fold in remaining egg whites. Transfer to a 9-in. square baking dish coated with nonstick cooking spray.

Bake at 300° for 40-45 minutes or until golden brown and a toothpick inserted near the center comes out clean. Cool. Cut into squares. **Yield:** 16 servings.

Nutritional Analysis: *One piece equals 177 calories, 5 g fat (trace saturated fat), 0 cholesterol, 83 mg sodium, 32 g carbohydrate, 2 g fiber, 3 g protein.*
  Diabetic Exchanges: *1-1/2 fruit, 1 fat, 1/2 starch.*
  ▲ ***Low-sodium***

Lemon Poppy Seed Cake

Family and friends will love this buttermilk cake...whether you serve tender slices with coffee at brunch or as a treat after dinner. The delicate lemon glaze adds a special touch.
—Kristen Croke, Hanover, Massachusetts

  6 tablespoons butter *or* stick margarine, softened
1-1/2 cups sugar, *divided*
  1 tablespoon grated lemon peel
  2 eggs
  2 egg whites
2-1/2 cups cake flour
  2 tablespoons poppy seeds
1-1/2 teaspoons baking powder
1/2 teaspoon baking soda
1/2 teaspoon salt
1/4 teaspoon ground allspice
1-1/3 cups 1% buttermilk
1/4 cup lemon juice

In a mixing bowl, cream butter and 1-1/4 cups sugar. Add lemon peel; mix well. Add eggs and egg whites, one at a time, beating after each addition. Combine the flour, poppy seeds, baking powder, baking soda, salt and allspice. Add to the creamed mixture alternately with buttermilk.

Transfer to a 10-in. tube pan heavily coated with nonstick cooking spray. Bake at 350° for 40-45 minutes or until a toothpick inserted near the center comes out clean. Cool in pan for 10 minutes. Carefully run a knife around the edge of pan and center tube to loosen. Remove to a wire rack.

Meanwhile, in a small saucepan, combine the lemon juice and remaining sugar. Cook and stir until mixture comes to a boil; cook and stir 1-2 minutes longer or until sugar is dissolved. Using a fork, poke holes in top of cake. Gradually pour hot syrup over cake. Cool completely. **Yield:** 2 dozen slices.

Editor's Note: The use of a fluted tube pan is not recommended for this recipe.

Nutritional Analysis: One serving (2 slices) equals 266 calories, 8 g fat (4 g saturated fat), 52 mg cholesterol, 318 mg sodium, 47 g carbohydrate, 1 g fiber, 5 g protein.
Diabetic Exchanges: 3 starch, 1 fat.

Cranberry Pear Compote

While simmering apples in brown sugar and cinnamon, I decided to add a ripe pear and a few cranberries to the mix. The result was a thick, tangy-sweet sauce that's terrific over frozen yogurt.
—Linda James, Greenfield, Wisconsin

- 1 medium pear, peeled and chopped
- 1 medium apple, peeled and chopped
- 1/4 cup fresh *or* frozen cranberries
- 1/4 cup water
- 3 tablespoons brown sugar
- 1/2 teaspoon ground cinnamon

In a small saucepan, combine all of the ingredients. Bring to a boil. Reduce heat; simmer, uncovered, until the berries pop and sauce thickens, about 15 minutes, stirring occasionally. Serve warm or chilled. Store in the refrigerator. **Yield:** 4 servings.

Nutritional Analysis: One serving (1/4 cup) equals 85 calories, trace fat (trace saturated fat), 0 cholesterol, 4 mg sodium, 22 g carbohydrate, 2 g fiber, trace protein.
Diabetic Exchange: 1-1/2 fruit.
△ *Low-fat*
▲ *Low-sodium*
▲ *Meatless*

🍎 Speedy Streusel Topping

WHENEVER I make banana pudding with sugar-free instant pudding mix and fresh bananas, I crush up cinnamon graham crackers and sprinkle them on top for a little different taste.

These nicely spiced crumbs also make a good streusel topping on pies and other baked goods.
—Janet Lusch, Vandalia, Illinois

Chocolate Peanut Butter Pie

(Pictured above)

Who can resist luscious chocolate and peanut butter paired up in a pie? With this recipe, you don't have to! Reduced-fat and sugar-free ingredients lighten up the dessert without slicing into its satisfying flavor. When I take it to gatherings, I get an empty pie plate and lots of compliments in return.
—Judy Barrett, Oklahoma City, Oklahoma

- 1/3 cup nonfat dry milk powder
- 1-1/4 cups cold water
- 1 package (1 ounce) sugar-free instant vanilla pudding mix
- 1/2 cup reduced-fat chunky peanut butter
- 1 reduced-fat graham cracker crust (8 inches)
- **CHOCOLATE LAYER:**
- 1/3 cup nonfat dry milk powder
- 1-1/4 cups cold water
- 1 package (1.4 ounces) sugar-free instant chocolate pudding mix
- 1 cup reduced-fat whipped topping
- 1/2 ounce semisweet chocolate, shaved into curls

In a mixing bowl, beat milk powder and water on low speed for 20 seconds. Add vanilla pudding mix; beat on low for 1-1/2 minutes. Add peanut butter; beat on low for 30 seconds. Pour into crust.

For chocolate layer, in a mixing bowl, beat milk powder and water on low for 20 seconds. Add chocolate pudding mix; beat on low for 2 minutes. Carefully spread over peanut butter layer. Top with whipped topping and chocolate curls. Cover and refrigerate for at least 2 hours. **Yield:** 8 servings.

Nutritional Analysis: One slice equals 257 calories, 10 g fat (3 g saturated fat), 1 mg cholesterol, 505 mg sodium, 34 g carbohydrate, 2 g fiber, 8 g protein.
Diabetic Exchanges: 2 starch, 2 fat.

Maple Pumpkin Pie

Since I have to watch my saturated fat, I was happy to find this recipe for a good pumpkin pie. We enjoy its mild maple flavor.
—Betty Leonard, Steinhatchee, Florida

1-1/2 cups all-purpose flour
1 tablespoon sugar
1/2 teaspoon salt
1/4 teaspoon baking powder
1/3 cup canola oil
1 teaspoon cider vinegar
2 to 4 tablespoons cold water
FILLING:
1 can (15 ounces) solid-pack pumpkin
3/4 cup egg substitute
1/2 cup maple syrup
1 teaspoon ground cinnamon
1/2 teaspoon ground ginger
1/2 teaspoon maple flavoring
1/4 teaspoon ground nutmeg
1 cup fat-free evaporated milk

In a bowl, combine the flour, sugar, salt and baking powder. Stir in oil and vinegar. Gradually add water, tossing with a fork until a ball forms. Shape into a 6-in. circle. Roll out between two pieces of plastic wrap to fit a 9-in. pie plate. Remove top piece of plastic wrap; invert pastry into a 9-in. pie plate coated with nonstick cooking spray. Remove remaining plastic wrap. Trim pastry to 1/2 in. beyond edge of plate; flute edges. Refrigerate for 20 minutes or until chilled.

In a large bowl, combine the pumpkin, egg substitute, syrup, cinnamon, ginger, maple flavoring and nutmeg; mix just until blended. Gradually stir in milk. Pour into pastry shell.

Bake at 450° for 10 minutes. Reduce heat to 350°; bake for 45-50 minutes or until a knife inserted near the center comes out clean. Cool on a wire rack. Store in the refrigerator. **Yield:** 8 servings.

Nutritional Analysis: One piece equals 282 calories, 10 g fat (1 g saturated fat), 3 mg cholesterol, 245 mg sodium, 42 g carbohydrate, 3 g fiber, 8 g protein.
Diabetic Exchanges: 2-1/2 starch, 2 fat.

Cranberry Parfaits

(Pictured at right)

Cranberry sauce and raspberry gelatin give this fluffy pink parfait from our Test Kitchen a sweet-tart flavor. Pretty enough for holiday company, the dessert is light and refreshing.

1 can (16 ounces) whole-berry cranberry sauce
1 cup reduced-calorie cranberry juice
1/2 teaspoon grated orange peel
1 package (.3 ounce) sugar-free raspberry gelatin
1 can (12 ounces) reduced-fat evaporated milk, chilled
1 teaspoon vanilla extract
Whole cranberries for garnish, optional

In a saucepan, bring the cranberry sauce, cranberry juice and orange peel to a boil; cook and stir until cranberry sauce

is melted. Stir in gelatin until dissolved. Refrigerate until mixture is the consistency of egg whites, stirring occasionally.

Place a mixing bowl with mixer beaters in the freezer. Chill until very cold. Add milk and vanilla to bowl; beat until soft peaks form. Fold into gelatin mixture. Spoon into parfait glasses. Chill 1-2 hours or until set. Garnish if desired. **Yield:** 6 servings.

Nutritional Analysis: One serving (1 cup) equals 174 calories, 1 g fat (1 g saturated fat), 5 mg cholesterol, 86 mg sodium, 37 g carbohydrate, 1 g fiber, 5 g protein.
Diabetic Exchanges: 2 fruit, 1/2 reduced-fat milk.
△ **Low-fat**
▲ **Low-sodium**

Applesauce Lattice Pie

(Pictured at right)

I had some apples that needed to be used up, so I combined them with a can of applesauce and turned out my best-tasting apple pie ever.
—Cherie Sweet, Evansville, Indiana

1-1/2 cups all-purpose flour
3 tablespoons sugar
1/4 teaspoon plus 1/8 teaspoon baking powder
1/4 teaspoon plus 1/8 teaspoon salt
6 tablespoons cold butter *or* stick margarine
4 to 6 tablespoons cold water
4-1/2 teaspoons fat-free milk
1-1/2 teaspoons cider vinegar
FILLING:
5 cups sliced peeled tart apples
1/4 cup raisins
Sugar substitute equivalent to 3 tablespoons sugar*
2 tablespoons all-purpose flour
4 teaspoons brown sugar
2 teaspoons ground cinnamon
1-1/2 cups unsweetened applesauce
2 teaspoons butter *or* stick margarine

In a bowl, combine the flour, sugar, baking powder and salt; cut in butter until mixture resembles coarse crumbs. Combine the water, milk and vinegar; gradually add to dry ingredients, tossing with a fork until dough forms a ball. Set aside a third of the dough. On a lightly floured surface, roll out remaining dough to fit a 9-in. pie plate. Transfer pastry to pie plate coated with nonstick cooking spray; trim even with edge of plate.

In a large bowl, combine the apples and raisins. Combine the sugar substitute, flour, brown sugar and cinnamon; add to apple mixture and toss to coat. Spoon 3 cups into the crust; cover with applesauce. Top with the remaining apple mixture; dot with butter. Roll out reserved pastry; make a lattice crust. Trim and flute edges. Bake at 375° for 40-45 minutes or until crust is golden brown and filling is bubbly. **Yield:** 8 servings.

*Editor's Note: This recipe was tested with Splenda No Calorie Sweetener. Look for it in the baking aisle of your grocery store.

Nutritional Analysis: One piece equals 281 calories, 10 g fat (6 g saturated fat), 26 mg cholesterol, 235 mg sodium, 47 g carbohydrate, 3 g fiber, 3 g protein.
Diabetic Exchanges: 2 fat, 1-1/2 fruit, 1-1/2 starch.

Buttermilk Chocolate Sauce

Our family received this delicious recipe from a dear friend. The thick sauce is not too sweet and makes a delightful topping for most desserts. Serve it warm over ice cream, cake or fruit.
—Leah Ramage, Saskatoon, Saskatchewan

3/4 cup sugar
1/4 cup baking cocoa
1 tablespoon cornstarch
3/4 cup 1% buttermilk
1 teaspoon vanilla extract
Reduced-fat ice cream

In a small saucepan, combine the sugar, cocoa and cornstarch. Whisk in milk. Bring to a boil over medium heat, stirring constantly. Reduce heat; simmer, uncovered, for 5-7 minutes or until slightly thickened. Remove from the heat; stir in vanilla. Serve warm over ice cream. Refrigerate leftovers. **Yield:** 3/4 cup.

Nutritional Analysis: One serving (1 tablespoon sauce, calculated without ice cream) equals 62 calories, trace fat (trace saturated fat), 1 mg cholesterol, 16 mg sodium, 15 g carbohydrate, trace fiber, 1 g protein.
Diabetic Exchange: 1 starch.
△ *Low-fat*
▲ *Low-sodium*

Raisin Cinnamon Bars

I've been making these simple iced bars for more than 40 years. They're easy to prepare for dessert or as a sweet treat with a cup of coffee.
—Jean Morgan, Roscoe, Illinois

1/4 cup butter *or* stick margarine, softened
1 cup packed brown sugar
1 egg
1/2 cup hot brewed coffee
1-1/2 cups all-purpose flour
1 teaspoon baking powder
1/2 teaspoon ground cinnamon
1/4 teaspoon baking soda
1/4 teaspoon salt
1/2 cup raisins
1/4 cup chopped pecans
ICING:
1 cup confectioners' sugar
1/2 teaspoon vanilla extract
4 to 5 teaspoons water

In a mixing bowl, combine butter and brown sugar until crumbly, about 2 minutes. Add egg; mix well. Gradually beat in coffee. Combine the flour, baking powder, cinnamon, baking soda and salt. Add to the coffee mixture; mix well. Stir in raisins and pecans.

Transfer to a 13-in. x 9-in. x 2-in. baking pan coated with nonstick cooking spray. Bake at 350° for 18-20 minutes or until edges begin to pull away from the sides of the pan and a toothpick inserted near the center comes out clean. Cool on a wire rack for 5 minutes.

Meanwhile for icing, in a bowl, combine the confection-
ers' sugar, vanilla and enough water to achieve spreading consistency. Spread over warm bars. **Yield:** 1-1/2 dozen.

Nutritional Analysis: One bar equals 158 calories, 4 g fat (2 g saturated fat), 19 mg cholesterol, 112 mg sodium, 30 g carbohydrate, 1 g fiber, 2 g protein.
Diabetic Exchanges: 1-1/2 starch, 1 fat, 1/2 fruit.
▲ *Low-sodium*

Mango Lemon Sorbet

(Pictured above)

You'll love the sunny color and fruity flavor of this light dessert developed by our home economists. If you can't find mangoes, substitute fresh peaches. To peel the peaches, drop them into boiling water for a few seconds. Then you can easily slip the skins right off.

3 cups chopped peeled mangoes *or* fresh peaches (about 2 pounds)
1/2 cup cold water
1 cup sugar
2 tablespoons lemon juice

In a food processor or blender, combine mangoes and water; cover and process until smooth. Add the sugar and lemon juice; cover and process until sugar is dissolved, about 1 minute. Freeze in an ice cream freezer according to manufacturer's directions. Transfer to a freezer container; cover and freeze for 1 hour or until firm. **Yield:** 6 servings.

Nutritional Analysis: One serving (1/2 cup) equals 184 calories, trace fat (trace saturated fat), 0 cholesterol, 2 mg sodium, 48 g carbohydrate, 2 g fiber, trace protein.
△ *Low-fat*
▲ *Low-sodium*

Strawberries 'n' Cream Trifle

(Pictured below)

My mother-in-law gave me this recipe, which I lightened up by using less milk, reduced-fat whipped topping and angel food cake instead of pound cake. It's good made with fresh peaches or blueberries, too.
—Pamela Gainer, Sand Ridge, West Virginia

- 1/2 cup sweetened condensed milk
- 1-1/2 cups cold water
- 1 package (1 ounce) sugar-free instant vanilla pudding mix
- 1 carton (8 ounces) reduced-fat frozen whipped topping, thawed
- 1 prepared angel food cake (9-ounce round)
- 4 cups sliced fresh strawberries
- 3 whole fresh strawberries

In a bowl, whisk the milk and water. Whisk in the pudding mix for 2 minutes. Let stand for 2 minutes or until soft-set; fold in the whipped topping. Cut cake into 1/2-in. cubes.

Spoon a third of the pudding mixture into a 4-qt. trifle or glass bowl. Top with half of the cake cubes and sliced strawberries. Repeat layers once. Top with the remaining pudding mixture. Garnish with the whole strawberries. **Yield:** 12 servings.

Nutritional Analysis: *One serving equals 156 calories, 3 g fat (3 g saturated fat), 4 mg cholesterol, 223 mg sodium, 28 g carbohydrate, 1 g fiber, 3 g protein.*
Diabetic Exchanges: *2 starch, 1/2 fat.*
△ **Low-fat**

Cocoa Banana Cupcakes

My family enjoys these moist cupcakes with mild banana flavor. The cocoa powder in the frosting boosts the chocolate flavor while the melted chocolate gives it a creamy texture, making it easier to spread.
—Rochelle Brownlee, Big Timber, Montana

- 2 cups all-purpose flour
- 1 cup sugar
- 1/2 cup baking cocoa
- 1 teaspoon baking powder
- 1/2 teaspoon *each* baking soda and salt
- 2 eggs
- 1-1/4 cups fat-free milk
- 1 cup mashed ripe banana (2 to 3 medium)
- 3 tablespoons canola oil
- 1 teaspoon vanilla extract

FROSTING:
- 4 ounces reduced-fat cream cheese
- 3 tablespoons fat-free milk
- 2 squares (1 ounce *each*) semisweet chocolate, melted and cooled
- 1 teaspoon vanilla extract
- 2 cups confectioners' sugar
- 1/3 cup baking cocoa

In a bowl, combine dry ingredients. In another bowl, combine eggs, milk, banana, oil and vanilla. Stir into dry ingredients just until moistened. Coat muffin cups with nonstick cooking spray or line with paper liners. Fill three-fourths full. Bake at 375° for 18-20 minutes or until a toothpick comes out clean. Cool for 5 minutes; remove to wire racks to cool completely.

Beat cream cheese, milk, chocolate and vanilla until smooth. Combine confectioners' sugar and cocoa; gradually beat into cream cheese mixture. Frost cupcakes. **Yield:** 1-1/2 dozen.

Nutritional Analysis: *One cupcake equals 224 calories, 6 g fat (2 g saturated fat), 29 mg cholesterol, 171 mg sodium, 40 g carbohydrate, 2 g fiber, 4 g protein.*
Diabetic Exchanges: *2-1/2 starch, 1 fat.*

Cover and refrigerate for at least 4 hours. Cut into squares. Top each piece with about 1 teaspoon of reserved whipped topping. Refrigerate leftovers. **Yield:** 15 servings.

Nutritional Analysis: One piece equals 215 calories, 4 g fat (3 g saturated fat), 9 mg cholesterol, 157 mg sodium, 40 g carbohydrate, 1 g fiber, 3 g protein.

Holiday Baked Apples

These appetizing oven-baked apples abound with fall flavor. The cored apples are filled with raisins, nuts and dried cranberries, then baked in a fragrant spiced sauce. Topped with white chocolate shavings, the apples will add a festive touch to your seasonal gatherings.
—Paula Marchesi, Lenhartsville, Pennsylvania

1/4 cup packed brown sugar
  1 teaspoon cornstarch
  1 teaspoon ground cinnamon
3/4 teaspoon ground ginger *or* 2 teaspoons fresh grated gingerroot
2-1/2 cups reduced-calorie cranberry juice
1/2 cup maple syrup
  1 tablespoon lemon juice
  1 teaspoon almond extract
1/3 cup dried cranberries
1/3 cup golden raisins
1/3 cup slivered almonds
  8 medium tart apples
1/2 ounce white baking chocolate, shaved

In a bowl, combine the brown sugar, cornstarch, cinnamon and ginger. Stir in the cranberry juice, syrup, lemon juice and almond extract until smooth; set aside. Combine the cranberries, raisins and almonds; set aside.

Core apples, then peel top half of each. Place in a 13-in. x 9-in. x 2-in. baking dish coated with nonstick cooking spray.

Fill each apple with 2 tablespoons of the cranberry mixture. Pour the juice mixture over and around apples. Bake, uncovered, at 350° for 55-65 minutes or until tender, basting occasionally. Reduce pan juices if desired. To serve, drizzle apples with pan juices and sprinkle with chocolate. **Yield:** 8 servings.

Nutritional Analysis: One apple equals 239 calories, 3 g fat (1 g saturated fat), trace cholesterol, 11 mg sodium, 53 g carbohydrate, 4 g fiber, 1 g protein.
  △ *Low-fat*
  ▲ *Low-sodium*

Peach Angel Dessert

(Pictured above)

This light and lovely dessert is absolutely heavenly! Try this with fresh strawberries, raspberries or blueberries, too, using the corresponding flavor of gelatin. It's delicious with any of them.
—Marge Hubrich, St. Cloud, Minnesota

3/4 cup sugar
  2 tablespoons cornstarch
  1 cup water
  2 tablespoons corn syrup
1/4 cup peach, apricot *or* orange gelatin powder
  1 loaf (10-1/2 ounces) angel food cake
  1 package (8 ounces) reduced-fat cream cheese
  2 tablespoons fat-free milk
2/3 cup confectioners' sugar
  1 carton (8 ounces) frozen reduced-fat whipped topping, thawed
  3 cups sliced peeled fresh *or* frozen peaches, thawed

In a small saucepan, combine the sugar and cornstarch. Gradually whisk in water and corn syrup until smooth. Cook and stir until mixture comes to a boil. Cook for 1-2 minutes or until thickened. Remove from the heat; stir in gelatin until dissolved. Cool to room temperature, stirring several times.

Cut angel food cake into nine slices. Line an ungreased 13-in. x 9-in. x 2-in. dish with the slices. In a mixing bowl, beat cream cheese and milk until blended. Gradually beat in confectioners' sugar. Set aside 1/3 cup whipped topping for garnish. Fold remaining whipped topping into cream cheese mixture; spread over cake. Top with peaches. Pour gelatin mixture over peaches.

Favorite Recipe Made Lighter

BIRTHDAYS at Julee Hay's home in Elkhart, Indiana wouldn't be the same without White Layer Cake. "My family always requests this cake for birthdays. I hope you can reduce the fat in it and still get a cake my family enjoys," she says.

Compared to the original, the pared-down dessert has nearly 60% less fat, just half the cholesterol and about a quarter less calories and sodium.

White Layer Cake

    1/4 cup butter *or* margarine, softened
    1/4 cup shortening
1-1/2 cups sugar
    4 egg whites
1-1/2 teaspoons vanilla extract
2-1/4 cups cake flour
    1 teaspoon baking powder
    1 teaspoon salt
    1 cup buttermilk
FROSTING:
    1/2 cup shortening
    1/4 cup butter *or* margarine, softened
    2 teaspoons vanilla extract
    1/8 teaspoon salt
    4 cups confectioners' sugar
    3 to 4 tablespoons milk

In a mixing bowl, cream butter, shortening and sugar until light and fluffy. Gradually add egg whites, beating well. Beat in vanilla. Combine the flour, baking powder and salt; add to creamed mixture alternately with buttermilk.

Pour into two greased and floured 9-in. round baking pans. Bake at 350° for 20-25 minutes or until a toothpick inserted near the center comes out clean. Cool for 10 minutes before removing from pans to wire racks to cool completely.

For frosting, in a mixing bowl, cream shortening and butter. Add vanilla and salt. Gradually beat in sugar. Add enough milk until frosting achieves spreading consistency. Spread between layers and over top and sides of cake. **Yield:** 14 servings.

Nutritional Analysis: One piece equals 449 calories, 17 g fat (9 g saturated fat), 20 mg cholesterol, 335 mg sodium, 72 g carbohydrate, trace fiber, 3 g protein.

Makeover White Layer Cake

(Pictured at right)

    1/4 cup shortening
1-1/2 cups sugar
    4 egg whites
    1/4 cup unsweetened applesauce
1-1/2 teaspoons vanilla extract
2-1/4 cups cake flour, sifted
    1 teaspoon baking powder
    1/2 teaspoon baking soda
    1/2 teaspoon salt
    1 cup 1% buttermilk
FROSTING:
    3 cups confectioners' sugar
    1/4 cup butter *or* stick margarine, softened
    1 tablespoon light corn syrup
    2 teaspoons vanilla extract
    1/8 teaspoon salt
    2 to 3 tablespoons 1% milk

Coat two 9-in. round baking pans with nonstick cooking spray and dust with flour; set aside. In a mixing bowl, cream shortening and sugar for about 2 minutes or until crumbly. Gradually add egg whites, beating well. Beat in applesauce and vanilla. Combine the flour, baking powder, baking soda and salt; add to batter alternately with buttermilk until combined.

Pour into prepared pans. Bake at 350° for 20-25 minutes or until a toothpick inserted near the center comes out clean. Cool for 10 minutes before removing from pans to wire racks to cool completely.

For frosting, in a mixing bowl, beat confectioners' sugar, butter, corn syrup, vanilla and salt. Beat in enough milk until frosting achieves spreading consistency. Spread between layers and over top and sides of cake. **Yield:** 14 servings.

Nutritional Analysis: One piece equals 330 calories, 7 g fat (3 g saturated fat), 10 mg cholesterol, 256 mg sodium, 65 g carbohydrate, 1 g fiber, 3 g protein.

Cantaloupe Sherbet

(Pictured below)

Melon lovers are sure to enjoy this frosty dessert. A dish of the sherbet is a refreshing ending to a light lunch or dinner during the summer. It's also a great way to use up overripe cantaloupe.
—Mary Dixson, Decatur, Alabama

1 small ripe cantaloupe
2 cups cold fat-free milk, *divided*
1/3 cup sugar
1 envelope unflavored gelatin
1/4 cup light corn syrup
1/4 teaspoon salt

Cut cantaloupe in half; discard seeds. Scoop out pulp (there should be about 4 cups of melon). Place cantaloupe and 1 cup milk in a blender or food processor; cover and process until smooth.

In a saucepan, combine sugar and remaining milk. Sprinkle gelatin over top; let stand for 1 minute. Heat over low heat, stirring until gelatin is completely dissolved. Stir in the corn syrup, salt and pureed cantaloupe. Pour into a 13-in. x 9-in. x 2-in. pan. Cover and freeze until partially frozen, about 3 hours, stirring occasionally.

Place cantaloupe mixture in a blender or food processor; cover and process until smooth. Return to pan. Cover; freeze until almost frozen, about 1 hour. **Yield:** 6 servings.

Nutritional Analysis: One serving (3/4 cup) equals 152 calories, trace fat (trace saturated fat), 2 mg cholesterol, 170 mg sodium, 35 g carbohydrate, 1 g fiber, 5 g protein.
Diabetic Exchanges: *1 starch, 1/2 fat-free milk, 1/2 fruit.*
△ **Low-fat**

Lemon Cooler Cookies

(Pictured above)

Baking soda helps brown these crisp, lemony shortbread-like goodies that were created by our Test Kitchen staff.

1/4 cup butter *or* stick margarine, softened
2 tablespoons canola oil
3/4 cup sugar
1 egg
1 egg white
1/4 cup lemonade concentrate
2 teaspoons grated lemon peel
2 cups all-purpose flour
1/2 teaspoon baking powder
1/4 teaspoon salt
1/8 teaspoon baking soda
1 tablespoon yellow decorating sugar

In a mixing bowl, beat the butter, oil and sugar. Beat in the egg, egg white, lemonade concentrate and lemon peel. Combine the flour, baking powder, salt and baking soda; gradually add to egg mixture.

Using a cookie press fitted with the disk of your choice, press dough 2 in. apart onto ungreased baking sheets. Sprinkle with yellow sugar. Bake at 350° for 8-10 minutes or until edges are lightly browned. Cool on wire racks. **Yield:** 3-1/2 dozen.

Nutritional Analysis: One serving (2 cookies) equals 116 calories, 4 g fat (2 g saturated fat), 26 mg cholesterol, 73 mg sodium, 18 g carbohydrate, trace fiber, 2 g protein.
Diabetic Exchanges: *1 starch, 1 fat.*
▲ **Low-sodium**

Desserts for Diabetics

• We have two diabetics in our family, so I'm always trying to come up with appropriate desserts for them. They like angel food cake, so I dress up cake batter with flavored sugar-free gelatin. I pour a third of the batter in the pan, sprinkle with a third of the dry gelatin powder and repeat two times.

The gelatin melts into the batter while baking to give the angel food cake a pretty look and different taste. —*Orris Caldwell*
Ponchatoula, Louisiana

• My husband and I both have diabetes, so I'm always trying to find delicious desserts that don't have a lot of sugar and fat. For a sweet treat, I simply spoon a can of light apricot halves (including syrup) into four parfait glasses.

Then I top them with sugar-free instant vanilla pudding prepared with fat-free milk. I chill them until set, then top with a maraschino cherry for a pretty look. —*Evelyn Krause*
Elizabeth City, North Carolina

Chocolate Mint Whoopie Pies

These cute sandwich cookies from our Test Kitchen would be a pretty addition to any holiday goodie tray.

    1/2 cup sugar
      3 tablespoons canola oil
      1 egg
      1 cup all-purpose flour
    1/4 cup baking cocoa
    1/2 teaspoon baking soda
    1/4 teaspoon salt
      4 tablespoons fat-free milk, *divided*
      2 tablespoons butter *or* stick margarine, softened
    1-1/3 cups confectioners' sugar
    1/8 teaspoon mint extract
      4 drops green food coloring, optional

In a bowl, beat the sugar and oil until crumbly. Add egg; beat for 1 minute. Combine the flour, cocoa, baking soda and salt. Gradually beat into sugar mixture. Add 2 tablespoons milk; mix well. With lightly floured hands, roll dough into 36 balls.

Place 2 in. apart on baking sheets coated with nonstick cooking spray. Flatten slightly with a glass coated with cooking spray. Bake at 425° for 5-6 minutes or until edges are set and tops are cracked. Cool for 2 minutes before removing to wire racks to cool. In a mixing bowl, combine butter and confectioners' sugar until crumbly. Beat in extract, food coloring if desired and remaining milk. Spread on the bottom of half of the cookies; top with remaining cookies. **Yield:** 1-1/2 dozen.

Nutritional Analysis: One sandwich cookie equals 122 calories, 4 g fat (1 g saturated fat), 15 mg cholesterol, 86 mg sodium, 21 g carbohydrate, trace fiber, 1 g protein.
Diabetic Exchanges: 1-1/2 starch, 1/2 fat.
▲ *Low-sodium*

Raspberry-Topped Cream Tarts

(Pictured below)

These tarts are as pretty to look at as they are good to eat! Crispy tortilla cups are filled with a cream cheese mixture and topped with fresh raspberries. They're also delicious with sliced strawberries.
—*Kathy Rairigh, Milford, Indiana*

      1 tablespoon brown sugar
    1/4 teaspoon ground cinnamon
    1/8 teaspoon ground nutmeg
      4 flour tortillas (8 inches)
Warm water
      1 package (8 ounces) reduced-fat cream cheese, softened
      3 tablespoons sugar
      1 to 2 tablespoons fat-free milk
    1/2 teaspoon almond extract
      1 cup fresh raspberries

In a bowl, combine the brown sugar, cinnamon and nutmeg; set aside. Cut tortillas with a 3-1/2-in. biscuit cutter; discard tortilla scraps. Brush both sides of tortilla rounds with warm water. Spray tops with nonstick cooking spray; sprinkle with brown sugar mixture. Press into ungreased muffin cups. Bake at 350° for 12-15 minutes or until lightly browned. Cool in pans on wire racks.

In a small mixing bowl, combine the cream cheese, sugar, milk and almond extract; mix well. Spoon into tortilla shells; top with raspberries. Store leftovers in the refrigerator. **Yield:** 16 servings.

Nutritional Analysis: One tart equals 93 calories, 3 g fat (2 g saturated fat), 8 mg cholesterol, 108 mg sodium, 13 g carbohydrate, 1 g fiber, 3 g protein.
Diabetic Exchanges: 1 starch, 1/2 fat.
△ *Low-fat*
▲ *Low-sodium*

Cinnamon Peach Crisp

This dessert is so good yet so easy to make. Fresh peaches and a sweet crunchy topping give it comforting flavor. I like to dish it up warm with a scoop of frozen yogurt.
—Leona Luecking, West Burlington, Iowa

4 cups sliced peeled fresh peaches
1/2 cup orange juice
2 tablespoons brown sugar
1/2 teaspoon ground cinnamon
1 cup all-purpose flour
1/3 cup sugar
1 teaspoon baking powder
1 egg, lightly beaten
2 tablespoons butter *or* stick margarine, melted
CINNAMON-SUGAR:
1-1/2 teaspoons sugar
1/8 teaspoon ground cinnamon

In a bowl, combine the peaches, orange juice, brown sugar and cinnamon. Transfer to an 8-in. square baking dish coated with nonstick cooking spray. Combine the flour, sugar and baking powder. Add egg and butter; mix until crumbly. Sprinkle over peaches. Combine sugar and cinnamon; sprinkle over batter. Bake at 350° for 40-45 minutes or until filling is bubbly and topping is golden brown. **Yield:** 6 servings.

Nutritional Analysis: One serving equals 245 calories, 5 g fat (3 g saturated fat), 46 mg cholesterol, 90 mg sodium, 48 g carbohydrate, 3 g fiber, 4 g protein.
Diabetic Exchanges: *2 starch, 1 fruit, 1 fat.*
▲ *Low-sodium*

Chocolate Chip Cheesecake

(Pictured at right)

No one will guess they're eating "light" when they take a bite of this creamy dessert. The cookie crumb crust holds a rich cream cheese filling dotted with mini chocolate chips.
—Connie Staal, Greenbrier, Arkansas

1 cup crushed reduced-fat chocolate sandwich cookies (about 11 cookies)
2 tablespoons butter *or* stick margarine, melted
2 packages (8 ounces *each*) fat-free cream cheese
1 package (8 ounces) reduced-fat cream cheese
1 can (14 ounces) sweetened condensed milk
3 eggs
2 teaspoons vanilla extract
1/2 cup miniature semisweet chocolate chips, *divided*
1 teaspoon all-purpose flour

In a bowl, combine cookie crumbs and butter; press onto the bottom of a 9-in. springform pan coated with nonstick cooking spray. Bake at 325° for 6-8 minutes. Cool on a wire rack.
In a mixing bowl, beat cream cheeses until smooth; beat in sweetened condensed milk. Add eggs; beat on low speed just until combined. Beat in vanilla just until blended. In a bowl, toss 1/3 cup chocolate chips and flour; stir into batter.

Pour into prepared pan. Sprinkle with remaining chocolate chips. Bake at 325° for 30-35 minutes or until almost set. Immediately run a knife around edge of pan to loosen; cool on a wire rack for 1 hour. Chill overnight. Remove sides of pan. Refrigerate leftovers. **Yield:** 12 servings.

Nutritional Analysis: One piece equals 303 calories, 14 g fat (8 g saturated fat), 87 mg cholesterol, 417 mg sodium, 33 g carbohydrate, 1 g fiber, 12 g protein.
Diabetic Exchanges: *2 starch, 2 fat, 1 lean meat.*

Cutout Sugar Cookies

(Pictured at right)

Our Test Kitchen home economists dreamed up these chewy sugar cookies with a lightly sweet flavor. Decorated for the holidays with colored sugar, sprinkles or frosting, they won't last long...so make sure you stash away a few for Santa!

6 tablespoons butter (no substitutes), softened
1/2 cup sugar
1/2 cup packed brown sugar
1 egg
1 teaspoon vanilla extract
2 tablespoons canola oil
1 tablespoon light corn syrup
1-1/2 cups all-purpose flour
1/4 cup cornmeal
1/2 teaspoon baking powder
1/2 teaspoon salt
1-1/4 cups colored sugar of your choice

In a mixing bowl, beat butter, sugar and brown sugar for 2 minutes. Add egg and vanilla; mix well. Gradually beat in oil. Gradually beat in corn syrup. Combine the flour, cornmeal, baking powder and salt. Add to creamed mixture just until blended. Divide in half; wrap each portion in plastic wrap. Refrigerate for at least 2 hours.
On a lightly floured surface, roll dough out to 1/4-in. thickness. Cut out dough with lightly floured 2-1/2-in. cookie cutter. Place 2 in. apart on baking sheets coated with nonstick cooking spray. Sprinkle each cutout with 2 teaspoons colored sugar. Bake at 350° for 7-9 minutes or until set and bottoms are lightly browned. Cool for 2 minutes before removing to wire racks. **Yield:** 2-1/2 dozen.

Nutritional Analysis: One cookie equals 117 calories, 3 g fat (2 g saturated fat), 13 mg cholesterol, 98 mg sodium, 21 g carbohydrate, trace fiber, 1 g protein.
Diabetic Exchange: *1-1/2 starch.*
△ *Low-fat*
▲ *Low-sodium*

Lemon Meringue Tarts

(Pictured above)

Eating less sugar meant limiting sweets, so I adapted this longtime favorite of my mother-in-law's. For a fun twist, spread the meringue into a regular-size pie tin, bake it and add the lemon filling.
—*Gloria Schwarting, Stuart, Virginia*

   3 egg whites
1/2 teaspoon cream of tartar
   3 tablespoons sugar
FILLING:
   3/4 cup sugar
Sugar substitute equivalent to 1/2 cup sugar*
   3 tablespoons cornstarch
1-1/3 cups cold water
   3 egg yolks, beaten
1/4 cup lemon juice
   1 teaspoon grated lemon peel
Lemon slices and mint sprigs

For meringue, in a mixing bowl, beat the egg whites and cream of tartar on medium speed until soft peaks form. Gradually add the sugar; beat on high until stiff peaks form. Drop meringue into six mounds on a parchment-lined baking sheet. Shape into 4-in. cups with the back of a spoon. Bake at 225° for 55 minutes. Turn oven off and do not open door; let meringues dry in oven for 1 to 1-1/2 hours.

For filling, in a saucepan, combine the sugar, sugar substitute and cornstarch. Gradually stir in the water until smooth. Bring to a boil over medium heat; cook and stir for 2 minutes or until thickened. Remove from the heat. Stir about half of the hot mixture into the egg yolks; return all to the pan, stirring constantly. Bring to a gentle boil. Cook and stir 2 minutes longer. Remove from the heat. Gently stir in lemon juice and lemon peel. Cool to room temperature without stirring. Cover and refrigerate for at least 1 hour. Just before serving, fill meringue shells with lemon mixture. Garnish with lemon slices and mint. **Yield:** 6 servings.

*Editor's Note: This recipe was tested with Splenda No Calorie Sweetener. Look for it in the baking aisle of your grocery store.

Nutritional Analysis: One tart equals 196 calories, 3 g fat (1 g saturated fat), 106 mg cholesterol, 33 mg sodium, 41 g carbohydrate, trace fiber, 3 g protein.
   Diabetic Exchange: 2-1/2 starch.
   △ *Low-fat*
   ▲ *Low-sodium*

Surprise Chocolate Fudge

(Pictured below)

This fun novelty recipe uses pinto beans to replace some of the butter typically found in fudge. Walnuts give the soft creamy squares a nice crunch.
—*Pattie Ann Forssberg, Logan, Kansas*

   1 can (15 ounces) pinto beans, rinsed and drained
   1 cup baking cocoa
3/4 cup butter *or* stick margarine, melted
   1 tablespoon vanilla extract
7-1/2 cups confectioners' sugar
   1 cup chopped walnuts

In a microwave-safe dish, mash beans with a fork until smooth; cover and microwave for 1-1/2 minutes or until heated through. Add cocoa, butter and vanilla. (Mixture will be thick.) Slowly stir in sugar; add nuts. Press mixture into a 9-in. square pan coated with nonstick cooking spray. Cover and refrigerate until firm. Cut into 1-in. pieces. **Yield:** about 3-1/2 pounds (81 pieces).

Nutritional Analysis: One piece equals 76 calories, 3 g fat (1g saturated fat), 4 mg cholesterol, 20 mg sodium, 13 g carbohydrate, 1 g fiber, 1 g protein.
   Diabetic Exchange: 1 starch.
   △ *Low-fat*
   ▲ *Low-sodium*

Fine Dining Pared Down

A special occasion calls for candles, fine china and a marvelous meal. But there's no need to add to your guests' waistlines at the same time. Pamper friends and family with these elegant but light menus.

Elegant Cornish Hens, Crumb-Topped Broccoli Medley and Gingersnap Pear Tart (page 250)

From-the-Sea Supper

Baked Salmon with Crumb Topping

Fishing for a new way to serve salmon that's special enough for company? Our Test Kitchen staff came up with this elegant entree. A generous topping of bread crumbs, almonds, green onion and seasonings gives moist salmon a tasty treatment.

1 cup soft whole wheat bread crumbs
1/3 cup sliced almonds, coarsely chopped
1 tablespoon finely chopped green onion
1-1/2 teaspoons minced fresh thyme *or* 1/2 teaspoon dried thyme
1/2 teaspoon salt
1/8 teaspoon pepper
2 tablespoons butter *or* stick margarine, melted
1 salmon fillet (2 pounds)

In a bowl, combine the bread crumbs, almonds, onion, thyme, salt and pepper; mix well. Add butter and toss lightly; set aside. Pat salmon dry. Place skin side down in a 15-in. x 10-in. x 1-in. baking pan coated with nonstick cooking spray. Spritz salmon with nonstick cooking spray; cover with crumb mixture. Bake, uncovered, at 350° for 20-25 minutes or until fish flakes easily with a fork. **Yield:** 8 servings.

Nutritional Analysis: One serving (3 ounces cooked salmon) equals 273 calories, 17 g fat (4 g saturated fat), 75 mg cholesterol, 276 mg sodium, 4 g carbohydrate, 1 g fiber, 24 g protein.
Diabetic Exchanges: *3 lean meat, 2 fat.*

Raspberry Tossed Salad

Our home economists tossed together mixed greens, fresh raspberries, mushrooms, feta cheese and more in this pretty salad. Toasted pecan halves add fun crunch...and a homemade raspberry dressing brings a delicious tang to the mix!

4 cups torn red leaf lettuce
1 package (5 ounces) spring mix salad greens
1 cup fresh raspberries
1 cup sliced fresh mushrooms
1/2 cup julienned red onion
1/4 cup crumbled feta *or* blue cheese
1/4 cup pecan halves, toasted
2 tablespoons 100% raspberry fruit spread, melted
2 tablespoons raspberry vinegar
2 tablespoons canola oil
1/8 teaspoon salt
Dash pepper

In a salad bowl, combine the first seven ingredients. In a jar with a tight-fitting lid, combine the fruit spread, vinegar, oil, salt and pepper; shake well. Pour over salad; toss gently to coat. **Yield:** 8 servings.

Nutritional Analysis: One serving (1-1/2 cups) equals 102 calories, 7 g fat (1 g saturated fat), 4 mg cholesterol, 108 mg sodium, 8 g carbohydrate, 3 g fiber, 3 g protein.
Diabetic Exchanges: *1-1/2 fat, 1 vegetable.*
▲ **Low-sodium**
▲ **Meatless**

Garlic Thyme Potatoes

Small red potatoes, partially peeled, make an eye-catching presentation in this simple side dish from our Test Kitchen. The potatoes are steamed, then tossed with oil and a flavorful combination of thyme and lemon peel.

2 pounds small red potatoes
4 garlic cloves, minced
1 tablespoon olive *or* canola oil
1 tablespoon minced fresh thyme *or* 1 teaspoon dried thyme
1/2 teaspoon grated lemon peel
1/4 teaspoon salt
1/4 teaspoon pepper

Peel a narrow strip of skin around the center of each potato. Place potatoes in a steamer basket; place in a saucepan over 1 in. of water. Bring to a boil. Cover and steam for 20-30 minutes or until tender. In a serving bowl, combine the remaining ingredients. Add potatoes and toss gently to coat. **Yield:** 8 servings.

Nutritional Analysis: One serving equals 102 calories, 2 g fat (trace saturated fat), 0 cholesterol, 78 mg sodium, 20 g carbohydrate, 2 g fiber, 2 g protein.
Diabetic Exchange: *1 starch.*
△ **Low-fat**
▲ **Low-sodium**
▲ **Meatless**

● Secrets to Buying Fresh Salmon

WHEN BUYING fresh salmon, let your eyes and nose help you judge its freshness.
- Select fresh salmon that is well-chilled and has bright color. It should be firm to the touch, giving slightly when you press it and then springing back.
- Salmon should have no fishy odor, but instead a fresh scent that hints of seaweed.
- Prepackaged salmon should contain only a minimal amount of liquid, if any.
- Store fresh salmon in the coldest part of your refrigerator for up to 2 days.
- If you will not be cooking fresh salmon within 2 days, re-wrap it well and freeze for use within 4 to 5 months.

Fix a Family-Style Feast

Beef Tenderloin with Balsamic Sauce

This beef tenderloin is quick and easy to prepare —but it's special enough to serve to guests, assures our Test Kitchen staff.

2 tablespoons minced fresh rosemary *or* **2 teaspoons dried rosemary, crushed**
2 tablespoons minced garlic
1-1/2 teaspoons salt
1 teaspoon coarsely ground pepper
1 beef tenderloin, trimmed (about 2 pounds)
SAUCE:
2 cups port wine *or* **1 cup grape juice and 1 cup reduced-sodium beef broth**
2 tablespoons balsamic vinegar
1 teaspoon butter *or* **stick margarine**
1/4 teaspoon salt
1/8 teaspoon pepper

Combine the rosemary, garlic, salt and pepper; rub evenly over tenderloin. Cover and refrigerate for 2 hours. Place meat on a rack in a shallow roasting pan. Bake, uncovered, at 400° for 50-70 minutes or until meat reaches desired doneness (for rare, a meat thermometer should read 140°; medium, 160°; well-done, 170°). Let stand for 10 minutes before slicing.

In a saucepan, bring wine or grape juice and broth to a boil; cook until reduced to 3/4 cup. Add vinegar; cook for 3-4 minutes or until reduced to a sauce consistency. Stir in butter, salt and pepper. Serve with beef. **Yield:** 8 servings.

Nutritional Analysis: One serving (3 ounces cooked meat with 3-1/2 teaspoons sauce) equals 242 calories, 9 g fat (3 g saturated fat), 72 mg cholesterol, 576 mg sodium, 6 g carbohydrate, 0 fiber, 24 g protein.
Diabetic Exchanges: *3 lean meat, 1 fat.*

Snappy Peas and Carrots

This brightly colored veggie side was stirred up by our home economists. It goes well with the peppery tenderloin.

3 quarts water
1-1/4 pounds baby carrots
1 pound fresh *or* **frozen sugar snap peas**
1-1/2 teaspoons canola oil
2 garlic cloves, minced
2 tablespoons reduced-sodium chicken broth *or* **vegetable broth**
1 teaspoon dried mint
1/4 teaspoon salt
1/4 teaspoon grated lemon peel
1/8 teaspoon pepper

In a Dutch oven, bring water to a boil. Add carrots; cover and boil for 4 minutes. Add peas; cover and boil 1 minute longer. Drain and pat dry. In a large nonstick skillet, saute vegetables in oil for 3 minutes. Add garlic; saute for 1 minute. Stir in the remaining ingredients; saute until heated through. **Yield:** 8 servings.

Nutritional Analysis: One serving (3/4 cup) equals 69 calories, 1 g fat (trace saturated fat), 0 cholesterol, 125 mg sodium, 11 g carbohydrate, 4 g fiber, 2 g protein.
Diabetic Exchange: *2 vegetable.*
△ **Low-fat**
▲ **Low-sodium**
▲ **Meatless**

Mahogany Devil's Food Cake

I found this recipe in a cookbook I bought at a garage sale. It's become one of my family's most-requested desserts.
—Jamie Regier, Omaha, Nebraska

2 tablespoons butter *or* **stick margarine, softened**
2 cups sugar
2 eggs
1 teaspoon vanilla extract
2-1/2 cups all-purpose flour
1/2 cup baking cocoa
2 teaspoons baking soda
1/2 teaspoon salt
1 cup 1% buttermilk
1 cup hot water
FROSTING:
1-1/4 cups sugar
3 egg whites
1/4 cup water
2 tablespoons light corn syrup
1/2 teaspoon cream of tartar
1 teaspoon vanilla extract
1/2 teaspoon almond extract

Coat three 9-in. round baking pans with nonstick cooking spray and sprinkle with flour; set aside. In a mixing bowl, beat butter and sugar until crumbly, about 2 minutes. Add eggs, one at a time, beating well after each addition. Beat in vanilla. Combine the flour, cocoa, baking soda and salt; add to creamed mixture alternately with buttermilk. Add water and mix well. Pour into prepared pans. Bake at 350° for 20-25 minutes or until a toothpick inserted near the center comes out clean. Cool for 10 minutes; remove from the pans to wire racks to cool completely.

For frosting, in a heavy saucepan, combine the sugar, egg whites, water, corn syrup and cream of tartar. With a portable mixer, beat mixture on low speed for 1 minute. Continue beating on low over low heat until a candy thermometer reads 160°, about 5 minutes. Pour into a large mixing bowl; add extracts. Beat on high until stiff peaks form, about 7 minutes. Spread frosting between layers and over top and sides of cake. **Yield:** 12 servings.

Editor's Note: A stand mixer is recommended for beating the frosting after it reaches 160°.

Nutritional Analysis: One piece equals 368 calories, 4 g fat (2 g saturated fat), 42 mg cholesterol, 378 mg sodium, 80 g carbohydrate, 1 g fiber, 6 g protein.

Grill-Side Specialties

Corn-Stuffed Pork Chops

For an eye-catching entree, grill pork chops filled with a colorful corn, pimiento and green pepper stuffing.
—Elizabeth Jussaume, Lowell, Massachusetts

    6 bone-in center loin pork chops (1 inch thick,
      about 10 ounces *each*)
  3/4 teaspoon salt, *divided*
  1/4 teaspoon pepper, *divided*
  1/4 cup chopped green pepper
  1/4 cup chopped onion
    1 tablespoon butter *or* stick margarine
1-1/2 cups bread cubes, toasted
  1/2 cup frozen corn, thawed
  1/4 cup egg substitute
    2 tablespoons chopped pimientos
  1/4 teaspoon ground cumin

Cut a pocket in each pork chop; sprinkle 1/4 teaspoon salt and 1/8 teaspoon pepper in pockets. Set aside. In a nonstick skillet, saute green pepper and onion in butter until tender. Transfer to a bowl. Add the bread cubes, corn, egg substitute, pimientos, cumin and remaining salt and pepper; mix well. Stuff into pork chops; secure with wooden toothpicks.

Before starting the grill, coat grill rack with nonstick cooking spray. Grill chops, covered, over medium indirect heat for 15-18 minutes on each side or until a meat thermometer inserted in stuffing reads 160°. **Yield:** 6 servings.

Nutritional Analysis: One serving (1 stuffed pork chop) equals 308 calories, 12 g fat (5 g saturated fat), 102 mg cholesterol, 458 mg sodium, 10 g carbohydrate, 1 g fiber, 38 g protein.
Diabetic Exchanges: 5 lean meat, 1/2 starch.

Outdoor Elegance

WHEN shorts and T-shirt season arrives, it doesn't mean you have to dress down your dinner. When the occasion warrants fine dining (and the weather cooperates!), move your meal outside. Here are a few ideas for creating an elegant outdoor atmosphere.

• Cover your picnic table or round wrought-iron table with a white tablecloth or a pretty bed sheet.

• Arrange fresh cut flowers from your garden in a clear glass or crystal vase for a centerpiece.

• Skip the paper plates and plastic utensils. Serve the meal on pretty dinnerware with tall or stemmed glasses, silverware and cloth napkins.

• Want to add a little glamour? Scout flea markets for a used chandelier and hang it from the porch or a sturdy tree branch.

Marinated Plum Tomatoes

Here's an easy, refreshing way to use the plump red tomatoes from your garden. Our Test Kitchen home economists simply sliced fresh tomatoes and tossed them in a cilantro-seasoned oil-and-vinegar marinade.

    2 tablespoons canola oil
    2 tablespoons balsamic vinegar *or* cider vinegar
    1 tablespoon lime juice
    1 tablespoon minced fresh cilantro *or* parsley
    1 teaspoon sugar
    1 teaspoon dried oregano
    1 garlic clove, minced
  1/2 teaspoon salt
  1/4 teaspoon pepper
   10 plum tomatoes, sliced

In a bowl, combine the first nine ingredients. Add tomatoes; toss gently to coat. Cover and refrigerate for at least 1 hour before serving. Serve with a slotted spoon. **Yield:** 6 servings.

Nutritional Analysis: One serving (3/4 cup) equals 71 calories, 5 g fat (trace saturated fat), 0 cholesterol, 206 mg sodium, 7 g carbohydrate, 1 g fiber, 1 g protein.
Diabetic Exchanges: 1 vegetable, 1 fat.
▲ **Meatless**

Frosty Peach Pie Supreme

This impressive dessert is just peachy! With only four ingredients, it's a snap to make.
—June Formanek, Belle Plaine, Iowa

    1 cup sliced fresh *or* frozen peaches, *divided*
    2 cups (16 ounces) fat-free reduced-sugar peach
      yogurt
    1 carton (8 ounces) frozen reduced-fat whipped
      topping, thawed
    1 reduced-fat graham cracker crust (8 inches)

Finely chop half of the peaches; place in a bowl. Stir in the yogurt. Fold in whipped topping. Spoon into the crust. Cover and freeze for 4 hours or until firm. Refrigerate for 45 minutes before slicing. Top with remaining peaches. **Yield:** 8 servings.

Nutritional Analysis: One piece equals 202 calories, 6 g fat (4 g saturated fat), 1 mg cholesterol, 127 mg sodium, 30 g carbohydrate, trace fiber, 3 g protein.
Diabetic Exchanges: 2 starch, 1 fat.
▲ **Low-sodium**

Showcase Summer Produce

Grilled Mango-Glazed Ham

I'm always looking for new ways to prepare ham ...but many of my cookbooks have the same old tried-and-true glazes. When I tried this one, I knew I had hit the jackpot!
—Sandy Lewis, Appleton, Wisconsin

1-1/2 cups red wine vinegar *or* cider vinegar
1/2 cup sugar
1 teaspoon finely chopped jalapeno pepper*
1/4 teaspoon ground ginger *or* 1 teaspoon grated fresh gingerroot
1 medium ripe mango *or* 2 medium ripe peaches, peeled and cut into wedges
1 bone-in fully cooked lean ham steak (about 2 pounds)
1/8 teaspoon pepper

In a saucepan, combine the vinegar, sugar, jalapeno and ginger. Bring to a boil. Reduce heat; simmer, uncovered, for 25-30 minutes or until glaze is thick and caramelized. Strain and cool. Place mango in a food processor or blender; cover and process until smooth. Stir into glaze; set aside.

Coat grill with nonstick cooking spray before starting the grill. Sprinkle both sides of ham steak with pepper. Grill, covered, over medium heat for 10 minutes on each side or until heated through. Brush both sides of ham with mango glaze; grill 5 minutes longer. Serve ham with remaining glaze. **Yield:** 8 servings.

*Editor's Note: When cutting or seeding hot peppers, use rubber or plastic gloves to protect your hands. Avoid touching your face.

Nutritional Analysis: *One serving (4 ounces cooked ham with 2 tablespoons glaze) equals 251 calories, 10 g fat (3 g saturated fat), 60 mg cholesterol, 1,454 mg sodium, 20 g carbohydrate, trace fiber, 21 g protein.*
Diabetic Exchanges: *3 lean meat, 1 starch, 1/2 fruit.*

Roasted Corn on the Cob

I've been grilling corn on the cob for years this way...our friends always insist on it!
—Sandy Szwarc, Albuquerque, New Mexico

8 medium ears sweet corn, husks removed
Refrigerated butter-flavored spray*
2 tablespoons butter *or* stick margarine, melted
2 tablespoons prepared horseradish
2 tablespoons Dijon mustard
2 garlic cloves, minced
1/2 teaspoon salt
1/8 teaspoon pepper
1/8 teaspoon paprika

Spray eight 12-in. x 10-in. pieces of foil with nonstick cooking spray. Place one ear of corn on each piece of foil; spritz corn evenly with butter-flavored spray. Fold foil over corn and seal tightly. Grill, covered, over medium indirect heat or bake at 400° for 25-30 minutes or until corn is tender. Combine the butter, horseradish, mustard, garlic, salt and pepper; brush over corn. Sprinkle with paprika. **Yield:** 8 servings.

*Editor's Note: This recipe was tested with I Can't Believe It's Not Butter Spray.

Nutritional Analysis: *One serving (1 seasoned ear of corn) equals 115 calories, 4 g fat (2 g saturated fat), 8 mg cholesterol, 291 mg sodium, 20 g carbohydrate, 2 g fiber, 3 g protein.*
Diabetic Exchanges: *1-1/2 starch, 1/2 fat.*
▲ Meatless

Mixed Berry Shortcake

This fruit-filled summer dessert looks so pretty served in parfait glasses. Strawberries, blueberries and a cool custard sauce are layered between tender cubes of homemade shortcake. Our Test Kitchen came up with the berry delicious treat.

1/2 cup plus 1/3 cup sugar, *divided*
3 tablespoons cornstarch
2-3/4 cups fat-free milk
2 egg yolks, lightly beaten
1 teaspoon vanilla extract
2 cups all-purpose flour
1 teaspoon baking powder
1/4 teaspoon baking soda
1/4 teaspoon salt
6 tablespoons cold butter *or* stick margarine
2/3 cup buttermilk
4 cups sliced fresh strawberries
4 cups fresh blueberries
8 whole strawberries, halved
1/2 cup reduced-fat whipped topping

In a heavy saucepan, combine 1/2 cup sugar and cornstarch. Stir in milk until blended. Bring to a boil over medium-low heat; cook and stir for 1-2 minutes or until thickened. Remove from the heat. Stir a small amount into egg yolks; return all to the pan, stirring constantly. Bring to a gentle boil, stirring constantly. Remove from the heat; stir in vanilla. Transfer to a bowl; press a piece of plastic wrap on top of custard. Refrigerate.

In a bowl, combine the flour, baking powder, baking soda, salt and remaining sugar. Cut in butter until mixture resembles coarse crumbs. Stir in buttermilk until a soft dough forms. Pat gently into a 9-in. square baking pan coated with nonstick cooking spray. Bake at 400° for 15-20 minutes or until lightly browned. Cool on a wire rack.

Cut shortcake into 3/4-in. cubes. In parfait glasses, alternate layers of shortcake, custard, sliced strawberries and blueberries. Garnish with halved strawberries and a dollop of whipped topping. **Yield:** 8 servings.

Nutritional Analysis: *One parfait equals 382 calories, 12 g fat (6 g saturated fat), 77 mg cholesterol, 290 mg sodium, 66 g carbohydrate, 5 g fiber, 6 g protein.*

A Healthier Holiday Meal

Cider Marinated Turkey

Make Thanksgiving dinner memorable by serving this golden-brown turkey from our Test Kitchen. Marinated in apple cider, kosher salt and spices, the turkey can be grilled or roasted.

8 cups apple cider *or* **unsweetened apple juice**
1/2 cup kosher salt
2 bay leaves
2 sprigs fresh thyme
8 whole cloves
5 garlic cloves
1 teaspoon whole allspice, crushed
2 medium navel oranges, quartered
3 quarts cold water
1 turkey (12 pounds)
1 medium onion, quartered
2 medium carrots, halved and quartered
2 sprigs fresh sage *or* **1 tablespoon rubbed sage**
1 tablespoon canola oil

In a large kettle, combine the first seven ingredients. Bring to a boil. Cook and stir until salt is dissolved. Stir in oranges. Remove from the heat. Add water; cool to room temperature.

Remove giblets from turkey; discard. Place a turkey-size oven roasting bag inside a second roasting bag; add turkey. Place in a roasting pan. Carefully pour cooled marinade into bag. Squeeze out as much air as possible; seal bag and turn to coat. Refrigerate for 12-24 hours; turn several times.

Drain and discard marinade. Rinse turkey under cold water; pat dry. Place onion, carrots and sage in cavity. Rub oil over skin. Skewer turkey openings; tie drumsticks together.

If grilling turkey, coat grill rack with nonstick cooking spray before starting the grill. Prepare grill for indirect heat, using a drip pan. Place turkey over drip pan; grill, covered, over indirect medium heat for 2 to 2-1/2 hours or until a meat thermometer reads 180°, tenting turkey with foil after about 1 hour.

If baking turkey, place breast side up on a rack in a roasting pan. Bake, uncovered, at 325° for about 3 hours or until a meat thermometer reads 180°.

If desired, thicken pan juices for gravy. Remove and discard skin and vegetables in cavity before carving turkey. Serve with gravy. **Yield:** 12 servings plus leftovers.

Editor's Note: It is best not to use a prebasted turkey for this recipe. However, if you do, omit the salt in the recipe.

Nutritional Analysis: One serving (4 ounces light and dark cooked turkey, skin removed, calculated without gravy) equals 198 calories, 6 g fat (2 g saturated fat), 86 mg cholesterol, 244 mg sodium, trace carbohydrate, 0 fiber, 33 g protein.
Diabetic Exchange: *4 lean meat.*

Green Beans with Peppers

Our Test Kitchen concocted this festive-looking side dish that's a snap to make for a holiday dinner.

2 pounds fresh green beans, trimmed
2 cups finely chopped sweet red peppers
1/2 cup finely chopped onion
2 tablespoons olive *or* **canola oil**
3 tablespoons chopped fresh basil *or* **1 tablespoon dried basil**
3/4 teaspoon salt
1/4 teaspoon pepper

Place beans in a steamer basket over 1 in. of water in a saucepan. Bring to a boil; cover and steam for 6-8 minutes or until crisp-tender. In a nonstick skillet, saute red peppers and onion in oil. Add seasonings and beans; toss. **Yield:** 12 servings.

Nutritional Analysis: One serving (3/4 cup) equals 53 calories, 2 g fat (trace saturated fat), 0 cholesterol, 152 mg sodium, 8 g carbohydrate, 1 g fiber, 2 g protein.
Diabetic Exchanges: *1 vegetable, 1/2 fat.*
△ **Low-fat**
▲ **Meatless**

Cranberry Hazelnut Dressing

This savory sausage stuffing gets a hint of sweetness from chopped apples, dried cranberries and orange juice.
—Virginia Anthony, Jacksonville, Florida

1/2 cup dried cranberries
1/4 cup orange juice
1-1/4 cups *each* **chopped celery and onions**
1 tablespoon canola oil
1 teaspoon poultry seasoning
1/2 pound reduced-fat pork sausage
4-1/2 cups seasoned stuffing croutons
2 cups chopped peeled apples
1 cup cooked wild rice
1/2 cup chopped hazelnuts *or* **pecans, toasted**
1/2 cup minced fresh parsley
1-1/4 cups reduced-sodium chicken broth
1 teaspoon salt
1/2 teaspoon pepper

In a saucepan, bring cranberries and juice to a boil. Remove from the heat; cover and set aside. In a nonstick skillet, saute celery and onions in oil. Stir in poultry seasoning. Place in a bowl.

In the same skillet, cook sausage over medium heat until no longer pink; drain and add to bowl. Add next five ingredients and reserved cranberry mixture; toss to combine. Drizzle with broth. Sprinkle with salt and pepper; toss. Place in a 13-in. x 9-in. x 2-in. baking dish coated with nonstick cooking spray. Cover; bake at 325° for 35 minutes. Uncover; bake 10-15 minutes or until lightly browned. **Yield:** 12 servings.

Nutritional Analysis: One serving (1 cup) equals 212 calories, 8 g fat (2 g saturated fat), 13 mg cholesterol, 657 mg sodium, 27 g carbohydrate, 3 g fiber, 7 g protein.
Diabetic Exchanges: *1 starch, 1 lean meat, 1 fat, 1/2 fruit.*

Lighter Yuletide Fare

Elegant Cornish Hens

(Also pictured on page 239)

This lovely entree not only looks special, it tastes special, too. Your holiday guests are sure to be impressed.

 1 teaspoon olive *or* canola oil
 2 Cornish game hens (20 ounces *each*), split lengthwise
1/2 teaspoon salt
1/2 teaspoon dried thyme
1/4 teaspoon pepper
MUSHROOM SAUCE:
1/2 pound fresh mushrooms, quartered
 4 teaspoons olive *or* canola oil, *divided*
1/4 teaspoon salt
1/4 teaspoon pepper, *divided*
1/3 cup finely chopped onion
 1 garlic clove, minced
 1 can (14-1/2 ounces) reduced-sodium chicken broth
1-1/2 teaspoons Dijon mustard
1-1/2 teaspoons balsamic vinegar
 1 teaspoon brown sugar
 1 teaspoon tomato paste
 1 bay leaf
 1 teaspoon *each* cornstarch and water
1/4 teaspoon minced fresh tarragon

Rub oil over hens; sprinkle with salt, thyme and pepper. Place skin side up on rack in shallow roasting pan. Bake, uncovered, at 400° for 35-40 minutes or until thermometer reads 180°. Broil hens for 3-4 minutes or until golden brown.

Meanwhile, toss mushrooms with 2 teaspoons oil, salt and 1/8 teaspoon pepper. Spread in a single layer on a 15-in. x 10-in. x 1-in. baking pan coated with nonstick cooking spray. Bake at 400° for 25-30 minutes, turning once. Set aside.

For sauce, in a saucepan, saute onion and garlic in remaining oil. Add the broth, mustard, vinegar, brown sugar, tomato paste, bay leaf and remaining pepper; bring to a boil. Cook, uncovered, over medium heat until mixture is reduced to 1 cup. Combine cornstarch and water until smooth; stir into sauce. Bring to a boil; cook and stir 1-2 minutes or until thickened. Stir in tarragon and mushrooms; heat through. Discard bay leaf. Serve sauce over hens. **Yield:** 4 servings.

Nutritional Analysis: One serving (1 hen half without skin and 1/4 cup sauce) equals 328 calories, 13 g fat (3 g saturated fat), 189 mg cholesterol, 873 mg sodium, 7 g carbohydrate, 1 g fiber, 45 g protein.
Diabetic Exchanges: 6 lean meat, 1 vegetable.

Crumb-Topped Broccoli Medley

(Also pictured on page 239)

Toasted almonds, Parmesan cheese and a full-flavored seasoning blend lend plenty of pizzazz to these steamed veggies.

1-1/2 pounds fresh broccoli, cut into florets (about 3 cups)
 2 small carrots, julienned (about 1 cup)
1/4 cup dry bread crumbs
 2 teaspoons butter *or* stick margarine
1/4 cup sliced almonds, toasted
 3 tablespoons shredded Parmesan cheese
1-1/2 teaspoons salt-free tomato basil garlic seasoning*
1/4 teaspoon salt

Place vegetables in a steamer basket in a saucepan over 1 in. of water; bring to a boil. Cover and steam for 8-10 minutes or until crisp-tender. In a small skillet, toast bread crumbs in butter. Add remaining ingredients; toss. Place vegetables in a bowl; sprinkle with crumb topping. **Yield:** 4 servings.

*Editor's Note: This recipe was tested with Mrs. Dash salt-free tomato basil garlic seasoning blend.

Nutritional Analysis: One serving (1 cup) equals 124 calories, 7 g fat (2 g saturated fat), 8 mg cholesterol, 307 mg sodium, 13 g carbohydrate, 3 g fiber, 6 g protein.
Diabetic Exchanges: 1 vegetable, 1 fat, 1/2 starch.
▲ *Meatless*

Gingersnap Pear Tart

(Also pictured on page 239)

This creamy cheesecake features a gingersnap crust and spiced pear slices on top.

 1 cup gingersnap crumbs (about 18 cookies)
 2 tablespoons butter *or* stick margarine, melted
 1 package (8 ounces) reduced-fat cream cheese
 1 package (8 ounces) fat-free cream cheese
1/3 plus 1/4 cup sugar, *divided*
 2 teaspoons all-purpose flour
 1 teaspoon vanilla extract
 2 eggs, lightly beaten
 2 large ripe pears, peeled and thinly sliced (about 3-1/2 cups)
1/2 teaspoon ground cinnamon

In a bowl, combine cookie crumbs and butter. Press onto the bottom and 1/2 in. up the sides of a 9-in. springform pan coated with nonstick cooking spray. Bake at 350° for 5-8 minutes or until set. Cool on a wire rack.

In a mixing bowl, beat cream cheeses until smooth. Beat in 1/3 cup sugar, flour and vanilla. Add eggs; beat on low speed just until combined. Pour into crust. Combine pears, cinnamon and remaining sugar; arrange pear slices over cream cheese mixture. Place pan on a baking sheet. Bake at 350° for 30-40 minutes or until almost set. Immediately run a knife around edge of pan to loosen; cool on a wire rack for 1 hour. Refrigerate for at least 2 hours. **Yield:** 8 servings.

Nutritional Analysis: One piece equals 301 calories, 13 g fat (7 g saturated fat), 85 mg cholesterol, 416 mg sodium, 38 g carbohydrate, 2 g fiber, 10 g protein.
Diabetic Exchanges: 2-1/2 starch, 1-1/2 fat, 1 lean meat.

Family-Style Suppers

In this chapter, you'll "meet" cooks
who share how they prepare good-for-you
fare for their families' tables. You'll
also find three dinners that don't
break your household budget.

Szechuan Chicken Noodle Toss, Mulled Cran-Apple
Juice and Orange Sponge Cake Roll (page 255)

A Meal for Just $1.75 a Plate!

Tamale Casserole

This family-pleasing main course is guaranteed to put a little kick in your menu.
—Kathleen Reid, Petaluma, California

1 pound lean ground beef
1 jalapeno pepper, seeded and diced*
2 cups frozen corn, thawed
1 can (28 ounces) diced tomatoes, undrained
1-1/2 cups fat-free milk
1 cup cornmeal
1 can (4 ounces) chopped green chilies, drained
1 can (2-1/4 ounces) sliced ripe olives, drained
2 egg whites, lightly beaten
1 envelope reduced-sodium taco seasoning
1 cup (4 ounces) shredded reduced-fat cheddar cheese
1 cup salsa

In a large nonstick skillet, cook beef and jalapeno over medium heat until meat is no longer pink; drain. Stir in the corn, tomatoes, milk, cornmeal, chilies, olives, egg whites and taco seasoning until blended. Transfer to a 13-in. x 9-in. x 2-in. baking dish coated with nonstick cooking spray.

Bake, uncovered, at 350° for 40 minutes. Sprinkle with cheese. Bake 5 minutes longer or until cheese is melted. Let stand for 10 minutes before cutting. Serve with salsa. **Yield:** 8 servings.

*Editor's Note: When cutting or seeding hot peppers, use rubber or plastic gloves to protect your hands. Avoid touching your face.

Nutritional Analysis: One serving (1 piece with 2 tablespoons salsa) equals 308 calories, 8 g fat (4 g saturated fat), 29 mg cholesterol, 839 mg sodium, 39 g carbohydrate, 4 g fiber, 22 g protein.
Diabetic Exchanges: 3 lean meat, 2 starch, 1 vegetable.

Southwestern Bean and Rice Salad

We enjoy fajitas and tacos, but finding a good side dish to go with them wasn't easy... until this recipe came along.
—Stephenie Liston, Ankeny, Iowa

3 cups cooked long grain rice, cooled
1 can (16 ounces) kidney beans, rinsed and drained
1 medium green pepper, diced
1 can (2-1/4 ounces) sliced ripe olives, drained
1/3 cup lime juice
1/4 cup chopped green onions
2 tablespoons canola oil
1 tablespoon minced fresh cilantro *or* parsley
2 garlic cloves, minced
1/2 teaspoon salt
1/2 teaspoon ground cumin

In a large bowl, combine the rice, beans, green pepper and olives. In a jar with a tight-fitting lid, combine the remaining ingredients; shake well. Pour over rice mixture and toss to coat. Cover and refrigerate for 1 hour or until chilled. Toss before serving. **Yield:** 8 servings.

Nutritional Analysis: One serving (3/4 cup) equals 154 calories, 5 g fat (trace saturated fat), 0 cholesterol, 404 mg sodium, 24 g carbohydrate, 3 g fiber, 4 g protein.
Diabetic Exchanges: 1-1/2 starch, 1 fat.
▲ *Meatless*

Fluffy Orange Gelatin Pie

This exceptionally light citrus dessert practically melts in your mouth.
—Frann Clark, DeRidder, Louisiana

1 can (15 ounces) mandarin oranges
1 package (3 ounces) orange gelatin
1 can (5 ounces) evaporated milk, chilled
1 reduced-fat graham cracker crust (8 inches)
1 medium navel orange, sliced

Drain liquid from oranges into a measuring cup. Add enough water to measure 1 cup; set oranges aside. Pour liquid into a saucepan; bring to a boil. Stir in gelatin until dissolved. Transfer to a large mixing bowl; place mixer beaters in bowl. Cover and refrigerate until mixture becomes syrupy.

Add milk. Beat on high speed until nearly doubled. Fold in oranges. Pour into crust. Refrigerate for 2-3 hours or until set. Garnish with orange slices. **Yield:** 8 servings.

Nutritional Analysis: One slice equals 202 calories, 4 g fat (2 g saturated fat), 6 mg cholesterol, 140 mg sodium, 37 g carbohydrate, 1 g fiber, 4 g protein.
Diabetic Exchanges: 1-1/2 starch, 1 fruit, 1 fat.
▲ *Low-sodium*

A Meal for Just $1.61 a Plate!

Easy Gazpacho

There's plenty of garden goodness in every bowl of this fresh-tasting soup. Served chilled, it's perfect for a summer meal.
—Marlene Muckenhirn, Delano, Minnesota

2-1/2 cups reduced-sodium tomato juice
   3 tablespoons white vinegar
   3 tablespoons olive *or* canola oil
   2 garlic cloves, minced
  1/4 teaspoon salt
   2 to 3 drops hot pepper sauce
   4 large tomatoes, chopped and *divided*
   1 medium onion, chopped
   1 medium cucumber, peeled, seeded and chopped
   1 medium green pepper, chopped
  1/4 cup fat-free croutons

In a blender or food processor, combine the tomato juice, vinegar, oil, garlic, salt, hot pepper sauce and half of the tomatoes; cover and process until smooth. Transfer to a bowl. Add the onion, cucumber, green pepper and remaining tomatoes. Cover and refrigerate for 4 hours or until chilled. Garnish with croutons. **Yield:** 4 servings.

Nutritional Analysis: One serving (1-1/2 cups) equals 203 calories, 11 g fat (2 g saturated fat), trace cholesterol, 285 mg sodium, 24 g carbohydrate, 4 g fiber, 4 g protein.
Diabetic Exchanges: 5 vegetable, 2 fat.
▲ *Meatless*

Spinach Corn Muffins

Chopped spinach adds green flecks to these golden muffins...and jalapeno peppers add a little heat.
—Jane Shapton, Tustin, California

   1 cup cornmeal
   1 cup all-purpose flour
  1/4 cup packed brown sugar
   2 teaspoons baking powder
  1/4 teaspoon salt
   1 egg
   1 cup fat-free milk
   2 tablespoons canola oil
   1 cup chopped fresh spinach
  3/4 cup shredded reduced-fat cheddar cheese
   2 jalapeno peppers, seeded and chopped*

In a large bowl, combine the cornmeal, flour, brown sugar, baking powder and salt. In another bowl, beat the egg, milk and oil; stir into dry ingredients just until moistened. Fold in the spinach, cheese and jalapenos.

Coat muffin cups with nonstick cooking spray; fill two-thirds full with batter. Bake at 400° for 18-22 minutes or until a toothpick comes out clean. Cool for 2 minutes before removing from pan to a wire rack. **Yield:** 1 dozen.

***Editor's Note:** When cutting or seeding hot peppers, use rubber or plastic gloves to protect your hands. Avoid touching your face.*

Nutritional Analysis: One muffin equals 153 calories, 5 g fat (1 g saturated fat), 23 mg cholesterol, 108 mg sodium, 23 g carbohydrate, 1 g fiber, 5 g protein.
Diabetic Exchanges: 1-1/2 starch, 1 fat.
▲ *Low-sodium*
▲ *Meatless*

Citrus Tossed Salad

The light and tangy dressing for this citrus salad is full of fruity flavor.
—Marge Werner, Broken Arrow, Oklahoma

   1 teaspoon cornstarch
  1/4 cup orange juice
  1/4 cup unsweetened grapefruit juice
   2 tablespoons cider vinegar
   2 tablespoons orange marmalade
   1 teaspoon Dijon mustard
  1/2 teaspoon grated orange peel
  1/8 teaspoon garlic powder
  1/8 teaspoon onion powder
   8 cups torn leaf lettuce
   1 medium grapefruit, peeled and sectioned
   1 medium navel orange, peeled and sectioned

In a saucepan, combine cornstarch and orange juice until smooth. Stir in the grapefruit juice, vinegar, marmalade, mustard, orange peel, garlic powder and onion powder. Bring to a boil; cook and stir for 2 minutes or until thickened. Remove from the heat; refrigerate until chilled. Divide lettuce and fruit among four salad plates; drizzle with dressing. **Yield:** 4 servings.

Nutritional Analysis: One serving (2 cups) equals 98 calories, 1 g fat (trace saturated fat), 0 cholesterol, 48 mg sodium, 24 g carbohydrate, 4 g fiber, 3 g protein.
Diabetic Exchanges: 1 fruit, 1 vegetable.
△ *Low-fat*
▲ *Low-sodium*
▲ *Meatless*

A Meal for Just $1.74 a Plate!

Szechuan Chicken Noodle Toss

My family loves Chinese food, so I came up with this recipe to use up leftover chicken, pork or beef.
—Carol Roane, Sarasota, Florida

  4 quarts water
  6 ounces uncooked thin spaghetti
  1 package (16 ounces) frozen Oriental vegetables
  1 tablespoon reduced-fat stick margarine*
  1 pound boneless skinless chicken breasts, cut
    into 2-inch strips
  2 garlic cloves, minced
1/8 teaspoon crushed red pepper flakes
  1 tablespoon canola oil
1/3 cup stir-fry sauce
  3 green onions, chopped

In a large saucepan or kettle, bring water to a boil. Add spaghetti; cook for 4 minutes. Add vegetables; cook 3-4 minutes longer or until spaghetti and vegetables are tender. Drain. Toss with margarine; set aside and keep warm. In a nonstick skillet, stir-fry the chicken, garlic and red pepper flakes in oil until chicken is no longer pink. Add stir-fry sauce; heat through. Add onions and spaghetti mixture; toss to coat. **Yield:** 4 servings.

*Editor's Note: This recipe was tested with Parkay Light stick margarine.

Nutritional Analysis: *One serving (1-1/2 cups) equals 394 calories, 7 g fat (1 g saturated fat), 66 mg cholesterol, 831 mg sodium, 44 g carbohydrate, 5 g fiber, 35 g protein.*
Diabetic Exchanges: *3 lean meat, 2-1/2 starch, 1 vegetable.*

Mulled Cran-Apple Juice

This beverage is a fun change from regular hot cider.
—Carol Mead, Los Alamos, New Mexico

 12 *each* whole cloves and allspice
2-1/2 quarts water
  1 can (12 ounces) frozen apple juice concentrate

  1 can (11-1/2 ounces) frozen cranberry juice
    concentrate
1/2 cup packed brown sugar

Place cloves and allspice on a double thickness of cheesecloth; bring up corners of cloth and tie with kitchen string to form a bag. Place the remaining ingredients in a large saucepan; add spice bag. Bring to a boil. Reduce heat; cover and simmer for 15-20 minutes. Discard spice bag. **Yield:** 13 servings.

Nutritional Analysis: *One serving (1 cup) equals 129 calories, trace fat (trace saturated fat), 0 cholesterol, 11 mg sodium, 33 g carbohydrate, trace fiber, trace protein.*
Diabetic Exchange: *2 fruit.*
△ **Low-fat**
▲ **Low-sodium**

Orange Sponge Cake Roll

This recipe looks hard, but it isn't. People will think you spent hours working on this pretty cake.
—Michelle Smith, Sykesville, Maryland

  7 egg whites
  1 cup cake flour
1/8 teaspoon salt
  4 egg yolks
3/4 cup sugar
  1 tablespoon grated orange peel
  1 tablespoon lemon juice
1/2 teaspoon vanilla extract
  2 tablespoons confectioners' sugar, *divided*
1-1/4 cups orange marmalade *or* apricot spreadable
    fruit

Let egg whites stand at room temperature for 30 minutes. Sift flour and salt; set aside. Coat a 15-in. x 10-in. x 1-in. baking pan with nonstick cooking spray; line with waxed paper and coat the paper with nonstick cooking spray.

In a mixing bowl, beat yolks until slightly thickened. Gradually add sugar, beating until thick and lemon-colored. Add orange peel, juice and vanilla. Add sifted flour mixture; mix well (batter will be thick). In another mixing bowl, beat egg whites on high speed until soft peaks form; fold into batter.

Spread into prepared pan. Bake at 350° for 12-15 minutes or until cake springs back when lightly touched in center. Cool in pan on a wire rack for 5 minutes. Turn cake onto a kitchen towel dusted with 1 tablespoon confectioners' sugar. Gently peel off waxed paper. Roll up cake in the towel jelly-roll style, starting with a short side. Cool completely on a wire rack.

Unroll cake; spread marmalade evenly over cake to within 1/2 in. of edges. Roll up again. Cover and refrigerate for 1 hour. Sprinkle with remaining confectioners' sugar. **Yield:** 8 servings.

Nutritional Analysis: *One slice equals 230 calories, 3 g fat (1 g saturated fat), 106 mg cholesterol, 89 mg sodium, 46 g carbohydrate, trace fiber, 5 g protein.*
Diabetic Exchanges: *2 starch, 1 fruit.*
△ **Low-fat**
▲ **Low-sodium**

Colorful Caribbean Cuisine

AN APPLE A DAY may keep the doctor away, but for Lee Ann Odell, it was a doctor's advice that changed her life for the better.

"After the birth of my second child, I found myself overweight and not able to lose the extra pounds," Lee Ann says from her home in Boulder, Colorado, where she lives with husband Dan and their two children, Patrick and Shannon.

"While on vacation in Mexico, I met a doctor who gave me some advice that changed my life and helped me shed the excess weight in a healthy, safe and nutritious way. I lost 44 pounds in 7 months simply by making a few changes in the types of food I was eating and by exercising moderately. I am down to my goal weight now and couldn't be happier. Dan has also lost 21 pounds."

The doctor's tips were simple. Lee Ann was advised to go lean on foods that were high in saturated fats and sodium.

"She told me to cut back on red meat...and eliminate fried foods and packaged sweets such as muffins and doughnuts," Lee Ann explains. "And she recommended eating more fruits and vegetables, chicken, fish, beans and whole grains."

Lee Ann began by reading food labels and avoiding anything with hydrogenated vegetable oil, which is high in saturated fat.

"Next, I focused on fresh produce," she says. "I started by eating the things I liked, then I experimented with those I hadn't tried. To season steamed vegetables, I used lemon, chicken broth and low-sodium teriyaki sauce. And I relied more on herbs and seasonings."

At first, Lee Ann made two suppers each day—a low-fat entree for herself, and a separate meal for Dan and the children. "I eventually began preparing healthy food for all of us, and no one seemed to mind," she shares.

Lee Ann combined her new outlook with exercise. "Dan and I like outdoor activities, so I was easily motivated to work out," she notes. "Hiking and biking helped keep the pounds off. And I started doing some yoga exercises as well."

Lee Ann enjoys playing the guitar and learning Spanish when she's not working at the auto shop she and Dan own.

"Looking for nutrition-focused Web sites is another favorite pastime," she adds. "I even started an Internet-based group for mothers trying to lose weight."

One of the meals Lee Ann serves often is a Polynesian-inspired menu. Chock-full of good-for-you fruits and veggies, the meal begins with Tangy Chicken.

"I had some leftover pineapple and decided to cook it with onion, tomato, soy sauce and a hint of brown sugar," she says. The result was a zesty chunky sauce, ideal for chicken and rice.

Simplicity is the key to cooking light for Lee Ann. "I don't mask tastes with heavy sauces, and I use oils sparingly," she says. Such is the case with Oriental Asparagus.

The easy-to-fix stir-fry offers a delightful garlic-orange sauce that keeps the spotlight on vegetables.

"And when it comes to dessert, I depend on pudding and chopped fruit," says Lee Ann. Her Paradise Parfaits, for instance, give fresh fruit, vanilla pudding and crunchy nuts a fun twist with cookie crumbs and coconut.

"This is a favorite with my gang," she confirms. "I'm sure your family will love it as well."

Tangy Chicken

  4 boneless skinless chicken breast halves (4 ounces *each*)
  3 teaspoons olive *or* canola oil, ***divided***
  1/2 small onion, chopped
  3/4 cup canned unsweetened pineapple tidbits, drained
  2 tablespoons reduced-sodium soy sauce
  1 tablespoon ketchup
  1 teaspoon brown sugar
  1 small tomato, chopped
  1 tablespoon minced fresh parsley
Hot cooked rice, optional

In a large nonstick skillet, cook chicken in 1 teaspoon oil for 5-10 minutes or until no longer pink. Remove and keep warm. In the same skillet, saute onion in remaining oil until tender. Add the pineapple, soy sauce, ketchup and brown sugar; bring to a boil. Reduce heat; simmer, uncovered, for 5 minutes.

Add the tomato; simmer 5 minutes longer. Return chicken to the skillet; sprinkle with parsley. Cook for 2-3 minutes or until heated through. Serve over rice if desired. **Yield:** 4 servings.

Nutritional Analysis: One serving (1 chicken breast half with 3 tablespoons sauce, calculated without rice) equals 214 calories, 6 g fat (1 g saturated fat), 67 mg cholesterol, 411 mg sodium, 13 g carbohydrate, 1 g fiber, 26 g protein.
Diabetic Exchanges: 3 lean meat, 1 vegetable, 1/2 fruit.

Oriental Asparagus

  2 tablespoons orange juice
  1 tablespoon white wine vinegar *or* cider vinegar
1-1/2 teaspoons reduced-sodium soy sauce
  1 garlic clove, minced
1/2 teaspoon sesame oil
1/8 teaspoon ground ginger *or* 1/2 teaspoon minced fresh gingerroot
Dash pepper
  1 pound fresh asparagus, trimmed and cut into 2-inch pieces
  1 teaspoon olive *or* canola oil
  6 cherry tomatoes, halved

In a bowl, combine the first seven ingredients. In a non-stick skillet, saute the asparagus in oil until tender, about 7 minutes. Add the orange juice mixture and tomatoes; heat through. **Yield:** 4 servings.

Nutritional Analysis: One serving (1 cup) equals 57 calories, 2 g fat (trace saturated fat), 0 cholesterol, 78 mg sodium, 7 g carbohydrate, 3 g fiber, 3 g protein.
Diabetic Exchanges: 1 vegetable, 1/2 fat.
△ *Low-fat*
▲ *Low-sodium*
▲ *Meatless*

Paradise Parfaits

2 cups cold fat-free milk
1 package (3.4 ounces) instant French vanilla pudding mix
1/4 teaspoon coconut extract
16 reduced-fat vanilla wafers, *divided*
1 medium firm banana, sliced
4 tablespoons chopped walnuts, toasted
1 cup sliced fresh strawberries
3/4 cup halved green grapes
2 tablespoons flaked coconut, toasted

In a bowl, whisk milk and pudding mix for 2 minutes. Whisk in extract. Refrigerate for 5 minutes. Coarsely crush 12 wafers; set aside. In parfait glasses, layer banana slices, half of the cookie crumbs, half of the walnuts and pudding and all of the strawberries. Top with the remaining cookie crumbs and pudding, all of the grapes and remaining nuts. Garnish with toasted coconut and a whole vanilla wafer. Serve immediately. **Yield:** 4 servings.

Nutritional Analysis: One parfait equals 313 calories, 7 g fat (2 g saturated fat), 3 mg cholesterol, 484 mg sodium, 57 g carbohydrate, 2 g fiber, 7 g protein.

The Skinny on Soup

GIVE OLD MAN WINTER the cold shoulder and keep fat and calories at bay with a steaming bowl of soup!

"When trying to trim down, I ate a lot more soup than usual," says Lee Ann Odell. "It filled me up without causing me to overeat.

"Soup is also great for finishing off leftovers such as chicken, and it's an easy way to fit an extra serving of vegetables into your day.

"Stay away from cream-based soups," she suggests. "If you like your soup on the thick side, puree white beans or cooked potatoes and stir the mixture into the broth."

Special Seafood Dinner

COOKING from scratch is Kate Selner's strategy for keeping her family healthy. That's why the St. Paul, Minnesota mom tries to avoid packaged foods when fixing dinner for her husband, Mike, and son, Griffin.

"I grew up enjoying typical comfort food," says Kate. "Over the years, however, it became apparent that I couldn't continue to eat that way without gaining weight.

"When I decided to change my family's meals, I started reading the nutrition labels on packaged goods. Ultimately, I began steering away from mixes and meal-starter kits.

"Instead of using boxed stovetop dinners, I turned flour, a little butter, fat-free milk and seasonings into my own sauces for skillet dishes and casseroles," she explains. "This cut back on calories, fat and salt, and I liked the added benefit of knowing what was in our food.

"Gradually, I began preparing most of our meals with fresh ingredients."

Kate says she's lucky because her gang loves vegetables. "I got out my steamer and put it to good use, cooking with fresh produce whenever possible."

Because she works full-time in the customer service area of a produce company, this busy mother didn't write off convenience items altogether. "I still resort to frozen vegetables at times," she says. "I also buy frozen meatless burgers for quick meals and occasionally use packaged low-salt spice mixes.

"But the majority of things we enjoy are made fresh. We even bake most of the bread we eat."

Kate also makes brownies, cookies and cakes from scratch. "I've found that oil can often be reduced in a recipe by substituting applesauce," she says. "I've also cut back on the number of eggs in some recipes."

When Kate made up her mind to serve her family more nutritious fare, she decided to scale back on meat entrees and use more fish. Maple-Glazed Grilled Salmon has become a popular mainstay at her home.

"My brother-in-law once made a sweet glaze for salmon," she says. "I lightened up a similar recipe."

Grilling gives the salmon palate-pleasing taste and eye-appealing flair, making it perfect for weeknight suppers as well as weekend dinner parties.

Kate's cheesy Au Gratin Red Potatoes are a perfect complement to the salmon. "I loved the creamy potatoes my mother prepared when I was young," she recalls, "so I created this lightened-up version that goes well with any main course."

She rounds out the mouth-watering meal with Fresh Fruit Compote, a colorful medley of apples, strawberries, peaches and pears that simmers in a simple lemon-and-honey sauce.

"Top off servings with low-fat vanilla yogurt, granola or both," she suggests. "It's a wonderful dessert that everyone will enjoy…and it features those good-for-you fruits that will help keep you and your family strong and healthy."

Maple-Glazed Grilled Salmon

    3/4 cup maple syrup
      2 tablespoons ketchup
      1 tablespoon brown sugar
      1 tablespoon cider vinegar
      1 tablespoon Worcestershire sauce
    1/2 teaspoon salt
    1/2 teaspoon ground mustard
    1/8 teaspoon hot pepper sauce
      1 salmon fillet (2 pounds)

In a bowl, combine the first eight ingredients; mix well. Pour 1/2 cup into a large resealable plastic bag; add the salmon. Seal bag and turn to coat; refrigerate for up to 2 hours. Cover and refrigerate remaining marinade.

Before starting the grill, coat grill rack with nonstick cooking spray. Drain and discard marinade from salmon. Grill salmon skin side up over medium-hot heat for 2-4 minutes. Transfer to a double thickness of heavy-duty foil (about 17 in. x 21 in.). Spoon some of the reserved marinade over salmon. Fold foil around fillet and seal tightly. Grill 5-6 minutes longer or until fish flakes easily with a fork. Brush with remaining marinade. **Yield:** 8 servings.

Nutritional Analysis: One serving (4 ounces cooked salmon) equals 254 calories, 12 g fat (2 g saturated fat), 67 mg cholesterol, 179 mg sodium, 12 g carbohydrate, trace fiber, 23 g protein.
Diabetic Exchanges: 3 lean meat, 1 starch.

Au Gratin Red Potatoes

      2 pounds red potatoes, peeled and sliced
      2 cups plus 2 tablespoons fat-free milk, *divided*
      2 garlic cloves, minced
      1 teaspoon dried basil
    3/4 teaspoon salt
    1/4 teaspoon pepper
      3 tablespoons all-purpose flour
    1/2 cup shredded cheddar cheese
    1/4 cup shredded Parmesan cheese
      2 tablespoons toasted wheat germ
    1/2 teaspoon olive *or* canola oil

In a large saucepan, combine the potatoes, 2 cups milk, garlic and seasonings. Bring to a boil. Reduce heat; simmer, uncovered, for 8-10 minutes or until potatoes are tender. With a slotted spoon, remove potatoes to a 1-1/2-qt. baking dish coated with nonstick cooking spray.

In a small bowl, combine flour and remaining milk until smooth; stir into hot milk mixture. Bring to a boil; cook and stir for 2 minutes or until thickened. Remove from the heat; stir in cheddar cheese until melted. Pour over potatoes; sprinkle with Parmesan cheese. Combine wheat germ and oil; sprinkle over the top.

Cover and bake at 375° for 20 minutes. Uncover; bake 5-10 minutes longer or until lightly browned and heated through. Let stand for 10 minutes before serving. **Yield:** 8 servings.

Nutritional Analysis: One serving equals 151 calories, 4 g fat (2 g saturated fat), 11 mg cholesterol, 351 mg sodium, 22 g carbohydrate, 2 g fiber, 8 g protein.
  Diabetic Exchanges: 1-1/2 starch, 1/2 fat.
  ▲ **Meatless**

Fresh Fruit Compote

1/2 medium lemon
1/2 cup water
1/4 cup honey
  2 cups sliced peeled apples
  2 cups sliced peeled peaches
  1 cup sliced peeled pears
1/3 cup 100% apricot spreadable fruit
  2 cups sliced strawberries
  1 cup seedless red grapes
  7 tablespoons reduced-fat vanilla yogurt

Cut two 1-in.-long strips from lemon peel. Squeeze juice from lemon. In a saucepan, combine water, honey, lemon juice and lemon peel strips. Bring to a boil. Reduce heat; cook, uncovered, for 15-20 minutes or until mixture is reduced by two-thirds. Add the apples, peaches and pears; cover and cook for 10-15 minutes or until fruit is softened.

Remove from heat; discard lemon peel. Using a slotted spoon, transfer fruit to a bowl; discard poaching liquid. Stir in spreadable fruit, strawberries and grapes. Cover and refrigerate for 4 hours or overnight. Serve with a slotted spoon. Top each serving with yogurt. **Yield:** 7 servings.

Nutritional Analysis: One serving (3/4 cup fruit mixture with 1 tablespoon yogurt) equals 166 calories, 1 g fat (trace saturated fat), 1 mg cholesterol, 14 mg sodium, 41 g carbohydrate, 4 g fiber, 2 g protein.
  Diabetic Exchange: 2-1/2 fruit.
  △ **Low-fat**
  ▲ **Low-sodium**

🍎 Tempting Tiny Tasters

LIKE most kids, Kate Selner's son, Griffin, isn't always excited to eat what's good for him.

"I give Griffin a small portion and require him to give it a try," says Kate. "When he's sampling a new food, I always tell him that it will taste delicious and by doing so, I feel that he is already thinking it might be true!

"I tell him to close his eyes and take a bite because his mouth will let him know if it's good…and he usually finds that it is."

Plan a Pleasing Pork Supper

THEY SAY that home is where the heart is...and that certainly rings true for Michelle Bishop. "I'm a stay-at-home mom," she says. "But I think I speak for most moms when I say that taking care of little ones is a full-time job."

Michelle and her husband, Fred, live in Peru, Indiana, where they raise their sons, Andrew and Samuel. While Michelle looks after the boys, Fred keeps busy at a local electronics factory.

"I love that I'm able to stay home and take care of our children," Michelle shares. "For me, nothing replaces the joy of watching our sons grow and the comfort of knowing I'm available whenever they need me."

While the boys are happily playing, Michelle likes to indulge in her favorite hobbies—cooking and baking.

"I've always enjoyed spending time in the kitchen," she notes. "One day, however, I realized that I needed to start changing the way I cooked and the things I ate. I decided it would do the entire family good to eat lighter."

"As I began to think about food differently, I re-evaluated our dinners and the way I prepared them," says Michelle. "I took a good look at the fat, calories and sodium in our favorite foods and began to consider healthier choices.

"Things like vegetable oil and butter were soon replaced with olive oil, flavored vinegar, and low-sodium soy sauce and chicken broth. I was happy to learn how much flavor herbs and low-salt spice blends offer," she shares.

Michelle continues to bake once a week, but she made changes in that area, too. "It wasn't hard to bake healthier goodies," she reports. "I reduced the sugar in many recipes and added good-for-you ingredients I hadn't considered before.

"For instance, I now thaw and drain frozen spinach, finely chop it and add it to brownie batter. The kids do not even know it is in there."

Michelle says her family has a great attitude when it comes to sampling her low-fat fare.

"The kids will try anything as long as I give them chopsticks to eat with," she says with a laugh. "They're also more likely to enjoy something if they help prepare it."

Consistently adding to her list of lightened-up recipes eventually led Michelle to the must-try menu shared here.

She begins the meal with moist Pineapple Pork Chops. Marinated in a delightful combination of pineapple, honey mustard and garlic, the entree is simple to prepare and tastes sensational.

"Since we cut back on red meat, the tasty chops and flavorful sauce fit perfectly with our eating plan," Michelle notes.

She relies on fresh rosemary to season Baked Garlic Sweet Potatoes. The herb comes through very well in the unique side dish, and garlic gives the tender potatoes a savory twist.

"Crunchy-Topped Chocolate Cake perfectly caps off this dinner without anyone guessing it's lighter than most desserts," assures the busy mom. Broiling the topping of oats, coconut and nuts creates a crispy texture that nicely complements the tender cake.

"I serve this meal regularly and everyone loves it," Michelle concludes. "I sincerely hope you and your family will enjoy it, too."

Pineapple Pork Chops

  1 can (8 ounces) crushed unsweetened
    pineapple, undrained
  1 tablespoon honey mustard*
  3 garlic cloves, minced
1/4 teaspoon salt
  4 bone-in pork loin chops (7 ounces *each*)
  2 teaspoons canola oil

In a bowl, combine the pineapple, mustard, garlic and salt; mix well. Pour 1/2 cup into a large resealable plastic bag; add the pork chops. Seal bag and turn to coat; refrigerate for up to 24 hours. Cover and refrigerate remaining pineapple mixture.

Drain and discard marinade from pork. In a nonstick skillet, brown chops on both sides in oil over medium heat. Add reserved pineapple mixture; cover and cook over low heat for 8-10 minutes or until juices run clear. **Yield:** 4 servings.

*Editor's Note: As a substitute for honey mustard, combine 1-1/2 teaspoons Dijon mustard and 1-1/2 teaspoons honey.

Nutritional Analysis: One serving (1 pork chop) equals 262 calories, 11 g fat (3 g saturated fat), 87 mg cholesterol, 238 mg sodium, 8 g carbohydrate, trace fiber, 31 g protein.
  Diabetic Exchanges: *4 lean meat, 1/2 fruit, 1/2 fat.*

Baked Garlic Sweet Potatoes

    1 tablespoon olive *or* canola oil
    4 garlic cloves
    1 teaspoon chopped fresh rosemary *or* 1/4
      teaspoon dried rosemary, crushed
  1/2 teaspoon salt
1-1/2 pounds sweet potatoes, peeled and cut into
      3/4-inch chunks
  1/4 cup reduced-sodium chicken broth *or*
      vegetable broth

In a large bowl, combine the oil, garlic, rosemary and salt; add sweet potatoes and toss to coat. Transfer to a 13-in. x 9-in. x 2-in. baking dish coated with nonstick cooking spray. Bake, uncovered, at 350° for 30 minutes. Add broth; bake 10-15 minutes longer or until potatoes are tender, stirring occasionally. **Yield:** 4 servings.

Nutritional Analysis: One serving (3/4 cup) equals 142 calories, 4 g fat (trace saturated fat), 0 cholesterol, 343 mg sodium, 26 g carbohydrate, 3 g fiber, 2 g protein.
  Diabetic Exchanges: *1-1/2 starch, 1/2 fat.*
  ▲ **Meatless**

Crunchy-Topped Chocolate Cake

   1 package (18-1/4 ounces) chocolate cake mix
1-1/4 cups water
   1/3 cup canola oil
   3 egg whites
TOPPING:
   1/2 cup packed brown sugar
   1/3 cup quick-cooking oats
   3 tablespoons cold reduced-fat stick margarine*
   2 tablespoons flaked coconut
   2 tablespoons chopped pecans

In a large mixing bowl, combine cake mix, water, oil and egg whites; beat on low speed for 30 seconds. Beat on medium for 2 minutes. Pour into a broiler-proof 13-in. x 9-in. x 2-in. baking dish coated with nonstick cooking spray. Bake at 350° for 30-35 minutes or until a toothpick inserted near the center comes out clean.

For topping, combine the brown sugar and oats in a bowl; cut in margarine until mixture resembles coarse crumbs. Stir in coconut and pecans; sprinkle over hot cake. Broil 4-6 in. from the heat for 1-2 minutes or until topping is bubbly. Serve warm. **Yield:** 15 servings.

*Editor's Note: This recipe was tested with Parkay Light stick margarine.

Nutritional Analysis: *One piece equals 245 calories, 10 g fat (2 g saturated fat), 0 cholesterol, 244 mg sodium, 37 g carbohydrate, 1 g fiber, 2 g protein.*

Marinating Magic

BEEFING UP flavor without adding much fat, calories or sodium is no trick. For her Pineapple Pork Chops (see recipe on opposite page), Michelle Bishop creates a terrific tropical marinade.

She uses canned pineapple and its juices as an acidic ingredient to tenderize the pork, and then adds garlic and honey mustard for seasoning. A pinch of salt carries flavoring and moisture throughout.

To get the most flavor out of a homemade marinade, use it for marinating and basting. Add a portion of the marinade to the meat and refrigerate the rest. Drain and discard the marinade from the meat when you're ready to cook. Then you can use the reserved marinade to baste the meat and give it an extra flavor boost.

Soup and Salad Delights

THERE'S no doubt about it—Martha Pollock's heart is in cooking healthy. "When my dad underwent a series of heart surgeries years ago, I quickly realized the importance of eating right," says the Maineville, Ohio cook.

"I immediately changed the way I prepared food. And I was happy to find that the longer I practiced light-cooking methods, the more automatic they became…and the more creative I got in the kitchen."

That was more than 10 years ago, and Martha now prepares trimmed-down meals for her husband, Doug, and their sons—Jonathan and David.

"When we got married, Doug had no trouble adapting to my cooking because good taste and texture are as important to me as good nutrition," she says.

"And our children are used to eating healthy because that's all they know. They enjoy an occasional snack, but it's usually low-fat ice cream or homemade banana bread."

Martha says she doesn't buy many packaged baked goods. "Those items often contain a lot of refined sugar or salt," she notes. "I prefer to bake all of our sandwich bread and most of our dinner rolls from scratch.

"I bake with wheat that I process through my miniature flour mill. It's sometimes a challenge to find fresh wheat kernels, and I need to take precautions to freeze the flour properly, but I find it's well worth the effort."

When she's not busy in the kitchen or looking after the little ones, Martha helps Doug with his work as a director of a missionary organization.

"I'm a stay-at-home mom because family is important to me," she explains. "But I can earn a full-time income by assisting Doug with paperwork and ministry projects from our house."

In her free time, Martha likes to sing, cook, jog and attend aerobics classes. "I also participate in a Bible study group, volunteer at our church's nursery program and lend a hand teaching a Sunday-school class for 4-year-olds," she adds.

Even though Martha keeps a busy schedule, she finds time to whip up family dinners that tempt taste buds without piling on the fat, calories or sodium.

"I love soup and serve it often," she says. "My favorite recipe is Broccoli Wild Rice Soup, which I received from my sister. Not only is it delicious, but it comes together quickly and freezes well."

The satisfying dish offers plenty of flavor while taking advantage of fat-free cream cheese and convenient canned soup, frozen broccoli and wild rice mix for easy preparation. Try it alongside Garden Salad with Lemon Dressing.

"I lightened up a tangy salad dressing by replacing some of the oil with lemon juice," Martha says. The revamped dressing lends a refreshing twist to mixed greens, tomatoes, pepper rings and cucumber slices.

In another of her trimmed-down delights, Martha relies on applesauce to keep crowd-pleasing Cran-Apple

Walnut Cake tender and moist.

"The blend of nuts, cranberries and apples complements the subtle hint of wheat flour for a terrific taste," she adds.

You'd never guess the mouth-watering treats are lower in fat and calories than other snack cakes, making them an ideal conclusion to Martha's sensational soup and salad supper.

Broccoli Wild Rice Soup

- 5 cups water
- 1 package (6 ounces) long grain and wild rice mix*
- 1 can (10-3/4 ounces) reduced-fat reduced-sodium cream of chicken soup, undiluted
- 1-1/2 cups 1% milk
- 1 package (8 ounces) fat-free cream cheese, cubed
- 1/4 teaspoon salt
- 1 package (10 ounces) frozen chopped broccoli, thawed
- 1 large carrot, shredded
- 1/4 cup sliced almonds, toasted

In a large saucepan, combine the water and rice mix with contents of seasoning packet; bring to a boil. Reduce heat; cover and simmer for 20 minutes. Add the soup, milk, cream cheese and salt; stir until cheese is melted. Add broccoli and carrot; cook over medium-low heat for 5-6 minutes or until vegetables and rice are tender. Garnish with almonds. **Yield:** 6 servings.

*Editor's Note: This recipe was tested with Uncle Ben's Original Long Grain and Wild Rice Mix.

Nutritional Analysis: One serving (1-1/2 cups) equals 232 calories, 5 g fat (1 g saturated fat), 10 mg cholesterol, 927 mg sodium, 35 g carbohydrate, 3 g fiber, 14 g protein.

Diabetic Exchanges: 1-1/2 starch, 1 vegetable, 1 lean meat, 1/2 fat-free milk.

Garden Salad with Lemon Dressing

- 8 cups torn salad greens
- 1 cup grape *or* cherry tomatoes
- 1 medium cucumber, sliced
- 1 large sweet yellow *or* green pepper, cut into rings
- 1/4 cup lemon juice
- 4 teaspoons honey
- 2 teaspoons minced chives
- 1 teaspoon ground mustard
- 1/2 teaspoon salt
- 1/4 teaspoon pepper
- 2 tablespoons olive *or* canola oil

In a large bowl, combine salad greens, tomatoes, cucumber and pepper rings. In a small bowl, whisk the lemon juice, honey, chives, mustard, salt and pepper until blended. Gradually whisk in oil until dressing thickens. Drizzle over salad; toss to coat. **Yield:** 4 servings.

Nutritional Analysis: One serving (2 cups) equals 143 calories, 8 g fat (1 g saturated fat), 0 cholesterol, 328 mg sodium, 19 g carbohydrate, 5 g fiber, 4 g protein.
    Diabetic Exchanges: 3 vegetable, 1-1/2 fat.
    ▲ **Meatless**

Cran-Apple Walnut Cake

    1 egg
    2 egg whites
1-3/4 cups packed brown sugar
    1/4 cup canola oil
    1/4 cup unsweetened applesauce
    1 teaspoon vanilla extract
    1 cup all-purpose flour
    1 cup whole wheat flour
    1 teaspoon baking soda
    1 teaspoon salt
    1 teaspoon ground cinnamon
    1/2 teaspoon ground nutmeg
    2 cups chopped peeled apples
    2 cups fresh cranberries, halved
    1/2 cup chopped walnuts
    2 teaspoons confectioners' sugar

In a mixing bowl, beat the egg, egg whites, brown sugar, oil, applesauce and vanilla. Combine the dry ingredients; stir into applesauce mixture just until blended. Fold in the apples, cranberries and walnuts. Pour into a 13-in. x 9-in. x 2-in. baking dish coated with nonstick cooking spray. Bake at 350° for 35-40 minutes or until a toothpick inserted near the center comes out clean. Cool on a wire rack. Dust with confectioners' sugar. **Yield:** 15 servings.

Nutritional Analysis: One piece equals 248 calories, 7 g fat (1 g saturated fat), 14 mg cholesterol, 262 mg sodium, 44 g carbohydrate, 3 g fiber, 4 g protein.

🍎 Flavorful Flair for Fun

EVEN THOUGH her gang is happy with her calorie-conscious cooking and health-minded meals, Martha Pollock still keeps a few tricks up her apron sleeve to ensure that everyone is eating right.

"I find that spinach is quickly gobbled up when it's wrapped in a tortilla with lean sandwich fixings," she says. "I also dice fresh spinach to garnish the top of homemade pizzas…and to mix into my filling for large pasta shells."

When snack time comes around, Martha gets on a roll. "My sons enjoy all kinds of melon," she says, "but they're sure to finish their helping when I use a melon baller to turn the fresh fruit into kid-friendly finger food."

Slimmed-Down Southern Meal

WHEN she's not cross-stitching or working on scrapbooks, you might find Dawn Harvey in her Bloomsburg, Pennsylvania kitchen lightening up a family favorite. But the stay-at-home mom acknowledges that cooking wasn't always a hobby.

"My mother is the best cook I've ever known," shares Dawn. "I grew up in Alabama and enjoyed the tasty Southern meals she made, but I never learned how to fix them myself.

"When I married Brad and moved to his home state of Pennsylvania, I had to quickly learn how to prepare my mom's dishes as well as the dishes Brad grew up eating.

"After I had our son, Colton, I wanted to lose weight, but I didn't want to try another diet. So I decided to change the way I cook and the way I eat," Dawn notes.

"By trimming fat and calories from our favorites and by watching portion sizes, we can eat healthier while still enjoying the comforting foods from our childhood."

When Dawn set out to revamp her menus, she received a few tips from her favorite cook…her mother.

"Just as I began to change our eating habits, my parents decided to lighten up their meals, too," she says.

"My mother shared invaluable pointers with me, explaining that one of the most important tools in a health-conscious kitchen is good-quality nonstick cookware," reports Dawn.

"She bought me my first nonstick skillet so I could fry meats with a very small amount of oil or butter. I also do all of my sauteing with nonstick cooking sprays instead of oil," she adds.

"Another trick I learned is to turn pan-fried meats with tongs or a spatula. This helps keep them moist compared to piercing items with a fork to turn them, which allows juices to escape.

"I do try to limit our servings of meat. When preparing stews and casseroles, for instance, I increase the vegetables and use smaller amounts of meat."

Dawn has been very successful reducing the fat, calories and sodium in regional recipes. Here, she shares a satisfying Southern entree of Pecan Parmesan Chicken.

"In the South, we love our fried chicken and we also love pecans," she relates. "This is my favorite way to combine the two." Dawn treats moist chicken breasts to a crunchy coating of pecans, Parmesan cheese, basil and oregano.

"To lighten the original dish, I replaced the egg yolks with egg whites and reduced the amount of nuts, cheese and bread crumbs," Dawn notes.

Eye-appealing Italian Mixed Vegetables is the ideal accompaniment to the chicken entree—or most any main course. Bottled salad dressing and herbs dress up frozen vegetables, making this a great stovetop side dish for hurried weeknights.

Dessert consists of a luscious longtime favorite. "I've enjoyed my mother's Warm Banana Pudding for as long as I can remember," shares Dawn. "She and I revised it, using a sugar substitute and reduced-fat ingredients.

"With its meringue-like top and soft vanilla wafer layer, it's a Southern dessert at its finest," Dawn concludes. "I hope your family will love it as much as mine does."

Pecan Parmesan Chicken

6 boneless skinless chicken breast halves (4 ounces *each*)
1-1/2 cups soft bread crumbs
1/3 cup grated Parmesan cheese
1/3 cup ground pecans
1 teaspoon dried oregano
1/2 teaspoon seasoned salt
1/2 teaspoon dried basil
1/4 teaspoon pepper
2 teaspoons cornstarch
2 egg whites
1 tablespoon olive *or* canola oil

Flatten chicken to 1/2-in. thickness. In a shallow bowl, combine the bread crumbs, Parmesan cheese, pecans, oregano, salt, basil and pepper. In another bowl, beat the cornstarch and egg whites. Dip chicken into egg white mixture, then coat with crumb mixture.

In a large nonstick skillet over medium heat, brown chicken in oil for 3-5 minutes on each side. Transfer to an ungreased 15-in. x 10-in. x 1-in. baking pan. Bake, uncovered, at 450° for 8-10 minutes or until juices run clear. **Yield:** 6 servings.

Nutritional Analysis: *One serving (1 chicken breast half) equals 238 calories, 10 g fat (2 g saturated fat), 66 mg cholesterol, 342 mg sodium, 8 g carbohydrate, 1 g fiber, 27 g protein.*
Diabetic Exchanges: *3 lean meat, 1/2 fat, 1/2 starch.*

Italian Mixed Vegetables

1 package (24 ounces) frozen California blend vegetables
1/4 cup water
1/4 cup reduced-fat Italian salad dressing
1/4 teaspoon salt
1/4 teaspoon dried basil
1/8 teaspoon dried oregano

In a large nonstick skillet, bring vegetables and water to a boil. Cover and cook for 10-12 minutes or until vegetables are crisp-tender. Uncover; cook and stir until liquid is reduced. Add the salad dressing, salt, basil and oregano. Cook and stir until heated through. **Yield:** 6 servings.

Nutritional Analysis: *One serving (3/4 cup) equals 51 calories, 1 g fat (trace saturated fat), trace cholesterol, 214 mg sodium, 6 g carbohydrate, 3 g fiber, 3 g protein.*
Diabetic Exchange: *1 vegetable.*
△ **Low-fat**
▲ **Meatless**

Warm Banana Pudding

Sugar substitute equivalent to 1/2 cup sugar
1/2 cup sugar, *divided*
   3 tablespoons cornstarch
   2 cups fat-free milk
   2 eggs, *separated*
   2 tablespoons reduced-fat stick margarine
   1 teaspoon vanilla extract
   2 large ripe bananas, sliced
   1 teaspoon lemon juice
  12 reduced-fat vanilla wafers

In the top of a double boiler, combine the sugar substitute, 1/4 cup sugar and cornstarch. Gradually stir in milk until smooth. Bring to a boil, stirring constantly. Cook and stir over simmering water until thickened. Remove from the heat. Stir a small amount of hot filling into egg yolks; return all to the pan, stirring constantly. Bring to a gentle boil; cook and stir for 2 minutes. Remove from the heat; stir in margarine and vanilla.

Pour half of the pudding into an ungreased 1-qt. baking dish. Toss bananas with lemon juice; layer over pudding. Arrange vanilla wafers in a single layer over bananas. Pour remaining pudding over wafers.

In a mixing bowl, beat egg whites on medium speed until soft peaks form. Beat in remaining sugar, 1 tablespoon at a time, on high until stiff peaks form. Spread evenly over pudding. Bake, uncovered, at 350° for 12-15 minutes or until golden brown. Refrigerate leftovers. **Yield:** 6 servings.

Editor's Note: This recipe uses both sugar and sugar substitute. It was tested with Splenda No Calorie Sweetener and Parkay Light stick margarine.

Nutritional Analysis: One serving equals 239 calories, 5 g fat (1 g saturated fat), 72 mg cholesterol, 116 mg sodium, 45 g carbohydrate, 1 g fiber, 6 g protein.
   Diabetic Exchanges: 2 starch, 1 fruit, 1 fat.
  ▲ *Low-sodium*

A Successful Strategy

WHEN Dawn Harvey decided to eat healthier, she formulated a plan. "I wanted to change my eating habits all at once, and the easiest way for me to do that was to create a weekly menu," she explains.

"By writing down everything I planned to eat for the upcoming week, I was less likely to purchase snacks and prepare meals that didn't fit my goal.

"The plan also helped ensure I ate something from each of the food groups every day," Dawn says. "I consumed more vegetables and fruit than I would have otherwise."

A Breakfast Beyond Compare

WORKING OUT, cooking light and eating healthy help Nicki Woods stay fit. But getting into shipshape wasn't high on her list of priorities until a few years ago.

"I wanted to lose about 5 pounds before my husband, Jeff, and I went on a cruise with friends," explains the Springfield, Missouri mother of two. "I gave up soda, fast food and red meat, and started doing exercises—stomach crunches and jumping jacks in the evening. I lost nearly 15 pounds right off the bat," Nicki says.

"Shortly after we returned from our vacation, I ordered a cheeseburger and fries from a fast-food restaurant. The food left such a bad taste in my mouth that I have not eaten fried food or red meat since.

"Now, I run about 70 miles each week, and Jeff and I lift weights every other day," Nicki notes. "I also like to bike and hike the beautiful trails in the Ozark Mountains with our son, Colton, and daughter, Kyra."

"At first, I prepared two separate dinners—a traditional one for my family and a lighter version for me. Then, over the course of a few months, I introduced healthy foods into their meals.

"I asked Jeff and the kids to take at least three bites of anything new," she says. "If they didn't like it, they didn't have to finish it, but they usually cleared their plates. Now, we all enjoy nutritious meals."

Nicki relies on her grill and oven nightly. "Grilling and roasting add flavor without fat," she notes. "I grill everything from chicken to fish to bread to pizza. I also use the oven frequently. For a tasty side dish, I just chop vegetables and put them in to roast."

Making sure her family gets enough nutrients is also important to her. "I sneak fiber into their diets by grinding Fiber One bran cereal into a powder," she explains. "Then I use the powder to replace some of the flour in homemade pizza crust dough, chicken breading and pancakes."

When she's not studying to earn a master's degree in education or working at a local law firm, you'll likely find Nicki in the kitchen trimming down recipes from her mother and grandmother.

"Rather than give up these family favorites, I did some homework, experimented and learned how to make them healthy while keeping their good flavor," she says. Such is the case with the breakfast menu she shares here.

Nicki starts the meal with Special Brunch Bake, an eye-opener featuring buttermilk biscuits. "If you don't have Canadian bacon, try it with turkey bacon or ham," she suggests.

For a colorful addition to the meal, Nicki blends up a batch of Raspberry Cream Smoothies. Frozen raspberries and banana chunks give the refreshing beverages plenty of frosty fruit flavor.

The health-conscious cook rounds out this brunch with soft chewy Cranberry Breakfast Pretzels. The tasty twists have a cinnamon-sugar topping and bits of bright cranberries throughout.

Special Brunch Bake

- 2 tubes (4 ounces *each*) refrigerated buttermilk biscuits
- 3 cartons (8 ounces *each*) frozen egg substitute, thawed
- 7 ounces Canadian bacon, chopped
- 1 cup (4 ounces) shredded reduced-fat cheddar cheese
- 1 cup (4 ounces) shredded reduced-fat mozzarella cheese
- 1/2 cup chopped fresh mushrooms
- 1/2 cup finely chopped onion
- 1/4 teaspoon pepper

Arrange biscuits in a 13-in. x 9-in. x 2-in. baking dish coated with nonstick cooking spray. In a bowl, combine the remaining ingredients; pour over biscuits. Bake, uncovered, at 350° for 30-35 minutes or until a knife inserted near the center comes out clean. **Yield:** 12 servings.

Nutritional Analysis: One serving (1 biscuit section) equals 160 calories, 5 g fat (3 g saturated fat), 20 mg cholesterol, 616 mg sodium, 13 g carbohydrate, 1 g fiber, 15 g protein.
Diabetic Exchanges: 2 lean meat, 1 starch.

Raspberry Cream Smoothies

- 2 cups orange juice
- 2 cups fat-free reduced-sugar raspberry yogurt
- 2 cups frozen vanilla yogurt
- 2 small ripe bananas, cut into chunks and frozen (1 cup)
- 3 cups frozen raspberries
- 2 teaspoons vanilla extract

In a blender or food processor, cover and process the ingredients in batches until blended. Stir if necessary. Pour into chilled glasses; serve immediately. **Yield:** 6 servings.

Nutritional Analysis: One serving (1 cup) equals 198 calories, 1 g fat (1 g saturated fat), 5 mg cholesterol, 98 mg sodium, 40 g carbohydrate, 2 g fiber, 7 g protein.
Diabetic Exchanges: 2 fruit, 1 fat-free milk.
△ *Low-fat*
▲ *Low-sodium*

Cranberry Breakfast Pretzels

- 3/4 cup dried cranberries
- 1/3 cup unsweetened applesauce
- 2 tablespoons sugar, *divided*
- 1 package (1/4 ounce) active dry yeast
- 1 cup warm fat-free milk (110° to 115°)
- 3 tablespoons canola oil
- 1-1/2 teaspoons salt
- 3-1/2 to 4 cups all-purpose flour
- 2 quarts water

TOPPING:
    1 egg white, beaten
    1/2 teaspoon ground cinnamon
    1 tablespoon sugar
Honey *or* cream cheese, optional

In a food processor or blender, place the dried cranberries, applesauce and 1 tablespoon sugar; cover and process until finely chopped. Set aside. In a mixing bowl, dissolve yeast in warm milk. Add the remaining sugar; let stand for 5 minutes. Add the cranberry mixture, oil, salt and enough flour to form a soft dough. Turn onto a lightly floured surface; knead until smooth and elastic, about 6-8 minutes. Place in a bowl coated with nonstick cooking spray, turning once to coat the top. Cover and let rise in a warm place until doubled, about 1-1/2 hours.

Punch dough down. Turn onto a floured surface. Divide dough into 15 balls. Roll each ball into a 14-in. rope and form into a pretzel shape.

In a large saucepan, bring water to a boil. Drop pretzels, one at a time into water; boil for 10 seconds on each side. Remove with a slotted spoon; drain on paper towels.

Place pretzels on baking sheets coated with nonstick cooking spray. Cover and let rise in a warm place until puffy, about 25 minutes. Brush with egg white. Combine cinnamon and sugar; sprinkle over tops. Bake at 375° for 12-14 minutes or until golden brown. Serve with honey or cream cheese if desired. **Yield:** 15 servings.

Nutritional Analysis: One pretzel equals 170 calories, 3 g fat (trace saturated fat), trace cholesterol, 248 mg sodium, 31 g carbohydrate, 1 g fiber, 4 g protein.
   Diabetic Exchange: 2 starch.
   △ *Low-fat*
   ▲ *Meatless*

🍎 Nutrition Know-How

IF you're looking to eat healthier, take a tip from Nicki Woods. "For one week, read Nutrition Facts panels on the foods you eat. Then record your fat, calorie and sodium intake," she suggests.

"I did, and I was amazed at how many items that I thought were good for me were jam-packed with anything-but-healthy ingredients. I was also surprised to learn what was considered a serving size.

"If you can't find the nutritional information on items such as produce or deli meats, ask the supermarket management for it," says Nicki. "There are also hundreds of resources in the library and on the Internet that offer this information.

"When the week is over, you'll have learned a lot about the foods you buy and your own eating habits."

Trimmed-Down Dishes for Two

Turn to this chapter if you're cooking for just two and neither of you cares to eat leftovers. These lighter recipes yield smaller quantities without sacrificing flavor.

Tarragon Turkey Patties and Zucchini Tomato Toss (page 270)

Berries with Banana Cream

This yummy dessert is just the thing for spring! The airy banana-orange cream and a hint of spice nicely complement the fresh berries.
—Kari Caven, Post Falls, Idaho

1-1/2 cups sliced fresh strawberries
1/2 cup fresh *or* frozen blueberries
1/3 cup reduced-fat sour cream
1/3 cup sliced ripe banana
1 tablespoon orange juice concentrate
1 teaspoon sugar
1/8 teaspoon ground cinnamon

Divide the berries between two serving bowls. In a blender, combine the sour cream, banana, orange juice concentrate and sugar; cover and process until smooth. Spoon over berries. Sprinkle with cinnamon. **Yield:** 2 servings.

Nutritional Analysis: One serving equals 156 calories, 4 g fat (3 g saturated fat), 13 mg cholesterol, 30 mg sodium, 28 g carbohydrate, 5 g fiber, 4 g protein.
Diabetic Exchanges: *2 fruit, 1/2 fat.*
△ **Low-sodium**

Berry Turkey Sandwich

(Pictured below)

Sliced fresh strawberries, Swiss cheese and a nutty cream cheese spread make this turkey sandwich different. It's tasty and easy to put together.
—Edward Meyer, Arnold, Missouri

4 slices whole wheat bread
2 lettuce leaves
2 slices reduced-fat Swiss cheese
1/4 pound thinly sliced deli turkey breast
4 fresh strawberries, sliced
2 tablespoons reduced-fat whipped cream cheese spread
2 teaspoons finely chopped pecans

On two slices of bread, layer the lettuce, cheese, turkey and strawberries. Combine cream cheese and pecans; spread over remaining bread. Place over strawberries. Serve immediately. **Yield:** 2 servings.

Nutritional Analysis: One sandwich equals 356 calories, 10 g fat (3 g saturated fat), 39 mg cholesterol, 932 mg sodium, 39 g carbohydrate, 5 g fiber, 28 g protein.
Diabetic Exchanges: *3 lean meat, 2-1/2 starch.*

Summer Squash Bundles

We love zucchini, and my husband enjoys cooking summer meals on the grill, so I came up with this idea to add to our outdoor dining menu.
—Juanita Daugherty, Cadet, Missouri

1 green onion
1 medium yellow squash (6 to 8 inches long)
1 medium zucchini (6 to 8 inches long)
1/4 cup chopped leek (white portion only)
2 tablespoons grated Parmesan cheese
2 teaspoons Italian seasoning
2 teaspoons butter *or* stick margarine, melted
1/4 teaspoon salt

Remove white portion of green onion (discard or save for another use). Trim the onion top to 8- or 9-in. lengths. In a saucepan, bring water to a boil. Add onion tops; boil for 1 minute or until softened. Drain and immediately place in ice water. Drain and pat dry; set aside.

Cut squash and zucchini in half lengthwise. Scoop out pulp from zucchini halves, leaving a 3/8-in. shell. Discard pulp. In a bowl, combine remaining ingredients; fill zucchini shells. Place yellow squash halves, cut side down, over filled zucchini halves. Tie each bundle with a blanched onion top.

Wrap each bundle in a double thickness of heavy-duty foil (12 in. square). Fold foil around squash and seal tightly. Grill, covered, over medium heat for 15-20 minutes or until tender. **Yield:** 2 servings.

Nutritional Analysis: One serving (one squash bundle) equals 114 calories, 6 g fat (3 g saturated fat), 14 mg cholesterol, 439 mg sodium, 12 g carbohydrate, 5 g fiber, 6 g protein.
Diabetic Exchanges: *2 vegetable, 1 fat.*
▲ **Meatless**

Ginger Apple Fizz

This refreshing hot-weather drink is a nice change of pace. It's not as sweet as regular sodas.
—Kimberly Wood, Caddo Mills, Texas

1/4 cup apple juice concentrate
1/8 teaspoon ground ginger
2 cups chilled club soda
Ice cubes

In a pitcher, combine apple juice concentrate and ginger. Slowly stir in soda. Serve over ice. **Yield:** 2 servings.

Nutritional Analysis: One serving (1 cup) equals 59 calories, trace fat (trace saturated fat), 0 cholesterol, 59 mg sodium, 15 g carbohydrate, trace fiber, trace protein.
Diabetic Exchange: *1 fruit.*
△ **Low-fat**
▲ **Low-sodium**

Tarragon Turkey Patties

(Pictured on page 268)

These ground turkey patties are excellent with rice or riced potatoes and a green vegetable for a quick supper.
—Lois Kinneberg, Phoenix, Arizona

1/2 cup crushed corn bread stuffing
1/4 cup egg substitute
  2 tablespoons minced fresh tarragon *or* 2 teaspoons dried tarragon
1/4 teaspoon pepper
1/2 pound lean ground turkey
TARRAGON-MUSTARD SAUCE:
  1 cup reduced-sodium chicken broth
  2 tablespoons minced fresh tarragon *or* 2 teaspoons dried tarragon
1-1/2 teaspoons Dijon mustard

In a bowl, combine the stuffing, egg substitute, tarragon and pepper. Crumble turkey over mixture and mix well. Shape into four patties. In a nonstick skillet coated with nonstick cooking spray, cook patties over medium heat for 4 minutes on each side or until juices run clear and a meat thermometer reads 165°. Remove and keep warm.

For sauce, add the broth, tarragon and mustard to the skillet; bring to a boil. Reduce heat; simmer, uncovered, for 5 minutes or until reduced by three-fourths. Serve with turkey patties. **Yield:** 2 servings.

Nutritional Analysis: One serving (2 patties with 2 tablespoons sauce) equals 259 calories, 10 g fat (3 g saturated fat), 90 mg cholesterol, 830 mg sodium, 13 g carbohydrate, 1 g fiber, 27 g protein.
Diabetic Exchanges: 3 lean meat, 1 starch.

Zucchini Tomato Toss

(Pictured on page 268)

Tomatoes, zucchini, green pepper and onion are seasoned with garlic and parsley in this side dish.
—Kathy Fielder, Dallas, Texas

1/4 cup chopped green pepper
  1 medium zucchini, cut into 1/4-inch slices
  1 small onion, thinly sliced and separated into rings
  1 garlic clove, minced
  1 teaspoon olive *or* canola oil
  2 small plum tomatoes, peeled and cut into wedges
1/2 teaspoon salt
Dash pepper
  1 tablespoon minced fresh parsley

In a nonstick skillet, saute green pepper, zucchini, onion and garlic in oil for 3-4 minutes or until crisp-tender. Add tomatoes, salt and pepper. Reduce heat to low; cover and cook until heated through. Sprinkle with parsley. **Yield:** 2 servings.

Nutritional Analysis: One serving (3/4 cup) equals 59 calories, 3 g fat (trace saturated fat), 0 cholesterol, 597 mg sodium, 9 g carbohydrate, 3 g fiber, 2 g protein.
Diabetic Exchanges: 1 vegetable, 1/2 fat.
△ **Low-fat**
▲ **Meatless**

Toasted Veggie Sandwich

Best when made with fresh garden ingredients, this sandwich is low in fat, packed with vitamins. It's a meal by itself.
—Gail Nonamaker, Saluda, North Carolina

  1 teaspoon fat-free mayonnaise
  1 teaspoon spicy brown *or* horseradish mustard
  2 slices rye bread
  1 slice (1 ounce) reduced-fat Swiss cheese, cut in half
  3 tablespoons grated carrot
  1 tablespoon finely chopped onion
  2 tablespoons sauerkraut, well drained and chopped
1/2 cup thinly sliced fresh spinach
Refrigerated butter-flavored spray*

Spread mayonnaise and mustard on each slice of bread. On one piece of bread, layer a half slice of cheese, carrot, onion, sauerkraut, spinach and remaining cheese. Cover with second piece of bread. Spray both sides of sandwich with refrigerated butter-flavored spray. In a small nonstick skillet, toast sandwich over medium heat until bread is browned on both sides. **Yield:** 1 serving.

***Editor's Note:** This recipe was tested with I Can't Believe It's Not Butter spray.*

Nutritional Analysis: One sandwich equals 290 calories, 9 g fat (5 g saturated fat), 19 mg cholesterol, 727 mg sodium, 37 g carbohydrate, 5 g fiber, 15 g protein.
Diabetic Exchanges: 2 starch, 1 vegetable, 1 lean meat, 1 fat.
▲ **Meatless**

Shrimp Creole

Our Test Kitchen staff came up with this recipe for shrimp simmered in a well-seasoned tomato mixture.

1/2 cup chopped green pepper
1/2 cup chopped onion
  1 celery rib, chopped
  1 garlic clove, minced
  2 teaspoons canola oil
  1 cup clam juice *or* chicken broth
1/4 cup tomato paste
  2 tablespoons minced fresh parsley
1/2 teaspoon seafood seasoning
1/2 teaspoon dried thyme
1/4 teaspoon pepper
1/8 to 1/4 teaspoon cayenne pepper
1/2 pound uncooked medium shrimp, peeled and deveined
Hot cooked rice

In a large nonstick skillet, saute the green pepper, onion, celery and garlic in oil until tender. In a small bowl, combine the clam juice or broth and tomato paste; add to the pan along with parsley and seasonings. Bring to a boil. Reduce heat; simmer, uncovered, for 15-20 minutes or until slightly thickened. Stir in shrimp; cook 5 minutes more or until shrimp turn pink. Serve over rice. **Yield:** 2 servings.

Nutritional Analysis: One serving (1 cup shrimp mixture, calculated without rice) equals 228 calories, 7 g fat (1 g saturated fat), 176 mg cholesterol, 640 mg sodium, 15 g carbohydrate, 3 g fiber, 27 g protein.
Diabetic Exchanges: 3 very lean meat, 3 vegetable, 1 fat.

Crispy Potato Wedges

Pass on the high-calorie french fries and opt for the tasty potato wedges our Test Kitchen home economists cooked up instead! Baked until crispy, the potatoes are zesty and satisfying.

1 teaspoon paprika
1 teaspoon dried parsley flakes
1/4 teaspoon onion salt
1/8 teaspoon pepper
2 medium potatoes, cut into wedges
Refrigerated butter-flavored spray*

In a resealable plastic bag, combine the paprika, parsley, onion salt and pepper. Spritz potato wedges with butter-flavored spray; place in the bag, a few at a time, and shake to coat. Arrange in a single layer on an ungreased baking sheet. Bake at 450° for 25-30 minutes or until tender. **Yield:** 2 servings.

*Editor's Note: This recipe was tested with I Can't Believe It's Not Butter Spray.

Nutritional Analysis: One serving equals 105 calories, trace fat (trace saturated fat), 0 cholesterol, 228 mg sodium, 27 g carbohydrate, 3 g fiber, 4 g protein.
Diabetic Exchange: 1-1/2 starch.
△ **Low-fat**
▲ **Meatless**

Baked Cod

(Pictured at right)

These fish fillets are quick to fix…and they bake in no time! Brushed with ranch salad dressing and coated with seasoned stuffing crumbs and parsley, the cod fillets are moist and flavorful. Our Test Kitchen sized the recipe just right to feed two.

1 cup seasoned stuffing croutons, crushed
1 tablespoon minced fresh parsley
2 cod fillets (about 6 ounces *each*)
1 tablespoon reduced-fat ranch salad dressing
Refrigerated butter-flavored spray*

In a shallow bowl, combine the crushed croutons and parsley. Brush cod with salad dressing, then coat with crumb mixture. Spritz with butter-flavored spray. Place in an 11-in. x 7-in. x 2-in. baking dish coated with nonstick cooking spray. Bake, uncovered, at 400° for 10-15 minutes or until fish flakes easily with a fork. **Yield:** 2 servings.

*Editor's Note: This recipe was tested with I Can't Believe It's Not Butter Spray.

Nutritional Analysis: One fillet equals 244 calories, 5 g fat (1 g saturated fat), 75 mg cholesterol, 423 mg sodium, 15 g carbohydrate, 1 g fiber, 33 g protein.
Diabetic Exchanges: 4 very lean meat, 1 starch, 1/2 fat.

Creamed Celery and Peas

(Pictured below)

Garden-variety peas really shine in this simple side dish. Dressed up with sauteed celery and a creamy white sauce, the peas are a perfect way to round out a meaty main course.
—*Evelyn Kennell, Roanoke, Illinois*

1 celery rib with leaves, chopped
1 teaspoon butter *or* stick margarine
1 cup frozen peas, thawed
1/4 cup reduced-fat sour cream
2 tablespoons fat-free milk
1 tablespoon minced fresh parsley
Dash white pepper

In a nonstick skillet, saute celery in butter for 6-8 minutes or until tender. Stir in peas; cook 3-4 minutes longer, stirring often. Add sour cream, milk, parsley and pepper; reduce heat. Cook and stir until heated through and blended. **Yield:** 2 servings.

Nutritional Analysis: One serving (1/2 cup) equals 127 calories, 5 g fat (3 g saturated fat), 16 mg cholesterol, 154 mg sodium, 14 g carbohydrate, 4 g fiber, 7 g protein.
Diabetic Exchanges: 1 starch, 1 fat.
▲ **Meatless**

General Recipe Index

This handy index lists every recipe by food category, major ingredient and/or cooking method, so you can easily locate recipes to suit your needs.

Alphabetical Index

*This handy index lists every recipe in alphabetical order
so you can easily find your favorite dish.*

Lentil Pepperoni Stew, 122
Light Guacamole, 30
Light Linguine Carbonara, 153
Light Pesto, 85
Lime Bean Medley, 85
Lo Mein Noodles, 93
Luscious Lime Angel Squares, 223

M

Mahogany Devil's Food Cake, 242
Makeover Almond Rhubarb Coffee
    Cake, 195
Makeover Au Gratin Hash
    Browns, 89
Makeover Butter Roasted
    Chicken, 143
Makeover Cranberry Pecan
    Scones, 203
Makeover Crispy Oat Cookies, 217
Makeover Four-Cheese Chicken
    Fettuccine, 133
Makeover Holiday Pumpkin
    Bread, 199
Makeover Honey French
    Dressing, 69
Makeover Pizza Pasta Salad, 63
Makeover Ranch Ham 'n' Cheese
    Pasta, 155
Makeover Strawberry Pretzel
    Dessert, 225
Makeover White Layer Cake, 233
Mandarin Couscous Salad, 72
Mandarin Orange Chicken
    Salad, 45
Mango Lemon Sorbet, 230
Maple-Glazed Grilled Salmon, 258
Maple Pumpkin Pie, 228
Marinated Plum Tomatoes, 244
Marinated Steak, 112
Marvelous Melon, 61
Mazurka, 226
Meatballs with Bean Sauce, 111
Mediterranean Herb Rub, 84
Mediterranean Pasta Salad, 68
Mexican Pizza, 145
Mexican-Style Stuffed Peppers, 116
Mexican Vegetable Pizza, 181
Minestrone Pasta Salad, 65
Minestrone Soup, 38
Mini Shrimp Rolls, 28
Mixed Berry Shortcake, 246
Mocha Dream Cake, 219
Montego Bay Chicken, 130
Mostaccioli Bake, 185
Mulled Cran-Apple Juice, 255
Mushroom Zucchini Lasagna, 180

N

No-Bake Chocolate
    Cheesecake, 206

O

Old-Fashioned Corn Relish, 77
Onion Bulgur Salad, 57
Onion-Rubbed Flank Steak, 110
Open-Face Tuna Melts, 177
Orange Chicken Salad, 58
Orange Cream Pops, 24
Orange Pecan Muffins, 193
Orange Rosemary Sorbet, 216
Orange Spiced Cider, 18
Orange Sponge Cake Roll, 255
Orange Tea Cake, 214
Oriental Asparagus, 256
Oriental Turkey Pitas, 135
Orzo Chicken Soup, 42
Oven Barbecued Chicken, 141
Oven-Roasted Root Vegetables, 94
Overnight Spinach Manicotti, 190
Overnight Vegetable Salad, 56

P

Paradise Parfaits, 257
Parmesan Catfish, 172
Parsley Pesto Spaghetti, 76
Pea Pod Carrot Medley, 93
Peach Angel Dessert, 232
Peanut Butter Pudding, 206
Peanut-Crusted Orange
    Roughy, 168
Pecan Parmesan Chicken, 264
Penne with Veggies 'n' Black
    Beans, 180
Pepper Potato Gratin, 83
Peppered Cilantro Rice, 91
Pepperoni Ziti Casserole, 119
Peppery Beef Stir-Fry, 110
Pineapple Almond Bars, 220
Pineapple Chicken with
    Spaghetti, 144
Pineapple Coleslaw, 48
Pineapple Grapefruit Salad, 44
Pineapple Pork Chops, 260
Pineapple Pudding, 216
Pineapple Shrimp Kabobs, 170
Pirate's Delight, 168
Pizza Lasagna, 108
Pizza Pasta Salad, 63
Poached Halibut, 174

Pork 'n' Veggie Packets, 149
Pork Cabbage Stir-Fry, 148
Pork Chops with Apple Stuffing, 158
Pork Chops with Red Cabbage, 154
Pork Loin with Currant Sauce, 159
Pork Paprika, 150
Pork Picante, 158
Pork Soft-Shell Tacos, 156
Pork with Sugar Snap Peas, 149
Potato 'n' Pea Salad, 65
Potato Spinach Pie, 187
Pretzel Snackers, 22
Pumpkin Angel Food Cake, 211
Pumpkin Chocolate Chip
    Muffins, 201
Pumpkin Spice Spread, 104

Q

Quick Crispy Snack Bars, 20
Quick Picante Sauce, 75
Quick Turkey Chop Suey, 132

R

Rainbow Melon Julep, 44
Rainbow Pasta Salad, 57
Raisin Brown Rice Pilaf, 77
Raisin Cinnamon Bars, 230
Raisin Wheat Bread, 204
Ranch Ham 'n' Cheese Pasta, 155
Ranch Yogurt Dip, 26
Raspberry Barbecue Sauce, 86
Raspberry Cream Smoothies, 266
Raspberry-Topped Cream
    Tarts, 235
Raspberry Tossed Salad, 240
Raspberry Whip, 218
Really Good Snack Mix, 27
Red Beans and Rice Salad, 57
Red, White and Blueberry Pie, 220
Rhubarb Custard Pie, 211
Rhubarb-Orange Angel Food
    Torte, 218
Rio Grande Pork Roast, 160
Ripe Tomato Relish, 86
Roasted Corn on the Cob, 246
Roasted Garlic Vinaigrette, 50
Roasted Ginger Green Beans, 75
Roasted Veggie Sandwiches, 184
Rosemary Chicken, 124
Rosemary Seasoned Lamb, 148
Rosemary Zucchini Sticks, 21
Rotini with Shrimp, 172
Rustic Round Herb Bread, 197

S

Sage Turkey Thighs, 118
Salmon-Stuffed Potatoes, 166
Salmon with Garlic and Ginger, 170
Salsa Fish Skillet, 177
Salt-Free Herb Blend, 74
Salt-Free Seasoning Mix, 91
Saucy Steak Strips, 106
Sausage Artichoke Pizza, 118
Sausage-Seafood Mini Corn
    Muffins, 196
Sauteed Spinach and Peppers, 88
Savory Herb Cheesecake, 28
Savory Pork Roast, 152
Savory Roasted Chicken, 122
Savory Skillet Noodles, 92
Scalloped Basil Tomatoes, 79
Seafood Pasta Delight, 174
Seasoned Lemon Chicken, 140
Sesame Chicken Couscous
    Salad, 45
Shredded Beef Barbecue, 116
Shrimp Creole, 270
Shrimp Shell Salad, 48
Shrimp Stir-Fry, 176
Sicilian Orange Salad, 50
Sirloin with Mushroom Sauce, 106
Slow-Cooked Coffee Beef
    Roast, 110
Smoked Sausage with Pasta, 124
Snappy Peas and Carrots, 242
Southern Barbecue Spaghetti
    Sauce, 132
Southwest Pasta Bake, 115
Southwestern Barley Salad, 66
Southwestern Bean and Rice
    Salad, 253
Southwestern Fried Rice, 120
Spaghetti Pie, 180
Spaghetti Squash Medley, 87
Spanish Fish, 166
Spanish Potatoes, 77
Special Brunch Bake, 266
Special Spicy Seafood Sauce, 90
Spiced Honey Pretzels, 19
Spiced Pear Cake, 215
Spicy Green Bean Saute, 78
Spicy Honey-Mustard Chicken
    Stir-Fry, 141
Spicy Kielbasa Soup, 32
Spicy Salmon Patties, 177
Spicy Turkey Stir-Fry, 138
Spinach Berry Salad, 65
Spinach Cheese Phyllo
    Squares, 102
Spinach Corn Muffins, 254
Spinach Lentil Stew, 188

Spinach Pinwheel Rolls, 192
Spinach Ricotta Tart, 189
Spinach-Stuffed Pizza, 183
Squash and Bean Saute, 76
Stir-Fried Asparagus, 182
Stir-Fried Chicken Marinara, 125
Stir-Fried Scallops, 178
Strawberries 'n' Cream Trifle, 231
Strawberry Cheesecake Torte, 210
Strawberry-Honey Salad
    Dressing, 70
Strawberry Pie, 226
Strawberry Pretzel Dessert, 225
Striped Fruit Pops, 25
Stuffed Mushrooms, 20
Sugar 'n' Spice Popcorn, 18
Sugar-Free Cocoa Mix, 29
Summer Squash Bundles, 269
Sunset Tomato Soup, 36
Superb Herb Bread, 201
Surprise Chocolate Fudge, 238
Sweet 'n' Sour Chicken, 136
Sweet 'n' Sour Sausage
    Stir-Fry, 134
Sweet 'n' Spicy Snack Mix, 30
Sweet 'n' Tangy Barbecue Sauce, 78
Sweet 'n' Tangy Pork Chops, 157
Sweet Potato Lentil Stew, 183
Sweet-Sour Kidney Beans, 186
Szechuan Chicken Noodle
    Toss, 255

T

Taco Soup, 40
Taco Twist Soup, 33
Tamale Casserole, 253
Tangy Chicken, 256
Tarragon Chicken with Apples, 128
Tarragon Turkey Patties, 270
Tart Orange Gelatin Salad, 70
Teriyaki Beef Stir-Fry, 108
Teriyaki Pork, 152
Three-Grain Pan Rolls, 202
Toasted Muesli, 99
Toasted Veggie Sandwich, 270
Tomato-Basil Chicken Spirals, 135
Tomato Herb Salad Dressing, 53
Tomato Sausage Ziti, 126
Tortellini Appetizers, 19
Tortellini Soup, 37
Tropical Fruit Dip, 24
Tuna Pasta Salad, 58
Turkey Avocado Sandwiches, 119
Turkey Barley Tomato Soup, 39
Turkey Casserole, 140
Turkey-Cheese Macaroni Bake, 122

Turkey Gyros, 125
Turkey Lasagna Roll-Ups, 128
Turkey with Orange Sauce, 131
Two-Bean Soup, 39

U

Unfried Refried Beans, 184

V

Vegetable Beef Soup, 35
Vegetable Beef Stew, 107
Vegetable Focaccia, 196
Vegetable Rice Casserole, 84
Vegetable Slaw, 72
Veggie Brown Rice Wraps, 185
Veggie Quesadillas, 190
Venezuelan Black Beans, 74
Venison Stew, 114

W

Walleye Veracruz, 172
Walnut Date Spread, 102
Warm Banana Pudding, 265
Warm Blackberry Cobbler, 212
Warm Chocolate Almond
    Pudding, 214
Warm Spiced Cider Punch, 26
Watermelon Ambrosia, 49
White Bean 'n' Barley Soup, 37
White Bean Fennel Soup, 35
White Chicken Enchiladas, 129
White Layer Cake, 233
White Turkey Chili, 40
Wild Rice Casserole, 94
Winter Floret Medley, 74
Winter Veggie Stir-Fry, 80

Y

Yogurt-Marinated Chicken, 150

Z

Zesty Potato Salad, 62
Zippy Rice Pilaf, 90
Zippy Slow-Cooked Chili, 42
Zucchini Beef Casserole, 106
Zucchini Corn Saute, 86
Zucchini Tomato Toss, 270

Reference Index

Use this index to locate the many healthy cooking hints located throughout the book.